AMERICAN EXPERIMENTAL POETRY
AND DEMOCRATIC THOUGHT

American Experimental Poetry and Democratic Thought

ALAN MARSHALL

OXFORD
UNIVERSITY PRESS

OXFORD
UNIVERSITY PRESS

Great Clarendon Street, Oxford OX2 6DP

Oxford University Press is a department of the University of Oxford.
It furthers the University's objective of excellence in research, scholarship,
and education by publishing worldwide in

Oxford New York

Auckland Cape Town Dar es Salaam Hong Kong Karachi
Kuala Lumpur Madrid Melbourne Mexico City Nairobi
New Delhi Shanghai Taipei Toronto

With offices in

Argentina Austria Brazil Chile Czech Republic France Greece
Guatemala Hungary Italy Japan Poland Portugal Singapore
South Korea Switzerland Thailand Turkey Ukraine Vietnam

Oxford is a registered trade mark of Oxford University Press
in the UK and in certain other countries

Published in the United States
by Oxford University Press Inc., New York

British Library Cataloguing in Publication Data

Data available

Library of Congress Cataloging in Publication Data

Data available

Typeset by SPI Publisher Services, Pondicherry, India
Printed in Great Britain
on acid-free paper by the
MPG Books Group, Bodmin and King's Lynn

ISBN 978-0-19-956192-6

1 3 5 7 9 10 8 6 4 2

For Maria

Contents

Acknowledgements

I can't do justice here to the innumerable occasions when a question or remark or perhaps just a moment of silence contributed to the process of thought that went to make this book, but there are some people I would like to thank by name for their conversation, friendship, and support: Alexandra Parigoris, Clive Bush, James Brophy, Michael Stone-Richards, and Shamoon Zamir. I have an old debt to Jacques Berthoud, who was generous enough to imagine that I might finish writing it sooner than I did. I owe thanks to more students than I can count, let alone name, and it would be thankless to name just one or two. I am grateful above all to Maria Kostaridou, for her steady critical intelligence and her good-humoured and unfathomable patience.

Parts of this book have appeared in cruder form. I would like to thank the National Poetry Foundation, Orono, Maine, for permission to quote from, 'Politics and Process', *Paideuma* 28/1 (1999) 25–61; and Talus Publications, King's College London, for permission to quote from 'Diffidence: An Essay on Robert Creeley', *Talus* 9/10 (1998), 145–75.

Grateful acknowledgement is made for the following: **Theodor Adorno:** extracts from *Minima Moralia* (Verso, 1984), reprinted by permission of the publisher; **Hannah Arendt:** extracts from *The Human Condition* (University of Chicago Press, 1958), reprinted by permission of the publisher; **Seyla Benhabib:** extracts from *Critique, Norm, and Utopia: a Study of the Foundations of Critical Theory* (Columbia University Press, 1986), reprinted by permission of the publisher; **Stanley Cavell:** extracts from *The Senses of Walden* (University of Chicago Press, 1972), reprinted by permission of the publisher; **Robert Creeley:** 'For W. C. W.' and 'To Bobbie' and extracts from 'The Turn' and 'Poem for D. H. Lawrence' from *Collected Poems, 1945–1975* (University of California Press, 1985), reprinted by permission of University of California Press and Marion Boyars Publishers Ltd; extracts from *The Collected Essays of Robert Creeley* (University of California Press, 1989), reprinted by permission of the publisher; **Alexis de Tocqueville:** extracts from *Democracy in America*, translated by George Lawrence, edited by J.P. Mayer and Max Lerner (Harper and Row, 1965), English translation copyright © 1965 by Harper & Row, Publishers, Inc., reprinted by permission of HarperCollins Publishers; **Emily Dickinson:** 'This Consciousness that is aware' (poem 822), 'I am alive—I guess—' (poem 470), 'The Way I read a Letter's—this—' (poem 636) and extracts from 'I dwell in Possibility—' (poem 657) and 'I cannot live with You—' (poem 640) from *The Poems of Emily Dickinson*, edited by Thomas H. Johnson (Cambridge, Mass.: The Belknap Press), copyright © 1951, 1955, 1979, 1983 by the President and Fellows of Harvard College, reprinted by permission of the

publishers and the Trustees of Amherst College; **Martin Heidegger:** extracts
from *Being and Time*, translated by John Macquarrie and Edward Robinson
(Blackwell, 1962), reprinted by permission of the publisher; **Mina Loy:** extracts
from 'The Effectual Marriage' and 'Der Blinde Junge' from *Lost Lunar Baede-
ker*, edited by Roger L. Conover (Noonday Press, 1997); **Marianne Moore:** an
extract from 'Poetry' from *The Collected Poems of Marianne Moore* (Macmillan
Publishing Company, 1979), copyright © 1935 by Marianne Moore; copy-
right renewed © 1963 by Marianne Moore and T. S. Eliot, reprinted by
permission of Scribner, a division of Simon & Schuster, Inc., and Faber &
Faber Ltd; **Lorine Niedecker:** 'The death of my poor father', 'Property is
poverty—', 'On a row of cabins / next my home', 'I am sick with the Time's
buying sickness', 'In the great snowfall before the bomb', 'What horror to awake
at night', 'To foreclose', 'Foreclosure', 'Terrible things coming up', 'When
brown folk lived a distance', 'She grew where every spring', 'What bird would
light', 'I've been away from poetry', 'In moonlight lies' and 'Don't tell me
property is sacred!' from *Collected Works*, edited by Jenny Penberthy (University
of California Press, 2002), © 2002 Regents of the University of California,
reprinted by permission of the University of California Press and the Estate of
Lorine Niedecker; **Frank O'Hara:** 'At the Old Place' and an extract from 'To
the Film Industry in Crisis' from *The Collected Poems of Frank O'Hara*, edited
by Donald Allen (Alfred A. Knopf, 1971), copyright © 1971 by Maureen
Granville-Smith, Administratrix of the Estate of Frank O'Hara, reprinted by
permission of Alfred A. Knopf, a division of Random House, Inc; **George
Oppen:** 'Leviathan' and 'White. From the' and extracts from 'Image of
the Engine' and 'World, World—' from *Collected Poems* (New Directions),
copyright © 1965, 1975 by George Oppen, reprinted by permission of New
Directions Publishing Corporation; 'The knowledge not of sorrow', and
extracts from 'Closed car—closed in glass—' and 'The evening, water in a
glass' from *New Collected Poems*, edited by Michael Davidson (New Directions,
2002), copyright © 1932, 1975 by George Oppen, reprinted by permission of
New Directions Publishing Corporation; **Muriel Rukeyser:** 'Effort at Speech
Between Two People' and 'Suicide Blues' from *The Collected Poems of Murial
Rukeyser*, edited by Janet Kaufman and Anne Herzog (University of Pittsburgh
Press, 2005), copyright © Muriel Rukeyser, 1978, reprinted by permission of
International Creative Management, Inc.; **Wallace Stevens:** extract from 'Not
Ideas About the Thing but the Thing Itself' from *The Collected Poems of Wallace
Stevens* (Faber & Faber, 1955), copyright 1954 by Wallace Stevens and renewed
1982 by Holly Stevens, reprinted by permission of Faber & Faber Ltd and
Alfred A. Knopf, a division of Random House, Inc; **William Carlos Williams:**
extract from Prologue to *Kora In Hell* from *Imaginations* (New Directions,
1970), copyright © 1970 by Florence H. Williams, reprinted by permission of
New Directions Publishing Corporation; extracts from *Spring and All* (IV and
XXVI) and 'The Red Wheelbarrow' (XXII) from *The Collected Poems: Volume I,*

1909–1939 (New Directions), © 1938 by New Directions Publishing Corporation, reprinted by permission of New Directions Publishing Corporation and Carcanet Press.

Every effort has been made to establish copyright and contact copyright holders prior to publication, but where there have been any errors or omissions the publisher will be pleased if contacted to arrange for their rectification at the earliest opportunity.

Introduction

Being seen and being heard by others derive their significance from the fact
that everybody sees and hears from a different position. This is the meaning
of public life.[1]

Hannah Arendt, *The Human Condition*

It is the argument of this book that American experimental poetry, from Walt
Whitman in the mid-nineteenth century to George Oppen in the mid–late
twentieth, has been animated by a communicative imperative, a power of
recognition, whose impulsive life and continuing resonance are insistently polit-
ical. For the past quarter of a century literary criticism has, for understandable
reasons, been too preoccupied with the elaborate formal achievements of the
experimental tradition and its complicated history, to consider the significance of
this democratic disposition. And it has been too captivated by the ideological
interpretation of politics to think about what else politics might be. In this book
the political is to be distinguished from the merely ideological, and with that in
mind I have drawn upon the work of the political philosopher Hannah Arendt.
The poets about whom I write have participated in the process—which is less a
process than a confluence of arguments and experiments running roughly side
by side—by means of which a democratic society comes to variable, pluralist,
multifaceted self-consciousness. The book's aim then is to measure the thought
of the poets or their poems against the thoughts of those who are more often
called thinkers by directing the reader to a series of exemplary constellations of
writings and ideas. In direct contrast to ideological history what I am proposing
is a visionary history, a series of intellectual experiments, whose free connections,
as I shall contend, correspond to deeper freedoms and connections.

I use the word experimental because of its nineteenth-century pedigree,
alluding to the self-conscious use of the term by the likes of Ralph Waldo
Emerson ('let me remind the reader that I am only an experimenter'), Emily
Dickinson, and Henry David Thoreau.[2] It gives me the scope to reach back
beyond the modernist, the innovative, the news that stays news, to America's

---

[1] Hannah Arendt, *The Human Condition* (Chicago: University of Chicago Press, 1958), 57.
Hereafter cited as *HC*.
[2] Ralph Waldo Emerson, 'Circles', *Essays and Lectures*, ed. Joel Porte (New York: Library of
America, 1983), 412.

two greatest nineteenth-century poets, Whitman and Dickinson, and then to reach forward again to the modernism of Ezra Pound and William Carlos Williams and beyond. Despite their differences, and the heady mixture of rivalry and condescension that bedevils Pound's attitude to Whitman, the two poets were similarly concerned with the relationship between experimental poetry and the turbulent political experiment going on around them in the name of democracy. 'I sometimes think the *Leaves* is only a language experiment', Whitman remarked.[3] And Pound similarly expressed the fear that his might be just a 'generation of experimenters, my generation, which was unable to work out a code for action'.[4]

It may be conceded at the outset that what is meant here by democratic thought is large and diffuse. The book's starting point, unsurprisingly, is Alexis de Tocqueville's *Democracy in America*, an acknowledged masterpiece of political anthropology in which, as James Schleifer has remarked, in one of the most frequently cited discussions of that work, the author struggled to define what he meant by democracy.[5] Nevertheless, Schleifer concludes that 'Tocqueville's very failure precisely to define *démocratie* accounts, in part, for the brilliance of his observations. If he had at one time fixed definitively upon a single meaning, all of the others would have been more or less lost from sight. His vision would have been at once restricted, his message narrowed, and his audience diminished' (273–4). In other words, Tocqueville was no more precise than Whitman was a quarter of a century later about what he was looking for, what he meant, and what he found:

> I was looking a long while for Intentions,
> For a clew to the history of the past for myself, and for these chants—and
>   now I have found it,
> It is not in those paged fables in the libraries, (them I neither accept nor reject,)
> It is no more in the legends than in all else,
> It is in the present—it is this earth to-day,

[3] Walt Whitman to Horace Traubel, qtd. in F. O. Matthiessen, *The American Renaissance: Art and Expression in the Age of Emerson and Whitman* (London: Oxford University Press, 1941), 517.
[4] Ezra Pound, *Guide to Kulchur* (1938; London: Peter Owen, 1978), 291.
[5] James T. Schleifer, *The Making of Tocqueville's* Democracy in America (Chapel Hill: University of North Carolina Press, 1980), 263. As Schleifer asks, did Tocqueville mean democracy as a fundamental social condition, or democracy as a form of government? Or did democracy really signify the people themselves? But then who were the people? Did it mean the triumph of the middle class, or the bourgeoisie? Schleifer writes that, 'In the margin of a description of the rising power and prominence of *la classe industrielle*, or bourgeoisie, he scribbled the following phrase: "*la classe Démocratique par excellence*"', (269). But could Tocqueville have meant the lower classes? For Schleifer notes that he 'continued to write of *la Démocratie* as if it were synonymous with the lower classes (*les classes inférieures*)' (267). And what part of the people were *they*? 'So, *démocratie*, on some occasions, could also mean *la classe moyenne*, as well as *les classes inférieures* or *le peuple*' (269). Is democracy synonymous, as it sometimes seems to be, with equality of conditions? And what is the relation of the former or the latter to what Schleifer calls the 'psychological dimension' of democracy, 'the unshakable conviction of equality' (*le sentiment de l'égalité*) (271)?

It is in Democracy—(the purport and aim of all the past,)
It is the life of one man or one woman to-day—the average man of to-day,
It is in languages, social customs, literatures, arts,
It is in the broad show of artificial things, ships, machinery, politics,
   creeds, modern improvements, and the interchange of nations,
All for the modern—all for the average man of to-day.[6]

Whitman seems here to express perfectly what Schleifer means when he declares that democracy, as Tocqueville understood it, 'was a pervasive tendency toward equality which affected property, *mœurs* [mores], laws, opinions, and ultimately all other areas of society as well' (264). This book then is concerned with how this 'pervasive tendency toward equality' gets recognized, expressed, or thought about in poetry.

I have used the term *thought*, then, rather than say *theory* or *philosophy* for the purpose of signifying something more indeterminate than these. There were moments when it was tempting to speak instead of democratic consciousness, but that would only substitute one set of problems for another. It has yet to be established whether poems are conscious, but that they are forms of thought is, I suppose, indisputable. In a famous essay, Hannah Arendt's contemporary Leo Strauss distinguished clearly between political philosophy and political thought. 'Political philosophy', he wrote, 'is the conscious, coherent and relentless effort to replace opinions about the political fundamentals by knowledge regarding them.'[7] Political thought, by contrast, 'finds its adequate expression in laws and codes, in poems and stories, in tracts and public speeches *inter alia* . . . Political thought is as old as the human race . . . but political philosophy appeared at a knowable time in the recorded past' (Strauss, 12–13). Thus political philosophy is concerned with knowledge and aspires to be a branch of knowledge, whereas political thought is something more diffuse, concerned with something more diffuse, and the forms it takes are more diffuse. To adapt an aphorism of Wallace Stevens's, thought is something more unofficial than philosophy. The distinction between thought and knowledge is central to Arendt. In her last great book, *The Life of the Mind*, she argues that whereas knowledge or cognition is concerned with truth, thought is concerned with meaning, and therefore has an entirely different remit. She writes urgently of the insatiable 'appetite for meaning we call thinking'.[8] Democratic thought then is any thought that thinks about the meaning of democracy.

[6] Walt Whitman, *Leaves of Grass*, ed. Sculley Bradley and Harold W. Blodgett (New York: W. W. Norton & Company, 1973), 387–8. Subsequent references to Whitman's poems are to this edition unless otherwise stated and for convenience generally cite both page and line.

[7] Leo Strauss, *What Is Political Philosophy? and Other Studies* (1959; Chicago: University of Chicago Press, 1988), 12–13.

[8] Hannah Arendt, *The Life of the Mind*, 1. *Thinking*; 2. *Willing*, 1-vol. edn., ed. Mary McCarthy (San Diego: Harcourt Brace & Company, 1978), 1. 62.

Whitman's poem also testifies to something more primordial than the pervasive tendency towards equality, which that same tendency nonetheless conditions and affects: which is the primary awareness of other people, people who are to be understood (it follows) as more or less one's equal. This then expresses itself in what I have called a communicative imperative: the wish to recognize these other people, and to communicate that recognition, and to be recognized and communicated with, in 'the life of one man or one woman to-day'. The poem is concerned to express this primordial and yet politically inflected awareness of others; and its wish to recognize and salute them is itself an aspect of the 'pervasive tendency toward equality' that Tocqueville observes.

To point to all this in Whitman is easy. No one seriously disputes that he has something to do with whatever democracy may be taken to mean. Let's take a more recondite example:

> This Consciousness that is aware
> Of Neighbours and the Sun
> Will be the one aware of Death
> And that itself alone
>
> Is traversing the interval
> Experience between
> And most profound experiment
> Appointed unto Men—[9]

'This Consciousness that is aware | Of Neighbours and the Sun', Dickinson begins, situating her neighbours in the natural cyclical background of things, part of the faceless diurnal round, a little dull beside the sun. In the foreground of the poem is what she must do alone—this 'most profound experiment'—which is to die her own death. 'Experiment escorts us last', she also wrote (1770). Poetry is her way of dying, as it was her way of living. It is to 'dwell in Possibility' (657)—the possibility of dying, as measure of the possibility of living. Poetry is in this sense a state of heightened anticipation, that practises dying as it practises living: 'And Finished knowing—then—' (280). On the other hand she also wrote that, 'Experiment to me | Is every one I meet' (1073). So experiment could mean the experiment of living; the experiment of dying; the experiment of poetry; and the experimental relationship to others. And it could also mean the complex relationship, itself an experiment, between these experiments.

Dickinson's proto-existentialist being-towards-death, like her renunciation of the public domain (where people appear to one another), poses the very question it was meant to dismiss: the problem of other people—the consciousness of neighbours, who might be more or less one's equal—which is to say the problem of democracy.

[9] Emily Dickinson, poem 822, *The Complete Poems of Emily Dickinson*, ed. Thomas H. Johnson (London: Faber and Faber, 1970). Numbers in parenthesis following quotations from Dickinson's poetry refer throughout to the poems as numbered by Johnson.

So the question of other people in a democracy has to be asked in the context of two potentially conflicting manifestations: on the one hand, the advance of equality, on the other the prospective sovereignty, the incorrigible centrality, of individual consciousness. 'Since plurality is one of the basic existential conditions of human life on earth,' writes Arendt, 'so that *inter homines esse,* to be among men, was to the Romans the sign of being alive, aware of the realness of world and self, and *inter homines esse desinere,* to cease to be among men, a synonym for dying—to be by myself and to have intercourse with myself is the outstanding characteristic of the life of the mind.'[10] For all its boundless confidence, even Whitman's poem raises the question of the nature of the relationship between 'one man' or 'one woman' (which is it to be?) and the universal 'average'; just as Dickinson's poem revolves around the individual, the neighbours, and the human race in general ('Appointed unto Men'). Now, individual consciousness, 'This Consciousness that is aware', can always decide to deal with the question of other people by having nothing to do with them. This is what Dickinson suggests she'll do here. It is the path of quietism, of the abnegation of the political, and it is mainly addressed in this book through two of its most profound exponents: Martin Heidegger and Sigmund Freud. Alternatively, this same consciousness may decide to deal with the problem of equality by turning it into a mainly ideological question and resolving it that way; above all, and for the past century and more, through the thought of Tocqueville's near contemporary, Karl Marx, and his followers.

At this juncture also the critical, pivotal figure is Arendt. She has been cast by her admirers and also by her critics as a successor to Tocqueville, a parallel which it isn't hard to accept. She is pivotal not only because of the way in which her own thinking about human and civic plurality shapes up, but also because of the way in which it positions her, or has helped others to position themselves, in relation both to Heideggerian quietism and to Marxism—Marxism, whether as represented by Marx himself, or in the twentieth century by the likes of Georg Lukács and Theodor Adorno. But Arendt has also had a powerful influence on the theory of communicative action—itself a manifestation, surely, of the secular democratic spirit in philosophy—whether as articulated by Jürgen Habermas or in the more feminist version set out by Seyla Benhabib. Both versions have marked out important critical distance from Marx, Lukács, and Adorno. On the other hand, I should emphasize that for all her importance to it this book is not primarily about Arendt, and her interpretation of the American Revolution, for instance, although I do make reference to it, seems to me to be less important than trying to see the latter as exemplifying the historical and practical efficacy of communicative action.

Now, if Heidegger gave definitive expression to one version of twentieth-century political quietism, then Freud, as I've said, gave another. 'Psychoanalysis',

[10] *Life of the Mind,* 1. 74.

Philip Rieff has written, 'undercuts the whole problem of the freedom of the individual in any society, emphasising instead the theme of the anti-political individual seeking his self-perfection in a context as far from the communal as possible.'[11] Psychoanalysis has discovered America to be peculiarly congenial territory, thanks to their mutual and more or less Emersonian preoccupation with what Walter Benjamin called that 'drug—ourselves—which we take in solitude'. And so, while I don't pretend that Arendt was very interested in psychoanalysis, I do attempt, in the opening chapter, to map the psychoanalytical picture of the human subject onto a more pluralistic picture of intersubjectivity to which Arendt, above all, gave expression. Among the writers I discuss in the following chapters, we can find in the work of David Riesman intersections of Tocqueville, Freud, Arendt, and existentialism; in the work of Stanley Cavell, intersections of Freud, Heidegger, and the eloquent American ordinary.

However, a book argues more than the sum of its parts, and it is through that triangular configuration constituted, in the main, by Arendt, Heidegger, and some version of Hegelian Marxism that I attempt to dramatize what is meant by democratic thought: for part of what I take to be democratic thought involves thinking through, with, alongside—however we may best express this constant facing up to—the claims of quietism on the one hand and Marxism on the other without acceding to them or turning one's back on them; and without, as I began by saying, subsuming politics in the question of ideology. In other words, democratic thought, as William Carlos Williams would say, is 'open', as history is 'open';[12] or as Maurice Merleau-Ponty would say, 'it is somehow open, which is to say that it is menaced'.[13] It is to the question of ideology and ideological criticism that I must now briefly turn.

The present study differs from such attempts as there have been—and there have been very few—to relate the experimental poetry of the nineteenth century, whose focal point is Whitman, to the experimental poetry of the twentieth, where the great exemplar is Pound, in so far as it makes democratic thought rather than poetics the basis of comparison; which is a way of saying that it takes poetics as being, as involving, a kind of democratic thought—or *unofficial*

---

[11] Philip Rieff, *Freud: The Mind of the Moralist* (London: Victor Gollanz Ltd, 1959), 256. The whole of ch. 7, 'Politics and the Individual', is of the utmost interest: 'However much Freudianism may itself function as an ideology', Rieff argues, 'it inculcates . . . scepticism about all ideologies except those of the private life. Psychoanalysis is the doctrine of the private man defending himself against public encroachment . . . Freedom is no more than a metaphor, for Freud, when applied to any form of society; it can be properly said to exist only within the person, when there is a right balance among parts of the psyche. The quest for *social* freedom is superficial, indeed, a contradiction in terms. . . . Thus Freud undermined the ancient concern of political philosophy and substituted for it the inquiry of a political psychology, asking in what manner and degree must the individual be constrained within his social relations' (pp. 255–6).

[12] William Carlos Williams, *In the American Grain* (1925; New York: New Directions, 1956), 189.

[13] Maurice Merleau-Ponty, *The Primacy of Perception* (Evanston: Northwestern University Press, 1964), 23.

political theory. And political theory which is, at the same time, not reducible to ideology. So, for example, where Stephen Fredman in his book *The Grounding of American Poetry: Charles Olson and the Emersonian Tradition* (1993), tries to find the common ground between nineteenth- and twentieth-century experimentation in an Emersonian concern to establish, in the absence of tradition, the basis of their literary authority, I am interested instead in the common ground of democracy—at once commonsensical and profoundly obscure: 'We want to say || "Common sense" | and cannot', as George Oppen writes, 'We stand on || That denial'.[14]

Nevertheless, Fredman was certainly on to something. For the most obvious reason why the two experimental lineages in American poetry haven't been brought together is that the most distinguished close readers of the Poundian tradition, the likes of Hugh Kenner, Marjorie Perloff, Donald Davie, and Kenneth Cox, have not been terribly interested in the Transcendentalist tradition.[15] And the Transcendentalists have not been terribly interested in Pound. Over the last thirty years or so, however, under the influence of ideological analysis and revisionist historicism the interpretation of both traditions has changed dramatically. The process has been gradual. It was on the interpretation of the nineteenth century that such criticism first made its mark, spearheaded by the work of Sacvan Bercovitch. But over the last decade or so the interpretation of modernism has been steadily catching up, and there have been numerous attempts to relate it, ideologically and discursively, to American social history.[16] This methodological confluence ought surely to have meant that it was only a matter of time before we saw a major study of ideological continuities in nineteenth- and twentieth-century experimental writing—except that ideological analysis tends by its very nature to encourage contextual saturation rather than the grander narratives of philosophical and historical comparison.

This book is more concerned with the latter than the former—with what I have called visionary history. And as I have indicated, my whole approach, or

[14] George Oppen, 'Of Being Numerous', *New Collected Poems*, ed. Michael Davidson (New York: New Directions, 2002), 178. Hereafter cited as *NCP*.
[15] One outstanding study which does bring together aspects of the two traditions is Elisa New's *The Line's Eye: Poetic Experience, American Sight* (Cambridge, Mass.: Harvard University Press, 1998), though in this instance Williams takes precedence over Pound. New's book also differs from mine in its thematic concerns (what might be called Protestant aesthetics rather than some congruence of aesthetics and politics) and despite some overlap (Dickinson, Williams) in its choice of poets. Nevertheless, what Fredman's work, New's, and my own all have in common is a responsiveness to the work of Stanley Cavell, whose writing these last forty years represents one of the most serious and imaginative alternatives to ideological criticism.
[16] I am thinking of such works as Frank Lentricchia's *Modernist Quartet* (Cambridge: Cambridge University Press, 1994), Alan Filreis's *Modernism from Right to Left: Wallace Stevens, the Thirties, and Literary Radicalism* (Cambridge: Cambridge University Press, 1994), Michael Szalay's *New Deal Modernism: American Literature and the Invention of the Welfare State* (Durham, NC: Duke University Press, 2000), and Joseph Harrington's *Poetry and the Public: The Social Form of U.S. Poetics* (Middletown, Conn.: Wesleyan University Press, 2002).

mixture of approaches, is premissed on the reservations I have about the cognitive pretensions of contemporary ideological criticism, which amply betray what Arendt calls 'the disrepute into which everything that is not visible, tangible, palpable has fallen' (*Life of the Mind*, 1. 12). The problems can be illustrated by looking at some of the essays collected together in Bercovitch's *The Rites of Assent: Transformations in the Symbolic Construction of America* (1993). Ideological criticism is presented there as 'a blend of cognitive and appreciative analysis', which defines ideology in a 'non-pejorative' way 'as the web of ideas, practices, beliefs, and myths through which a society, any society, coheres and perpetuates itself'.[17] What Bercovitch calls his 'concept of ideology' insists on: '(1) the ideological context of common-sense eclecticism; (2) the truth-value of ideology, as a key not to the cosmos but to culture... and (3) the de facto coherence of American culture', as revealed in its 'ideological symmetries'.[18]

The claim that society may be thought of in terms of 'ideas, practices, beliefs, and myths' seems perfectly reasonable and is easy enough to test empirically: but that these things constitute an ideological web, a pattern of 'ideological symmetries', which the concept of ideology equips us to unravel, turns out to be a circular argument: i.e. society is consensual; social consensus, or culture, is ideological; ideology is best understood through ideological analysis; consensus, culture, and society are best understood through ideological analysis. If one assumes that everything is or becomes ideological, these propositions make sense. But why make that assumption? Why assume that there is an underlying coherence that may be understood in these particular (ideological) terms? Like any idealism, in other words, the concept of ideology presupposes what it sets out to prove. Ideology as premiss requires a leap of faith. It is no more cognitive than Emerson's Oversoul.

Bercovitch attempts to shrug off the contradictions in the argument by seeming at first to concede them:

Ideology, we have seen, arises out of historical circumstances, and then re-presents these, rhetorically and conceptually, as though they were natural, universal, inevitable, and right... And lest I seem to have exempted myself from that process, I would like to declare the principles of my own ideological dependence. I hold these truths to be self-evident: that there is no escape from ideology; that so long as human beings remain political animals they will always be bounded in some degree by consensus; and that so long as they are symbol-making animals they will always seek to persuade themselves and others that in some sense, by relative measure if not absolutely, the terms of *their* symbology are objective and true. (*Rites*, 356)

If all belief systems are ideological, then the concept of ideology is also ideological, and 'arises out of historical circumstances': this severely compromises

---

[17] Sacvan Bercovitch, *The Rites of Assent: Transformations in the Symbolic Construction of America* (New York: Routledge, 1993), 13.
[18] *Rites of Assent*, 14.

its explanatory power as key to all mythologies. To the Arendtian pluralist, there is no key to all mythologies. To suppose that there is such is theology, not criticism. There is a histrionic fatalism apparent in Bercovitch's choice of metaphors: 'there is no escape from ideology'; human beings will always be 'bounded in some degree by consensus'. The author was in fact free to choose different metaphors. For one might just as well contend (there is no less *reason* to contend) that one is liberated by consensus, or liberated by the bounds of consensus, and that freedom occurs within and on the basis of what binds us. But 'art', he writes, 'can no more transcend ideology than an artist's mind can transcend psychology' (360)—as if the loose conceptual amalgam that is designated by 'psychology' were the arbiter of the life of the mind.

In 'The Music of America', the introductory chapter of *Rites*, Bercovitch deploys most of the barren universals of ideological criticism. From this point of view, for instance, critical interpretations are seen as 'constructions', to emphasize the way in which ideological consensus constructs a past to suit its present. But by the same logic, what Bercovitch calls a *construction* is itself a *construction*, arising out of historical circumstances, for ideological purposes. And if a construction is a construction, then clearly the concept is inadequate to the critical process it would name, to the several things that whatever we are calling a construction does. It is to the idea of these several things that the criticism in this present book is dedicated. There is a similar problem with the use of the term 'hegemony'. The concept of hegemony explains nothing in the last analysis, for every culture is or can be described as hegemonic—including the culture of ideological criticism and the use of the term 'hegemonic'. Indeed nothing is more hegemonic than this last.

Throughout Bercovitch's discussion of ideology, the burden is shifted from one term to another without the theological premiss of underlying coherence ever being satisfactorily explained: ideology, culture, consensus, myth, rhetoric, totality. But 'totality' is no more total—and no less a totalizing assumption—for being called 'complex' (369). In the final pages of *Rites*, Bercovitch aims to present ideological analysis as a dialogue: but ideology can only take part in a dialogue if it does not claim to be the soul and substance of the dialogue; if it is seen as just one concept rubbing up against others rather than as a 'master discourse'. What we end up with is a kind of parody of Emersonian identity-thinking, which is especially ironic given Bercovitch's critique of Emerson and Emersonians: everything corresponds to everything else because everything is a manifestation of the wholeness of the whole, the ideological whole from which there is no escape.

So much turns on one's choice of words, and that goes for criticism as well as freedom. As Stanley Cavell has written, the 'mind is chanced, but not forced, by language'.[19] Whenever we write criticism we have a chance to choose the language that will give us a chance—or not.

---

[19] Stanley Cavell, *The Senses of Walden* (1972; Chicago: University of Chicago Press, 1992), 67.

I would like to give one further illustration of what I mean by this question of critical freedom by glancing briefly at Michael Davidson's recent study, *Guys Like Us: Citing Masculinity in Cold War Poetics* (2004). Despite its main focus on the post-1945 period, this work does reach back to Whitman and, to a lesser extent, to Pound, and so shares some of the historical span of my own. At the same time, Davidson's constant references to 'consensus' indicate his alignment with Bercovitch. Davidson is concerned with how 'compulsory heterosexuality' and 'homosocial community' are articulated within the theory and practice of American poetry during the second half of the twentieth century; in other words with how the flux of intersubjectivity takes on, hardens into, recognizable ideological 'subject positions', that may be, for example, gendered, macho, misogynistic, patriarchal, panic-ridden, and so on. There is no doubt that this is useful historical work. And when Davidson picks up on the prominence of the masculine pronoun in Charles Olson's famous essay on 'Projective Verse' (1950), he seems to have a point. He continues:

It is clear that the body from which poetry is projective belongs to a male heterosexual whose alternating pattern of tumescence and detumescence, penetration and projection, dissemination and impregnation structures more than the poem's lineation. Despite his repudiation elsewhere in the essay of traditional figuration (the 'suck of symbol') Olson uses a familiar metaphor of the male as generative principle operating on a passive female nature, 'that force to which he owes his somewhat small existence'. Such sustained masculinization of poetry gives the first syllable of 'Manifesto' new meaning.[20]

I see what Davidson is driving at, even though part of me is tempted to reply that if Olson is using the word man with the same repetitiveness that, for instance, Thoreau uses the first person in *Walden*, it may be reasonable to ask whether he has not a parallel dialectical purpose in mind; defiantly to raise the stakes. 'I should not talk so much about myself if there were any body else whom I knew as well':[21] I should not speak of men if I could speak of angels. Methodologically, ideological criticism often seems to function like a magnet —with a literal-minded focus on the manifest filings of ideological content. This is apparent even in the way the argument comes to rest a little disingenuously on a pun, *manifesto*, which seems to flag up the possibility that Davidson doesn't really expect us to take him quite literally—at the very moment that he chooses to take Olson literally. The critic avails himself of just that poetic licence he denies to the poet. There is a similar equivocation about some of Davidson's other puns, 'homo-textual' for instance (*Guys Like Us*, 14). Or the literal way in which the biography of Elizabeth Bishop is read into her poem 'Crusoe in England'.[22] It

---

[20] Michael Davidson, *Guys Like Us: Citing Masculinity in Cold War Poetics* (Chicago: Chicago University Press, 2004), 33-4.

[21] Henry David Thoreau, *Walden*, in *Walden and Civil Disobedience*, ed. Owen Thomas (1854; New York: W. W. Norton & Company, 1966) ch.1, p. 1.

[22] 'Since Bishop's Friday *was* a woman, Crusoe's desire for a heterosexual relationship . . . reverses itself' (*Guys Like Us*, 178).

feels incredibly straight, and one wants to queer it, so as to cherish the queerness—I should say the *queernesses*—of the poem. And perhaps inevitably, Wordsworth's famous definition of the poet as a man speaking to men is also invoked, in the same tendentious spirit, for what it says about gendering (3). Interestingly, however, Davidson chooses to make only passing reference to George Oppen, a poet whose work he has beautifully edited, and quotes, in personal terms, in the acknowledgements to *Guys Like Us*, a poet whose work falls squarely into the historical context with which the author is principally concerned, and whose writing is not only markedly gendered, but reverberates in places with what sound like distinct echoes of Wordsworth's monumental formulation, as for instance: 'But I will listen to a man, I will listen to a man, and when I speak I will speak, tho he will fail and I will fail. But I will listen to him speak' (*NCP*, 167–8).

Had Davidson chosen to discuss Oppen in similar terms to those in which he discusses Olson, he might easily have had a point. Here Wordsworth's poet has found his ideal listener, a man who listens to a man, as the poet speaks to one, in the exclusive periods of homosociality. What stops Davidson? I would suggest that it is that sense of imaginative freedom and discretion that knows better than to seize upon the literal merely because it is offered to us, which is what Cavell is talking about when he writes, 'our mind is chanced, but not forced, by language'. The literal is always an attempt to force the mind, a reluctance to chance it. And this is the wilfulness at the heart of ideological analysis. It is obliged to discount the fact that what looks like force (ideology) once felt like chance; which is to say, that the exercise of freedom may be critically dependent on our ability to imagine or remember it of others; in other words, to remember that their writings are always more than just the works of ideological manikins or subject positions. The freedom of an Oppen or an Olson may be strangely intermixed with our own.

This book is not intended as a systematic history of American experimental poetry. Instead it attends to a series of exemplary moments relating to the work of a number of exemplary poets. As the book proceeds, a number of themes or motifs, ideas and questions, trace a kind of zigzag movement from chapter to chapter.

Chapter 1 begins with a discussion of the envisioning of democracy in Tocqueville, before embarking on a re-examination of the role of vision in Whitman. It looks at how a certain dominant and domineering model of human subjectivity, referred to in the chapter as narcissistic subjectivity, fails to account for what I call Whitman's posture, the intersubjective and democratic nature of which, I argue, is better expressed in what may be characterized as the invisible physiognomy of the poetry. The chapter deepens the question of narcissistic subjectivity by engaging with the thought of Sigmund Freud, which is then contrasted with the work of Donald Winnicott. It argues that the distance from Tocqueville's picture of democracy to Whitman's finds a correlative in the distance from Freud to Winnicott.

Chapter 2 looks, from a very different perspective, but with comparable phenomenological intensity, at the complexion of intersubjectivity in Ezra Pound. Building on areas of common interest between Pound and Arendt, including their critical engagement with Marx, their admiration for the American Revolution, and for the heroic phase of ancient Greek society, the chapter considers the case for an Arendtian interpretation of Pound's politics. In the process it examines the tension between Pound's dialogical and dialectical tendencies, between his disposition to democratic openness and his systematic idealism. This tension strikingly foreshadows Arendt's argument with Hegelian Marxism.

After the favourable account of Arendt's political theory in Chapter 2, Chapter 3 begins by considering the controversy surrounding her distinction between the public and the private. It then looks at the debate within the American context, anchoring itself in Stanley Cavell's interpretation of Thoreau in *The Senses of Walden*. Cavell's attempt to generate a model of politically meaningful double consciousness out of transcendental privacy brings into stark relief Arendt's cosmopolitan emphasis on plurality. It also reintroduces the psychoanalytical motif and establishes a framework for looking at the dynamics of public and private identity in three women poets: Emily Dickinson, Mina Loy, and Lorine Niedecker.

Chapter 4 begins by looking back to that first and most radical moment in American democratic history, the American Revolution, examining its importance not for Ezra Pound this time but for William Carlos Williams. It takes Williams's response to the Revolution as a starting point for examining the significance of the poetic dialogue between him and Wallace Stevens, focusing particularly on the centrality of the notion of representation. The chapter deliberately draws on the work of Theodor Adorno here, particularly the way he develops the distinction between values in use and values in exchange, to try to get the measure of Williams's formal radicalism, to which Stevens proves such a resourceful foil. The proposed opposition between the two poets also picks up again from Chapter 2 the argument between dialogical (humanist) and dialectical (Marxian) modes of thought, to which the book will return one final time in Chapter 6.

Chapter 5 is a reinterpretation of Robert Creeley's poetry. It starts with a detailed consideration of the poet's formal achievement, beginning with his indebtedness to William Carlos Williams. It thus builds on the discussion of Williams in the previous chapter. It then moves on to consider the particular formal qualities of Creeley's poetry, exemplified by the diffidence of the characteristic Creeley line ending, in relation to the social theory of David Riesman, a figure whose ideas may be situated somewhere between the thought of Tocqueville, Arendt, Freud, and Heidegger.

Chapter 6 focuses primarily on the poetry of George Oppen, a poet acutely aware of both Marx and Heidegger, and provides a reinterpretation of how his poetry may be seen to engage with their ideas. Nobody exemplifies better than Oppen the difficulty of living in the face, or more accurately in the teeth, of the twin allures of ideology and silence—being in the difficulty of what it is to be, in Wallace Stevens's terms—i.e. being democratically. The chapter begins by re-examining the tension between vision and speech that is a constant feature of Oppen's writing. It goes on to look at Oppen in relation to the broad tenor of Arendtian thought, with its celebration of communicative action over work. It ends by comparing him with two writers who confronted similar issues at roughly the same time as he, albeit from different angles and in different ways, the novelist Richard Wright and the poet Muriel Rukeyser.

The Conclusion begins by referring back to Tocqueville, as it offers some reflections on the nature of human greatness in democratic societies, more particularly in relation to the nature of human difference. It considers the role of names and recognition and elaborates on Arendt's concept of the 'space of appearance'. Within this frame of reference it proposes a new and distinctive reading of the poetry of Frank O'Hara.

I

The Flag of His Disposition:
Whitman's Posture

Perhaps it was an effect of what Emerson called the 'distant line of the horizon', but the pre-eminence of the eye as a perceptual organ seems freshly exposed, laid bare, in mid-nineteenth-century American literature: Hawkeye, Emerson's eye, Whitman's 'space of a peach-pit'. It is a point that has been widely noted, and recognition of its significance is probably best understood as part of a much larger critique, affecting the interpretation of culture generally, from history to philosophy, of the ubiquity and imperiousness of ocular metaphors. The eye at the heart of the American Renaissance has been discovered to be an organ and a metaphor of empire: the visionary company were, this argument goes, secret agents of Manifest Destiny—a secret that was kept, as in some degree all ideological secrets are kept, even from them. Paradoxically, then, the eye had been the organ of a profound ideological insensibility—blind to any suffering that it could not simply see, blindly envisioning precisely when it failed to see.[1]

No American writer rests more on the eye than Whitman. 'I lean and loaf at my ease', he says, at the beginning of *Leaves of Grass*, 'observing a spear of

---

[1] The point has been made with great force and eloquence by Elisa New. Citing such 'exemplary studies' as Angela Miller's *The Empire of the Eye* (1994), Donald Pease's *Visionary Compacts* (1987), Myra Jehlen's *American Incarnation* (1986), and Carolyn Porter's *Seeing and Being* (1981), New observes that they have rendered positively normative the current critical notion of a 'polity compacted by vision alone, of nation secured in the self's incarnation, of Being achieved in immaculate seeing' (New, *Line's Eye*, 2). She contends that the 'equation of American originality and expansionist vision' is 'the critical axiom of our day' (ibid.). It holds that the American poet's nationality is 'confirmed by a will to see piercing and exceeding any mere experience of sight' (ibid.). What she then argues in detail and at length is that poetry and seeing alike are altogether more complicated. Her 'poetic reorientation of American sight', reveals, as she says, 'a different set of Protestant provenances than those customarily invoked in studies of American vision . . . Its purview is the poem rather than poetics, *parole* rather than *langue*, choice rather than possibility, freedom rather than fate, work rather than discourse' (10, 14). This would be rhetoric—or worse, it would be mere ideology—if it were not backed up by readings of poems that show New to be as good as her word. Although my own book focuses on mostly different poets, and in a somewhat different experiential context, I am in sympathy with a great deal of this—the exceptions occurring in just those thorny 'discursive' circumstances where poetry, experience, and ideology, if they do not quite concur, commingle inextricably; where part of a given experience is, if you like, the experience of ideology.

summer grass'.[2] What I want to do is to try and be more precise about what we mean by Whitman's vision, by bringing into the discussion his angle of vision, which is to say his posture, how he sees himself standing as and when he sees (for instance, leaning and loafing) and fleshing out all that identifies or means. His posture is, as Maurice Merleau-Ponty might say, his point of view on the world; the seat so to speak of his powers of observation.[3] What I am getting at is suggested in slightly bolder terms in a few sentences by the art historian Michael Fried writing of Gustave Courbet:

> Beholding in Courbet so profoundly implicates the body, goes by way of the body, that all discussion of the issue of theatricality as it pertains to his work will necessarily be concerned with issues of embodiedness and corporeality, including, so to speak, the corporeality of painting... I take this aspect of Courbet's oeuvre to be characteristic of a vital strain in mid- and late nineteenth-century cultural production in Europe and America, the poetry of his exact contemporary, Walt Whitman, being very nearly analogous to his paintings.[4]

One impulse for this chapter comes then from a feeling that no critic has yet seen Whitman as Whitman sees—or indeed as Fried sees Courbet.

But by complicating our sense of how Whitman sees I also want to challenge some of the givens of the ideological argument about insensibility. For the ideological critic such insensibility, the thick-skinned eye of the West, is always, of course, at the expense of difference. We fail to see beyond ourselves. As for example when Whitman writes: 'I do not ask the wounded person how he feels, I myself become the wounded person, | My hurts turn livid upon me as I lean on a cane and observe' ('Song of Myself', p. 67, lines 845–6). We don't have to share the Nietzschean exaltation of D. H. Lawrence to baulk at the presumption that seems to be embedded in the vision.[5] Despite this, it remains my contention that when we do get a properly complex picture of how Whitman's poetry sees, it works something like a miracle of recognition, which is in turn the only possible basis for the appreciation, rugged and imperfect as that always is, of the diverse, democratic, differentiated other—always 'different from what you suppose' (*Calamus*).

The ideological critique of the visual is, then—to put it plainly—neither wholly right nor wholly wrong. But it is at any rate too limiting. In what follows I mean first to use it (for that it is useful seems to be undeniable); then to expose

---

[2] 'Song of Myself' (1881), *Leaves*, p. 28, line 5.

[3] See Merleau-Ponty, *Primacy of Perception*, 5: 'the body... is our *point of view on the world*, the place where the spirit takes on a certain physical and historical situation.'

[4] Michael Fried, *Courbet's Realism* (Chicago: University of Chicago Press, 1992), 50.

[5] I am thinking here of Lawrence's brilliant but essentially Nietzschean assault on how the potentially constructive fund of sympathy in Whitman is diverted by Christian love and charity. D. H. Lawrence, *Studies in Classic American Literature* (1923; Harmondsworth: Penguin, 1971), 182.

the limitations of it (to go about as far as such analysis can go); and then if I can to transcend it (to go back as it were before and beyond ideology).

The chapter begins by examining Tocqueville's critique of the seeming epistemological narcissism of American democracy, the core of an endemic cultural narcissism. It is easily overlooked that this aspect of Tocqueville's work anticipates the more sophisticated critique mounted by late twentieth-century cultural studies of the ideological coherence of American mythmaking.[6] From the latter's more acerbic, more uncompromising point of view such coherence is always, finally, self-serving and insensate.

In the next section of the chapter I make the focus on the notion of epistemological and cultural narcissism more explicit again by bringing in Freud, the greatest, if also, by definition, the most reductive modern thinker on the subject. This also enables me to read at least one aspect of Whitman's apparent homosexuality through Freud's (nineteenth-century) theory of sexual inversion—but no less importantly, it enables me to reverse the terms, and to read Freud back through Whitman. Having thus read Freud back through Whitman, we shall read Tocqueville back through both, meanwhile reading ideological analysis, by implication, through all three. In each case I depend fundamentally on the singular richness of Whitman's poetry. My aim is to show how it can represent precisely what is missing from Tocqueville's picture of democracy, as well as what is missing from Freud's theory of narcissism. Perhaps nothing has hidden the complexity of the poetry quite so much as its fine easy manner of address: 'I lean and loafe at my ease'. These great writers, framing chronologically Whitman's own oeuvre, will help us to engage with some part of that complexity; they will give us, I hope, a different sort of handle on the peculiar intensiveness with which Whitman sees.

1.1 'ON SOME SOURCES OF POETIC INSPIRATION IN DEMOCRACIES'

1.1.1

I want to begin with an image, a point of view. It comes from the 'Author's Introduction' to *Democracy in America*, and I begin here because it shows up the difficulty not just of what Tocqueville was trying to address, but the difficulty, let us say, of address as such—the problem of having a point of view:

---

[6] See Sacvan Bercovitch, *The American Jeremiad* (Madison: University of Wisconsin Press, 1978), 167: '*Democracy in American* is a foreigner's inside view of the consensus, and, like D. H. Lawrence's *Studies in Classic American Literature*, it is profoundly in touch with the ritual dynamics of the myth.'

Whither, then, are we going? No one can tell, for already terms of comparison are lacking...

To me the Christian nations of our day present an alarming spectacle; the movement which carries them along is already too strong to be halted, but it is not yet so swift that we must despair of directing it; our fate is in our hands but soon it may pass beyond our control. . . .

A new political science is needed for a world itself quite new.

But it is just that to which we give least attention. Carried away by a rapid current, we obstinately keep our eyes fixed on the ruins still in sight on the bank, while the stream whirls us backward—facing toward the abyss.[7]

From a figurative point of view, the significance of the passage lies not in the comparison between rapid current and static ruins, which is unremarkable enough, but in the reorientation of the metaphor, the sudden transition which becomes apparent when the reader tries to work out where Tocqueville himself might be supposed to be standing *in relation to the current and the ruins*—in other words, where Tocqueville sees himself as *looking from*. In the second of these paragraphs he is facing towards the 'alarming spectacle', from the banks, it would appear, of the old aristocratic order. He stands over against, as subject to object, the Christian nations—*they/them*—who are carried swiftly along. In the fourth paragraph, however, he has joined the 'rapid current', and becomes part of the alarming spectacle which a moment ago he was watching; what he looks at now, he tell us, is the ruins he had stood among. But he is looking back at them *with us*, and Tocqueville seems to imply that it is we ourselves who create the 'abyss' by thus fixing on the *past*, leaving the revolutionary stream ('the social state imposed by Providence'),[8] to confront blindly, to *face* unattended, the irresistible future. There's a fine balance throughout the passage of caution and apocalypse.

As he paints this scene for us, Tocqueville's freedom with visual metaphors is a function of his objectivity, which is figured, conventionally enough, as disembodied. If we try to read the stance or body or posture of the speaker into the picture

[7] Alexis de Tocqueville, *Democracy in America*, trans. George Lawrence, ed. J. P. Mayer (1966; London: Fontana, 1994), 12–13. I have used the Lawrence translation because of its readability, because it enables me to make the points I need to make without misrepresenting the original, because it is the one with which I am most familiar, and because it bears the imprimatur of Mayer, editor of Tocqueville's *Œuvres complètes*. The more recent translation by Harvey C. Mansfield and Delba Winthrop (Chicago: University of Chicago Press, 2000) provides a more strictly literal rendering of Tocqueville's French, for which it has been criticized as well as praised. See e.g. Arthur Goldhammer, 'Remarks on the Mansfield-Winthrop Translation', <http://www.people.fas.harvard.edu/~agoldham/articles/Mansfield.htm> last accessed 2 Dec. 2008. Happily, the reader can linger somewhere between all the available versions, including, now, Goldhammer's own. Meanwhile it can be seen, I think, that for the purposes of my argument the ocular metaphors in Lawrence's translation are a sufficiently accurate reflection of the French. '*Mais c'est à quoi nous ne songeons guère: placés au milieu d'un fleuve rapide, nous fixons obstinément les yeux vers quelques débris qu'on aperçoit encore sur le rivage, tandis que le courant nous entraîne et nous pousse à reculons vers des abîmes.*' Alexis de Tocqueville, *Œuvres complètes, 1. De la Démocratie en Amérique*, ed. J. P. Mayer, vol. 1 (Paris: Gallimard, 1961), 5.

[8] *Democracy in America*, 12.

then it becomes confused. Yet the passage raises the question, inadvertently, of whether the problems of relation and critical attention can be adequately framed as problems of point of view—of whether this is the best way to think about *whither we are going* or whether the problem doesn't partly consist in identifying 'science' with having a point of view at all. Perhaps, that is, to have a point of view that is literally a *view* is already to be out of things, to stand over against the object we would understand. Tocqueville exposes the problem of point of view, and he exposes it by transposing it. In either instance, democracy is only a 'spectacle': it is where he is *going*, not where he is coming from.

Tocqueville confessed that he had written his entire book under 'a kind of religious dread' inspired by the 'contemplation' of the democratic revolution that was advancing all around him (12). He wanted to educate society as to the nature of this 'irresistible' revolution, to give an account of its manifold weaknesses and failings, and yet at the same time to do justice to its virtues. In some of its most celebrated and influential pages, like the chapter on political associations, Tocqueville seemed to see democracy as complex, multilayered, manifold.[9] In the American political association, he found, people combine together freely and voluntarily for a specific purpose—they form 'something like a separate nation within the nation and a government within the government' (190). Democracy, in other words, comprises of democracies, of a volatile plurality. Moreover, 'freedom of association has become a necessary guarantee against the tyranny of the majority . . . No countries need associations more . . . than those with a democratic social state' (192). Associations can be extreme, that is to say, they can be revolutionary. But 'extreme freedom corrects the abuse of freedom, and extreme democracy forestalls the dangers of democracy' (195). Such nuanced perspectives certainly account for a great deal of Tocqueville's work. But in other moods and at other moments, as we saw above, the author seems almost to hypostasize democracy, to view it as one vast faceless social substance, an object of 'religious dread'. At such points ocular metaphors come powerfully to the fore, emphasizing the sense of distance, estrangement, and epistemic bafflement.[10]

---

[9] See vol. 1, pt. 2, ch. 4: 'Political Association in the United States'.

[10] So far, then, I concur with the ideological critique, and it isn't difficult to see the relevance to Tocqueville's vision of democracy of Georg Lukács's concept of 'reification' as explicated by Carolyn Porter. 'In the broadest sense,' Porter writes, 'reification refers to a process in the course of which man becomes alienated from himself. This process is generated by the developing autonomy of a commodified world of objects that confronts man as a mystery "simply because", as Marx put it, "in it the social character of men's labour appears to them as an objective character stamped upon the product of that labour." The effects of this process as Lukács describes them . . . infiltrate the consciousness of everyone living in a society driven by capitalist growth. The reifying process endemic to capitalism produces a new kind of world and a new kind of man. It generates, on the one hand, a "new objectivity", a "second nature" in which man's own productive activity is obscured, so that what he has made appears to him as a given, an external and objective reality operating according to its own immutable laws. On the other hand, it generates a man who assumes a passive and "contemplative" stance in the face of that objectified and rationalized reality—a man who seems to himself to stand outside that reality because his own participation in producing it is

Consider another of Tocqueville's points of view. It comes from the discussion of the American 'aptitude' for 'general ideas'. He writes: 'The Deity does not view the human race collectively. With one glance He sees every human being separately and sees in each the resemblances that make him like his fellows and the differences which isolate him from them' (*Democracy in America*, 437). And he goes on to say, somewhat dryly, 'that God has no need of general ideas, that is to say, He never feels the necessity of giving the same label to a considerable number of analogous objects in order to think about them more conveniently' (ibid.).[11] The strain on the visual metaphor is still more obvious in this example. It is the eye which is the conceptual-metaphorical engine, driving the idea of recognizing, taking in, all human beings separately and at once—that is to say, at a glance (*un seul coup d'œil*). The notions of semblance and difference, along with the notion of the glance that combines them, are all part of a conspicuous optical metaphor that is simultaneously intended to elude, to laugh to scorn, the restrictions which we readily attribute to ordinary human vision. The very limitations Tocqueville attributes to it when for instance he evokes the literal-mindednes of democratic historians—who take mere vision for cause and effect—or else when he evokes, as Melville does after him, the epistemological narcissism of democratic individualism.[12] The paradox is that Tocqueville uses optical metaphors to convey the idea of God's omniscience *and* the idea of human ignorance (*insuffisance*).

---

mystified.' Carolyn Porter, *Seeing and Being: The Plight of the Participant Observer in Emerson, James, Adams, and Faulkner* (Middletown, Conn.: Wesleyan University Press, 1981), p. xi. The 'pattern' Porter detects in 'American literary history' seems to describe Tocqueville's attitude very well: 'A new political science ... for a world itself quite new': the science of passive contemplation infused with religious dread. Fancying that it stands outside the reality it tries to understand, this reified consciousness has no conception of its historical agency, of how it is helping to produce the conditions of its own mystification. Reification occurs, then, wherever we are alienated from our own activity, the deeds and doings that we do with others. Where I would differ from Lukács is in the supposition—very much a part of its historical moment—that the only answer to reification is the 'sensuous human activity' of the awakened proletariat. For instance, why should we imagine that the political associations discussed by Tocqueville were not an example of a form of life that transcended reification—an active part of the political process based on an active understanding of it?

[11] '*Dieu ne songe point au genre humain en général. Il voit d'un seul coup d'œil et séparément tous les êtres dont l'humanité se compose, et il aperçoit chacun d'eux avec les ressemblances qui le rapprochent de tous et les différences qui l'en isolent. Dieu n'a donc pas besoin d'idées générales; c'est-à-dire qu'il ne sent jamais la nécessité de renfermer un très grand nombre d'objets analogues sous une même forme afin d'y penser plus commodément.*' Tocqueville, *De la Démocratie en Amérique*, 2. 20.

[12] Tocqueville writes for example that 'If a human intelligence tried to examine and judge all the particular cases that came his way individually he would soon be lost in a wilderness of detail and not be able to see anything at all. In this pass he has recourse to an imperfect though necessary procedure which aids the weakness that makes it necessary. After a superficial inspection of a certain number of objects he notes that they resemble each other and gives them all the same name. After that he puts them on one side and continues on his way' (437). '*Si l'esprit humain entreprenait d'examiner et de juger individuellement tous les cas particuliers qui le frappent, il se perdrait bientôt au milieu de l'immensité des détails et ne verrait plus rien; dans cette extrémité, il a recours à un procédé imparfait, mais nécessaire, qui aide sa faiblesse et qui la prouve. Après avoir considéré superficiellement un certain nombre d'objets et remarqué qu'ils se ressemblent, il leur donne à tous un même nom, les met à part et poursuit sa route*' (*De la Démocratie*, 2. 20).

Among the many questions we could ask one sequence seems to me to be overwhelming and goes to the heart of what this book is about: *why was it that Tocqueville could not grant to democracy as such what he was willing to grant to God's perception of humanity as such? Why did he think that a democratic society would not be capable of recognizing its own diversity? Why was it in the gift, in the glance, of God? And how far are these visual metaphors symptomatic of Tocqueville's thinking, enabling it and confusing it all at the same time?* Could it be the case that democracy doesn't lend itself to visual metaphors—that to the observer who feels quite out of it all democrats look the same, as they did, for example, to the convalescent narrator of Poe's 'The Man of the Crowd'? As George Oppen would put it more than a century later: 'We are not coeval | With a locality | But we imagine others are' ('Of Being Numerous').[13] It would be fatuous to say that Tocqueville was confused. What is interesting rather is just this apparent inadequacy of ocular metaphors to the democratic relation they are trying to describe; to what William Carlos Williams might have called, as he worked to complicate his and our *visual* preoccupation with the *visual* nature of the poetic image, the democratic complex. In subsequent chapters of this book we shall be looking at American poetry's discovery and elaboration of alternative metaphors for the democratic relationship it too, like Tocqueville, began by visualizing. In the meantime, however, we have to look again at Whitman, for he is the champion of the visual conception *and* the democratic relation. The critical difference is, however, that Whitman's vision, unlike Tocqueville's, is embodied: how does this affect the representation of democracy?

To grasp the full significance of what Whitman was doing it helps to look a little longer at what Tocqueville was doing.

1.1.2

Images, metaphors, are powerful things—life-shaping things—as Tocqueville understood. Nowadays, however, we have a more developed and explicit understanding of the relationship between metaphysics and metaphor—so much so in fact that it has been argued that attention to metaphor has reinvigorated the study of metaphysics and epistemology, brought them back from the dead.[14] We know about the metaphysics of metaphor then, but what about the politics of it?

---

[13] *NCP*, 164.

[14] While consideration of the role of metaphor in philosophy has come to be primarily associated with Jacques Derrida and his followers, it was also, as Richard Rorty has explained, a significant part of the work of those two most influential of twentieth-century philosophers, Wittgenstein and Heidegger. However, it is worth noting that even before Rorty had argued this point in his epochal book, *Philosophy and the Mirror of Nature* (Oxford: Basil Blackwell, 1980), Hannah Arendt had already made similar connections in the chapters on 'Language and Metaphor' and 'Metaphor and the Ineffable' in vol. 1 of *The Life of the Mind*, in which, with mercurial prescience, she also cites Ezra Pound.

Here then is a third image. It comes from volume 2 of Tocqueville's book, from the discussion of 'Characteristics of Historians in a Democracy'. He is trying to account for the tendency towards determinism among contemporary historians, a tendency with which he is intellectually and morally at odds.[15] 'Once the trace of the influence of individuals on the nations has been lost', he writes, 'we are often left *with the sight of the world* moving without anyone moving it' (495, my emphasis).[16] The specific point Tocqueville wishes to make here is that we often cannot see a set of historical actors for looking at the scale of events—so we jump to the conclusion that human action is involuntary. Tocqueville challenges this conclusion by exposing the metaphor on which it rests. Determinism, he is saying, is an optical illusion ('the sight of the world moving without anyone moving it')—an effect of size and distance.

We can compare this with the point which was made in the first example. The determinist, like the aristocrat clinging to the ruins, is a man *staring at history*. He stands back from it, a non-participant, but a non-participant in the same way that, as he himself understands it, we are all non-participants. We come to feel, Tocqueville says, that we cannot individually act on history: that history acts on us. But this too is a problem of point of view, a problem of metaphor: that is to say, determinism is an effect of distancing and objectification. Tocqueville, on the contrary, wants to put freedom and politics before history. There is no action without freedom and no history without action. Politics is not just the history of force (the history of involuntary movement) but the history of freedom. So, if determinism is how you see the world, that is one of the ways you act on it: *that is your politics*.

It is more than possible to agree with Tocqueville, to share some of his urgency, have a comparable sense perhaps of wanting to resist a similarly deterministic historicizing tendency which dominates contemporary cultural materialist criticism. All the same, part of what makes Tocqueville so interesting is the contradiction in his method—or in that aspect of his method which requires the agreement of argument and metaphor. For in order to characterize

---

[15] See James T. Schleifer, 'Tocqueville as Historian: Philosophy and Methodology in the *Democracy*', in Abraham S. Eisenstadt (ed.), *Reconsidering Tocqueville's* Democracy in America (New Brunswick: Rutgers University Press, 1988), 146–67 (155–6): 'The allure of determinism, like that of materialism, seemed almost irresistible to Tocqueville's contemporaries. His original manuscript discloses, for example, that his chapter on historians was in part a dissent from the historical philosophy of François Mignet, who in his work on the French Revolution excused the Terror as a *necessary* response to historical developments.'

[16] '*Lorsque la trace de l'action des individus sur les nations se perd, il arrive souvent qu'on voit le monde se remuer sans que le moteur se découvre*' (*De la Démocratie*, 2. 91). The Mansfield and Winthrop translation, while it draws closer to the French, makes no difference to the point at issue: 'When any trace of the individuals on nations is lost, it often happens that one sees the world moving without discovering its motor.' Tocqueville, *Democracy in America*, trans. and ed. Mansfield and Winthrop, 471.

democracy he draws on a set of metaphors which are, fundamentally, just as unfavourable to freedom as the ones whose determinism he sets out to expose.

To illustrate what I mean by this, I want to look at a sequence of images taken mainly from one chapter of the *Democracy*, the chapter on 'sources of poetic inspiration'. Throughout this section, as Tocqueville sets out his familiar, broadly Aristotelian position that poetry is concerned with the representation of the ideal, he refers to painting as much as to poetry, and often speaks of poetry as if it were painting. But what I mean by ocular metaphors, a visual conception of the mind, runs much deeper than that. Here are some instances then of this visual conception at work:

In democracies . . . doubt brings the poet's imagination back to earth and shuts it up in the actual, visible world. (483)

In democratic societies where all are insignificant and very much alike, each man, as he looks at himself, sees all his fellows at the same time. (484)[17]

The very likeness of individuals, which rules them out as subjects for poetry on their own, helps the poet to group them in imagination and make a coherent picture of the nation as a whole. Democracies see themselves more vividly than do other nations. (485)

It is not only the members of a single nation that come to resemble each other; the nations themselves are assimilated, and one can form the picture of one vast democracy in which a nation counts as a single citizen. Thus for the first time all mankind can be seen together in broad daylight. (486)[18]

At one level of course these visual metaphors are just commonplace figures of speech. They are so ingrained in us that to avoid them would sound false or suspicious.[19] Nevertheless, we are concerned with what follows from the seemingly incontestable fact that in his figurative conception of democracy—in the figural language on which his generalizations depend—Tocqueville repeatedly

---

[17] This is more or less the sentiment expressed by Captain Ahab: 'Starbuck is Stubb reversed, and Stubb is Starbuck; and ye two are all mankind'. Herman Melville, *Moby Dick; Or, the Whale*, ed. Harold Beaver (1851; Harmondsworth: Penguin, 1972), 663; ch. 133. Or as Poe's great admirer Paul Bowles has one of his characters put it a century later: 'You might say there's only one person in the world, and we're all it.' Paul Bowles, *Let It Come Down* (1952; Santa Rosa, Calif.: Black Sparrow Press, 1990), 35.

[18] '*Le doute ramène alors l'imagination des poètes sur la terre et les renferme dans le monde invisible et réel*' (*De la Démocratie*, 2. 77); '*Dans les sociétés démocratiques, où les hommes sont tous très petits et fort semblables, chacun, en s'envisageant soi-même, voit à l'instant tous les autres*' (2. 78); '*La similitude de tous les individus, qui rend chacun d'eux séparément impropre à devenir l'objet de la poésie, permet aux poètes de les renfermer tous dans une même image et de considérer enfin le peuple lui-même. Les nations démocratiques aperçoivent plus clairement que toutes les autres leur propre figure*' (2. 79); '*Ce ne sont donc pas seulement les membres d'une même nation qui deviennent semblables; les nations elles-mêmes s'assimilent, et toutes ensemble ne forment plus à l'œil du spectateur qu'une vaste démocratie dont chaque citoyen est un peuple. Cela met pour la première fois au grand jour la figure du genre humain*' (2. 79–80).

[19] See e.g. Schleifer, 'Tocqueville as Historian': 'Resurrecting a discarded paragraph or an essay, unpolished and not intended for public view, presents undeniable dangers. The intrinsic interest in watching Tocqueville's mind at work will have to be my excuse' (Eisenstadt, 147).

represents democratic man's idea of society, or, equally, democratic society's idea of itself, as a visualization, a visual or visible relation. Democratic man looks at himself and sees all his fellows at the same time. 'One can form', he writes, 'the picture of one vast democracy in which a nation counts as a single citizen. Thus for the first time all mankind can be seen together in broad daylight.'

In passages like this it is clear that Tocqueville takes the visible relation he describes, which is to say the democratic relation, as constituting an impoverishment of human understanding. The idea that the relationship between man and his world can be understood as seeing the world, the idea that the relation is a view, that the world you are part of is the world you see, is premature and hubristic—carried away by the scope of the eye, we lose any feeling for our saving limitations.[20] It leads Tocqueville to conceive of democracy as a kind of cultural narcissism: a specular correspondence that is total, symmetrical, and reciprocal.

What complicates the matter further and makes it more interesting again is the realization that this idea of democracy's impoverished self-understanding (understanding reduced to projective self-imaging) is itself founded, first of all, on that much older idea, the widespread philosophical assumption, that the mind is an essentially visual instrument. This brings about a methodological contradiction. Tocqueville conceives of conceiving, of knowing and understanding, thinks of what we generally call epistemology, in predominantly visual terms. In other words he trusts his own eye while doubting the eye of democracy; he presumes to see metaphorically into the poverty of this new way of seeing—this seeing literally. The problem is particularly apparent toward the end of the chapter on 'Poetic Inspiration', when he seems to hope for the recovery of the ideal from within democracy as the new world grows introspective:

The language, dress, and daily actions of democratic man are repugnant to conceptions of the ideal. Such things are not poetic in themselves, and anyhow, too great familiarity would spoil them for the audience. The poet must therefore look beyond external appearance and palpable fact to glimpse the soul itself. . . .

There is no need to traverse earth and sky to find a wondrous object full of contrasts of infinite greatness and littleness, of deep gloom and amazing brightness, capable at the same time of arousing piety, wonder, scorn, and terror. I have only to contemplate myself; man comes from nothing, passes through time, and disappears forever in the bosom of God. He is seen but for a moment wandering on the verge of two abysses, and then is lost.

If man were wholly ignorant of himself he would have no poetry in him, for one cannot describe what one does not conceive. If he saw himself clearly, his imagination would remain idle and would have nothing to add to the picture. But the nature of man is sufficiently revealed for him to know something of himself and sufficiently veiled to leave much in impenetrable darkness, a darkness in which he ever gropes, forever in vain, trying to understand himself. (486–7)

---

[20] '*Les idées générales*', writes Tocqueville, '*n'attestent point la force de l'intelligence humaine, mais plutôt son insuffisance*' (*De la Démocratie*, 2. 20).

Tocqueville is still drawing throughout passages like this on the underlying idea that the mind functions like an eye. Nevertheless this eye differs from the democratic eye. For here Tocqueville is led by way of seeing to consider what he cannot see—yet even so, on the very edge of darkness, seeing continues to be the decisive metaphor. 'I have only to contemplate myself':[21] we seem to have arrived at the state of contemplation as such, which for Tocqueville is founded on the self-conscious perception of human insufficiency—seeing with an inner light, out of, *and because of,* inner dark, seeing, that is to say, shaped by man's realization of his vulnerable and dependent place in the great chain of being. But just as seeing continues, paradoxically, to act as a metaphor for understanding what cannot be seen, so it readily functions as a metaphor for the understanding of what apparently *can be seen*—or so Tocqueville thinks: in this case the social and political world. Tocqueville presumes to see democracy (that 'spectacle'), while *complaining* that democracy presumes to see itself.

The problem is that under democracy, as Tocqueville sees it, the light, 'the broad daylight', *appears* to be total:

Being accustomed to rely on the witness of their own ideas, [Americans] like to see the object before them very clearly. They therefore free it, as far as they can, from its wrappings and move anything in the way and anything that hides their view of it, so as to get the closest view they can in broad daylight [*en plein jour*]. This turn of mind soon leads them to a scorn of forms, which they take as useless, hampering veils put between them and truth.[22]

The world has become what can be seen of it: it has been rendered literal: the process of contemplation has been aborted. This now becomes the foundation of Tocqueville's critique of individualism for leaving people alone with their respective wits, all of them equally equipped, so they assume, to understand the meaning of the world around them with the help of pantheistic metaphysics—all of them identifying one with all. This is vision all right, but vision flattened out, a vision of unity rather than of order; without perspective, chronology, gradation, or degree; vision with a 'scorn of forms'. In this vast but all too visible world 'the concept of unity becomes an obsession'.[23]

So, the danger for the democratic world is that it will be a world *reduced to appearances*. The world as what I see of it, where nothing is hidden from me. What prevented this vast flattening out of the world picture from happening before was inequality of condition or station: but the two main sources of inequality have vanished: supernatural inequality—'Gods and heroes gone' (484)—and social inequality: the president is to be seen doffing his hat to the

---

[21] '*Je n'ai qu'à me considérer moi-même*' (*De la Démocratie*, 2. 81): the French verb *considérer* comes from the Latin *considerare*, meaning to inspect the stars.
[22] See vol. 2, pt. 1, ch. 1: 'Concerning the Philosophical Approach of the Americans', 430.
[23] See vol. 2, pt. 1, ch. 7: 'What Causes Democratic Nations to Incline toward Pantheism', 451.

people, not they to him. Nothing inhibits or obscures our newfound centrality. Like Edmund Burke, Tocqueville was not morally disturbed by social inequality. It was just one compelling aspect of the larger cosmic inequality which everyone lived with and which only religion could hope to make sense of. More than that, it was a metaphor, a visible allegory, of our *insuffisance.* 'One might suppose', he writes, 'that all the laws of moral analogy had been abolished' (16).[24]

There is one final point I want to make about Tocqueville's eye before we move on. I said that this book is concerned with a series of questions; in the first place: *why was it that Tocqueville couldn't grant to democracy as such what he was willing to grant to God's perception of humanity as such? Why did he assume that a democratic society would not be capable of recognizing its own diversity?*

So far I have been mainly concerned with the subject of democracy, the point of view. But what about the object? What does the idea of knowing as viewing, seeing, contemplating, do to the manifold external world, to what is viewed, seen, contemplated, to everything that Emerson will lump together under the category of the 'Not Me'? We notice that for Tocqueville, democratic society, epistemologically speaking, replicates itself; it looks up and sees itself, and the object that it sees is undifferentiated: we are not to think of that object as eluding or resisting the subject, as implying some remainder which will always be to some extent external to itself—irreducibly plural at the core, in what becomes, metaphorically, its heart of hearts. It is not devolved, indefinite, conflicted, or obscured. Another way of saying this is to say that the subject presumes that there is an object—an object it can see, or represent in terms of seeing, a visual, visible unit. The question is, how far is this homogenizing of the object a consequence of democracy's all-seeing literal-minded eye, and how far is it a consequence of the ocular metaphors which Tocqueville also thinks in terms of, and which he uses whenever he conceives of democracy or perhaps of anything else?

My point is that Tocqueville attributes to democracy the very habit of deceptive objectification to which he himself subjects democracy when he objectifies it as a 'spectacle'; for what he sees as the narcissism of democracy (its self-replicating presumption of centrality) is the product, first of all, of the optical and always potentially narcissistic structure he already attributes to the mind. Now, the claim that Tocqueville has somehow assumed that the mind functions like an eye is not important by itself. It has been amply demonstrated that everyone has been more or less assuming this since Plato.[25] What is more

---

[24] 'Each citizen of an aristocratic society has his fixed station, one above another, so that there is always someone above him whose protection he needs and someone below him whose help he may require. So people living in an aristocratic age are almost always closely involved with something outside themselves' (507). *Something outside themselves:* timeless fixed externals stop us from lodging our self-centredness at the centre of the world. They, as the saying goes, *remind us of our place.* They are a continual humbling.

[25] See e.g. Martin Heidegger, *Being and Time,* trans. John Macquarrie and Edward Robinson (Oxford: Basil Blackwell, 1962), 214–15: 'Even at an early date . . . cognition was conceived in

interesting is, first of all, the way in which Tocqueville binds this picture of the mind to a political anthropology—a political anthropology whose concerns are then echoed in some of the finest American literature of the next fifty years (say from Emerson to *Huckleberry Finn*); secondly, the way in which his critique of narcissistic individualism prefigures certain problems in the current ideologically minded reception of modernism which in turn mould our understanding of the relationship between poetry and democracy—or between poetry, you might say, and the world.

My aim, then, as I have said, is to lay bare some alternative metaphors for this endlessly vexing relationship—and of course to complicate some old ones. And we shall start by looking again at the way Whitman sees: the point being to show how Whitman's altogether deeper and as it were more postured vision—so of a piece with the *bearing* of the poet that we have to ask ourselves finally if vision is what it is—while it seems at first to illustrate perfectly Tocqueville's entire argument, transcends it altogether. Tocqueville's satire of democracy's simple-minded narcissism shows as interestingly but essentially superficial.

Before we turn to the poetry, however, we need to say a little more about this term narcissism, which for a century and a half, now, has been an important and pervasive one in American cultural criticism.

1.2 FREUD AND NARCISSISM

1.2.1

It was Melville who proposed in the opening chapter of *Moby Dick* that when the adventurer in humanity who discovered America originally put out to sea he was driven by narcissism. 'And still deeper the meaning of that story of Narcissus, who because he could not grasp the tormenting, mild image he saw in the fountain, plunged into it and was drowned. But that same image, we ourselves see in all rivers and oceans' (*Moby Dick*, 95). And what Narcissus assumes we shall assume: 'If they but knew it, almost all men in their degree, some time or other, cherish very nearly the same feelings towards the ocean with me' (93). America, in other words, is just the latest and greatest projection of 'the un-graspable phantom of life' (95). In the quest for 'this new yet unapproachable America', as Emerson called it,[26] one is, like Ishmael or Bulkington, 'always tying

terms of the "desire to see" . . . This Greek Interpretation of the existential genesis of science is not accidental . . . Being is that which shows itself in the pure perception which belongs to beholding, and only by such seeing does Being get discovered. Primordial and genuine truth lies in pure beholding. This thesis has remained the foundation of western philosophy ever since.'

[26] Emerson, 'Experience', *Essays and Lectures*, ed. Joel Porte (New York: Library of America, 1983), 485.

up | and then deciding to depart'.[27] One is always disembarking; or being already there, never quite arriving. The Transcendentalist individualist is a narcissist; the colonists were; the artist always is; demagogue and democrat are narcissists alike; and even the Calvinist God is a narcissist—for what is narcissism if it is not predestination and foreknowing? This is the real meaning of the tautologies of Ahab. 'Is Ahab, Ahab?' (*Moby Dick*, p. 653; ch. 132). Answer: 'Ahab is for ever Ahab' (p. 672; ch. 134).

For Tocqueville, as for Edmund Burke, what saves us from endless social replication, from endless sameness, is social hierarchy and tradition. The trouble with America was that narcissism could reign there virtually unchecked. Melville's critique of narcissism ranges more widely than Tocqueville's, just as it plunges deeper: it is political, historical, anthropological, sexual, metaphysical, aesthetic, and religious. The problem of democracy is just one manifestation of this oceanic problem. Melville anticipates Freud in his feeling that the story of Narcissus 'is the key to it all' (*Moby Dick*, p. 95; ch. 1). We all know how important the Oedipus Complex was for Freud, but before there was Oedipus there was Narcissus. And without the narcissistic infrastructure to hold the individual more or less intact there would be no Oedipus Complex and no dissolution of it.

Freud's work remains the cornerstone of the theoretical discussion of narcissism. It is also acutely relevant when considering Whitman—never mind Melville—because it is through narcissism that Freud tries to explain (and in a sense explain away), homosexuality. And just as Whitman would seem to be the exemplary instance of what Tocqueville understands as the bland self-replicating demon of democratic individualism ('I celebrate myself, and sing myself, | And what I assume you shall assume'),[28] so, and for surprisingly similar reasons, he might seem to illustrate the cogency of Freud's account of the psychogenesis of male homosexuality. And there is the rub. For we can say that the same logical limitations are present in Tocqueville's critique of democratic individualism as are at work in Freud's critique of homosexuality. The logic of narcissism as Freud understands it is essentially self-fulfilling; or to put it another way, the theory of narcissism is narcissistic in itself: it presupposes what it sets out to prove.

In suggesting that Freud's account of narcissism can function as a cognitive analogue of Tocqueville's account of democracy, I am also drawing attention to the fact that both writers build on a presumption of sameness that is based on the same underlying visual metaphor. What Tocqueville attributes to the democratic self, Freud attributes to the narcissistic adult self. In other words Tocqueville charges democracy with narcissism as Freud understands it—a failure to see beyond itself. It is an epistemological and cognitive condition. What holds

---

[27] Frank O'Hara, 'To the Harbormaster', *The Collected Poems of Frank O'Hara*, ed. Donald Allen (New York: Alfred A. Knopf, 1971), 217.
[28] 'Song of Myself', p. 28, lines 1–2.

democracy's attention is democracy itself, and when it thinks to see another what it sees is still itself. It is no accident that Whitman manages to inspire both kinds of trepidation simultaneously—the trepidation before democracy and the trepidation before homosexuality, for his democracy frequently resembles what Melville called a 'paradise of bachelors'.

As we shall see, Tocqueville and Freud were both on to something, and they were both wrong for interesting and similar reasons, reasons that help to reveal the lasting magnificence of Whitman's democratic conception.

1.2.2

We are interested in two related ideas: narcissism (*Narzissmus*) and identification (*Identifizierung*). By narcissism Freud means self-love, a profound satisfaction in and with the self; by identification he means the process whereby the ego forms itself, models itself, by introjecting (identifying with) the object or objects, other or others, to which it finds itself libidinously (and more than libidinously) attached.

'Love for oneself', writes Freud, 'knows only one barrier—love for others, love for objects.'[29] According to the great essay 'On Narcissism' of 1914, this *barrier* is where the sexual instincts separate off from the ego-instincts—the instinct to reproduce ('love for others') from the instinct of self-preservation ('love for oneself').[30] The 'path of narcissism', as Freud calls it, is a nice way of negotiating this barrier. As for instinct, we can think of it as a *drive* (*Trieb*), *pressure*, or *demand*, which occurs at the frontier of mind and body ('the demand made upon the mind for work in consequence of its connection with the body'),[31] throwing them together, driving the organism to act in a certain way, to aim at a certain end.[32] As instinct or drive, mind and body are now aimed at an object: 'The object is not necessarily something extraneous: it may equally well be a part of the subject's own body' (Freud, 11. 119).

In childhood, at the stage of *primary narcissism*, there is 'an original libidinal cathexis of the ego' (11. 68): that is, the ego and sexual instincts coincide, the self loves itself: 'The first auto-erotic sexual satisfactions are experienced in connection with vital functions which serve the purpose of self-preservation. The sexual instincts are at the outset attached to the satisfaction of the ego-instincts'

---

[29] Sigmund Freud, 'Group Psychology and the Analysis of the Ego', *Penguin Freud Library*, 12. *Civilization, Society and Religion*, ed. Albert Dickson (1985; Harmondsworth: Penguin, 1991), 132.

[30] Sigmund Freud, 'On Narcissism: An Introduction', *Penguin Freud Library*, 11. *On Metapsychology*, ed. Angela Richards (1984; Harmondsworth: Penguin, 1991), 59–97.

[31] Sigmund Freud, 'Instincts and Their Vicissitudes', *Penguin Freud Library*, 11. 118.

[32] Freud's English translators have used 'instinct' to translate both *Instinkt* and *Trieb*. See Jean Laplanche and Jean-Bertrand Pontalis, *The Language of Psychoanalysis*, trans. Donald Nicholson-Smith (1973; London: Karnac Books, 1988), 214: 'Freud makes use of two terms that it is quite possible to contrast with each other, though no such contrast has an explicit place in his theory.'

(11. 80–1). Thus attached, thus absorbed, the self basks in the sun of unbounded self-love, which the adult will come to remember as the innocent and irrecoverable bliss of childhood (11. 83). It is only later that some of this libido is 'given off to objects' (11. 68). Once this happens the sexual-instinct—reaching out to objects—has to compete with the ego-instinct to which it was originally attached and which it once helped to satisfy. Freud does not try to hide the difficulty of making out the separation of the instincts. Their proximity and intermittent co-existence means that, 'to begin with . . . our analysis is too coarse to distinguish between them; not until there is object-cathexis [*Objektbesetzung*] is it possible to discriminate a sexual energy—the libido—from an energy of the ego-instincts [*Ichtriebe*]' (11. 68).

One of the most compelling parts of Freud's 1914 essay is his account of the formation of the ego ideal in 'normal adults' (11. 87), on the ruins of primary narcissism. As the child grows up what Freud had referred to as its once 'unassailable libidinal position' (11. 83) succumbs to the critical pressure that experience and the admonitions of a hostile world bring unremittingly to bear (11. 88). Cut down to size, the adult sets up an ideal of himself within himself and displaces his self-love onto that: 'This ego ideal is now the target of the self-love [*Selbstliebe*] which was enjoyed in childhood by the actual ego [*das wirkliche Ich*]. The subject's narcissism makes its appearance displaced on to this new ideal ego, which, like the infantile ego, finds itself possessed of every perfection that is of value' (11. 88).

By the 1920s Freud was developing in more systematic form the picture of the self that had emerged in the essay 'On Narcissism'. The ego ideal is the prototype of what becomes, in 'The Ego and the Id' (1923), *das Über-Ich*, traditionally translated as the super-ego—or in more ordinary terms the con-science. The conscience 'acts as a watchman' on behalf of the ego ideal (11. 90). Alongside the super-ego, the term id (*das Es*), with its Nietzschean pedigree, was also introduced to replace the looser 'unconscious' and its variants (Laplanche and Pontalis, 197). With the assistance of these new terms, Freud produced a topography of the psyche, complete with rudimentary diagram. He extends and clarifies the role of identification—underlining that it is our identifications which lead to the formation of the ego and super-ego: 'We have said repeatedly that the ego is formed to a great extent out of identifications which take the place of abandoned cathexes by the id; that the first of these identifications always behave as a special agency in the ego and stand apart from the ego in the form of a super-ego'.[33]

As it happens, Whitman describes this process of ego-formation by identifica-tion as well as one could wish for in a remarkable poem included in the original *Leaves of Grass*, 'There Was a Child Went Forth':

---

[33] 'The Ego and the Id', *Penguin Freud Library*, 11. 339–407 (389).

> There was a child went forth every day,
> And the first object he looked upon and received with wonder
>   or pity or love or dread, that object he became,
> And that object became part of him for the day or a certain part
>   of the day . . . or for many years or stretching cycles of years.[34]

Freud thinks that the single most important identification that any of us makes is with the father, for this is what brings about the dissolution of the Oedipus Complex. The father is perceived as the overwhelming obstacle to the child's Oedipal desire, so the child internalizes the father, 'erecting this same obstacle within itself' (Freud, 11. 374).[35] In the case of male homosexuality, however, the determinate act of identification is with the mother. Freud gives a lucid summary of the process in his essay on Leonardo from 1910. As the boy's 'intense erotic attachment to the mother' comes under pressure:

The boy represses his love for his mother: he puts himself in her place, identifies himself with her, and takes his own person as a model in whose likeness he chooses the new objects of his love. In this way he has become a homosexual. What he has done in fact is to slip back to auto-erotism: for the boys whom he now loves as he grows up are after all only substitutive figures and revivals of himself in childhood— boys whom he loves in the way in which his mother loved *him* when he was a child. He finds the objects of his love along the path of *narcissism,* as we say; for Narcissus, according to the Greek legend, was a youth who preferred his own reflection to everything else.[36]

The later elaborate metapsychology only hardens the causal outline apparent here. In a further footnote added to the 'Three Essays' in 1915, Freud speaks tersely of 'narcissistic object-choice' as one of the 'essential characteristics' of what he refers

---

[34] Walt Whitman, *Leaves of Grass* (1855), in *Poetry and Prose,* ed. Justin Kaplan (New York: Library of America, 1982), 138.

[35] It is interesting to look at the way Whitman revises the lines from 'There was a child went forth'. By 1881 the expansive second line is dramatically truncated:

> There was a child went forth every day,
> And the first object he look'd upon, that object he became,
> And that object became part of him for the day or a certain part of the day,
> Or for many years or stretching cycles of years. (p. 364, lines 1–4)

In the original version there is, as we see, a verbal lingering over those prodigious feelings by way of which one identifies or becomes ('and received with wonder or pity or love or dread'), as if the words are meant to re-enact the conflicted process of emotions from out of which the self goes forth. The older poet on the other hand just cuts through to the *result* of the process, as if he has resolved it, Oedipally, for good or ill.

[36] Sigmund Freud, 'Leonardo Da Vinci and a Memory of His Childhood', *The Penguin Freud Library,* 14. *Art and Literature,* ed. Albert Dickson (1985; Harmondsworth: Penguin, 1990), 143–231 (191). The editor of the Penguin Freud Library notes that 1910 was also the year of Freud's first published reference to narcissism, in a footnote added to the second edition of 'Three Essays on Sexuality' (14. 192).

to, in nineteenth-century terms, as inversion (*die Inversion*).[37] And in 1921, just two years before he recasts his understanding of the unconscious in 'The Ego and the Id', Freud virtually paraphrases the sentence about the boy's identification with the mother from the Leonardo essay: 'The young man does not abandon his mother, but identifies himself with her; he transforms himself into her, and now looks about for objects which can replace his ego for him, and on which he can bestow such love and care as he has experienced from his mother' (Freud, 12. 138).

We can see these conflicting identifications, with the father and with the mother, at work in Whitman's poem:

> His own parents . . he that had propelled the fatherstuff at night, and fathered
> him . . and she that conceived him in her womb and birthed him . . . . they gave this
> child more of themselves than that,
> They gave him afterward every day . . . . they and of them became part of
> him.
>
> The mother at home quietly placing the dishes on the suppertable,
> The mother with mild words . . . . clean her cap and gown . . . . a wholesome
> odor falling off her person and clothes as she walks by:
> The father, strong, selfsufficient, manly, mean, angered, unjust,
> The blow, the quick loud word, the tight bargain, the crafty lure,
> The family usages, the language, the company, the furniture . . . . the
> yearning and swelling heart.

> (*Leaves*, ed. Kaplan, 138–9)

It seems that the child's identification with the quiet wholesomeness of the mother is put in its place in due course by his identification with the father—and indeed the succession of adjectives that describes him, 'strong, selfsufficient, manly, mean, angered, unjust,' approximates rhythmically at least to Whitman's manly description of himself in 'Song of Myself': 'Turbulent, fleshy, sensual, eating, drinking and breeding' (line 498).[38] However, there is also the quiet implication that the poem knows this masculine character in the same way that the mother knows it; knows that it is 'mean, angered, unjust'; the implication,

---

[37] Sigmund Freud, 'Three Essays on the Theory of Sexuality', *The Pelican Freud Library*, 7. *On Sexuality*, ed. Angela Richards (Harmondsworth: Penguin, 1977), 31–169 (57). On the history of the term 'inversion' see George Chauncey, Jr., 'From Sexual Inversion to Homosexuality: Medicine and the Changing Conceptualization of Female Deviance', *Salmagundi*, 58–9 (Fall 1982–Winter 1983), 114–45.

[38] In the 1881 version of this same passage Whitman deletes altogether the explicit phrase, 'he that had propelled the father stuff at night' but leaves intact 'she that conceived him in her womb and birthed him'. It is a fascinating change—not least from the point of view of Freudian psychoanalysis: is it that Whitman had by then, in Freud's words, *erected the obstacle within himself* to such an extent that it had become superfluous to belabour the point? Or was it that he no longer cared to look, at any rate to imagine this propelling of the fatherstuff at night? In which case, would it be fair to surmise that in the wake now of the dissolution of the Oedipus Complex, he might be able to draw upon the father within him, the super-ego, to ensure that he averted his eyes? As with n. 35 above, it would be interesting to dwell for much longer than is appropriate here on the relationship between repression and revision.

then, that the apparent identification with the father is not finally as decisive as the subtle and more constant identification with the mother from whose standpoint the father is perceived and, if not exactly judged, held up to judgement.

Returning now to Freud, I want to try and summarize some of the problems in the theory of narcissism as they bear on the interpretation of Whitman. First of all, then, male homosexuality, as Freud understands it, is narcissism flourishing through identification with the mother. In what Philip Rieff calls Freud's 'strictly evolutionist' model of sexual normalcy, identification has a pivotal and ambiguous role.[39] As Freud put it in 1921: 'First, identification is the original form of emotional tie with an object; secondly, in a regressive way it becomes a substitute for a libidinal object-tie, as it were by means of introjection of the object into the ego' (Freud, 12. 137). From this point of view then male homosexuality is regressive: *but only, we note, because of the regressive role assigned to this aspect of identification.* However, as Paul Ricoeur has argued, there are very good grounds for not restricting identification to the narrowly regressive role allocated to it from Freud's evolutionist perspective. 'But is the loss of the object always and fundamentally a regressive process, a return to narcissism?' asks Ricoeur plaintively.[40]

Then there is the problem exemplified by Freud's assumption that identification with the mother is narcissistic: and that once this identification has occurred, each act of cognition—i.e. of the cognizing of another—will be only an act of re-cognition, the mere re-cognizing of the self. This is the analogue, I have ventured, of Tocqueville's assumption that democracy, or to express it in more technical terms the democratic epistemic social subject, sees only itself, that *democracy sees no difference.*

Thus we are only a step away from saying, allegorically at least, that democracy is inverted—that it refers to a society in which identification with the mother has got the upper hand of identification with the father. Whitman the democrat is one and the same with Whitman the invert—both are instinct with a fundamental narcissism. However, once we stop taking it for granted that the same is the same, that *homo* is *homo* (stop thinking in visual, that is to say narcissistic terms), the possibility of inversion, homosexuality, or whatever we prefer to call it, can be understood after all as being somewhere near the heart of Whitman's democracy—it is the difference at the heart of difference, different even from itself. It is expressed for example in the great lyrics of *Calamus*—where Whitman makes it clear that you can't tell democracy, or deviation, by appearances:

> Whoever you are holding me now in hand,
> Without one thing all will be useless,

---

[39] Rieff, *Freud: The Mind of the Moralist,* 157.

[40] Paul Ricoeur, *Freud and Philosophy: An Essay on Interpretation,* trans. Denis Savage (New Haven: Yale University Press, 1970), 481.

> I give you fair warning before you attempt me further,
> I am not what you had supposed, but far different.[41]
>
> Are you the new person drawn toward me?
> . . . I am surely far different from what you suppose[42]

We might consolidate the bridge from Tocqueville to Freud not just with Whitman, whom we shall consider in more detail in a moment, but with a brief reference to another Frenchman of aristocratic perspectives, Marcel Proust. Like Freud, Proust fastens his sexual straitjackets onto an idea of psychic plurality which ought to be as potent as Whitman's. In *À la recherche du temps perdu*, what links together the critique of the bourgeoisification of society and the critique of inversion is the narrator's specular distance from both: he is, first of all, a non-aristocrat with aristocratic sympathies, for whom the aristocracy of pure, that is to say, spontaneous memory—in other words of art—takes up the aristocratic burden of authenticity which blood and pedigree prove too ridiculous to uphold; he is also a non-invert with thoroughly inverted friends. It is difficult to resist the conclusion that like Freud, Proust casts inversion as he casts bourgeois society—*as Tocqueville casts democracy*—as essentially regressive— a retreat from alterity rather than a radicalization of it.[43] Yet inversion can also be seen (as is the case in Whitman and Melville, and is pretty much the case even so in Proust), as a sign not for the *sameness* of relations, or for the *relating of the same*, but for the living out of the difference which any relationship is ('I am not what you had supposed, but far different'); as seen, however, by a subject who, despite his philosophical claims to pluralized subjectivity, pretends to think that the relationship between two such subjectivities is a relationship between the same. As Eve Sedgwick so succinctly puts it: 'How does a man's love of *other* men become a love of the *same*?' (160). Caricature as it is, inversion in the nineteenth century emerges as an ill-concealed and highly ambivalent metaphor for the repressed radical potential of the democratic relation as such—it conceals within itself what democracy is supposed to be. Without one's exoticizing it as difference per se, inversion nevertheless comes into view as that difference which is cast as sameness; and in this way it exemplifies the fate of democracy—or the fate of difference—when that difference is seen (as by a Tocqueville or a Proust) from outside.

However, the provenance and symbolic misrepresentation of what is now-adays called—no more satisfactorily—same-sex desire is not my primary concern in this chapter. What I want to do instead is to look more closely at this notion of identification with the mother and its part in Whitman's poems.

---

[41] Whitman, 'Whoever You Are Holding Me Now in Hand', *Leaves*, p. 115, lines 1–4.

[42] 'Are You the New Person Drawn toward Me?', *Leaves*, p. 123, lines 1–2.

[43] See Eve Kosofsky Sedgwick, 'Proust and the Spectacle of the Closet', *Epistemology of the Closet* (Berkeley and Los Angeles: University of California Press, 1990), 213–51.

1.3 'BENEATH THY LOOK O MATERNAL'

If we are familiar with Whitman's poetry, then his testimony regarding his mother, that 'Leaves of Grass is the flower of her temperament active in me', this woman who 'was illiterate in the formal sense but strangely knowing', ought, I feel, to come as no surprise.[44] Nevertheless the image of motherhood in Whitman's poetry has provoked mixed reactions: for if, as Whitman put it in his celebrated letter to Emerson of 1856, 'the body of a man or woman, the main matter, is so far quite unexpressed in poems; but . . . the body is to be expressed, and sex is' (*Leaves*, 739), then why did he confine himself, when it came to expressing the body of a woman, to the expression of her role as mother, monumental as that may be? According to one critic, 'Whitman tends to collapse the many possibilities contained in the word "Woman" into the single word "Mother" and then to extol the preeminence of maternal work in contradistinction to other contributions that women might make to culture, especially those that depend on self-determining thought and self-determining language.'[45] Despite his revolutionary ambition, Whitman reaffirms 'the mid-nineteenth-century American cult of the mother', and so embraces the 'institution and practice of idealizing maternity as a depoliticizing, universalizing trope' (Pollack, 92). Lewis Hyde's incredulous response to Whitman's women perhaps best sums it up: 'It is a persistent quirk of Whitman's imagination that heterosexual lovemaking always leads to babies. His women are always mothers. No matter how graphically Whitman describes "the clinch," "the merge," within a few lines out pops a child. This has the odd effect of making Whitman's sexually explicit poems seem abstract: they have no emotional nuance, just biology. The women are not people you would know, nor anyone you feel Whitman knew.'[46] Whitman's women lack any particular sexual presence: they don't provoke us, seduce us, attract us, or disturb us.

Betsy Erkkila represents a more positive view. She argues that in line with the tradition of popular American feminism that runs from Margaret Fuller and Charlotte Perkins Gilman down to Adrienne Rich, 'Whitman sought to remove motherhood from the private sphere and release the values of nurturance, love, generativity, and community into the culture at large.'[47] In novels like *Uncle Tom's Cabin*, *Little Women*, *Herland*, the mother is 'a utopian figure who

---

[44] Horace Traubel, *With Walt Whitman in Camden*, vol. 2 (New York: D. Appleton and Company, 1908), 113.

[45] Vivian R. Pollack, '"In Loftiest Spheres": Whitman's Visionary Feminism', in Betsy Erkkila and Jay Grossman (eds.), *Breaking Bounds: Whitman and American Cultural Studies* (New York: Oxford University Press, 1996), 92–111 (92).

[46] Lewis Hyde, *The Gift: Imagination and the Erotic Life of Property* (New York: Vintage Books, 1983), 185–6.

[47] Betsy Erkkila, *Whitman: The Political Poet* (New York: Oxford University Press, 1989), 259.

represented a radical critique of the capitalist industrial order and the possibility of an alternative matriarchal economy' (Erkkila, 316): so, in a similar way, Whitman's 'good' or 'perfect motherhood' is one that exceeds 'the bounds of home, marriage, and the isolate family' (259). Whitman seems to anticipate the now familiar feminist insight that the private is political—in other words, that the definition of what constitutes the private is a politically interested matter. Certainly, democracy like feminism gets a great deal of its polemical energy from expressing in public what had been hidden behind doors. 'Unscrew the locks from the doors! | Unscrew the doors themselves from their jambs!' cries Whitman[48]—for 'the body is to be expressed, and sex is'.[49] Erkkila cites several contemporary examples of women who found Whitman's expression of the body, whether male or female, emotionally and imaginatively empowering, from highly literate public figures like Fanny Fern and the Englishwoman Anne Gilchrist, to the obscure working women of Connecticut (311–12).[50]

However, I am not so much interested in Whitman's representation of women as mothers as in what I will call the maternal posture of his poetry as such. And this is where Freud's notion of identification with the mother seems, at least to begin with, helpful. Here is an elementary instance, from 'I Sing the Body Electric':

> This is the female form
> A divine nimbus exhales from it from head to foot,
> It attracts with fierce undeniable attraction,
> I am drawn by its breath as if I were no more than a helpless vapor, all falls
>   aside but myself and it,
>
> .   .   .   .
>
> This the nucleus—after the child is born of woman, man is born of woman,
> This is the bath of birth, this the merge of small and large, and the outlet
>   again.
>
> .   .   .   .
>
> The female contains all qualities and tempers them,
> She is in her place and moves with perfect balance,
> She is all things duly veil'd, she is both passive and active,
> She is to conceive daughters as well as sons, and sons as well as daughters.

---

[48] 'Song of Myself', lines 501–2.

[49] *Leaves*, 739.

[50] According to Traubel, Whitman claimed in a now famous passage that 'Leaves of Grass is essentially a woman's book: the women do not know it, but every now and then a woman shows that she knows it: it speaks out the necessities, its cry is the cry of the right and wrong of the woman sex—of the woman first of all, of the facts of creation first of all—of the feminine: speaks out loud: warns, encourages, persuades, points the way' (Traubel, 2. 331). The statement that 'the women do not know it, but every now and then a woman shows that she knows it' might pass for a definition of the phrase that he used of his mother: *strangely knowing*. See also Sherry Ceniza, ' "Being a Woman . . . I Wish to Give My Own View": Some Nineteenth-Century Women's Responses to the 1860 *Leaves of Grass*', in Ezra Greenspan (ed.), *The Cambridge Companion to Walt Whitman* (Cambridge: Cambridge University Press, 1995), 110–34.

As I see my soul reflected in Nature,
As I see through a mist, One with inexpressible completeness, sanity, beauty,
See the bent head and arms folded over the breast, the Female I see.[51]

Clearly this is the sort of imagery that critics like Lewis Hyde have in mind when they protest that Whitman only ever sees women as mothers. 'The female form', as the poet calls it, is always one that gives 'birth', that 'conceives', and her demure breast is only for the nursing and comfort of the 'babe'. There is nothing sexually or socially disturbing about her. As mother she is 'perfect' (she 'contains all qualities and tempers them'), and 'She is in her place'. But the question as to the ultimate significance of the mother in Whitman cannot be adequately addressed so long as we see motherhood in mainly ideological terms.

There are some other things that are interesting about the passage: for instance the assertion that the woman 'is both passive and active'—which I take it means active in her passivity, in her receptivity; in other words she is what Whitman elsewhere calls *compassionating*. Then there is the woman's posture, with 'bent head and arms folded over the breast'. The striking thing about this is that it recalls the bent or bending posture of the poet, as Whitman habitually describes himself: 'Bending with open eyes over the shut eyes of sleepers';[52] 'An old man bending I come among new faces';[53] 'I look where he lies white-faced and still in the coffin—I draw near, | Bend down and touch lightly with my lips the white face in the coffin.' [54] The image of the mother's 'bent head' and the intuition that she is 'both passive and active' make something particular, something more idiosyncratic of the poet's otherwise vague claim (in 'I Sing the Body Electric') to find his soul 'reflected' there. For, as we shall see, Whitman will bend over humanity with the same selflessness—the same active passivity—with which a mother bends over her child.

It is not just the downward inclination of the figure that is important: the capacity to nurse indicated by the breast matters equally. Together they constitute the maternal posture as Whitman sees it. Take the brief poem 'Mother and Babe', which was originally published alongside the great Civil War poems of *Drum Taps*—which was not inappropriate, as we shall see shortly: 'I see the sleeping babe nestling the breast of its mother, | The sleeping mother and babe—hush'd, I study them long and long' (*Leaves*, 275). The mother is not seen in isolation but in relation to her child: likewise the child is seen specifically in relation to the mother. As the psychoanalyst and paediatrician Donald Winnicott would put it, 'If you show me a baby you certainly show me also someone caring for the baby . . . One sees a "nursing couple." '[55]

[51] *Leaves*, pp. 96–7, lines 52–5, 64–5, and 68–74.
[52] 'The Sleepers', *Leaves*, p. 424, line 3.
[53] 'The Wound-Dresser', *Leaves*, p. 308, line 1.
[54] 'Reconciliation', *Leaves*, p. 321, lines 5–6.
[55] D. W. Winnicott, *Through Paediatrics to Psychoanalysis: Collected Papers* (1975; London: Karnac Books, 1992), 99.

But the relationship is not just between mother and child: it is between mother, child, and poet. The mother has nursed the child to sleep: and the child or the poet, or the child in the poet, has nursed, reciprocally, the mother. Note that the poet, like the child, is 'hush'd'—like the child *and* like the mother, indicating his symbiosis with both. Meanwhile his concerned watching ('I study them long and long'), is itself motherly. There is a somewhat similar moment in 'Song of Myself', after Whitman has been celebrating 'mothers and the mothers of mothers' (p. 35, line 142): 'The little one sleeps in its cradle, | I lift the gauze and look a long time, and silently brush away flies with my hand' (lines 148–9). Here Whitman virtually takes the place of the mother and his active passivity is once again expressed in terms of duration, the persistence of attention: he 'look[s] a long time'. The 'hush'd' quality of it all is wonderfully emphasized when the poet tells us that he 'silently brush[es] away flies with [his] hand'—as if it were possible for the hand to brush flies away noisily! or as if the hand had been tempted to speak but had remembered to be quiet. It is also possible that this brushing of the flies might express, divert, and conceal an impulse to reach out and touch the child. We shall come back to Whitman's hands later on.

Remember now what Freud said about the genesis of male homosexuality: 'The young man does not abandon his mother, but identifies himself with her; he transforms himself into her, and now looks about for objects . . . on which he can bestow such love and care as he has experienced from his mother.' The movement as Freud sketches it looks simple enough: the boy moves from passive recipient (of the other's action), to active agent (of that same action), looking round for an object, which, even as he identifies with his mother, is identified with *him*. From passive, then, to active, and we might say that the movement is a blindly selfish one. The boy's focus is always on himself and his satisfactions: unable to give the mother up, he identifies with her, so as to give himself what she had given him: he wants to have his cake and eat it, to be as it were in both places at once—and one thinks inevitably of the cannibalism Freud detected at the core of identification. The mother is never seen in and for herself. There is no disinterested cognitive moment. Her place, when she leaves it, is devoured. Narcissism is the order of the day, the only epistemology. Accordingly the only way to perceive an object will be to lose it. The mother is only another by default.

Now here is Freud in another context on the transition from passive to active behaviour:

The first sexually coloured experiences which a child has in relation to its mother are naturally of a passive character. It is suckled, fed, cleaned, and dressed by her, and taught to perform all its functions. A part of its libido goes on clinging to those experiences and enjoys the satisfactions bound up with them; but another part strives to turn them into activity. In the first place, being suckled at the breast gives place to active sucking.

As regards the other experiences the child contents itself either with becoming self-sufficient . . . or with repeating its experiences in an active form in play; or else it actually makes its mother into the object and behaves as the active subject towards her.[56]

In this passage the movement from passive to active is sketched in a more nuanced, more gradual way: at some stage 'being suckled at the breast gives way to active sucking'; the child 'makes its mother into the object and behaves as the active subject towards her'. At some point then, and before there is any determinate homosexual identification with the mother, the child reverses the terms of their relationship: he becomes active to her passive. I want to suggest that just this swapping of roles might provide the basis for another cognitive moment—for an intuition that isn't reducible to narcissism, or to what is forced on narcissism by loss. And this has a direct bearing on Whitman's depiction of mother and child.

1.4 WHITMAN AND WINNICOTT

Profoundly influenced by Melanie Klein, from whom he nonetheless differed fundamentally, much of Donald Winnicott's extraordinary contribution to psychoanalytical thought expands and develops Freud's rather mechanical understanding of the mother–child relationship.[57] In his essay 'The Development of the Capacity for Concern', Winnicott takes his bearings from Freud's discussion of the child's first experience of ambivalence vis-à-vis the maternal object. 'This is the achievement of emotional development in which the baby experiences erotic and aggressive drives toward the same object at the same time.'[58] The infant is nurtured, so to speak, by this experience of ambivalence:

the infant is beginning to relate himself to objects that are less and less subjective phenomena, and more and more objectively perceived 'not-me' elements. He has begun to establish a self, a unit that is both physically contained in the body's skin and that is psychologically integrated. The mother has now become—in the child's mind—a coherent image, and the term 'whole object' [i.e. an object in respect of which one is able to feel ambivalence] now becomes applicable . . .

This development implies an ego that begins to be independent of the mother's auxiliary ego, and there can now be said to be an inside to the baby, and therefore an outside. The body-scheme has come into being and quickly develops complexity. From

[56] Freud, 'Female Sexuality', *Penguin Freud Library*, 7. 367–92 (384).

[57] See Julia Kristeva, *Melanie Klein*, trans. Ross Guberman (New York: Columbia University Press, 2001), 252 n. 26: 'Klein acknowledged that she was not a "natural-born mother," whereas she believed that Winnicott had "a strong maternal identification, even though he had no children of his own."'

[58] D. W. Winnicott, 'The Development of the Capacity for Concern', *The Maturational Processes and the Facilitating Environment: Studies in the Theory of Emotional Development* (1965; London: Karnac Books, 1990), 73–82 (74).

now on, the infant lives a psychosomatic life. The inner psychic reality which Freud taught us to respect now becomes a real thing to the infant, who now feels that personal richness resides within the self. This personal richness develops out of the simultaneous love-hate experience which implies the achievement of ambivalence, the enrichment and refinement of which leads to the emergence of concern. (75)

Winnicott ventures to suggest that it might be 'helpful to postulate the existence for the immature child of two mothers': the 'object-mother' and the 'environment-mother' (75). The 'object-mother' is the target of the infant's 'crude instinct tension' (76). As object the mother is the breast, and the child wishes to devour it: to take possession of it and to destroy it all at once. Nevertheless the child discovers in good time that the breast survives this attack—and this experience is fundamental to its realization that there is a world outside the self: the Emersonian 'not-me', as Winnicott also calls it. It is the environment-mother's role to hold the child together while it thus finds the world out. The child becomes concerned about the world—that is, the not-me—and its own excited relationship to it. It feels guilty. It accepts responsibility. In time it makes what Winnicott calls a 'restitutive gesture': in other words, finding itself still there, and the breast still there, it wants to partake in the give and take of the world. Having taken, ruthlessly, it now also wants to give. As the infant matures (a process of maturation Winnicott most succinctly describes in fact as the experience, the reassurance, of just 'going on being') so the object-mother and the environment-mother come together through the child's acceptance of responsibility, its developing concern. 'Gradually as the infant finds out that the mother survives and accepts the restitutive gesture, so the infant becomes able to accept responsibility for the total fantasy of the full instinctual impulse that was previously ruthless. Ruthlessness gives way to ruth, unconcern to concern.'[59]

Winnicott plots the subtle growth of the child then from anxiety, through guilt, to maturing concern. To begin with, the child is anxious 'because if he consumes the mother he will lose her', but the mother enables the child 'to hold' that anxiety—in effect to live with it, so as not to be overwhelmed by it (76–7). The mother's holding of the child enables the child to hold the anxiety. Because she is there, *the child can be there*. It can live with the anxiety. Anxiety that is held in this way is in turn mollified, ameliorated.

We see that for Winnicott the child's egotism develops alongside and in relation to its developing ability to be *concerned about*, i.e. to empathize. (It is not just the 'transitional object' or the mother as object that are transitional. The whole mother, including the environment-mother, is transitional.) Its inner-life emerges alongside its developing awareness of life outside, the life it lives *in relation to*.

[59] Winnicott, 'Psycho-analysis and the Sense of Guilt', *Maturational Processes*, 15–28 (23–4).

It seems that after a time the individual can build up memories of experiences felt to be good, so that the experience of the mother holding the situation becomes part of the self, becomes assimilated into the ego. In this way the actual mother gradually becomes less and less necessary. The individual acquires an internal environment. The child thus becomes able to find new situation-holding experiences, and *is able in time to take over the function of being the situation-holding person for someone else, without resentment.*[60]

The mother 'becomes less and less necessary' in the sense that the child is learning *to hold itself.* It learns to hold and as it were to hold on; to bear up; to carry on being. The inner space that the child has discovered and filled out is obviously fundamental here. The mother falls away—that is she reverts, as a *whole object* (a whole object being, as we have said, an object one has learned to feel ambivalent about) to the not-me world, where she may then become someone to whom the child can healthily extend its newfound capacity for empathy.

One could go so far as to say that the dominant, the characteristic mood of Whitman's poetry, from the opening lines of 'Song of Myself' on, recapitulates the child's acquisition of an internal environment (the taking on of the environment-mother's role) simultaneously with its finding itself to face to face —without anxiety—with the not-me world. It is doubtful whether any poet has conveyed more copiously than Whitman the satisfaction in just going on being, the contentment in just being oneself, which is the mother's gift to the child—the cushion on which its ego rests. No poet is more robustly benign, more affectionate, and more detached. And no poet takes his health and wholeness more for granted, or is more willing to meet with it in others; is more accepting of the good and bad—call it the whole-object nature of the not-me world:

> Trippers and askers surround me,
> People I meet, the effect upon me of my early life or the ward and city I live in,
>   or the nation,
> The latest dates, discoveries, inventions, societies, authors old and new,
> My dinner, dress, associates, looks, compliments, dues,
> The real or fancied indifference of some man or woman I love,
> The sickness of one of my folks or of myself, or ill-doing or loss or lack of
>   money, or depressions or exaltations,
> Battles, the horrors of fratricidal war, the fever of doubtful news, the fitful
>   events;
> These come to me days and nights and go from me again,
> But they are not the Me myself.

---

[60] Winnicott, 'The Depressive Position in Normal Emotional Development', *Through Paediatrics*, 262–77 (271), my emphasis.

Apart from the pulling and hauling stands what I am,
Stands amused, complacent, compassionating, idle, unitary,
Looks down, is erect, or bends an arm on an impalpable certain rest,
Looking with side-curved head curious what will come next,
Both in an out of the game and watching and wondering at it.

Backward I see in my own days where I sweated through fog with linguists
   and contenders,
I have no mockings or arguments, I witness and wait.

('Song of Myself', p. 32, lines 66–81)

The internalizing of environmental beneficence or bounty, this 'impalpable certain rest', transforms or, more accurately, matures anxiety into a concerned and empathetic relationship to others.

Following Winnicott then, I want to suggest that there is a moment, a first moment, perhaps not recognized there and then but recognized in time, when the child or boy, or the child or boy remembered and remembering in the man, recognizes the passive position in which he has put his mother as a position which he himself was in. I want to say that he recognizes passivity as such, and is helped by that recognition, quite inadvertently, to see the person over there, the mother, as over there, separate: to perceive her dimly as one who can, dimly, suffer the fate of passivity. At which point, to quote from Whitman's Preface of 1855: 'He judges not as the judge judges but as the sun falling around a helpless thing' (*Leaves*, 715). The mother herself is seen in what is now her childlike helplessness. This literally compassionate recognition (in that last long quotation from 'Song of Myself', Whitman calls his disposition 'compassionating', a usage which has the merit of expressing compassion as an activity, as something one *does*), lies at the emotional heart of Whitman's poetry as one of his central epiphanies. It is perhaps best to formulate it by saying that it is an epiphany the poetry is always in the process of having—and it is, I think, what makes Whitman's images of the child at the breast so extraordinarily charged and affecting: the mother no less than the child is both active and passive—and this is precisely what the image sees, is what makes it cognitive.

Christian archetypes and iconography inevitably inflect our response to the mother–child relation—though oddly enough Winnicott, as far as I'm aware, does not discuss them. Indeed I would argue that the line I just quoted from Whitman's Preface activates rather magnificently the conventional, stylized sun/son homonym which is such a familiar Christian trope: what Whitman gets at is *the son's feeling for the mother's feeling for the son*, his feeling for what she goes through, as bearing on what he goes through, for which the notion of empathy, disparaged as it is, is perhaps too crude. It seems to me that it was just this feeling of compassion which, a century later, Pier Paolo Pasolini managed to express in the film *The Gospel According to Matthew* (1964) by having the spiritual 'Motherless Child' accompany the image of the childlike Mary, now confirmed, orphan-like, in her adult motherhood. The motif of the mother as motherless child, like its corollary the childless mother, which is also emphasized ('Rachel weeping for her children' after the slaughter of the innocents),[61] introduces the motif of Christ as motherless child (the song recurs shortly before the adult Christ is baptized); of Christ as he who will repudiate motherhood[62]—a point the film makes repeatedly and emphatically; which is to say, the motif of separateness and forsaking which will find its ultimate expression on the cross ('My God, my God, why hast thou forsaken me?').[63] The viewer's pity for the mother becomes one with Christ's pity for her.

1.5 'A SIGHT IN CAMP IN THE DAYBREAK GRAY AND DIM', 'THE WOUND-DRESSER', *CALAMUS*

Whitman's gift for motherhood is expressed through his passivity, or better, his receptivity, the patience that we find in his voice and the way he waits on us and for us: 'I stop somewhere waiting for you', as the last line of 'Song of Myself' has it. It is in the maternal posture of the poetry as it contemplates others, who are those 'objects', as Freud says, 'on which he can bestow such love and care as he has experienced from his mother'. This quality of mothering is what Whitman refers to as his capacity for acceptance ('I accept Time absolutely'; 'I accept Reality'), or else of not resisting ('I resist anything better than my own diversity'), of, in the pregnant opening verb of 'Song of Myself', *celebrating*.[64] The state of waiting, where observation is a kind of patience, the being there to attend or suffer with, recalls the importance of time in Winnicott's conception of the mother's work of holding.[65] For Whitman witnessing is also a kind of waiting ('I witness and wait'), it does not bring waiting to an end but prolongs it, waits upon it ('I witness the corpse with its dabbled hair, I note where the pistol has fallen').[66] If passivity is one aspect of identification with the mother, by which Whitman recalls that he was originally the recipient of the love he waits to

---

[61] Matthew 2: 18.

[62] Matthew 10: 35–7.

[63] Matthew 27: 46.

[64] Whitman, 'Song of Myself', p. 51, lines 480, 483; p. 45, line 349. See Allen Grossman, 'The Poetics of Union in Whitman and Lincoln: An Inquiry toward the Relationship of Art and Policy', in Walter Benn Michaels and Donald E. Pease (eds.), *The American Renaissance Reconsidered* (Baltimore and London: Johns Hopkins University Press, 1985) 183–208 (208 n. 29), where it is suggested that '"Celebration" in Whitman (as in "I celebrate myself") invokes the meaning of pluralization which inheres in all cognates of Latin *celebrare*'.

[65] See e.g. Winnicott, 'The Depressive Position in Normal Emotional Development', *Through Paediatrics*: 'Let us see what happens if the "quiet" mother holds the situation in time, so that the baby may experience "excited" relationships and meet the consequences' (267); 'All the while the mother is holding the situation in time' (269).

[66] Whitman, 'Song of Myself', p. 36, line 153.

bestow, and bestows in waiting (and he is always waiting), and which he bestows for the most part with his eye—his 'look O Maternal'—then his affirmation of suffering ('I am the man, I suffer'd, I was there'),[67] one might almost speak of his pleasure in it, at any rate of love aroused in the presence of it (as if love required just that combination, the opportunity to give what one received, to activate reception), recalls him to his pleasure in that maternal affection. The recollection is at the heart of the affirmation, or rather affirmation is recollection. In the posture of Whitman's poetry, then, we find both the mother waiting to bestow her love and care, or reaching out carefully to bestow it, *combined with the memory of waiting for that love and care* (the memory of dependence, of having to wait for her). In the light of Whitman's poetry of the American Civil War, another way of expressing all this is to speak of the posture of nursing in his poetry, his dressing of wounds; in the complex sense of addressing himself to what, because it is uncovered, not dressed, addresses itself to him; wants to be dressed, to be covered—which for Whitman will mean covering it with his eye, the act of seeing as a kind of bandage.

I want to discuss now one of the poems which most perfectly demonstrates what I mean by this, a poem rightly regarded as one of Whitman's finest achievements.

'A Sight in Camp in the Daybreak Gray and Dim' begins in the half-light of daybreak, with the poet rising early from his tent:

> A sight in camp in the daybreak gray and dim,
> As from my tent I emerge so early sleepless,
> As slow I walk in the cool fresh air the path near by the hospital tent,
> Three forms I see on stretchers lying, brought out there untended lying,
> Over each the blanket spread, ample brownish woollen blanket,
> Gray and heavy blanket, folding, covering all.

(Leaves, pp. 306–7, lines 1–6)

One is reminded for a moment of the beginning of 'The Sleepers', the angle and movement of the 'sleepless' walking poet in relation to the supine bodies around him ('Bending with open eyes over the shut eyes of sleepers, | . . . | How solemn they look there, stretch'd and still').[68] 'Slow I walk' suggests not just the calmness of the speaker, or a concern not to wake the sleeping and the dead, but the sense of adjusting one's eyes to the light: slowly I wake. This quality of slowness and the poem's realistic focus on this one 'sight' are obviously quite different from the visionary confusion of 'The Sleepers'—still, the posture practised there in the earlier poem prepares the way here (in the final line of 'The Sleepers' the poet calls the night his 'mother'). The brown blankets which cover the dead forms suggest burial as well as sleep, while the fact that there are

---

[67] Ibid., p. 66, line 832.
[68] Whitman, *Leaves*, p. 424, lines 3, 6.

three of them, a number which is also imaged on the page by the three verse paragraphs, suggests the scene at Golgotha, the crucified Christ and the two men crucified beside him.

The second stanza begins by again limning the erect stance of the speaker in relation to the supine bodies—reminding us (all the while subliminally) of how they lie at right angles to the one vertical figure. What we have here is almost a pietà scene; that is, a scene in which the principal human figures (the dead Christ laid across the lap of his mother) are formed into a pattern that recalls the upper half of the Cross. However, the underlying iconographical structure is beautifully concealed by the almost offhand realism:

> Curious I halt and silent stand,
> Then with light fingers I from the face of the nearest the first just lift the
>   blanket;
> Who are you elderly man so gaunt and grim, with well-gray'd hair, and flesh
>   all sunken about the eyes?
> Who are you my dear comrade?
>
> (lines 7–10)

As the poet bends, presumably, over the first body we note that his fingers are described as 'light': that is, they are, in the first instance, weightless, pressureless, and what is more *they do not actually touch* the body of the man. What they touch is the blanket. This lifting of the blanket underscores the point that the poet's fingers are also as it were *shedding light.* Then, as he shifts the emphasis from what he sees to this man who cannot see, Whitman turns the meaning round further, from the 'sight' of the eye to the 'flesh' of it ('sunken' also suggests graves—holes in the earth, the Day of Judgement), bringing the act of touching, something one does with the flesh, up alongside the act of seeing. Whereas Whitman's fingers become his eyes, the dead man's eyes express the transition in reverse and become flesh—but flesh that is insensate, and therefore blind. Whitman, by contrast, touches because he sees and only because he sees; he preserves intimate distance, as expressed in the exquisitely tentative 'the nearest the first just'—sounds which draw consummately near. We can compare the whole gesture to that moment in 'Song of Myself' cited earlier where Whitman examined the cradled infant: 'I lift the gauze and look a long time'.

The three lines of the third stanza, in which the poet now looks at the third body, make the crucifixion theme explicit, and automatically bring to mind the question of resurrection:

> Then to the third—a face nor child nor old, very calm, as of beautiful yellow-
>   white ivory;
> Young man I think I know you—I think this face is the face of the Christ
>   himself,
> Dead and divine and brother of all, and here again he lies.
>
> (lines 13–15)

The poignancy of this stab of recognition ('I think I know you') is pretty much as if Christ at the Day of Judgement busily raising up the dead should suddenly come across himself—his own dead body lying there—and find its calm forgiveness surpassing his own: Christ in his humanity forgiving God his supernatural inhumanity. This is one of the things that, apart from the authors' common fondness for the word *bloom*, makes Whitman seem at times to anticipate James Joyce's gentle voyeuristic urban democrat—and perhaps only Joyce imagined the Day of Judgement with anything approaching Whitman's unruffled humanness. Here the shock of recognition is underscored by the astonishing splash of colour—the first colours to be named since all that grey and brown: 'beautiful yellow-white ivory'.

But this is not really the Day of Judgement any more than Joyce's is: the angle of vision is the angle here on earth. In keeping with the previous stanzas, the biblical precedent is rather that strange new day after the Crucifixion and the Sabbath. After Christ's body was taken from the cross, Mary Magdalene was the first, or among the first, depending on which apostle one reads, to approach the sepulchre: 'And very early in the morning . . . they came into the sepulchre at the rising of the sun', says Mark (16: 2). A sight in camp in the daybreak grey and dim . . . Mary sees the resurrected Christ—sees him, doesn't touch him. Indeed according to John, Christ says to Mary Magdalene: 'Touch me not; for I am not yet ascended to my Father' (John 20: 17). Seeing is as close as she can get. Mary seems to be a sort of surrogate at this point for Christ's mother, who had been with her at the Cross (John 19: 25). And this is where Whitman's perspective remains, this is whom he identifies with—not with Christ but with those who tend his death, the Marys of this world, the mothers and their surrogates.[69] Meanwhile his humanist resurrection of Christ consists not in having Christ rise again but in having him die again: 'Dead and divine . . . *and here again he lies*' (my emphasis).

The fact that 'the Christ' is described as lying reminds us again that the speaker is standing, therefore bending, implicitly stooping or perhaps even kneeling, over the body (the notebook entry which Sculley Bradley and Harold W. Blodgett, Whitman's editors, quote as the source of the poem is no more specific). This posture affords, I think, Whitman's habitual angle of vision, his being more or less vertical to the other's more or less horizontal—glancing down through an angle of roughly 90 degrees: which is the angle of the mother to the child at her

[69] The point is made again beautifully in 'When Lilacs Last in the Dooryard Bloom'd' (*Leaves*, p. 336, lines 179–84):

> I saw the debris and debris of all the slain soldiers of the war,
> But I saw they were not as was thought,
> They themselves were fully at rest, they suffer'd not,
> The living remain'd and suffer'd, the mother suffer'd,
> And the wife and the child and the musing comrade suffer'd,
> And the armies that remain'd suffer'd.

breast, to the dead Christ in her lap, of the nurse to his or her patients, of the
somnambulist to the surrounding sleepers (consider the fifth line of 'The Slee-
pers': 'Pausing, gazing, bending, and stopping')—one might even add, of the
reader or the writer to the book. It is also the angle of the person at prayer to his
or her praying hands. The marvellous image of 'the mechanic's wife with her
babe at her nipple interceding for every person born', from 'Song of Myself'
(p. 75, line 1043), takes at least some of its force from the way it evokes the
prayer-like posture of breast-feeding—and vice versa. It is also of course the angle
at which Whitman must examine that first 'spear of summer grass',[70] and it is
evoked as well as anywhere in the passage from 'Song of Myself' we looked at
earlier:

> Apart from the pulling and hauling stands what I am,
> Stands amused, complacent, compassionating, idle, unitary,
> Looks down, is erect, or bends an arm on an impalpable certain rest
> Looking with side-curved head curious what will come next,
> Both in and out of the game and watching and wondering at it.

> (lines 75–9)

Whitman 'Stands' and 'Looks down', and the descending angle of vision is
then echoed in the changing posture, which is first 'erect' and then 'bends'. Also
interesting here is that word *impalpable*: 'an impalpable certain rest' is one that
the bent arm rests on without going so far as to touch, feel, or handle it. It has
become part of the self—part of the outside that is inside (the gift, as Winnicott
would say, of the 'environment-mother').

In what becomes section 6 of 'Song of Myself' the grass is identified with a
child: 'A child said *What is the grass?* fetching it to me with full hands' (p. 33, line
99). And again: 'Or I guess the grass is itself a child, the produced babe of the
vegetation' (p. 34, line 105). True, neither the grass nor the child is described as
lying, and the grass itself is often pointedly erect, at least to begin with: neverthe-
less, the glance is implicitly angling downward, in a way that is at once disarming,
deflationary, and compassionate: 'And limitless are leaves stiff or drooping in the
fields' (p. 33, line 96). 'Stiff or drooping' suggests the transformation of one (stiff)
into the other (drooping), along the angle of deflation, the angle of vision,
something already caught once and for all in the beautifully poised ambiguity
of Whitman's great title—not spears, not blades, but leaves: at once flatter, less
erect, more recumbent than blades. (It is also the peculiar achievement of Whit-
man's lines to extend tumescently and flatten out gently.)[71] As the passage
proceeds it is full of images that drift beautifully between the vertical and the

[70] 'Song of Myself', p. 28, line 5.
[71] Compare the marvellous description of Leopold Bloom in the bath, 'in a womb of warmth',
with his 'limp father of thousands, a languid floating flower'. James Joyce, *Ulysses* (1922;
Harmondsworth: Penguin, 1986), 71; ch. 5.

horizontal: from 'the flag of my disposition', which in turn becomes 'the hand-kerchief of the Lord, | . . . designedly dropt' (p. 33, lines 101–3)—Christian archetypes again but with an admixture of *Othello*—to 'mothers' laps' (mentioned three times in eight lines: 114, 115, and 122), which could be said to enact the very posture of what Whitman calls 'compassionating' (p. 32, line 76).

I want to give one further instance of why it seems to me that in Whitman the question of what I am calling posture comes before questions of ideology. In one of the most comprehensive treatments of Whitman's politics, Betsy Erkkila has this to say of 'The Wound-Dresser':

> Harold W. Blodgett and Sculley Bradley, the editors of the New York University edition of *Leaves of Grass*, describe the content of this poem as 'a faithful description of Walt Whitman's ministrations to the war-wounded in Washington hospitals' . . . Rarely, however, did Whitman actually dress the wounds of soldiers during his service in the Washington hospitals: rather, the image of wound-dresser is a metaphor for the role he played both in the hospitals and in his war poems as the soother, reconciler, and psychic healer who dared to look—as others could not—on the dismembered bodies and bloody corpses produced by the war.[72]

One might well agree that the image of the wound-dresser is in some part a metaphor for the role Whitman played as 'figurative dresser of the amputated body and wounded psyche of the American republic' (Erkkila, 219), but to separate the literal and the metaphorical as starkly as Erkkila does, and to give primacy to what she sees as that literal historical distinction, is to take for granted what the poetry so singularly and powerfully does. And part of what it does is to open up the question of what is literal and what is metaphorical.

Once again the striking thing about this poem is how touching resolves into seeing—so much so in fact that Whitman can, as Erkkila says, represent himself as 'actually dress[ing] . . . wounds':

> From the stump of the arm, the amputated hand,
> I undo the clotted lint, remove the slough, wash off the matter and blood,
> Back on his pillow the soldier bends with curv'd neck and side-falling head,
> His eyes are closed, his face is pale, he dares not look on the bloody stump,
> And has not yet look'd on it.[73]

This is the most detailed individual encounter in 'The Wound-Dresser' and lies at the heart of the poem. There are two features that I would like to note. First, the undressing of the soldier, the exposure of the wound, with the poet intimately compassionating: 'undo the clotted line, remove the slough, wash off the matter and blood'. What Whitman does with his hands he automatically and simultaneously registers with his eyes—indeed it might be said that the actions of hand

[72] Erkkila, *Whitman: The Political Poet*, 219.
[73] 'The Wound-Dresser', *Leaves*, pp. 310–11, lines 45–9.

and eye are so interchangeable, so coordinated, that the unflinching attention of the eye is what dresses or undresses the wound. Or perhaps what we ought to say (given Erkkila's point that Whitman only rarely actually dressed wounds), is that what is remarkable is how the hand (Whitman never describes the action of his hand as such or the feel of the wounded flesh under his fingers) becomes a natural extension of the eye, does the work of the eye (or vice versa—the eye does for Whitman what for most people would be the work of the hand). Secondly, in a complementary way we note that the soldier's 'eyes are closed', that 'he dares not look' at his wound, 'And has not yet look'd': this emphasis on the soldier's understandable reluctance or inability to see rhymes with the fact that it is his hand which has been 'amputated'—as if the poem were implying that one needs a hand to see; that not to have a hand is to be blind. Whitman, however, has his hands and his eyes; that is, his hands are in his eyes. And he has to see and touch on behalf of this other man whom he sees and touches; this man whom he touches by seeing, as if out of respect for the fact that he will no longer be able to touch for himself. At least not with his hand. Henceforth seeing is the form that touching must take.

The figurative density doesn't dissolve the separateness of the two men. But it draws attention to the fact that Whitman's seeing is embodied: it is physical, fleshly, postured. The density of it all is remarkable—the emotional density coming from the figurative density. And one could of course say more. We have yet to discuss the soldier's posture or the angle of his head, how it echoes the way the poet succumbed earlier on in the poem, consciously—or conscientiously—to a feeling of psychic impotence ('my fingers fail'd me, my face drooped').[74] In all this 'The Wound-Dresser' takes up where 'The Sleepers' left off: we can see from his posture that the 'old man bending' (p. 308, line 1) over the wounded, 'With hinged knees' (p. 310, line 23), 'in silence, in dreams' projections' (line 20), is recognizably the one who a decade earlier had been 'Bending with open eyes over the shut eyes of sleepers' (p. 424, line 3).

Thus the old critical commonplace about the importance of seeing in Whitman, which we are accustomed to finding inflected by the relatively new (or newer) critical commonplace about the overbearing power of the eye, its gaze, its dominating scope, its imperialism, narcissism, etc., needs to be inflected again not just by an alertness to the way seeing is postured, held, embodied, but also by consideration of the possibility that for Whitman not to look is not to make contact at all: in other words, it is not looking rather than looking which is more likely to signal or become the condition of narcissism in Whitman.

Having considered the closeness of hand and eye in *Drum-Taps*, it's worth going back for a moment to that earlier, equally definitive sequence *Calamus*, with its celebration of 'The institution of the dear love of comrades' (*Leaves*,

---

[74] 'The Wound-Dresser', *Leaves*, p. 308, line 5.

p. 128). 'It is to the development, identification, and general prevalence of that fervid comradeship', Whitman wrote, 'that I look for the counterbalance and offset of our materialistic and vulgar American democracy, and for the spiritualization thereof.'[75] The question of what democracy is, who it's for, goes to the heart of the poems, as images of 'fervid comradeship', or what might seem to be the poet's mystically articulated, effaced and ineffaceable, homosexuality, search out and interrogate what is meant by democracy. The word homosexuality seems in some ways inadequate to the indefiniteness of the poetry, its historic ambiguity, but one has to use it so as not *not* to use it.[76] The poems necessarily raise the question, if not for Whitman then for us, of how free the 'free association' or relation between men really is. Nevertheless, what *Calamus* also makes clear— and this is where those who want to insist unambiguously on Whitman's homosexuality risk oversimplifying the texture of the poems—is that the nature of comradeship, like the nature of democracy, cannot be understood simply by *looking* at it. In 'A Glimpse', for example, the emotional anxiety about what the sighting of a young man through the 'interstice' of a 'bar-room' means is stilled by the same man's 'silently approaching and sitting himself near, that he may hold me by the hand' (*Leaves*, pp. 131–2). The uncertainty experienced at eye-level is ameliorated by the immanence of the body in space, which is communicated primarily by way of the hand. Again and again in *Calamus* hand and eye work together in a vivid process of adjustment.

If some of this is suggested merely by the title of 'Whoever You Are Holding Me Now in Hand', the poem 'Of the Terrible Doubt of Appearances' is just as potent. And once again the anxiety that 'May-be the things I perceive, the animals, plants, men, hills', and so on are 'only apparitions', is resolved by 'holding' and being 'held'.

> To me these and the like of these are curiously answer'd by my lovers, my
>   dear friends,
> When he whom I love travels with me or sits a long while holding me by the
>   hand,

---

[75] Whitman, qtd. in *Leaves*, p. 112.

[76] As far as the question of sexuality in Whitman's poetry is concerned, Robert K. Martin's *The Homosexual Tradition in American Poetry* (Austin: University of Texas Press, 1979), which argued that 'Whitman intended his work to communicate his homosexuality to his readers', was in its day a useful polemical corrective to the wilful ignorance of much of the criticism that preceded it, but the reading of the poetry is too tendentious, and readers are better served by Michael Moon, *Disseminating Whitman: Revision and Corporeality in Leaves of Grass* (Cambridge, Mass.: Harvard University Press, 1991). Commenting on Martin's reading of section 11 of 'Song of Myself', Moon rightly observes: 'Whitman might have opposed such a literally "sexual" reading of these lines . . . not so much because such a reading would be inaccurate or irrelevant as because limiting the determinate grounds for the exchanges which are represented in a passage like this one to specifically sexual ones is inevitably to produce a hermeneutic dead-end in a text which was designed to retain its fluidity and mobility of meaning(s)' (41).

> When the subtle air, the impalpable, the sense that words and reason hold
>   not, surround us and pervade us,
> Then I am charged with untold and untellable wisdom, I am silent, I require
>   nothing further,
> I cannot answer the question of appearances or that of identity beyond the
>   grave,
> But I walk or sit indifferent, I am satisfied,
> He ahold of my hand has completely satisfied me.
>
> (*Leaves*, p. 120, lines 10–16)

The 'long while holding me' is first contrasted here with 'the sense that words and reason hold not', then consolidated by 'He ahold of my hand'. In one or two poems the sense of the intimate environment created by holding is amplified by an unexpected movement indoors, as for instance in 'A Glimpse' or 'O You Whom I Often and Silently Come' ('As I walk by your side or sit near, or remain in the same room with you');[77] or by the way the poet sees or longs to see comrades similarly embraced ('I wish to infuse myself among you till I see it common for you to walk hand in hand';[78] 'Who oft as he saunter'd the streets curv'd with his arm the shoulder of his friend, while the arm of his friend rested upon him also').[79] The point in either case is that hand and vision work in tandem. What Whitman calls in 'Of the Terrible Doubt of Appearances' his 'point of view' is only really satisfied when it is accompanied by this holding or handling—as in 'When I Heard at the Close of the Day' ('his face was inclined toward me, | And his arm lay lightly around my breast—and that night I was happy').[80] The gaze doesn't function by itself: *the gaze holds and is held*.

And just as we saw in Winnicott, this holding, as realizing, communicating the reality of self and others, is not to be confused with clinging or grasping. It is able to let go; what is held can be released. Reality remains *transitional*: 'let go your hand from my shoulders, | Put me down and depart on your way' (*Leaves*, p. 116).

1.6 'IS THIS THEN A TOUCH?'

To recapitulate then: my starting point was that according to Tocqueville democratic seeing is not a function of difference, of the relationship between the me and the not-me, but a projection of sameness: 'each man, as he looks at himself, sees all his fellows at the same time'. A line like that could almost sound like Whitman, and yet it couldn't be further from him. As far as Whitman is concerned seeing is always postured, held, embodied: and its being so is a

---

[77] *Leaves*, pp. 135–6.   [78] Ibid., p. 132.
[79] Ibid., p. 122.   [80] Ibid., p. 123.

sign of the seer's relation to another; instead of being self-centred, a narcissistic projection, seeing is a form of acknowledgement, recalling the child's acknowledgement of its mother's acknowledgement of him (the child is not wholly self-centred, Winnicott would say, precisely because he is centred; is not self-absorbed precisely because he has once been absorbed). Seeing for Whitman presupposes a relational holding, an environmental munificence that goes beyond mere touching. Seeing presupposes touch and also transcends it—as the mother's holding of the child transcends the mere touching of it. Seeing is the fruit of one's being in relation, of the acceptance of the not-me. Without sight, touch is blind.

There is one more passage in particular from 'Song of Myself' on which this argument cries out to be tested. This is the sequence in the middle of the poem, relating the crisis provoked by touch. Working from her ideological perspective Erkkila interprets it as follows:

Read closely, the sequence provides a useful corrective to the popular image of Whitman as the poet of sexual excess. Whitman does not celebrate masturbation in 'Song of Myself.' On the contrary, his attitude is closer to the antimasturbation tracts published by Fowler and Wells, the distributors of the first edition of *Leaves of Grass*. Whitman presents masturbation as an instance of bodily perturbation—a muted sign, perhaps, of the unruliness of his own homosexual passion—and a trope for disorder in the political sphere. As a figure of democratic unruliness in body and body politic, masturbation becomes the sexual ground on which Whitman tests the democratic theory of America. By demonstrating the restoration of bodily balance after taking democracy to 'the verge of the limit' in a masturbatory fit, Whitman tests and enacts poetically the principle of self-regulation in individual and cosmos that is at the base of his democratic faith. But while he successfully manages the onslaught of touch within the symbolic order of the poem, the unruly body—both his own and the bodies of others—would remain a source of anxiety and perturbation in his dream of democracy. (106)

It is easy to see what Erkkila is getting at here: the poem does indeed seem to represent masturbation as a threat to the self-regulating body politic ('Treacherous tip of me', 'I am given up by traitors') which duly comes to rest on the moral hygiene of each individual ('I and nobody else am the greatest traitor'). From this perspective Whitman's anxious encounter with masturbation, with the poem dilating to contain it and restore the body politic, is, when we get down to it, ideologically determined. It is for ideological reasons—not cosmic ones—that touch ends up tamed by the poem's cosmic rhythm. In Erkkila's words: 'In the gloriously regenerative economy of "Song of Myself," (homo)erotic touching is safe and natural, quivering the poet not to a new and marginal identity as a homosexual in heterosexual America but toward an experience of cosmic community' (106). The problem here is that by making ideology the determining factor Erkkila passes over whatever it is in the poem's experiential make-up (in its way of experiencing the world, or of mediating the experience of the world—which comes to the same thing), in what I call its posture, that precedes or anticipates the ideological factor. For Erkkila, masturbation is rejected for ideological reasons: but what if it were rejected for what I want to call experiential reasons—because of some intuition the self has about itself; about itself in relation to the world? This intuition may not be incompatible with Whitman's ideological investment in democracy. But it may also mean that Whitman chooses democracy, or has developed what might be called a democratic tendency, for reasons that cannot be fully understood in such blanket ideological terms. The ideological cart seems to come before the horse—and the horse has been obscured altogether.

Here is the passage—the cart and the horse together:

> Is this then a touch? quivering me to a new identity,
> Flames and ether making a rush for my veins,
> Treacherous tip of me reaching and crowding to help them,
> My flesh and blood playing out lightning to strike what is hardly different from
>   myself,
> On all sides prurient provokers stiffening my limbs,
> Straining the udder of my heart for its withheld drip,
> Behaving licentious toward me, taking no denial,
> Depriving me of my best as for a purpose,
> Unbuttoning my clothes, holding me by the bare waist,
> Deluding my confusion with the calm of the sunlight and pasture-fields,
> Immodestly sliding the fellow-senses away,
> They bribed to swap off with touch and go and graze at the edges of me,
> No consideration, no regard for my draining strength or my anger,
> Fetching the rest of the herd around to enjoy them a while,
> Then all uniting to stand on a headland and worry me.
>
> The sentries desert every other part of me,
> They have left me helpless to a red marauder,
> They all come to the headland to witness and assist against me.
>
> I am given up by traitors,
> I talk wildly, I have lost my wits, I and nobody else am the greatest traitor,
> I went myself first to the headland, my own hands carried me there.
>
> You villain touch! what are you doing? my breath is tight in its throat,
> Unclench your floodgates, you are too much for me.
>
> (pp. 57–8, lines 619–41)

The problem with Erkkila's reading of this passage is that it seems to miss out altogether on the dynamics of touching and seeing in Whitman's poetry, on the intrinsic experiential posture of the poetry, which is the source of its tenderness and its peculiar eroticism, and which is moreover its handle on the world.

As I read it, it is not primarily for ideological reasons that touch is problematical, but because of the way in which it effects a regression in Whitman's receptive posture, which is not in the first place an ideological matter. Let us be clear about that receptive posture. In the first verse paragraph alone, the speaker is, or some part of him is, the direct or indirect object of at least thirteen verbal actions ('quivering me'; 'making a rush for my'; 'tip of me reaching'; 'stiffening my limbs'; 'Straining the udder of my'; 'Behaving . . . toward me'; 'Depriving me'; 'Unbuttoning my'; 'holding me'; 'Deluding my'; 'graze . . . of me'; 'no regard for my'; 'worry me'): he is associated with the subject of the verb only once, at line 622 ('My flesh and blood playing out . . . to strike'), and here too the object, if it is touched at all—and it isn't clear that it is—is 'hardly different from myself'. The first-person pronoun has not occurred once, and won't occur until line 637. When it does come, it comes with a rush: five times in three lines—but what is interesting even then is the failure of the 'I' to activate a verb so as to make contact with an object other than himself. In each case the speaker will turn out to be the recipient of any action described by a verb, while it is central to the whole effect that the subject as such is dissociated: the 'I' dissociated from 'my own hands' or 'My flesh and blood'; and the string of verbs dissociated from the 'prurient provokers', who get only one more concrete but indefinite pronoun reference ('They', line 630). We can agree that there seems to be an element of anxious sexual fantasy about the passage, as the perpetrators who masturbated the poet turn out to have been figments of his imagination. Meanwhile the dissociation is such that he will tell us 'my breath is tight in *its* throat' (my italics).[81]

Let us now consider the passage from the point of view of the mother–child relation as discussed by Winnicott and Freud. It seems to conflate imagery derived from two experiences. To begin with, there is the guilty recollection of erotic excitement in the child. 'In simplest possible terms', Winnicott writes, 'the excited baby, scarcely knowing what is happening, becomes carried away by crude instinct and with ideas of the powerful kind that belong to instinct.'[82] The child experiences its excitement as violent and invasive—as a threat to its fragile equilibrium—but on the other hand it 'is hardly different from myself'. The poem conveys the sense of being carried away by desire: 'my own hands carried me there' (not, for example, *I carried myself there by my own hands*)—and the difficulty the child has in accepting responsibility for its desire. The problem, if you like, of *becoming a subject*.

Compounded with this, there is a suggestion of growing identification with passive or patient maternity. As the speaker is attacked by its own desire, it feels as if it were nothing but the helpless object of another's desire. In other words, the speaker is like the mother at the point where she, or her breast, was attacked by the child—before the restitutive (empathic) gesture. Thus the poem is or recalls

---

[81] The wording of the entire passage is nearly identical in the original 1855 version.
[82] Winnicott, *Through Paediatrics*, 267.

that gesture. But first of all, it must allow, endure, and survive the attack. The imagery suggests a dairy cow in a pasture ('Straining the udder of my heart for its withheld drip'; 'pasture-fields'; 'graze at the edges'; 'the rest of the herd') suckled by a libidinous but invisible calf.

The stress falls, as was said, on the question of touch. The speaker cannot touch, he can only be touched. Nowhere in the passage does he actually succeed in touching another. He can fantasize, as we can see, about reaching out, but in so far as he touches rather than gets touched all he touches is himself. Otherwise the action is out of his hands. The question, 'Is this then a touch?' is not an empty question. If you touch yourself are you really touched?

The crucial point, then, is that there is no reciprocation—which for Whitman would take the form not of touching but of seeing. In Whitman touching by itself is blind ('Blind loving wrestling touch', line 642): to touch another you have to be able to see that other. But this seeing, as opposed to the kind of seeing that we find in Tocqueville, is always postured, embodied: that is to say, seeing is premissed on touching, and above that on holding. And holding goes beyond mere touching. 'The experience of the mother holding the situation becomes part of the self, becomes assimilated into the ego . . . The child thus becomes able to find new situation-holding experiences, and is able in time to take over the function of being the situation-holding person for someone else, without resentment.' Seeing is not just seeing but the expression of a holding, a being held, that can in turn hold: of compassionate recognition and relation. It is an acceptance of mutuality. It does not do away with difference but depends on it. It is mature perception. It is, in Whitman or indeed in Winnicott, the epistemic core of democracy.[83]

As I said earlier in relation to Tocqueville's critique of historical determinism, the ideological critic likes to look from a distance—and from a distance Whitman might indeed look like, as he is contiguous in time and place to, an anti-masturbation tract. Close up, however, he seems more like the relational being described by Winnicott. Nor should we forget entirely that while prudery may be a poor reason to find fault with masturbation, it is after all only masturbation. In other words, the coming to terms with infantile desire, mediated as it seems to be through the confrontation with masturbation, presents us with an extraordinarily hopeful interpretation of why we might want to be, feel that we are most ourselves insofar as we can be, citizens in a democracy: according to this theory we become citizens or democrats, not for reasons of ideology, nor even, more significantly, because we are resigned to the social contract, but rather because we have learned, and learned intimately, that that way recognition lies.

---

[83] In his short excellent book on Winnicott, Adam Phillips notes that Winnicott 'would suggest that there was a precarious but "innate democratic tendency" in the developing individual'. Adam Phillips, *Winnicott* (London: Fontana, 1988), 71. The essay Phillips is referring to here is not one of Winnicott's best unfortunately but as I understand it the notion is implicit throughout his work. See D. W. Winnicott, 'Some Thoughts on the Meaning of the Word Democracy', *The Family and Individual Development* (1965; London: Brunner-Routledge, 2001), 155–69.

2

The Poet in the Dark: Ezra Pound, an Arendtian Perspective

Das Licht der Öffentlichkeit verdunkelt alles.
(The light of the public obscures everything.)
Martin Heidegger, quoted by Hannah Arendt,
Preface to *Men in Dark Times*

In the gloom, the gold gathers the light against it.
Ezra Pound, canto 11

In the previous chapter I looked at how a certain model of human subjectivity, which I referred to as the narcissistic model, was inadequate to describe what I called Whitman's posture, the intersubjective and democratic nature of which, I argued, is expressed in what may be characterized as the invisible physiognomy of the poetry. In this chapter, I want to look, from a completely different perspective, but with the same sort of phenomenological intensity, at the complexion of intersubjectivity in Ezra Pound. The argument is that we can better understand Pound's visionary humanism by examining it in the light of the political thought of Hannah Arendt. It is an aim that might seem at first to be arbitrary, paradoxical, and perverse. Might it not dishonour the thought of Arendt to draw comparisons between her work and Pound's? After all, it is not too much to say that her book *The Origins of Totalitarianism* (1951) was, as one scholar recently observed, 'for a number of years the most comprehensive and influential effort to come to terms with what came to be called the "Holocaust"'.[1] It traced the origins of totalitarianism to the impact of colonialism and imperialism, to what Arendt called 'the decline of the nation-state and the end of the rights of man', and to the history of European anti-Semitism. In the philosophical consideration it gave to specific historical phenomena, it has been likened to Tocqueville's *Democracy in America*,[2] and it remains to this day, 'an

---

[1] Richard H. King, *Race, Culture, and the Intellectuals, 1940–1970* (Washington: Woodrow Wilson Center Press; Baltimore: Johns Hopkins University Press, 2004), 96.

[2] The comparison to Tocqueville is familiar, but see Margaret Canovan, *Hannah Arendt: A Reinterpretation of Her Political Thought* (Cambridge: Cambridge University Press, 1992), 60: 'Like Burke on the French Revolution, Montesquieu on the British Constitution or Tocqueville on America (all of whom she greatly admired) she [Arendt] was less interested in writing history than in presenting a model of the political possibilities and dangers of her time.' Canovan suggests that

enormously suggestive effort to understand the political and social experience of continental Jewry between emancipation and extermination'.[3] Ezra Pound by contrast had emerged by the middle of the twentieth century as a public spokesperson for the totalitarian cause, a propagandist of downright criminal proportions. And the many desultory pieces he wrote on Jews and economics prior to this obscene wartime manifestation, in which names like Rothschild recur like a mantra, read like perfect examples of the obsessive *fin-de-siècle* anti-Semitic mindset Arendt documented in *Origins*. The biographies seem to sum up the differences: the European Jewess who had to flee her continent and found refuge in America, and the American Protestant who charged off to Europe and betrayed his democratic heritage. One of these authors seemed to know the twentieth century inside out, the other to bubble in the froth of it, or to mistake it for another century altogether.

Yet it is the terms of Arendt's own thought that justify the comparison. In *The Human Condition* (1958) Arendt argued for the special place of forgiveness in human affairs. It could even be said that it is forgiveness that makes them possible at all: 'Only through this constant mutual release from what they do can men remain free agents, only by constant willingness to change their minds and start again can they be trusted with so great a power as that to begin something new' (*HC*, 240). But 'nobody can forgive himself; here, as in action and speech generally, we are dependent upon others, to whom we appear in a distinctness which we ourselves are unable to perceive' (*HC*, 243). The fact that 'nobody can forgive himself' is the paradox with which Pound is confronted in the *Drafts and Fragments*, and it is what makes them, in their Lear-like way, so moving, as Pound, in his broken and yet lucid hubris, tries to say the words that only another —a Cordelia, say—could utter.

However, forgiveness does not come easily: it is tied to the obligation to make a judgement, another concept dear to Arendt's heart. There can be no forgiveness without the willingness to make a judgement, which like all things political is a risky, fallible, in a word human, thing to do. If you mean to forgive Pound you will have to judge him first.

This issue of judgement and forgiveness had a very particular bearing on Arendt's own life in an instance that invites direct comparison with the case of Pound. Arendt had been one of Martin Heidegger's students at Freiburg, and became, as is now well known, the philosopher's youthful lover. To Arendt's dismay, Heidegger became (as is also well known) an enthusiastic supporter of National Socialism, joining the Nazi Party on 1 May 1933, and turning his back on his Jewish mentor at Freiburg, Edmund Husserl.[4] This is not the place to go

---

when she 'lectured on Tocqueville at the University of California in 1955, she was evidently struck by the similarity of his approach to her own' (67 n. 16).

[3] King, *Race, Culture, and the Intellectuals*, 110.

[4] See Hugo Ott, *Martin Heidegger: A Political Life*, trans. Allan Blunden (London: Harper Collins Publishers, 1993).

into Arendt's relationship to Heidegger. But the fact is that she continued throughout her life to speak of the great philosopher with admiration and gratitude, even while she dismissed his political obtuseness. Her contribution, in 1969, to Heidegger's eightieth birthday *Festschrift,* eventually published in English as 'Martin Heidegger at 80', exemplifies, as Arendt's biographer Elisabeth Young-Breuhl puts it, 'her willingness to forgive Heidegger for his year in the Nazi Party'.[5] Indeed commentators as distinct as Seyla Benhabib and Julia Kristeva invoke this same concept of forgiveness to describe Arendt's attitude.[6]

It would be hard to find a more appropriate philosopher to help us to forgive Pound. But forgiveness is only a beginning, as Arendt says. What I also want to argue is that the extraordinary residual power of *The Cantos,* the way they may be said to hang fire, finds an almost perfect philosophical correlative in Arendt's concept of the 'space of appearance' which 'comes into being wherever men are together in the manner of speech and action' (*HC,* 199). *The Cantos* might well be the most remarkable image in twentieth-century Anglo-American literature of what Arendt understood the *polis* to be. In their meditations on the glory and frailty of human affairs, both writers were beset by archetypal images of light and dark. The light of *The Cantos* is the reciprocated light of the space of appearances, with its deceptive aura of antiquity, and the darkness that shadows them is that same darkness which Arendt felt benighted the public sphere in the modern age: the darkness of Bertolt Brecht's *finsteren Zeiten.*

If Arendt's work tries to explain the rarity of meaningful political life in the twentieth century, then there are of course many other philosophical writers of whom one could say as much. There are not so many though who have been able to light up, to illumine, its occurrence—of whom it would be possible to say that their work is more remarkable for its charity than its despair. It is one of the things that distinguishes Arendt. She is blessedly and refreshingly free of the too piquant pessimism, the not entirely stoical resignation of Theodor Adorno (too often the resignation of the dialectical *Besserwisser*) and the Frankfurt School or the ecstatic nihilism of Michel Foucault.[7] This willingness to see the virtue in things, a high-mindedness that is at the same time a kind of open-mindedness, is invaluable when it comes to making sense of the politics of Pound.

[5] Elisabeth Young-Bruehl, *Hannah Arendt: For Love of the World* (New Haven: Yale University Press, 1982), 531–2 n. 9.

[6] Seyla Benhabib, *The Reluctant Modernism of Hannah Arendt* (Thousand Oaks, Calif.: Sage, 1996), 103; Julia Kristeva, *Hannah Arendt,* trans. Ross Guberman (New York: Columbia University Press, 2001), 234.

[7] For the affinity between Adorno and Foucault, we have, among other things, Foucault's own testimony: 'A decade and a half after Adorno's death . . . Foucault . . . said: "If I had known about the Frankfurt School in time, I would have been saved a great deal of work. I would not have said a certain amount of nonsense and would not have taken so many false trails trying not to get lost, when the Frankfurt School had already cleared the way" '. Rolf Wiggershaus, *The Frankfurt School: Its History, Theories and Political Significance,* trans. Michael Robertson (Cambridge: Polity Press, 1994), 4.

As for arbitrariness, this chapter will try to show that when it came to political orientation Pound and Arendt had a number of critical affirmations and resistances in common: first, a tremendous esteem for the American Revolution and the men who fathered it; secondly, a long critical engagement with the writings and influence of Karl Marx, which expresses itself in both as an anti-capitalistic anti-communism; thirdly, against the grain of American individualism or European existentialism, a tendency to take their profoundest bearings from the life we have in common, not from the consciousness of the individual subject; fourthly, the desire to cast this life in heroic terms, the terms of ancient Greek art and thought, where men are 'what they do and say and suffer', and action and identity are one[8]—which has left both writers open to the charge of nostalgia; and finally, contrary to the Romantic ethos summed up by Goethe and haunting the psyche of poets ever since, both writers insist on the political responsibilities of poets: they are not to be exempt from the claims of citizenship.

Arendt makes this point with steady irony in her famous essay on Brecht:

To talk about poets is an uncomfortable task; poets are there to be quoted, not to be talked about. Those whose specialty is literature, and among whom we now find the 'Brecht scholars,' have learned how to overcome their unease, but I am not one of them. The voice of the poets, however, concerns all of us, not only critics and scholars; it concerns us in our private lives and also insofar as we are citizens. We don't need to deal with *engagé* poets in order to feel justified in talking about them from a political viewpoint, as citizens, but it seems easier for a non-literary person to engage in this activity if political attitudes and commitments have played an all-important role in the life and work of an author, as they did in Brecht's.

The first thing to be pointed out is that poets have not often made good, reliable citizens; Plato, himself a great poet in philosopher's disguise, was not the first to be sorely worried and annoyed by poets. There has always been trouble with them; they have often shown a deplorable tendency to misbehave, and in our century their misbehaviour has on occasion been of even deeper concern to citizens than ever before. We need only remember the case of Ezra Pound. The United States government decided not to put him on trial for treason in wartime, because he could plead insanity, whereupon a committee of poets did, in a way, what the government chose not to—it judged him—and the result was an award for having written the best poetry of 1948. The poets honoured him regardless of his misbehaviour or insanity. They judged the poet; it was not their business to judge the

---

[8] See Alasdair MacIntyre, *After Virtue: A Study in Moral Theory* (1981; London: Duckworth, 1985), 122–3: 'A man in heroic society is what he does. Hermann Fränkel wrote of Homeric man that "a man and his actions become identical, and he makes himself completely and adequately comprehended in them; he has no hidden depths. . . . In [the epics] factual report of what men do and say, everything that men are, is expressed, because they are no more than what they do and say and suffer" [Hermann Fränkel, *Early Greek Poetry and Philosophy*, trans. M. Hadas and J. Willis (1973), 79]. To judge a man therefore is to judge his actions. By performing actions of a particular kind in a particular situation a man gives warrant for judgement upon his virtues and vices; for the virtues just are those qualities which sustain a free man in his role and which manifest themselves in those actions which his role requires'. In short, a heroic society is one in which 'morality and social structure are in fact one and the same'.

citizen. And since they were poets themselves, they might have thought in Goethe's terms: '*Dichter sündgen nicht schwer*' [poets don't sin heavily] . . .

Undeniably, Ezra Pound's sins were more serious [than Brecht's] . . . In his vicious radio broadcasts, he went far beyond Mussolini's worst speeches, doing Hitler's business and proving to be one of the worst Jew-baiters among the intellectuals on either side of the Atlantic. . . .However, Pound could plead insanity and get away with things that Brecht, entirely sane and highly intelligent, was not able to get away with. Brecht's sins were smaller than Pound's, yet he sinned more heavily, because he was only a poet, not an insane one.[9]

Arendt's greatest irony is reserved for those who have attempted to judge Pound as a poet without also judging him as a citizen—that is, without actually judging him at all. For judgement as Arendt understands it asserts the common ground between literary specialists and 'non-literary persons', poets and politicians. Judgement presupposes the common ground of citizenship. There is a sense in which by failing to judge Pound we leave him muttering to himself. The implication is that the poets who honoured Pound's poetry 'regardless of his misbehaviour', by granting him madness denied him forgiveness.[10]

2.1 SUBJECTS AND OBJECTS

2.1.1

If we dare to think of it for a moment as a political programme, then humanism may mean preserving the possibility of action against the incursions of violence, a definition that presupposes a distinction between action and violence. In circumstances in which the meaning of a given distinction is unclear, it is the heroism of humanism—and of poetry in particular—to preserve the terms. Along with other poets and philosophers, Pound struggled with the abstract categories on which we depend to make distinctions. But there can be no doubt that one way or another he preserved the terms.

Pound's dislike of abstraction was not confined to poetry. 'The incapacity of abstract statement to retain meaning or utility is perhaps nowhere more apparent

---

[9] Hannah Arendt, 'Bertolt Brecht: 1898–1956', *Men in Dark Times* (San Diego, Calif.: Harcourt Brace & Company, 1983), 207–49 (210–12).

[10] Arendt could not have known that Pound had been judged privately and directly by some of the poets closest to him, such as William Carlos Williams and Basil Bunting. In a letter to Pound in 1938, the English poet Bunting denounced the anti-Semitic 'rot' of his friend's heart and mind. See Keith Alldritt, *The Poet as Spy: The Life and Wild Times of Basil Bunting* (London: Aurum Press, 1998), 94: 'It was a critical moment in the history of his friendship with Ezra Pound, the most important and determining one in Basil's life.' Henceforward contact was restricted to an exchange of letters. For Williams's vexed relationship to Pound, judging first, forgiving later, see Paul Mariani, *William Carlos Williams: A New World Naked* (New York: McGraw-Hill Book Company, 1981).

than in the declaration of the rights of man,' he wrote in the 1940s.[11] 'Liberty', he argued, 'is not defendable on a static theory.'[12] We need, he maintained, an 'opportunist politics' for a 'flowing world' (274). Freedom, he suggests, is energy applied—particular, vivid, and effective. Pound acknowledges there must be rule of law: the individual, 'to be free . . . must know his law . . . the law of his country or countries, he must know his history' (275). The 'constitution' must not be 'violated' (ibid.). Nevertheless, the law should not be a sequence of abstractions. It depends upon 'a quick and ready perception of when the given case fits the general formula' (273). 'Machiavelli's democracy', he protests, was too 'theoretic', yet we need 'not less theory but more' (275): i.e. theory that is 'quick and ready perception', theory that is too alive and supple to be fixed. It must be informed by a 'conception' of the 'flow' and 'time-spirit' of events (ibid.). What Pound was seeking of course, here as in his poetry, was a perfect coincidence of idea and action—a concept that wouldn't fail of its object. Nevertheless, it is interesting to see which article of the Declaration of the Rights of Man and Citizens (1789), as published by France's revolutionary National Assembly, Pound singled out as exemplifying abstract obsolescence: 'Liberty is the right to do anything that does not injure others' (273). Pound's most sustained attempt to safeguard liberty, to cherish the freedom of mind that art and individuality exemplify, while simultaneously cherishing the law, is worked out in his lifelong meditation on action, where what begins as the solution to an epistemological problem, a problem of aesthetics or perception, emerges as a political problem in the broadest sense.

In one of the most cogent treatments of the subject, James Longenbach has argued that between the original version of the Browningesque *Three Cantos*, first published in 1917, and the publication of *A Draft of XVI. Cantos* in 1925, Pound makes the radical break from a subjectivist attitude to history, i.e. 'blooded' history, or what Fredric Jameson calls 'existential historicism', to an objectivist conception of history—the 'neopositivist' idea of history as a 'concatenation of facts'.[13] The key points of Longenbach's argument can be summarized as follows. The early Pound, the Pound who set out to write *The Cantos*, was reacting against the impersonal nineteenth-century tradition of German philology. Accordingly, he deliberately endorsed a subjectivist position that can be helpfully summarized by Wilhelm Dilthey's dictum that 'the first condition for the possibility of the study of history lies in this: that I myself am an historical being, that the man who studies history is the man who makes history'.[14] The most compelling evidence for Longenbach's argument is the frequency with

---

[11] Ezra Pound, 'Freedom de Facto', *Selected Prose 1909–1965*, ed. William Cookson (London: Faber, 1973), 273.

[12] Ibid. 275.

[13] James Longenbach, *Modernist Poetics of History: Pound, Eliot, and the Sense of the Past* (Princeton: Princeton University Press, 1987), 18, 13, 141.

[14] Ibid. 14.

which Pound uses the first-person pronoun in *Three Cantos*, as compared with his pronounced omission of it in *The Cantos* as such. Pound also used a distinctively subjectivist approach in his criticism, and this method is what breathes life into the scholarship of *The Spirit of Romance* (1910) and *I Gather the Limbs of Osiris* (1911–12). Other obvious examples of Pound's 'existential historicism' would be his free translations, translations that are also selections and interpretations. However, about 1919 Pound apparently rejected this historicist stance, and in *The Cantos* he increasingly rejects or disguises the conditions of his own subjectivity as he tries to 'give the impression of the tribe's own heritage narrating itself' (here Longenbach adopts the terms of Michael Bernstein's influential work).[15] Longenbach's interpretation of what seems to be an absolute volte-face raises, on straightforward epistemological grounds, many of the important questions about Pound, art, politics, and history. He writes, 'Pound's removal of the signs of authorial presence from *The Cantos* is finally a political strategy designed to make his idiosyncratic interpretations of history and economics seem as inevitable as nature itself. Unless we want to excuse Pound's unattractive politics, we cannot accept his fiction that the poem "narrates itself." The history included in *The Cantos* is not factual or inevitable in any absolute sense; it is one man's interpretation' (142–3).

As a conclusion this is familiar and persuasive. Nevertheless, I want to try and break down some of its constitutive omissions and assumptions. From the point of view of Arendt, for instance, the first condition for the possibility of the study of history is not that 'I myself am an historical being' but that people have come together in the manner of speech and action to create history: I can be a historical being only by virtue of the being of others. Moreover there is something in their speaking and acting together—call it the quality of plurality or togetherness itself, a quality which Pound and Arendt identify with light—that transcends 'one man's interpretation'. For Longenbach it is clear that Pound's politics are unattractive because they are undemocratic, and he takes it for granted that the interpretative priority—and with it the fallibility—of the individual subject can stand for democracy. For Arendt, however, democracy is no guarantor of politics: politics begins when people in their plurality act and speak. Nevertheless, Longenbach's discussion of the individual subject in Pound's early work ('authorial presence') paves the way for his observation that it is eventually and successfully reinstated in *The Pisan Cantos*.

One of the starting points for this chapter is that Longenbach's emphasis on individual subjectivity, with its attendant subject–object dualism, simplifies and rigidifies a complex of problems that Pound was trying to negotiate dynamically. In order to understand Pound's politics in relation to his poetics, we need to see how far his writing intuited the creative and political bankruptcy of what we are

---

[15] Michael Bernstein, *The Tale of the Tribe: Ezra Pound and the Modern Verse Epic* (Princeton: Princeton University Press, 1980), 171.

today in a better position to classify as subject-centred reason ('one man's interpretation').[16] Like his best poetic effects, Pound's politics are inseparable from this basic insight, endlessly breaking out on the surface of the text. Longenbach's failure to engage the poem's struggle for expressive means, its crisis of innovation, where articulacy and inarticulacy converge, begging our intervention, is reductive in the strictest sense of the word.

What follows can be divided into several broad stages. First, I would like to present an alternative context for the evidence that Longenbach assembles, by reconsidering Pound's concern with *identity* and *facts*, that is, with the subjective and the objective, and referring what emerges to one instance in the wider cultural context of that concern, the revival of interest in the theory and possibilities of the epic. In subsequent sections I will try to clarify the nature of Pound's revolutionary humanism through a more detailed comparison with the political thought of Arendt.

2.1.2

Pound traces the dynamic ramifications of his theory of the image, ramifications that led him to Vorticism, in *Gaudier-Brzeska: A Memoir* (1916): in other words, right at the beginning of his movement away from resolutely centred subjectivity. In his instinct for the inadequacy of the epistemic subject, and in his desire to find a new way of coming at the actuality of the object, Pound was dealing in his own philosophically untutored way with one of the characteristic crises of Western thought in the early twentieth century, in response to which thinkers as distinct as Georg Lukács and Martin Heidegger were trying to move beyond the limitations of subjectivism while steering clear of a coldly rationalistic positivism.[17] In this context, Pound's reflections on the image, despite their familiarity, are worth re-examining. Referring to 'In a Station of the Metro', he explains, 'I dare say it is meaningless unless one has drifted into a certain vein of thought. In a poem of this sort one is trying to record the precise instant when a thing outward and objective transforms itself, or darts into a thing inward and

---

[16] The most important contemporary theorist in this respect has been Jürgen Habermas, who sets out to replace the subject–object paradigm of epistemology with the subject–subject paradigm of communicative rationality. The conceptual history of decentred subjectivity's 'stubborn self-disclosure', which finally 'assumed objective shape' in the twentieth-century avant-garde, is developed in Jürgen Habermas, *The Philosophical Discourse of Modernity*, trans. Frederick Lawrence (Cambridge: Polity Press, 1987), 122.

[17] Heidegger was certainly influenced by the emphasis on immanent interpretation that is found in Dilthey's hermeneutics, but as J. L. Mehta puts it, he 'rejected the psychological concept of *Erlebnis* [lived experience], along with all that was subjectivistic in Dilthey's way of thinking'. J. L. Mehta, *The Philosophy of Martin Heidegger* (New York: Harper & Row, 1971), 18. Habermas writes in *Philosophical Discourse of Modernity* that while Heidegger 'takes up' certain 'impulses' from 'Dilthey, Bergson and Simmel', he 'recognizes the inadequacy of the basic concepts of the philosophy of consciousness dragged along with them' (142).

subjective.'[18] This statement is more complicated than it seems, since the emphasis is not on a static resolution (the aftermath of the internalization of the thing) but on the verb 'transforms', i.e. on the 'precise instant' of the 'dart [ing]' movement—the process of transformation. The poem itself gives neither the 'outward and objective' nor the 'inward and subjective' priority, but sets up a dialogue between subjective images (the 'apparition of these faces' is not less subjective, or more plausible as an object, than 'petals on a wet, black bough'), in which the internal is meaningless without the external, and in which the dialogical, subject–subject relationship, between juxtaposed aesthetic utterances, comprehends, outlasts, and effectively destabilizes (reactivates) any determinate subject–object relationship.

Pound's criticism constantly emphasizes the activity of the image. What analysis tends to show is that this activity is created dialogically, through the bringing together of subject statements. Instead of endorsing the linear *telos* of the subject–object paradigm, the image produces a lateral space, a 'complex'[19] or a 'vortex' (*Gaudier-Brzeska*, 92), with no one epistemic end in sight. Cognition is not contained and confined by epistemological certainty, but has become on the contrary an effect of uncertainty, an effect of 'liberation; that sense of freedom from time limits and space limits' (*Literary Essays*, 4). Cognition happens alongside or within the dialogue of possibilities. Similarly, whereas Longenbach reads Pound's contention, of 1915, that the 'first difficulty in a modern poem is to give a feeling of the reality of the speaker',[20] as meaning that the reality of things is conditioned, first and foremost, by psychological reality, much as history in Dilthey is conditioned by the 'I' (*Modernist Poetics*, 143), I would point to the significance of *spokenness* itself—with which Dilthey is not concerned: *the reality of things as an effect of speech*. I would say that this helps to account for the exaggerated intimations of spokenness that we find in early Pound, something which Longenbach's reading frequently exposes, particularly in *Three Cantos*, but does not actually address.

In *Gaudier-Brzeska*, Pound had written:

If I am to give a psychological or philosophical definition 'from the inside,' I can only do so autobiographically. The precise statement of such a matter must be based on one's own experience.

In the 'search for oneself,' in the search for 'sincere self-expression,' one gropes, one finds some seeming verity. One says 'I am' this, that, or the other, and with the words scarcely uttered one ceases to be that thing. (85)

---

[18] Ezra Pound, *Gaudier-Brzeska: A Memoir* (1916; New York: New Directions, 1970), 89.
[19] See Ezra Pound, 'A Retrospect', *The Literary Essays of Ezra Pound*, ed. T. S. Eliot (London: Faber and Faber, 1954), 3–14 (4): 'An "Image" is that which presents an intellectual and emotional complex in an instant of time'.
[20] 'Remy de Gourmont', *Selected Prose*, 383–93 (388).

Here the subject, conceived as an individual, cannot wholly grasp his 'experience'. This apparently untroubled statement of modernist dissociation (usually read as an ominous portent of a later, supposedly schizoid Pound), with its heavy emphasis on voiced realities, tends to bear out that alongside the dynamics of the image there was, as we might expect, a complementary dynamics of the self. The self here is conceived in relation to itself, intersubjectively, emerging and disappearing in a flux of speech (something nicely brought out by Pound's use of quotation marks, interrupting the monotone that accompanies the logic of the sentence). Something survives the self's self-expression: something that apparently is also the self; but this self is not quite the self that was just expressed; or if it is it seems different. Pound does not go on to say that the important energy lies in the continuing relationship between separate temporary acts of self-expression; nevertheless, the theory and practice of Imagism are already moving him away from a static notion of centred subjectivity towards a complex affirmation of the importance of relationship, an intersubjective or dialogical way of looking at self and world.

If we bear in mind this suggestion of dialogical or intersubjective reason, a mobile knowing subject to which neither a single voice nor a single identity seems adequate (a subject not so much divided against itself, as freely and creatively *divided*), it can be seen I think to anticipate a statement which Longenbach cites, Pound's 1919 formulation, in 'Pastiche: the Regional', of the *historical concept*: 'Any historical concept and any sociological deduction from history must assemble a great number of violently contrasted facts, if it is to be valid. It must not be a simple paradox, or a simple opposition of two terms' (*Modernist Poetics*, 140). Pound's habitual resistance to reductive binaries, including the subject–object binary, was inscribed in the language that he used to invoke the epistemic vortex in *Gaudier-Brzeska*: '"I am" this, that, or the other' (85): 'from which, and through which, and into which' (92)—triads that evoke complicated constellations not just paradoxical alternatives. And what Longenbach's interpretation of the quotation from 'Pastiche: the Regional' ignores is its emphasis on the energizing nature of a complex relationship, in which the assembled facts are 'violently contrasted'. This is to ignore what all Pound's art will keep driving at: the energy between the facts, moving from one to another, the intersubjective, dialogical dynamic. We can get some sense of what it means to think in this way, to think through and with (and not against) the violently contrasted, historical transit of the image, by comparing Pound's stance with Henry Adams's more desperate recourse to imagistic thinking, which had been expressed only a few years earlier (both writers use the same evocatively scientific language), but which in Adams's case is so much more apologistic: 'Images are not arguments, rarely even lead to proof, but the mind craves them, and, of late more than ever, the keenest experimenters find twenty images better than one, especially if contradictory; since the human mind has already learned to deal in contradictions.'[21] Adams saw the recourse to images as the inevitable and inadequate consequence of the unicellular mind's inability to keep pace with progress, the 'law of acceleration'; he maintained that the mind can only 'react' to progress, it cannot intervene.[22] However, his concept of imagist reaction depends, like his concept of ultimate futility, on the assumption that there is an ahistorical language for the constitution of the mind, from which transcendental perspective it may indeed seem that history accelerates away. Pound does not make the same assumption. His imagist states of mind are not distanced from that history which they try to understand. They are part of history, not cast out of it. They are there among the 'facts'.

But what did Pound mean by 'facts'? According to Longenbach, who takes his bearings from Karl Popper (via Bernstein) and T. S. Eliot ('whose understanding of the intricacies of historiography surpassed Pound's in these matters'), Pound's interest in facts is 'predicated on the questionable belief that anything we could call a "fact" exists independently from the interpretive strategy that presents it' (*Modernist Poetics*, 143). On this reading Pound succumbs to his self-created 'illusion of impersonal objectivity' (142). However, as against this troublingly undynamic, curiously unhistorical notion of Pound's neopositivism, what I am trying to suggest is that there is another way of thinking about what Pound was doing, whereby the word 'fact' becomes a polemical weapon in his not yet fully articulate struggle with the straitjacket of his own late-Romantic, subjectivist vocabulary. This is (as Longenbach helps to show) a struggle which is to some extent worked out in dialogue with Browning. And in 1919, one of the years at the heart of Longenbach's argument, we find some interesting instances of the word 'fact' in a short article on Browning's translations of Aeschylus. Pound writes:

'Thought' as Browning understood it—'ideas' as the term is current, are poor two-dimensional stuff, a scant, scratch covering. 'Damn ideas, anyhow.' An idea is only an imperfect induction from fact.

The solid, the 'last atom of force verging off into the first atom of matter' is the force, the emotion, the objective sight of the poet. In the *Agamemnon* it is the whole rush of the action.[23]

What Pound means by fact, it seems, is 'matter' in 'action'. Pound emphasizes 'fact' not because he wants to ignore the individual, but because he wants to emphasize action over subjectivity and linguistic obfuscation. He is probably never closer to Aristotle than he is here. In keeping with the emphasis of Aristotle's *Poetics*, it is not individuality but *action* which is the centre of things.

[21] Henry Adams, *The Education of Henry Adams* (1918; Boston: Houghton Mifflin Company, 1973), 489.
[22] Ibid. 489–98.
[23] 'Translation of Aeschylus', in 'Translators of Greek: Early Translators of Homer', *Literary Essays*, 267–75 (267).

For both men 'the whole rush of the action' is what Aristotle calls the 'soul of the tragic art', corresponding to that 'superiority of activities over states', which Gerald F. Else rightly describes as an Aristotelian commonplace.[24] Moreover, as we shall see, it is via the action that the speaker will be recognized, will become 'Klutaimnestra actual' (*Literary Essays*, 270). In order to drive home what he sees as the failure of Browning's translation Pound whets his axe and gives his own:

> 'This is Agamemnon,
> My husband,
> Dead by this hand,
> And a good job. These, gentlemen, are the facts'.

No, that is extreme, but the point is that any natural wording, anything which keeps the mind off theatricals and on Klutaimnestra actual, dealing with an actual situation, and not pestering the reader with frills and festoons of language, is worth all the convoluted tushery that the Victorians can heap together. (*Literary Essays*, 270)

This is what Pound means by the 'objective sight of the poet': a technique that can meet, in quick, economical language, the demands of the whole rush of action. Pound does not forget the individual actor who contributes to the action, but finds her most 'actual' in her dealings with an 'actual situation'. 'These, gentleman, are the facts': i.e. this is the 'matter', the 'solid', the 'force'; this is where the 'emotion' is, if it is anywhere. Pound uses 'facts' to convey, as directly as possible, aspects of the surface of the matter. It is certainly true to say that the emphasis has changed. As an Imagist, Pound might be said to have simply pared down romanticism's inheritance of the subjective. But now he is cutting through to what Imagism had already implied: that the objective is the first to find out the subjective; that the objective comprehends it through the integral of action. As far as Pound is concerned, action increasingly approximates to the ideal epistemic situation.

Unlike Pound, Longenbach never tries to imagine or project an alternative to the either/or, subjective or objective history dilemma. And so he reads the poem without yielding anything to the nascent, experimental element which I take it is another part of its foothold in time, and which has its issue in the question of action—almost as explicit in 1919 as it will be in *Guide to Kulchur* (1938).[25] However, it is only by addressing the 'Charybdis of action' (canto 74/445) that one can hope to address Pound's politics, and to work out its relation to his poetics.[26]

---

[24] Gerald F. Else, *Aristotle's Poetics: The Argument* (Cambridge, Mass.: Harvard University Press, 1967), 252–3. The main section of *The Poetics* in question is ch. 6, 15a15.

[25] See Pound, *Kulchur*, 182: 'Not only is the truth of a given idea measured by the degree and celerity wherewith it goes into action, but a very distinct component of truth remains ungrasped by the non-participant in the action.'

[26] Ezra Pound, *The Cantos* (1954; London: Faber and Faber, 1987). In this and all subsequent references to *The Cantos* I cite both canto and page.

2.1.3

Pound explicitly protests against the assumption that the artist can know what he is doing—can somehow describe it all in the appropriate general philosophical terms—as well as *do* what he is doing. This is also a protest against the ingrained idea of a single knowing subject. To define what has been generally attested to be the most influential breakthrough in English poetic technique this century as, in effect, the subjective representing itself as the objective, is to simplify beyond recognition the continuing disintegration of the subjective into the fragmentary intersubjective (with all its attendant 'violent contrasts'), a *complex of knowing* which constitutes one of the abiding features of modernity. Now obviously there are many different ways of representing the phenomenon of the disintegrating subject. In Pound's case I am arguing that it led to the gradually more intense discovery of the integral power of action.

In the piece on Browning's Aeschylus, Pound distinguishes between two different kinds of obscurity: 'obscurities' embedded in the 'wording', and 'obscurities inherent in the thing': 'Obscurities inherent in the thing occur when the author is piercing, or trying to pierce into, uncharted regions; when he is trying to express things not yet current, not yet worn into phrase; when he is ahead of the emotional, or philosophic sense (as a painter might be ahead of the colour-sense) of his contemporaries' (*Literary Essays*, 268–9). This is an important digression on Pound's part, as he wanders away from a discussion of translation into a more personal reflection on the time lag between a technical innovation and its concept, i.e. between a change in one's way of writing and the conceptualization of that change. In order to find a conceptual parallel for the historical project at the heart of Pound's epic, we might usefully consider the ideas of one of his more strictly philosophical contemporaries. Not Dilthey this time, whom Longenbach cites, but Lukács. Pound's rehabilitation of the epic poem for an irreversibly post-Homeric age corresponds in several significant respects to Lukács's extraordinary exposition of the post-Homeric epic of the novel. Instead of reducing Pound's objective bias to the simple opposite of Dilthey's subjectivism, Lukács helps us to see it as an attempt to submit the egotism of the subject to the particularity of the historical process. What both writers finally share is an inversion of the values found in *The Poetics*, where Aristotle distinguishes between universality and history and exalts the first over the second.

However, timing is probably the most obvious part of the parallel with Lukács, who tells us that *The Theory of the Novel*, which finally appeared in 1920, was actually begun in 1914 and completed during the first winter of the Great War.[27] Looking back nearly fifty years later, Lukács explained that a considerable part of what motivated him was his deeply personal 'rejection of the war and, together with it, of the bourgeois society of that time' (12). He would make larger and

---

[27] Georg Lukács, *The Theory of the Novel*, trans. Anna Bostock (London: Merlin, 1971), 11.

more communal sense of this rejection, and as it were ground his utopian vision, after he had written *The Theory of the Novel* and when he eventually came to terms with what Marx had defined as the economic bedrock of Western civilization. In the same way, a fuller realization of the socio-economic was what Pound experienced, as he moved away from the narrowly aesthetic nineteenth-century aloofness of the Mauberley persona (the type to whom the war was indeed fought 'For a few thousand battered books'),[28] to the conviction, in *The Cantos*, that the larger social questions, the questions of people en masse, need in the first place to be understood economically: 'There is no serious history without study of the social texture wherein IS the money factor' (*Kulcher*, 277). In *Guide to Kulchur* Pound would take a critical position on cultural treasures as uncompromising and as idealistic as any rudimentary Marxist base-superstructure model: 'I suggest that finer and future critics of art will be able to tell from the quality of a painting the degree of tolerance or intolerance of usury extant in the age and milieu that produced it' (27).[29]

But the more immediate relevance of the comparison to Lukács lies in the latter's complicated exposition of the subject's encounter with the historical process, in what Lukács calls the 'meta-subjective . . . grace' of this encounter, a grace in excess of the subject's subjectivity (*Theory of the Novel*, 50). In an argument that recalls Pound's insistence that matter (fact) is more important than ideas, Lukács writes that epic has an 'indestructible bond with reality *as it is*', and that this is 'the crucial difference between the epic and the drama' (47). As against the epic acknowledgement of life 'as it is', the form of the drama is predetermined by what '*should be*' (47). That is, in order for tragedy to arrive at what Else in his commentary on *The Poetics* calls the 'typology of human nature' (Else, 305), all particulars must be bent to the unities of action, time, and place. In chapter 9 of *The Poetics* Aristotle makes his famous assertion that 'the writing of poetry is a more philosophical activity, and one to be taken more seriously, than the writing of history; for poetry tells us rather the universals, history the particulars' (Else, 301). Lukács repudiates this, and jumps to the other side: 'The "should be" kills life, and every concept expresses a "should-be" of its object; that is why thought can never arrive at a real definition of life, and why, perhaps, the philosophy of art is so much more adequate to tragedy than it is to the epic' (*Theory of the Novel*, 48). Or as Pound puts it, 'An idea is only an imperfect induction from fact.' Lukács sees the epic writer as someone who immerses his art in the extra-conceptual particulars of life, and thereby makes the return into

[28] Ezra Pound, *Collected Shorter Poems* (London: Faber and Faber, 1968), 208.

[29] Citing Pound's own heavily marked edition of *Capital* as evidence of his substantial dialogue with Marxism, Tim Redman has written, 'In his cultural and social writings, Pound came to share with Marx the view that the economic level was the fundamental level of analysis of society. The health, the art, the justice of any culture was determined by whether or not it had a just economic sense. In that sense, Pound can be considered a Marxist.' Tim Redman, *Ezra Pound and Italian Fascism* (Cambridge: Cambridge University Press, 1991), 147–9.

history. The modern epic writer knows instinctively that he is not ready for Aristotelian generalities. For these it is both too late and too early. In philosophical terms he is condemned to immaturity. But by the same token, the Aristotle of *The Poetics* is forever condemned to be on the verge of history.

Pound, who was always ambivalent about Aristotle anyway, as we shall see, cuts a very ironical figure when he remembers him at Pisa:

> because as says Aristotle
> philosophy is not for young men
> their *Katholou* can not be sufficiently derived from
> their *hekasta*
> their generalities cannot be born from a sufficient phalanx
> of particulars
>
> (canto 74/455)

History makes man universal by revealing more particulars to him, that is, by revealing his latent callowness. History makes Pound young and old. Lukács parallels Pound's anti-Aristotelian aesthetic, in its groping, nascent post-First World War manifestation, as well as anticipating its more explicit manifestation during the 1930s and beyond. He also inadvertently provides what now seems like a powerful theoretical statement of what will eventually come to be known as Objectivist poetics.[30]

Longenbach sees the omission of the first person in the early cantos merely as an attempt to deny subjectivity, rather than trying to consider what its omission means or discovers as an aesthetic technique. What makes this reading so difficult to accept is that the energy that poetry releases by omitting the individual subject was one of the most important effects of Imagism. The absent or inexplicit subject is a constitutive part of the psychic economy of the whole Imagist procedure:

> The apparition of these faces in the crowd;
> Petals on a wet, black bough.
>
> (*Collected Shorter Poems*, 119)[31]

Here the semicolon enters the space vacated by the missing first person, refusing to foreclose on the newly emotive energies of the compared, contrasted subject statements, which in their turn activate perception. In terms of authorial presence, the distance from the persona to the image is more or less that traversed between *Three Cantos* and *A Draft of XVI. Cantos*. In this light, it is equally misleading to present *The Pisan Cantos* as returning the 'I' to its accountable

---

[30] This is discussed further in Ch. 6.

[31] As originally published, the poem was punctuated by a colon rather than a semicolon, and each of the two lines was broken up into three rhythmic units. See K. K. Ruthven, *A Guide to Ezra Pound's Personae (1926)* (Berkeley and Los Angeles: University of California Press, 1969), 152.

place, vis-à-vis history/nature. The 'I' comes and goes. The economy of means discovered in Imagism is still present, if still further refined.

In what could easily stand as a statement of the new poetics of particularity (Objectivist poetics), Lukács writes:

> In the epic, totality can only truly manifest itself in the contents of the object: it is meta-subjective, transcendent, it is a revelation and grace. Living, empirical man is always the subject of the epic, but his creative, life-mastering arrogance is transformed in the great epics into humility, contemplation, speechless wonder at the luminous meaning which, so unexpectedly, so naturally, has become visible to him, an ordinary human being in the midst of ordinary life. (*Theory of the Novel*, 50)

As far as Pound is concerned, action denominates the realm of this 'meta-subjective' grace. It is also worth paying attention to Lukács's prophetic characterization of the 'minor epic', wherein *form* is surprised by a 'fragment of life' (50–1)—as Pound so memorably is in canto 74, surprised by what 'exists only in fragments unexpected excellent sausage, | the smell of mint, for example' (74/ 452). Whereas thirty years earlier Pound would have paused (on a colon?) between 'fragments' and 'unexpected', form now approximates, mimetically, to the unexpected nature of remembered apperception; not only because the pause/ lack of pause is itself unexpected, but because through the absence of grammar and even of a line break, the poem presents an unstable image, the only plausible image, of the rapid play of contradictions inherent in the temporary relief from chronological time. A more explicit invocation of the subject would ruin the emotional balance, whereas its absence coincides with, just as it contributes to, the all-important syntactical leap. Pound's '*paradis*', if it is possible at all, is inseparable from this insertion of epistemological and syntactical suspense, from which the inevitable momentum of the line then draws the poet forward, gently, deceptively, as it unwinds (the sudden flurry of commas). The projective structural tendency of the line in *The Cantos* is outward, empirical, and historic. Within a page in fact, Pound's momentary wonder at, salvation in, what Lukács calls the ordinariness of life is thrown back upon the cross of history ("'. . . all of 'em fascists'").[32] And again we are left to contemplate the understated elegiac irony, whose tone had been established at the outset:

> The enormous tragedy of the dream in the peasant's bent
> shoulders.
> Manes! Manes was tanned and stuffed,
> Thus Ben and la Clara *a Milano*
>   by the heels at Milano
> That maggots shd/ eat the dead bullock
> DIGONOS, Δίγονος, but the twice crucified
>   where in history will you find it?

[32] *The Cantos*, 74/453.

> yet say this to the Possum: a bang, not a whimper,
>   with a bang not with whimper,

(74/439)

Repetition in *The Cantos* has always this quality: it conveys both the wish to resist time ('now in the mind indestructible'),[33] and the fate of being dragged simultaneously into it; processed, crucified by it. That certain words occur twice ('Manes! Manes'; '*a Milano* | . . . at Milano'; 'DIGONOS, Δίγονος'; 'whimper, | . . . whimper') amplifies the suggestion that Mussolini was 'twice crucified';[34] and the implication further, that since 'Time is not, Time is the evil' (74/458), it is in fact history which is the second crucifixion (Pound/Ulysses bound to the mast comes to recall Christ at the 'cross'),[35] always effectively incomplete.

2.2 ACTIONS: ARISTOTLE, MARX, MARXISTS, ARENDT

2.2.1

So far I have been tracing the borderline between Pound's developing poetics of cognitive action and his commitment to history. I want now to consider what is problematical about this relationship. It will be helpful then, in the first instance, to go more deeply into what Pound means by action.

His most sustained discussion of the question of action is to be found in *Guide to Kulchur* (1938). The initial discussion can be broken down into three converging areas: the test of action and the Confucian attack on Aristotle; the relationship between a style and an idea, and by extension between the ethical and the whole; the distinction between the public and the private.

The question of the extent to which the Pound of *Guide to Kulchur* has misrepresented Aristotle is not what concerns me here. What matters is how far Pound's interpretation or conception is consistent in itself. *Guide to Kulchur* is obviously as flawed as it is general. But the book is remarkable for its attempt to think politically; it discusses action and the arts within the context of a concept of the state. This political emphasis is crucial—and unless it is respected, everything Pound has to say about language, economics, and Aristotle becomes easily and unnecessarily confused.

From the beginning Pound seems to enter into a kind of covenant with the reader, whom he always credits with the intelligence to read him, to work the system out from the available clarities ('and with one day's reading a man may

[33] Ibid. 74/456.
[34] See Carroll F. Terrell, *A Companion to* The Cantos *of Ezra Pound* (Berkeley and Los Angeles: University of California Press, 1993), 362.
[35] *The Cantos*, 74/457.

have the key in his hands').[36] In keeping with this, Pound's critical attack on Aristotle begins by concentrating on his written 'style', on what Pound sees as the slipshod presentation of his thinking: 'words slide about like oil on surface of pond' (*Kulchur*, 313); 'the terminology is unsatisfactory' (322). Thus presented, Aristotle's lack of verbal precision provides Pound with an exemplary image: it exemplifies a thoughtlessness that goes beyond the *Nichomachean Ethics*, to the partial nature of Greek society: 'greek philosophic thought...is at no point impregnated with a feeling for the whole people' (29). Aristotle 'anchored human thought for 2000 years...But he did not engender a sense of social responsibility' (39). Confucius provides Pound with an antithetical image, in which social responsibility is first registered at the level of 'exact' terminology (16): 'As working hypothesis say that Kung is superior to Aristotle by totalitarian instinct. His thought is never something scaled off the surface of facts. It is root volition branching out, the ethical weight is present in every phrase' (279). The consistency of Pound's thinking is apparent here (at some level he seems to think in an essentially spatial way, architecturally, in terms of outlines, relations, configurations, and distances), in the clear echo of his attack on Browning's preoccupation with ideas, made some twenty years earlier: 'An idea is only an imperfect induction from fact'; i.e. its ethical weight (rooted in experience) is not present in its every phrase. Social irresponsibility has been written into the Western philosophical tradition, and is apparent in its prolixity and in its lack of concern for accountable terminology—its unwillingness to express a thought that *anyone* can act on. As against the Confucian optimum, the Aristotelian 'splintering' of 'mind' from 'morals', the failure, that is, to weigh every phrase, gave birth to the inertias of the modern 'amoral tradition' (331), in which art is as culpable as philosophy: 'a generation of experimenters, my generation, which was unable to work out a code for action' (291).

To Pound then, the question of written 'style' and the question of action are inseparable: it is impossible 'to act on one's definition' (144) if there is no definition in the first place: 'Man...will die out for want of simplicity' (135). A simple idea is 'a code for action'. Action is the proving ground of an idea; an idea in action illuminates a style, a plurality of such ideas illuminates a culture: 'Knowledge is NOT culture' (134); 'Ideas are true as they go into action. I am not resurrecting a pragmatic sanction, but trying to light up pragmatic PROOF' (188). There is no real difference between a defective definition and a defect in the idea itself. A defective idea, however, because it inhibits action, is a social problem. If this seems too uncomplicated it is worth bearing in mind that Pound's insistence on the monad-like correlation, or what we may call the expressive correlation, between idea, style, and society is basic to the critical apparatus of some of the most sophisticated critical thinkers of the century, determined, in their various ways, to convict seemingly autonomous aesthetic

[36] *The Cantos*, 74/441.

forms of ideological and sociological content.[37] If an idea and style are one and the same, and their sameness has a social meaning, as Pound's holistic or 'totalitarian' maxims repeatedly insist, this gives his notion of style a largely unacknowledged, socially orientated, dialectical thrust. Indeed his pithy provo-cation that 'ideas are true as they go into action' is decidedly close in spirit to Marx's celebrated observation, in the 'Theses on Feuerbach' (*c.*1845), that 'the philosophers have only interpreted the world, in various ways: the point is to change it'.[38] By demanding a living relationship between thought and change, Marx was punching what Pound's would call his ethical weight.

As for dialectics, as Jameson has admirably put it: 'The peculiar difficulty of dialectical thinking lies indeed in its holistic, "totalizing" character: as though you could not say any one thing until you had first said everything; as though with each new idea you were bound to recapitulate the entire system.'[39] The difficulty implicit from the word 'totalizing' is in fact double. The totalizing thought, for example, of the historical materialist, implicit in his dialectical method, which seems impelled to say everything where it says anything, endea-vours to recover the total conditions, the socio-economic conditions, of the object under analysis. Pound also writes in a totalizing style, a style that implies the whole (the inseparability of style and idea), in order to draw from the style that he is writing about the material conditions of the whole (the inseparability of style and the socio-economic). Pound calls this 'totalitarian'. He is always trying to say the same thing more or less (style = idea = society), in a slightly different way. To take a passage cited earlier, 'I suggest that future and finer critics of art will be able to tell from the quality of a painting the degree of tolerance or intolerance of usury extant in the age and milieu that produced it' (*Kulchur*). Here, the clarity of the 'age and milieu' as an *idea* (we would say, as ideology), inseparable from the idea (if there is one) of legitimate economic conduct, expresses itself at the level of *image*, in the 'style' of a work of art. It is important not to be snobbish about

---

[37] See Fredric Jameson, *The Political Unconscious: Narrative as a Socially Symbolic Act* (1981; London: Routledge, 1989), 27–8: 'The construction of a historical totality necessarily involves the isolation and the privileging of one of the elements *within* the totality (a kind of thought habit, a predilection for specific forms, a certain type of belief, a "characteristic" political structure or form of domination) such that the element in question becomes a master code or "inner essence" capable of explicating the other elements or features of the "whole" in question ... The fullest form of what Althusser calls "expressive causality" (and of what he calls "historicism") will thus prove to be a vast interpretive allegory in which a sequence of historical events or texts and artefacts is rewritten in terms of some deeper, underlying, and more "fundamental" narrative, of a hidden master narrative, which is the allegorical key or figural content of the first sequence of historical materials. This kind of allegorical master narrative would then include providential histories (such as those of Hegel or Marx), catastrophic visions of history (such as that of Spengler), and cyclical or Viconian visions of history alike.'
[38] Karl Marx, *Selected Writings*, ed. David McLellan (Oxford: Oxford University Press, 1977), 158.
[39] Fredric Jameson, *Marxism and Form: Twentieth-Century Dialectical Theories of Literature* (Princeton: Princeton University Press, 1974), 306.

Pound's terminology. Like the dialecticians, he responded to the impossible task of giving exhaustive expression to the social totality by having recourse, as we have seen, to the fragment, the image, or the monad.

Despite his careful reading of Marx, Pound had more in common with Aristotle than he could be said to have had with Hegel. But as we have seen from the comparison with the Hegelian Lukács, it is as if, in Pound, an essentially Aristotelian ethical mindset was adapting itself to a world (or a world-historical process) more amply described by Hegel.[40] Of course the many significant differences between Pound's position and the positions adopted by the Hegelian Marxists cannot be simply swept aside. For the purposes of this chapter, one of the most prominent and instructive of these differences is that Pound, in the first half of the twentieth century, and in his Confucian-humanist way, should have thought it possible *to be clear*, was prepared to chance his arm on some half-chance of communication. By contrast, a writer such as Theodor Adorno, who similarly emphasized style and its analysis (so as to disabuse us of a 'wholeness', a relation, which capitalism had in effect hollowed out from inside), felt—as the pre-Marxist Walter Benjamin had already felt—that clarity was impossible; that communicability had become, directly or indirectly, the unthinking language of the despised bourgeoisie (advanced capitalist in Adorno's case, usurious in Pound's). Accordingly, it is his unsparing distrust of the conditions of reception, the belief that art must resist the triviality of reception, which makes Adorno one of the most significant theorists of modernism: 'A writer will find that the more precisely, conscientiously, appropriately he expresses himself, the more obscure the literary result is thought, whereas a loose and irresponsible formulation is at once rewarded with a certain understanding.'[41] It is interesting to compare Adorno's invocation to 'rigorous formulation . . . conceptual effort' in *Minima Moralia* (101), widely regarded as his best-written book, with what Pound sees as Aristotle's slide into the unexacting language of contemporary journalism (*Kulchur*, 309). Meanwhile, Adorno's reflections on how light reveals light, object finds object and quotation quotation, evoke 'the swift perception of relations' which is the logical heart of *The Cantos*:

> The soundness of a conception can be judged by whether it causes one quotation to summon another. Where thought has opened up one cell of reality, it should, without violence by the subject, penetrate the next. It proves its relation to the object as soon as other objects crystallize around it. In the light that it casts on its chosen substance, others begin to glow. (*Minima Moralia*, 87)

---

[40] See MacIntyre, *After Virtue*, 150: 'It is worth remembering Aristotle's insistence that the virtues find their place not just in the life of the individual, but in the life of the city and that the individual is indeed intelligible only as a *politikon zoon*.' It follows that, 'on an Aristotelian view law and morality are not two separate realms, as they are for modernity' (152). My point is that it is Hegel, by contrast, who may be said to describe our modernity.

[41] Theodor W. Adorno, *Minima Moralia: Reflections from Damaged Life*, trans. E. F. N. Jephcott (London: Verso, 1978), 101.

Compare Pound's claim in *Guide to Kulchur* that 'A REAL book is one whose words grow ever more luminous' (317). In the passage from Adorno the crucial phrase is 'without violence', because a violent association would block the 'light'. What both writers have in mind is uninhibited cognitive action. The basic difference turns on what they are prepared to take for granted. Adorno exhorts himself to write *purely* from the impure writer's point of view, from his closed-off den in the midst of late capitalism, where he must commit himself only to paper, barred from invoking the disenfranchised, superannuated reader.[42] Pound leaves more to trust. In the words of Leo Frobenius, as quoted by Pound: 'It is not what a man says but the part of it which the auditor considers important which determines the amount of the communication.'[43] This exemplifies what I referred to earlier as Pound's humanistic determination to preserve the terms—to give the reader a plain chance.

Looking back at the end of the twentieth century, when a great many poets and critics alike aspired to a difficult style, we might want to endorse Adorno's call for 'conceptual effort', for 'rigorous formulation', without agreeing that the 'advocates of communicability' are the pre-eminent 'traitors to what they communicate'.[44] The critical tables have turned for the worse and now nothing seems more difficult than to write simply. From this point of view, Pound's emphasis is timely. His economically responsible holism differs from modern Marxist dialectics in its belief that a clear and simple idea, 'a precise definition', can be as revolutionary as a more intractable, difficult one. In the following passage, for example, Pound's argument with communism makes a critical distinction that needs to be sorted out from what is merely condescending and cantankerous:

Communism as a revolt against the huggers of harvest was an admirable tendency. As a revolutionary I refuse a pretended revolution that tries to stand still or move backward . . .

A movement, against capital, that cannot distinguish between capital and property is a blind movement . . .

There is a borderline between public and private things. Sanity bids us observe it. (*Kulchur*, 191–2)

Here Pound is making an important distinction between property and wealth, and with his habitual rapid powers of association he connects that to the distinction he consistently tries to observe between the public and the private. 'The drear horror of American life', he wrote, in 1927, 'can be traced to two damnable roots, or perhaps it is only one root: 1. The loss of *all* distinction

---

[42] See, e.g. Adorno, *Minima Moralia*, 87: 'In the end, the writer is not even allowed to live in his writing.'

[43] Qtd. in Pound, *Selected Prose*, 90.

[44] Adorno, 'Morality and Style', *Minima Moralia*, 101.

between public and private affairs' (*Selected Prose*, 186).[45] Moreover, the distinction between the public and the private, like that between property and wealth, is inseparable from the emphasis on 'borderlines' and definition as such—inseparable from the precise terminology that facilitates action. As we saw from the critique of Aristotle's style, Pound seems to hold that definition and conceptualization are in some sense a public or political matter. 'The ethical weight is present in every phrase': or rather, the critic aspires to makes an ethical test of every phrase, to weigh up the presence or the absence of the ethical. Again Pound here seems close to Adorno: in the absence of a just polity, in the absence of a genuine public sphere, in the absence, that is, of the political, the writer falls back upon the ethical—i.e. *not the whole as such but the feeling for it*. But this brings us hard up against the inflected Marxian thesis that distinguishes the two writers. To Adorno, the 'whole' is lost, sold out to capital and power; any manifestation of it is necessarily 'false'.[46] Such a protestation of impotence is the ethical corollary of historical materialism, and leads in this case to an ironic solipsism. Jameson rightly asks of Adorno, 'To whom can one present a writer whose principal subject is the disappearance of the public?' (*Marxism and Form*, 3). With the disappearance of the public as a reliable accessible domain, Pound continues to insist on it as an unreliable experiential possibility. Nevertheless this has some grotesque consequences—as Adorno would have appreciated, such as the Rome radio broadcasts, which give us a vivid example of how a supposedly public demeanour comes across in the absence of a properly public sphere, and in conditions which grossly parody the concept.

Leaving its more grotesque manifestations aside, we can find strong support for Pound's position on public and private in the work of one of Marx's most powerful modern critics, Hannah Arendt. Arendt argues that 'property, as distinguished from wealth and appropriation, indicates the privately owned share of a common world and therefore is the most elementary political condition for man's worldliness' (*HC*, 253). In other words it is only on the basis of one's having a private life, a property or shelter that serves one's body and one's needs, that one can enter into the larger common world. Property as guarantor of health, a concession to necessity, an expression of one's privacy, is prior to its aggrandizement as capital and wealth. This distinction lies behind Pound's

---

[45] See *Kulchur*, 116: 'No biography of a public man or of a ruler or prime minister can henceforth be accepted as valid unless it contains a clear statement of his finances, of his public acts in relation to public financing.' The point is illustrated in *The Cantos* by the following quotation from John Quincy Adams: 'I called upon Nicholas Biddle . . . and recd. two dividends | of my bank stock . . . . . as I might be called to take part in/public measures . . . . . I wished to divest myself | of all personal interest. . . . Nov. 9. '31' (canto 34/169). The emphasis in both instances is on public identity conceived as accountability. It was basic to Pound's criticism of his fellow artists that they had given up all claims to citizenship: a 'generation of experimenters . . . unable to work out a code for action'.

[46] As Adorno's translator notes, 'the whole is the false' is an 'inversion of Hegel's famous dictum: *Das Wahre ist das Ganze*' (*Minima Moralia*, 50).

injunction to Stalin: 'you need not, i.e. need not take over the means of production' (canto 74/440).

Neither Pound nor Arendt is against utopian commonalty (the public, the *polis*); on the contrary, what concerns them is what precisely our commonalty is for, what it means, if it is given over to managing the means of production. Arendt argues that there is a 'fundamental contradiction which runs like a red thread through the whole of Marx's thought' (*HC*, 104). On the one hand Marx sees labour as that activity which most distinguishes human beings from animals; on the other hand he contends that 'the realm of freedom begins only where labour determined through want and external utility ceases' (ibid.).[47] The freedom to experience our humanity is made to depend on the transcendence of that very same humanity (i.e. labour), at least as Marx understands it. What seems to be missing from Marx is a categorical distinction between *pre-political labour* and the subsequent *political action* which would make revolution worthwhile ('as a revolutionary', said Pound, 'I refuse a pretended revolution').

At the start of canto 74 Pound links several seemingly unrelated aspects of the lost public domain: the annihilation of 'free speech' is juxtaposed to the doomed attempt to make property a public concern. As if property could ever be more than a step towards the freedom that would be characterized in the first place by 'free speech'. Alongside these images Pound sets the Judaeo-Christian notion of labour not as an end in itself ('the peasant's bent shoulders'), but as 'preparation' for an end:

> that free speech without free radio speech is as zero
>   and but one point needed for Stalin
> you need not, i.e. need not take over the means of production
> money to signify work done, inside a system
>   and measured and wanted
> 'I have not done unnecessary manual labour'
> says the R. C. chaplain's field book
>   (preparation before confession)
> squawky as larks over the death cells
>   militarism progressing westward
> im Westen nichts neues
> and the Constitution in jeopardy
> and that state of things not very new either

>   (74/440)

---

[47] In the *Grundrisse*, for example, Marx writes of 'real freedom, whose activity is precisely labour' (Marx, 368). Arendt is citing the famous passage from *Capital* that Jameson quotes at the beginning of *The Political Unconscious*, in which Marx speaks of *freedoms* that lie both *within* and *beyond* 'the realm of necessity' (*Political Unconscious*, 19).

Pound goes beyond what would be his basic concurrence with Marx's analysis of the iniquity of surplus labour, in his wish to dignify, or sanctify, what men do after labour—which is not merely to rest but, above all, to commune together: 'preparation before confession'. There is some irony here, as throughout *The Pisan Cantos* the proximity of work to rest, and of rest to death is pronounced. Nevertheless, with 'the Constitution in jeopardy', the Roman Catholic Church provides the only available retreat in which men can be more than the labour of their bodies—albeit in parenthesis. Here again Pound's instinct is in keeping with Arendt's historical analysis: 'It has been rightly remarked that after the downfall of the Roman Empire, it was the Catholic Church that offered men a substitute for the citizenship which had formerly been the prerogative of municipal government'; this 'corresponds in many respects to the rise from the private to the public in antiquity' (*HC*, 34). The Church's historic role in providing a substitute for citizenship helps to account for the nostalgic allusions to religious observance that we find in *The Pisan Cantos*. As long as the dream remains lodged in the peasant's bent shoulders, as long as labour is seen as an end in itself (as objectless as 'militarism progressing westward'), the properly post-political, the sacred, has to fill the space vacated by the properly political.

2.2.2

Having drawn on Arendt to elucidate Pound's humanism, I want now to place him in the context of Arendt's critique of process, for this will help to clarify the serious threat posed to politics, as the proper space of action, by the sometimes contradictory terms of his approach to history. In order to do this, I need first to say something more about Arendt's conception of the complicated relationship between action and process—part of a critique of modernity, which is also to some extent a critique of modernist art.

According to Arendt action takes place in 'the space of appearance'; that is, it takes place or happens between people, in a space that is only incidentally a topographical space. The space is constituted first and foremost by a plurality of persons, whom Arendt calls citizens. People become citizens only when they are free from the violence of work and the painfulness of labour. In the violence of work, means are used to ends, and the material worked upon is, in Kantian terms, violated, turned to something else, not treated as an end in itself (155–6).

Nevertheless, Arendt acknowledges that 'This element of violation and violence is present in all fabrication' (*HC*, 139). Furthermore, only the violence of work and the painfulness of labour can establish the conditions for public life: 'violence is the pre-political act of liberating oneself from the necessity of life for the freedom of the world' (*HC*, 31). The pre-political is the private, and at the core of the private is the body. The body, the household, labour in general, everything that has to do with the securing of 'wealth and health', are pre-political phenomena (*HC*, 31). In the oblivion of labour, man's potential for separate individual identity is absorbed into nature, and he becomes what Marx calls his 'metabolism with nature' (*HC*, 98). The labourer is not free for action, that is, free to be recognized as a citizen among citizens, but is in thrall to the cycle of necessity, the general indifference of the life process.

Action by contrast, as Arendt understands it, is the general category only of those revelatory events and performances into which we enter spontaneously and which happen in a public space, the space of citizens plural. Here it is that in virtue of our acts, in the presence of others, our identities are revealed and bestowed. The complement of action therefore is speech: 'Without the accompaniment of speech, at any rate, action would not only lose its revelatory character, but, and by the same token, it would lose its subject [the actor]' (*HC*, 178). Indeed, 'No other human performance requires speech to the same extent as action' (*HC*, 179). It is speech that completes the act of disclosure: 'Without the disclosure of the agent in the act, action loses its specific character and becomes one form of achievement among others' (*HC*, 180). Action and speech together are the very basis of identity. The *polis* is where *who men are* is disclosed. In Arendt's categorical map of classical Athens, it designates the reciprocal realm of speech and action, where speech evidences the political and metaphysical priority of the communal, the intersubjectivity of being as being-with.

Arendt argues that politics takes place in a world that people have made for themselves out of and alongside nature. Even so, politics, as action, has a different character from making, for action, unlike making, is not violent (is not something used for the sake of something else). And while making makes something durable, the acts of action are by contrast transient, though they are characteristically remembered in the form of stories. All acts are distinguished by natality, or beginning, and by their sheer unpredictability. This second point is fundamental: action by definition has not the designated end of work, so its consequences are anarchic and uncertain (compare for example Pound's 'Charybdis of action').

Nevertheless, for Arendt the world is a durable artifice. She defines it against nature, which she understands as 'process'. Describing 'the central position of the concept of process in modernity' (*HC*, 307), she writes:

Historically, political theorists from the seventeenth century onward were confronted with a hitherto unheard-of process of growing wealth, growing property, growing acquisition. In the attempt to account for this steady growth, their attention was naturally drawn to the phenomenon of a progressing process itself, so that . . . the concept of process became the very key term of the new age as well as the sciences, historical and natural, developed by it. From its beginning, this process, because of its apparent endlessness, was understood as a natural process and more specifically in the image of the life process itself. (*HC*, 105)

Arendt argues that the concept of process, a concept based on nature and necessity, the apparent 'endlessness' of 'growth', has invaded the traditional spheres both of making (*HC*, 301) and of politics (*HC*, 230–6). This is another source of her significance for Pound, the would-be maker-politician. Politics no longer exists as the distinctive realm of speech and action. Instead we have society, where we get stuck upon the horns of 'political economy'—bodily need (survival) and acquisitive wealth (i.e. capital, survival in its autonomous fetishized form).

In this new social world, images of the life process have come to dominate our self-images as human beings. 'The introduction of the concept of process into making' (*HC*, 301) led to the '*modern shift of emphasis from the "what" to the "how," from the thing itself to its fabrication process*' (*HC*, 307, my emphasis). With modernity—and this would also apply to many of the works of art characteristic of modernism—work is no longer undertaken with a 'fixed and permanent' end in sight, but in a spirit of open-endedness whose model is nature. The world has lost its durability, the essence of its character as world; the maker has relinquished his or her hold on permanence; work has become indistinguishable from process; action has become indistinguishable from both; speech has lost its relation to the actor; the new narratives of human identity do not have a beginning or an end.

For Pound, as we have seen, action and definition are intimately related: 'The truth of a given idea [is] measured by the degree and celerity wherewith it goes into action' (*Kulchur*, 182). This is one of the points that Pound keeps making about the American Revolution: that it took place first 'in the minds of the people' (cantos 32, 33, and 50); its truthfulness as an idea, an idea that had *taken place* (had been given definition or conceived), was demonstrable from the action that had followed. But in canto 74, with the 'Constitution in jeopardy', the republican ideal seems to have become a 'dream'—as 'a precise definition' it continues to be 'transmitted' only through works of art (74/439). Politics and action are so endangered as to have become almost other-worldly. But Pound will mollify this danger through a eulogy to 'process' in which nature and history are conflated. The immolation of Mussolini and the 'end' of the 'world' (the end of the Republic which in a sense is all republics) are merged with Confucian allusions to the 'process' of nature. Observe that nature is not conceived here as *processes*, but as one indistinguishable *process*: 'rain also is of the process', 'the wind also is of the process' (74/439). The word 'also' embraces all Pound's historical data, without specifying them, as parts of the one now natural-historical process. In this way Pound is able to see the historical setbacks around him as part of an essentially fecund natural process. The dream of ultimate victory is therefore salvaged from defeat via what has been characterized as the myth of continuing revolution: 'The real revolution *continua*, it goes on, propaganda or no propaganda. The historian or he who introduces his reader to the study of history must at least *know* of this process' (*Kulchur*, 259). This is history as *natural* process. Like other American writers before him, Pound seems to hand the revolution over to the safe keeping of nature.[48]

According to canto 74 the American Constitution is natural, its present 'jeopardy' is natural, and its ultimate 'resurrection' is natural. What is 'now in the mind indestructible' is *nature* (74/456). The problem with this scenario is that it effectively squeezes out the possibility of recognizing what is unique—and uniquely human—about political activity. It squeezes out the recognition on which political life depends. Whether we act or fail to act the result is exactly the same, natural ('of the process'). Prior to *The Pisan Cantos* it had never been Pound's intention thus to dissolve altogether the singularity of the human act. *The Cantos* may not be *imitations of action* in the full Aristotelian sense, but they conjure, like no other twentieth-century poem, *the space of appearance* in which action comes to light. They celebrate the realm of human efficacy that Pound sought to exemplify in the Malatesta cantos: 'No one has claimed that the Malatesta cantos are obscure. They are openly volitionist, establishing, I think clearly, the effect of the factive personality' (*Kulchur*, 194). It was not Malatesta's subjectivity that Pound was interested in; he was concerned with his public 'personality', what he calls the 'the effect of the factive', the now familiar language of crafts, facts, and surfaces.

Similarly, in the John Adams cantos (cantos 62–71), the last cantos before *The Pisan Cantos*, the Constitution is constantly in jeopardy—along with America and the Revolution itself. Constitution and constitutions is the great theme of the sequence. But Adams's words, his vigilance, whom he agrees with, where he differs (quoting others as Pound quotes him), humanize that jeopardy; which is to say they keep it political—political, I mean, as Arendt understands it—by giving voice to the effect of the factive personality, and by making it self-evident that government is in men's hands ('no more agreeable employment | than the study of the best kind of government'[49]—though 'mankind dare not yet think upon | CONSTITUTIONS').[50] Here politics is something quite distinct from nature.

On the other hand, Pound's reading of Confucius on 'equity' or justice in canto 74,[51] by making individuals not so much the custodians of the law as bearers of the internalized historical process, has the effect of neutralizing volition and naturalizing history. Politics and nature become the same:

> not words whereto be faithful
> nor deeds that they be resolute

---

[48] One thinks for example of Whitman's great Preface to *Leaves of Grass* of 1855, with its repeated and deliberate conflation of the two words *nature* and *nation*. The American mythology of 'continuing revolution' has been analysed by Sacvan Bercovitch, notably in *Rites of Assent*.

[49] *The Cantos*, 67/392.

[50] Ibid., 68/395.

[51] See Terrell, 365.

> only that bird-hearted equity make timber
> and lay hold of the earth
>
> (74/440)

Pound cancels out the fragile sphere of self-responsible human action even as he alludes to it—in the *making* of timber, the *laying hold* of the earth.[52] There is a comparable if less drastic moment at the end of Pound's first Confucian canto, canto 13, when Kung's allusion to the apricot blossoms ('I have tried to keep them from falling'),[53] pits the slightness of human volition ('I have tried') *against* the magnitude of natural process ('But that time seems to be passing'),[54] in the cause, paradoxically, of a morality of process ('correctly . . . each in his nature').[55]

In *Guide to Kulchur* Pound seems to be falling between two stools, one that is exemplified by the heroic assertion that a defective idea does not go into action (188–9), and another best illustrated by an antithetical statement (originally from Dante) and the question mark that Pound places after it: '"All things that move, move by reason of some imperfection in themselves"?' (243).[56] His problem is that there is no way of knowing what the difference between these two positions is. How to tell the perfection that acts from the imperfection that moves? Nature reconciles everything. In canto 74 likewise the surrendering of politics turns out to be, paradoxically, a kind of resigned utopianism. An example from the Hegelian Marxists might help to clarify what is at stake. Fredric Jameson gets himself into a comparable knot in the conclusion to *The Political Unconscious*, when he goes so far as to argue that the ideological unity of the oppressor-class can serve as a figure for the utopian impulse (289–91). This is all well and good, and as ingenious as it is reassuring. However, it really gets us nowhere, since it only begs the question—the question begged by both Pound and Arendt—of how we can actually distinguish between freedom and injury to others, between political action and violence. It is a form of dialectical inertia.

I have been suggesting that the strength of the revolutionary humanist position versus the Marxist position is that it is able to insist on a categorical distinction between action and natural-historical process, which in turn corresponds to the distinction between public and private. These are distinctions which Pound sometimes intuits and observes, but at other times suspends. Where he observes

---

[52] See Arendt, *HC*, 137: 'The things of the world have the function of stabilizing human life, and their objectivity lies in the fact that—in contradiction to the Heraclitean saying that the same men can never enter the same stream—men, their ever-changing nature notwithstanding, can retrieve their sameness, that is their identity, by being related to the same chair and the same table.'

[53] *The Cantos*, 13/60.

[54] Ibid.

[55] Ibid., 13/58.

[56] Pound doesn't give the source, but Louis Zukofsky gives it as Dante. Louis Zukofsky, *Prepositions+: The Collected Critical Essays*, additional prose ed. Mark Scroggins (Hanover, NH: Wesleyan University Press, 2000), 63.

them, he goes against the anti-humanistic grain of his time, but where he suspends them he becomes a representative, even typical figure.

2.3 REVOLUTIONS AND RECOGNITIONS

Having made the basic distinction between the public and the private, Pound seems to confirm Arendt's analysis of action and to share her respect for the Enlightenment; that is, both writers concur in maintaining that action is essentially innovatory and the exemplary instance of political action in the modern age was the American Revolution.

Arendt writes that 'Only where this pathos of novelty is present and where novelty is connected with the idea of freedom are we entitled to speak of revolution.'[57] As far as Pound is concerned, it is its more comprehensive pathos of novelty that exalts the Fascist revolution over the Russian revolution, notwithstanding his evident admiration for Lenin. The Fascist revolution '*is not a revolution according to preconceived type*'.[58] True action surprises the public sphere. 'The specific lesson', he writes, in the context of a typically syncretic discussion of Chinese-American history, 'might be to recognize the U.S. Constitution as an innovation' (*Kulchur*, 275). For Pound innovation is the Confucian principle: 'Day by day make it new' (canto 53/265); 'NOT mistaking recurrence for innovation' (*Kulchur*, 274). In *Jefferson and/or Mussolini* and *Guide to Kulchur* he readily associates action with men making a beginning: 'The ideas of genius, or of "men of intelligence" are organic and germinal, the "seed" of the scriptures. You put down one of these ideas somewhere, i.e. somewhere in a definite space and time, and something begins to happen. "All men are born free and equal."'[59] Here Pound distinguishes action as inception, as beginning, even as he assimilates it into metaphors of organic process. Action is characterized by the actor's *presence in performance*. 'Happy is the man who can start where he is, and *do* something' (*Kulchur*, 266). The emphasis is on the breakthrough character of action, on newness or innovation, which is what defines act as act in the first place, revolution as revolution. Pound asks of Thomas Jefferson, 'What did he really *do*? Through what mechanisms did he act?' (*Jefferson and/or Mussolini*, 15). And he concludes that, 'No man in history had ever *done* more and done it with less violence' (ibid. 5).

Arendt endorses Pound's emphasis on the distinctive character of action as beginning, 'an unconnected, new event breaking into the continuous sequence of historical time' (*On Revolution*, 205). Indeed for both writers the whole concept of revolution has a revelatory Christian feel: 'The modern concept of revolution, inextricably bound up with the notion that the course of history suddenly begins

---

[57] Hannah Arendt, *On Revolution* (1963; Harmondsworth: Penguin, 1973), 34.
[58] Ezra Pound, *Jefferson and/or Mussolini* (1935; New York: Liveright, 1970), 24.
[59] Ibid., 21.

anew, that an entirely new story, a story never known or told before, is about to unfold, was unknown prior to the two great revolutions at the end of the eighteenth century' (*On Revolution*, 28). It is central to their interpretations of the American Revolution that it was in certain fundamental respects non-violent. *The Cantos* keep reminding us that, as far as John Adams was concerned, the Revolution had already taken place in the 'minds of the people | in the fifteen years before [the battle of] Lexington' (50/246). No men in history had *done* more, and done it with *less violence*. In order to offset the threat of violence, Pound and Arendt both give centre stage to the words that facilitate, disclose, or effectively constitute an action. Arendt writes: 'No doubt there is a grandeur in the Declaration of Independence, but it consists not in its philosophy and not even so much in its being "an argument in support of an action" as in its being the perfect way for an action to appear in words' (*On Revolution*, 130). Or as she says in almost Poundian terms: 'Obviously, each new appearance among men stands in need of a new word' (35).

Earlier on in *On Revolution*, Arendt dwells suggestively on the complex relationship between words, acts, and the violence of all pre-political beginnings:

Whatever brotherhood human beings may be capable of has grown out of fratricide, whatever political organization men may have achieved has its origin in crime. The conviction, in the beginning was a crime—for which the phrase 'state of nature' is only a theoretically purified paraphrase—has carried through the centuries no less self-evident plausibility for the state of human affairs than the first sentence of St John, 'In the beginning was the Word', has possessed for the affairs of salvation. (20)

We can compare the associations and insights going on in this passage with what is happening in the first few pages of canto 74. Pound makes the selfsame leap from the pre-political violence on which the ideal city apparently has to be founded to the transcendence of that violence once the city has been established:

> yet say this to the Possum: a bang, not a whimper,
>   with a bang not with a whimper,
> To build the city of Dioce whose terraces are the colour of stars.
>
>   (74/439)

Here is a darker example:

> Ouan Jin spoke and thereby created the named
>   thereby making clutter
>   the bane of men moving
>   and so his mouth was removed
>   as you will find it removed in his pictures
>   in principio verbum
>   paraclete or the verbum perfectum: sinceritas
> from the death cells in sight of Mt Taishan @ Pisa
>
>   (74/441)

In Pound's world, pre-political violence remains justified where it protects the domain of what Arendt calls politics (speech and action) from those insincere or superfluous words that could inhibit action and prevent 'men moving'. The beginning of political language proper (which is to say the beginning of politics), like the beginning of salvation, cannot disown responsibility for the crime or violence that all beginning originally is. Political man tries to acknowledge his relationship to that crime, to that violence, by establishing a space that will be free of it (Pound's 'stillness outlasting all wars').[60] For both Pound and Arendt, the immemorial adage that in the beginning was violence, is overcome in time by a humanist political beginning, graced by the forgiveness of the Gospel: 'in principio verbum'. The political sphere has a responsibility to be self-forgiving: it is incumbent upon it to begin anew.

At one level, this is Pound in his Fenollosa mode, putting the verbal before the static nominal, process before substance, action before definition.[61] 'Clutter' reminds us of his criticism of Browning's Aeschylus ('frills and festoons of language... convoluted tushery'). But there is a lingering ambivalence that complicates the passage and gives a different significance to the looming 'sight of Mt Taishan'. For the poet is also a speaker and a name-giver; and the poet in the death cells has had 'his mouth... removed'; while 'men moving' might just be another reference to 'militarism progressing westward'. At what point does a set of aesthetic convictions turn into an ideological psychosis? Pound seems to catch a glimpse of himself here—effectively, ironically, absurdly self-condemned.

I want to have a look now at an earlier instance of the poet as name-giver. Canto 1, based on book 11 of *The Odyssey*, Odysseus's journey to the under-world, also dramatizes the Christian humanist credo of a new beginning. The poem reveals the extraordinary power language has to reflect upon the silence and anonymity of violence ('These many crowded about me'),[62] thereby transform-ing its negative aftermath by bringing it into the communal space of recognition. What is depicted here is not violence as such, the fact of injury to others, but violence seen from the point of view of politics, the beginning of which is the word:

> I sat to keep off the impetuous impotent dead,
> Till I should hear Tiresias.
> But first Elpenor came, our friend Elpenor,
> Unburied, cast on the wide earth,
> Limbs that we left in the house of Circe,
> Unwept, unwrapped in sepulchre, since toils urged other.

---

[60] *The Cantos*, 74/441.
[61] See George Kearns, *Guide to Ezra Pound's Selected Cantos* (Folkestone: Dawson, 1980), 6: 'To the willful or wishful eyes of Pound and Fenollosa the ideogram retains—persistently transmits— the energy, the process, the verbness' of the thing.
[62] *The Cantos*, 1/4.

> Pitiful spirit. And I cried in hurried speech:
> 'Elpenor, how art thou come to this dark coast?
> 'Cam'st thou afoot, outstripping seamen?'
>   And he in heavy speech:
> 'Ill fate and abundant wine. I slept in Circe's ingle.
> 'Going down the long ladder unguarded,
> 'I fell against the buttress,
> 'Shattered the nape-nerve, the soul sought Avernus.
> 'But thou, O King, I bid remember me, unwept, unburied,
> 'Heap up mine arms, be tomb by sea-bord, and inscribed:
> '*A man of no fortune; and with a name to come.*'
>
>   (1/4)

Fending off the nameless dead, Odysseus has been waiting to 'hear' Tiresias, but in fact it is Odysseus who speaks first because he recognizes Elpenor. This sets up a structural parallel in which Odysseus becomes Tiresias ('Tiresias . . . knew me, and spoke first') to Elpenor's Odysseus (a man of 'ill-star', who has lost 'all companions'). Odysseus gives the dignity of a name to the nameless Elpenor (*'A man of no fortune, and with a name to come'*), just as Tiresias will give a name to him: 'Odysseus | Shalt return' (1/4–5). So far the poem has been faithful to its Homeric source, the Latin translation by Andreas Divus, but Pound now adds another dimension to this system of parallels by *naming* Divus: 'Lie quiet Divus. I mean, that is Andreas Divus' (1/5).

The dead Divus now takes Elpenor's position: his 'name to come' is a name given by Pound to him. This layering of one act of recognition on top of another expands the circle of appearances, in which violence and namelessness are freely transformed. The poem becomes an exemplary instance of mutual individuation in the public sphere ('establishing . . . the effect of the factive personality'), in which actions speak louder by virtue of words, by virtue of names. Having established the technique, Pound expands the circle again by beginning canto 2 with a name: 'Hang it all, Robert Browning' (2/6).

It is interesting to compare canto 1 with Joyce's brilliant adaptation of the Hades episode in *Ulysses*. For Joyce, as for Pound, Ulysses (Leopold Bloom) is a poet, a name-giver. But Joyce makes the ceremony of naming more oblique and arbitrary than it is in *The Cantos*, when Bloom catches himself naming, at Paddy Dignam's funeral, a person whom he does not know, a person whom he names accidentally, wrongly, without any knowledge of his name: 'that fellow in the . . . Macintosh'.[63] Macintosh promptly disappears, into the death-like anonymity of Dublin. Joyce presents us with an acutely comic image of modernist insignificance and agoraphobia, which has the effect of breaking up the circle of reciprocal recognition that characterizes the public sphere. It may be that to an even greater extent than Pound, Joyce creates the sense of something unique and

---

[63] Joyce, *Ulysses*, 92.

numinous about the poetic act of name-giving, but it is a numinousness tinged with banal sadness—as of a domesticated god cut off from his creation. And so whereas Joyce gets considerable mileage out of what Walter Benjamin calls the 'bourgeois view of language', which 'maintains that the word has [only] an accidental relation to its object', Pound refuses to pay this familiar tribute to the spiritual and creative isolation of his contemporaries.[64] Benjamin wrote that 'Man is the namer, by this we recognize that through him pure language speaks' (111). In *The Cantos* this speaking of language is what evidences the metaphysical priority of commonalty. On the basis of linguistically experienced commonalty, Pound articulates the dynamic compact of appearances, spelling out the luminous relationship between acts and words, agents and names, the element of cognition within recognition.

2.4 CRAFT OR CONSENSUS?

2.4.1

Having set out Pound's humanist agenda, his emphasis on dialogical action over the drama of individual subjectivity, I will try to complete my analysis with a consideration of what Longenbach calls Pound's 'unattractive politics', focusing again on the role of violence in *The Cantos*.

It may be helpful, to begin with, to make some general points about Pound and Fascism. Two of the most informed and sympathetic treatments of the subject are Wendy Flory's *The American Ezra Pound* and Redman's *Ezra Pound and Italian Fascism*. Both studies make important historical distinctions between Fascism and Nazism, and between Italian Fascism and anti-Semitism (until 1938, Flory writes, 'Italy was the least anti-Semitic of all the countries in Europe'), arguing that Pound's support for Mussolini was founded primarily on the latter's consolidation of state and society through an integrated, socialistic economic programme, in the light of which Fascism can be seen as a 'Marxist heresy'.[65] In *The Origins of Totalitarianism*, Arendt interpreted Italian Fascism in a very similar way, distinguishing it from totalitarianism, i.e. Nazism and

---

[64] Walter Benjamin, 'On Language as Such and on the Language of Man' (1916), *One Way Street and Other Writings*, trans. Edmund Jephcott and Kingsley Shorter (London: Verso, 1985), 107–23 (116–17).

[65] See Wendy Stallard Flory, *The American Ezra Pound* (New Haven: Yale University Press, 1988), 137, 94. Redman endorses the definition of Fascism as a 'Marxist heresy', and also points out that there is no evidence that Pound was aware of the Nazi death camps (Redman, 3, 5). Nevertheless, when in one of his notorious broadcasts Pound tells the audience that 'Had you had the sense to eliminate Roosevelt and his Jews or the Jews and their Roosevelt at the last election, you would not now be at war', and that the next step 'towards a bright new world', is, again, 'to eliminate him and all his damned gang from public life in America', the careless repetition of *eliminate* is, at the very least, an instance of the slipshod terminology for which he condemned Aristotle in *Guide to Kulchur*, and makes for dispiriting reading. Qtd. in Julian Cornell, *The Trial of*

Stalinism, and seeing Mussolini's ideal of the corporate state as a deliberate attempt to secure the nation's future, by, first, solving the conflict between the classes and, second, making the people as a whole identical with the state.[66]

Pound beautifully captures this idea in the magnificent opening line of canto 74. But here the image is also indicative of a certain top-heavy idealism (the dream is in the anonymous peasant's shoulders, not in his head), and Pound remains, for most of the canto, trapped in the pre-political violence of an indefatigably ideal city: 'the city of Dioce', which is both unbuilt and in ruins. There is a great deal of pathos in Pound's repeatedly mentioned but elegiacally understated proximity to the death cells, a place which continues to mark, as throughout the history of civilization it has always marked, the outer boundary of an unrealized utopia—the point at which the idea refused to go into action. According to Arendt, an act which is not an end in itself, i.e. whatever is done purely in order to achieve something else (what is done in order to 'build the city of Dioce', for instance), is not an action at all, but is caught up in human violence, the world of means to ends.

Furthermore, if we follow Arendt in holding that the complement of action is speech, then it would seem to follow that the complement of violence is silence. Hence the silencing of Ouan Jin (a perfect example of violence making silence), the silence of the death cells (beautifully suggested by the reference to the larks squawking over them), the 'stillness outlasting all wars' (the antithesis of 'militarism progressing westward'), and the incarceration of the failed propagandist poet, are all profoundly related; they are all forms of silence emerging out of violence, a violence that has failed to metamorphose into action, of which the proper complement is speech. Canto 74 is in fact a classic example of the dream-like way in which Pound's poetry discovers deeper meaning by association, beneath, that is, the level of association at which the poet seems to have been working in the first place (in which Ouan Jin would have been merely a pedantic instance of someone who failed to meet the Confucian ethical standard).

I have been arguing all along that Pound had an instinctive pre-modern contempt for what he saw as the political impotence of modernism, its inability to bring about and sustain the conditions for action; this is what defines the modernity of the modernists, who are 'unable to work out a code for action'. At the same time, however, he himself failed to distinguish the category of action, the category of politics, from the two deceptively contiguous categories of violence and art. As we saw earlier on, he confuses voluntary human action with anonymous natural process. A related ambiguity occurs in the Preface to *Jefferson and/or Mussolini*, where history is both 'made' by Mussolini (p. viii) and

---

Ezra Pound: A Documented Account of the Treason Case by the Defendant's Lawyer (London: Faber and Faber, 1967), 140–1.

[66] Hannah Arendt, *The Origins of Totalitarianism* (1951; San Diego, Calif.: Harcourt Brace & Company, 1975), 258–9.

a self-determining 'process' (p. v). But these confusions, which are pervasive, pale beside the more drastic confusion, as far as the destiny of art is concerned, of art and politics. Pound finally models politics, the realm of human affairs, in which people in their plurality act and appear, on the craft of the artist, working in isolation. Thus he writes of Mussolini: 'I don't believe that any estimate of Mussolini will be valid unless it *starts* from his passion for construction. Treat him as *artifex* and all the details fall into place. Take him as anything save the artist and you will get muddled with contradiction' (*Jefferson and/or Mussolini*, 33–4). This could hardly be more emphatic. And it leads, in canto 74, to Pound's deliberate identification of the revolutionary statesman with the artist/ sculptor who cuts through to nature as it really is. The statesman is he whose statesmanship reveals, in Mussolini's terms, the historical process:

> Sunt lumina
> that the drama is wholly subjective
> stone knowing the form which the carver imparts it
> the stone knows the form

> (74/444)

This passage is one of the great vindicatory moments in the whole of *The Cantos*, as Pound/Odysseus retrospectively negotiates the 'Charybdis of action' by eliminating what Arendt describes as action's inherent uncertainty, the uncertainty which is the very hallmark of its freedom. The 'stone knows the form', i.e., the revolution will happen because mentally it has already happened, because the city of Dioce is 'in the mind indestructible' (74/456). Pound has eliminated uncertainty precisely as Plato did, by falling back upon the notion of the cerebral artisan, the philosopher-king. As F. M. Cornford writes, the philosopher-king is compared by Plato to 'an artist working with constant reference to an unchanging model, which irrevocably determines the outline and basic principles of his work'.[67] The significance of this image for Pound and for us is that it constitutes the 'degradation' of politics as the realm in which human actions freely appear (*HC*, 230). Politics is now identified with work, with instrumentality, with the world of means to ends. Instead of trying to read an instrumentalist Italian revolution through the consensual, pluralistic American Revolution, Pound ends up reducing the latter to the shape of his Fascist-Platonic model, and despite all the insistence on innovation Jefferson and Mussolini become the 'preconceived type[s]' of each other.[68]

From this interpretive perspective another ambiguity emerges more clearly: it now seems that throughout *The Cantos* Pound may have seized on Adams's proposition that the revolution had already taken place *in the minds* of the people '15 years before Lexington', because it is consonant with the artisanal model of

---

[67] Plato, *The Republic*, trans. F. M. Cornford (Oxford: Clarendon Press, 1941), 200.
[68] *Jefferson and/or Mussolini*, 24.

public life. Whereas Arendt understood the American Revolution to be a matter of people talking to one another, an action appearing in words, Pound seems to be equally drawn to another aspect of the image, which is, despite the invocation of the 'people'—and the constant presence of the loquacious Adams—that of the artist's *mind* quietly contemplating *form*. Like the peasant with the dream in his shoulders, 'the people' are as taciturn as they are anonymous. The revolution is surrounded by the silence, lack of speech, that accompanies the artist in his task of fabrication. The people are the silent artist of their own revolution, in the same way that the stone is the silent knower of its own carved form. The paradox is that Pound wants to limit revolutionary violence to the absolute minimum— which is why he says the revolution had already happened. But he could hardly have picked a more critical historical moment in respect of which to emphasize art over politics, revolution as craft, as construction, over revolution as dialogue and consensus.

From Bercovitch's *Rites of Assent* to Michael Davidson's *Men Like Us*, 'consensus' is a word in bad odour in American literary studies. That is because it is always understood as the endgame of an ideological assent that reproduces itself discursively. But from an Arendtian perspective, consensus is always fraught with the phenomenological knowledge that it is an agreement not just between ideologues but between human beings; that it is no more strictly rational than it is purely ideological; that it is seldom easily arrived at and can be broken off at any moment; and that it is by definition volatile and imperfect. From Arendt's point of view, then, the language spoken in the marketplace is not just what ideological criticism calls discourse, for it is surely a considerable part of her point that people don't free themselves from labour and work in order to speak—they don't first become free as it were and then speak—rather they become free *when* they speak. They find themselves in the act, the intersubjective act, of being found by and alongside others. Habermas too, in his different way, writes of the 'central experience of the unconstrained, unifying, consensus-bringing force of argumentative speech, in which different participants overcome their merely subjective views'.[69] Though Habermas does without Arendt's gift for histrionic phenomenology, this overcoming is first reasonable before it is ideological, and it must coexist with everything that threatens it, including our humanity.

2.4.2

Names have an important auratic role throughout *The Cantos*. But Odysseus's name has a special epic significance, and the ambiguity that attaches to it, which has its Homeric basis in Odysseus's deception of the Cyclops, becomes an important motif in canto 74, where the hero reiterates the words, 'I am

[69] Jürgen Habermas, *The Theory of Communicative Action*, 1. *Reason and the Rationalization of Society*, trans. Thomas McCarthy (London: Heinemann, 1984), 10.

noman, my name is noman' (74/440). The identity-through-unidentifiability of Odysseus contrasts him with Ouan Jin, who 'created the named | thereby making clutter' (74/441):

> Odysseus
> the name of my family.
> the wind also is of the process,
>
> (74/439)

From having been the name of a family, Odysseus becomes the name of a process, as substance is effectively drained from the substantive. The problem with this can be expressed as follows: either Odysseus's name brings with it what Pound refers to elsewhere as 'the effect of the factive personality', or else its nominative power is dispersed in the natural-historical flow; either there is individuation ('my name') or there is nature/history ('no man'). This is also the dichotomy that Longenbach's reading of Pound leaves us with, subjective or objective history. I have tried to argue that something else is going on beyond the strict antithesis such a reading proposes, and that the poem locates a third realm within that potentially dichotomized terrain. This is the realm of action, in which the 'effect of the factive personality', as distinct from the endlessly introspective reflexes of subjectivity ('that the drama is wholly subjective'), is an effect of recognition, constituted dialogically: a cognitive event in the event of our being—in the event of our being free to perceive.

3

'I am alive—because I I do not own a House': Emily Dickinson, Mina Loy, and Lorine Niedecker

In this chapter we shall stay, in the first instance, with Arendt, but with the aim now of opening up one of the most controversial aspects of her work, the distinction between the public and private spheres. Not surprisingly, feminist critical responses have been among the most fruitful here, a circumstance that is all the more piquant in that Arendt was notoriously indifferent to feminism. I shall be using her thought and the feminist critique of it to shed light on the experimental poetry of three women in particular, Emily Dickinson, Mina Loy, and Lorine Niedecker—though with the idea as always that the poetry illuminates both Arendt's work and the critique. Obviously I am not concerned to offer a comprehensive survey, but to make sense of certain common emphases— emphases that already resonate profoundly within the American literary context. What the chapter will also do is to continue the dialogue of the previous chapter between Hegelian-Marxist Critical Theory and communicative reason (in other words, between the dialectical and communicative wings of Critical Theory), while using poetry to compensate as far as possible for the missing phenomenological dimension of communicative reason—which is to say, using poetry as phenomenology.

3.1 THE PHILOSOPHER'S HOUSE: FROM ARENDT TO CAVELL

3.1.1

Here, to begin with, is a typically ambivalent passage from *The Human Condition*:

[It] is striking that from the beginning of history to our own time it has always been the bodily part of human existence that needed to be hidden in privacy, all things connected with the necessity of the life process itself, which prior to the modern age comprehended all activities serving the subsistence of the individual and the survival of the species.

Hidden away were the laborers who 'with their bodies minister to the [bodily] needs of life' [Aristotle, *Politics*], and the women who with their bodies guarantee the physical survival of the species. Women and slaves belonged to the same category and were hidden away not only because they were somebody else's property but because their life was 'laborious,' devoted to bodily functions . . . The fact that the modern age emancipated the working classes and the women at nearly the same historical moment must certainly be counted among the characteristics of an age which no longer believes that bodily functions and material concerns should be hidden. (*HC*, 72–3)

As we have seen, Arendt's distinction between public and private (what 'should be shown' and what 'should be hidden') is inseparable from a number of other critical distinctions, including those between action and work, and, further down the scale, between work and labour. 'It is indeed the mark of all laboring that it leaves nothing behind, that the result of its effort is almost as quickly consumed as the effort is spent. And yet this effort, despite its futility, is born of a great urgency . . . because life itself depends upon it' (*HC*, 87). The immediate problem with this position from a feminist point of view is not the distinction between labour and work as such, but the way in which it gets applied to women, the fact that Arendt is content to define what the majority of women have been doing all through history in such categorically restrictive and unimaginative terms. Household labour, the bearing and raising of children in particular, is not work because it makes nothing durable: it is not world-making—in the very specific sense in which Arendt understands the world, as man-made artifice, constructed over against nature. It is a slave to necessity and vanishes in the effort.

The problem is compounded by Arendt's apparently rarefied notion of public life, which holds that everything that touches on necessity, on the life process, is not really a public matter at all. From this point of view, everything that pertains to political economy amounts to a usurpation of politics by the life process and its derivatives. The space of appearance has been given over to what should be hidden; action has been displaced by the realm of necessity. Where once there was a strict demarcation between public and private, now there is the boundlessness of the *social*. From a feminist point of view, the trouble with such a world picture is that it strips the women's and labour movements of historical freedom and political dignity. Arendt has mystified the realm of politics beyond common-sense recognition (it has nothing to do with society), and left us with no decent word for the exercise and augmenting of power by millions of men and women, working reasonably, laboriously, sometimes invisibly, individually, and collectively, over two hundred years.

In an outstanding critical study of Arendt, the political philosopher Seyla Benhabib discusses the oversimplifications and contradictions embedded in what she rightly describes as this 'systematic kernel of Arendt's political thought'.[1] She

---

[1] Benhabib, *Reluctant Modernism*, 137.

argues that no real human activity ever conforms to just one of Arendt's categories—whatever we undertake, we are apt to find ourselves *working, acting and labouring* more or less simultaneously and in endlessly varied and variable ratios (*Reluctant Modernism*, 131). Nothing reveals this more clearly than 'if we insert gender as a category of analysis' into the discussion (135). 'Several consequences follow', she writes:

We see that household labour, as it has been traditionally identified with the women's domain, includes not only housework but child rearing as well. This activity, in turn, bears more the marks of 'world-protection, world-preservation, and world-repair,' which Arendt normally associated with work, than of the cyclical necessity characteristic of labour. For in raising a child, one is also transmitting to that child through every word and gesture, every sound and action, a world . . . We teach the child 'what the world is like'; we teach the child which aspects of the world around us we consider worthwhile to preserve and cultivate, which aspects make us feel at home in the world. And this work is not just work but action, in the emphatic Arendtian sense, 'of the disclosure of the who through speech and action.'[2]

As for Arendt's apparently rarefied concept of politics, it was her friend Mary McCarthy who best summed up the difficulty:

Now I have asked myself: 'What is somebody supposed to do on the public stage, in the public space, if he does not concern himself with the social? That is, what's left?' . . . On the other hand, if all questions of economics, human welfare, busing, anything that touches the social sphere, are to be excluded from the political scene, then I am mystified. I am left with war and speeches. But the speeches can't be just speeches. They have to be speeches about something.[3]

We might say that Arendt's concept of politics could end up looking as empty as a piazza in a painting by Giorgio de Chirico.

Despite the force and clarity of these criticisms, Benhabib argues for the continuing value of Arendt's political conception, but in a revitalized, out-ward-looking form. She argues along two distinct lines. First, drawing on the work of other feminist critics, she tries to bring to light what she sees as the hidden 'normative core of the Arendtian conception of the political' (*Reluctant Modernism*, 166):

The constitution of a public space always involves a claim to the generalizability of the demands, needs, and interests for which one is fighting . . . Whichever class or social group enters the public realm, and no matter how class or group specific its demands may be

---

[2] See Benhabib, *Reluctant Modernism*, 135, where it is observed that Arendt makes this very same point, despite herself: 'The child, this in-between to which the lovers now are related and which they hold in common, is representative of the world in that it also separates them; it is an indication that they will insert a new world into the existing world. Through the child, it is as though the lovers return to the world from which their love had expelled them' (*HC*, 242).

[3] Mary McCarthy, qtd. in *Reluctant Modernism*, 155.

in their genesis, the process of public-political struggle transforms the *attitude of narrow self-interest into a more broadly shared public or common interest.* This, I think, is the fundamental distinction between the 'social-cum-economic' and 'political' realms for Hannah Arendt. Engaging in politics does not mean abandoning economic or social issues; it means fighting for them in the name of principles, interests, values that have a generalizable basis, and that concern us as members of a collectivity. (145)

We must work to disclose the common significance of the private, which we do whenever we attempt to bring generalizable 'principles, interests, values' to bear on the socio-economic. This is of enormous significance for feminist historians, indeed for any historian who attempts to give narrative life to some part of that muted majority who, as Benjamin famously put it, make up history's victims and oppressed. The generalizable basis of public space is *not just the prerogative of the present, but can be extended back in time wherever we claim to recognize a common interest. We disclose in retrospect the political dignity and efficacy of the generations that preceded us.*

Secondly, Benhabib emphasizes the qualitative phenomenological dimension of the space of appearance that was at the centre of my discussion of Pound's *Cantos.* This is of course where action resonates. The integral power of action, as I described it, flows right through the realm of intersubjectivity as it is established between persons communicating freely. 'All things that are are lights', as Pound says, quoting Johannes Scotus Erigena (74/443), or to adjust the phrase a little, all persons in the public domain are lights—by virtue of the light they elicit from one another, and by virtue of the light they shed on one another.

As I understand it, the problem with the first line of defence is that it almost inevitably underestimates this second line of defence—that is to say, the argument from normativity and socio-economics tends to underestimate the significance of the phenomenological argument. But the reverse is also the case: the phenomenological argument tends to underestimate the argument from socio-economics. I don't propose in this chapter to undo that aporia, but just to observe its ramifications.

In any case, whatever misgivings feminists have had about Arendt's distinction between public and private, they have seized gratefully on her concept of natality: 'The very capacity for beginning is rooted in *natality,* and by no means in creativity, not in a gift but in the fact that human beings, new men, again and again appear in the world by virtue of birth.'[4] Julia Kristeva comments that, 'no one else, in modern times, has reflected upon birth as a constant succession of new beginnings.'[5] 'Our freedom is not', she continues, 'a psychic construction, but the result of our . . . being born.'[6] Freedom is a product of our first appearing, the new beginning enacted in our birth, so that action itself, wherein we

---

[4] Arendt, *The Life of the Mind,* 2. 217.
[5] Kristeva, *Hannah Arendt,* 44.
[6] Ibid. 45.

appear—and where we are seen to begin—has its origins in natality. Kristeva concurs with Benhabib, and with other Arendt scholars, in finding here a joyful riposte to Heidegger's fateful notion of our being *thrown* into the world. 'And, surely, it is no accident that the thinker who countered Western philosophy's love affair with death with her category of "natality"—that a child is born to us— was a woman' (*Reluctant Modernism*, 135).

Benhabib's book on Arendt ends with an excellent discussion of her concept of privacy. While allowing that the latter's 'affirmation of the private realm so often reads like an ahistorical justification of a specific gender division of labour that historically confined modern bourgeois women to the home', she argues that 'the binarity of the public and the private spheres must be reconstructed', and that the 'recovery of the public world is impossible and unlikely without a parallel reconstruction of the private sphere' (213–15). For this Arendt is an 'indispensable guide' (215). In *The Human Condition* she insists that while the distinction between the private and the public 'coincides with the opposition of necessity and freedom, of futility and permanence, and, finally, of shame and honour, it is by no means true that only the necessary, the futile, and the shameful have their proper place in the private realm' (*HC*, 73). The private is also a place of shelter, restoration, and replenishment. And here there are (though Benhabib chooses not to say it) altogether more positive echoes of the Heidegger of *Being and Time*:

A life spent entirely in public, in the presence of others, becomes, as we would say, shallow. While it retains its visibility, it loses the quality of rising into sight from some darker ground which must remain hidden if it is not to lose its depth in a very real, non-subjective sense. The only efficient way to guarantee the darkness of what needs to be hidden against the light of publicity is private property, a privately owned place to hide in. (*HC*, 71)[7]

Despite more than a suggestion of sympathy for 'the abolition of private ownership of wealth' (*HC*, 70), Arendt still champions—and in words that are reminiscent of Virginia Woolf's famous essay, *A Room of One's Own* (1929) —'private property in the sense of a tangible, worldly place of one's own' (*HC*, 70). It is as if in this respect at least a little private property is the best we can do. Benhabib refers to this as Arendt's 'concept of the "home"' (*Reluctant Modernism*, 213).

I want now to develop this discussion and relate it to the American context.

3.1.2

Arendt's notion of the decay of the public domain is well and truly anticipated in what has become the canonical literature of nineteenth-century America. But

[7] See e.g. Arendt's brief comments on Heidegger's *Being and Time* in the Preface to *Men in Dark Times*, p. ix.

whereas she would try to outline a new vision of republican commonalty—an endeavour that coincides with Pound's re-visioning of public life—nineteenth-century men of letters had preferred to itemize the corruption of the public domain, and to invest all real value, spiritual, moral and even, paradoxically, political, in Emerson's infinite private man, who 'shall leave governments to clerks and desks': 'This revolution is to be wrought by the gradual domestication of the idea of Culture . . . The private life of one man shall be a more illustrious monarchy, more formidable to its enemy, more sweet and serene in its influence to its friend, than any kingdom in history.'[8] In a similar spirit the reader of James Fenimore Cooper's *The Pioneers* (1823) is encouraged to sympathize with the loner Natty Bumppo rather than with Judge Temple, the man trying to hold the body politic together. Hawthorne begins what is generally regarded as his greatest novel, *The Scarlet Letter* (1850) with a preface, 'The Custom House', that stresses the intimacy rather than the publicity of being read, and reiterates—in a striking echo of Emerson's 'Introduction' to *Nature* (1836)—the inviolable privacy of the 'inmost Me'.[9] Emerson himself, as the quotation illustrates, invents the metaphysics of self-reliance and in the process domesticates the American Revolution. And democratic republicans like Melville and Twain are no more inclined than the reactionary Poe had been to represent the gathering together of the 'kingly commons' (*Moby Dick*) as free and efficacious.

The century's most systematic treatment of the distinction between public and private, however, has got to be Henry James's novel *The Bostonians* (1886). James not only lampoons the blue-stockinged 'inverts' of the women's movement, he satirizes the conditions of contemporary public life, and then ridicules women for their determination to enter it—the essential charge being that it, public life, has been commercialized through and through, given up to the Selah Tarrants of the world—in a sense the Walt Whitmans. And if Tarrant may stand, in retrospect, for Whitman the vulgarian, the newspaper hack, who can't be photographed too often and quotes Emerson's correspondence on his book cover; then Olive Chancellor, with her privacy like an open wound, may be allowed to stand for the opposite extreme, for someone like Emily Dickinson, who could not bear to be photographed, and flirted with publication with a kind of holy terror. It seems that for all his instinctive cosmopolitanism, James's valuation of private life ends up coinciding with the valuation given to it by the supposedly antithetical Emerson. But it's not as simple as that. Critics and general readers have remarked that, in the final passage of *The Bostonians*, when Olive is left to address the baying crowd, and the lovers, taking up their privacy, move beyond the ken of both Olive and the narrator, there is more than a hint of hard times ahead. But the point isn't simply that marriage without means is hard.

---

[8] Emerson, 'The American Scholar' (1837), *Essays and Lectures*, 67.
[9] Nathaniel Hawthorne, *The Scarlet Letter*, ed. Seymour Gross, Sculley Bradley, Richmond Croom Beatty, and E. Hudson Long (1850; New York: W. W. Norton & Company, 1988), 5.

The sense of trepidation comes quite as much from the prospect of imminent darkness ('so far from brilliant')—an image of the unrelieved obscurity of unremitting private life.[10] (It is no accident surely that the last sentence recalls that 'solitary' exit at the end of Milton's *Paradise Lost*.) The overriding point, then, consists in the full contrast between the unacceptable publicity of public life, its tawdry glare, and the unedifying prospect of total privacy. Public life may be a travesty, but to ask for nothing but privacy is, in James's view, to ask too much of it.[11]

I want to show how the trajectory I am tracing here can also be observed in the poetry of Emily Dickinson. There is nothing controversial in claiming that Dickinson's poetry represents the extreme development of privacy in the lyric. But precisely as a result, I argue, it demonstrates the exhaustion and ultimate inadequacy of privacy, its metamorphic dependency on a contiguous public realm. Here privacy points beyond itself, despite itself, over its own dead body. I will show what I mean more precisely by focusing on the motif of the house in a handful of Dickinson's poems, but before I do that I want to look at an important philosophical attempt to reinterpret and redeploy the nineteenth-century American preoccupation with privacy.

3.1.3

Women have not been alone in opposing 'Western philosophy's love affair with death' with the concept of 'natality' and in discerning in this last a source of political freedom. We can find elements of it in Emerson's claim that 'Every man is an impossibility until he is born' ('Experience');[12] in the mildness of Winnicott's response to Freud and Klein; and in Gaston Bachelard's importantly playful rejoinders to Heideggerian existentialism. In a passage that chimes significantly with Arendt's response to the somewhat *fin-de-siècle* Heideggerian concept of being *thrown* into the world, the French phenomenologist has written:

Before he is 'cast into the world,' as claimed by certain hasty metaphysics, man is laid in the cradle of the house . . . Life begins well, it begins enclosed, protected, all warm in the bosom of the house . . .

From the phenomenologist's viewpoint, the conscious metaphysics that starts from the moment when the being is 'cast into the world' is a secondary metaphysics. It passes over

---

[10] Henry James, *The Bostonians*, ed. Charles R. Anderson (1886; Harmondsworth: Penguin, 1984).

[11] This is another way of thinking about why Isabel Archer turns down the uncompromising privacy offered her by Caspar Goodwood in the slightly earlier novel *The Portrait of a Lady* (1882), in favour of the compromised privacy of her husband's Roman salon. Compromised privacy is by no means the same thing as authentic public life, but at least it is not unrelieved privacy either.

[12] Emerson's thought is echoed (like so many of his thoughts) in Thoreau's *Walden*: 'Every child begins the world again, to some extent' (p. 18; ch. 1).

the preliminaries, when being is being-well, when the human being is deposited in a being-well, in the well-being originally associated with being.[13]

Though the American scene hardly figures in Bachelard's reflections on *The Poetics of Space*, this image of the house of being, of being as a house, is, in keeping with the pre-eminence accorded to private life, one of the archetypal images of nineteenth-century American literature. We find it repeatedly in Hawthorne and Poe; we find it in *Uncle Tom's Cabin* (1852), in Louisa May Alcott, in Emerson's paean to the domestication of culture, even in Basil Ransom's response to Olive Chancellor's drawing room. As we shall see shortly, it has also been argued that the image of house or home is 'perhaps the most penetrating and comprehensive figure' that Emily Dickinson employs. But perhaps the greatest single instance of it, the exemplary instance, and the most affirmative, is Henry David Thoreau's *Walden* (1854). *Walden* is also exemplary for having inspired a response of nearly comparable philosophic and poetic richness in Stanley Cavell's *The Senses of Walden*—a book wherein Thoreau's book is made to resonate, as Bachelard would say, phenomenologically. In the chapter 'Where I Lived, and What I Lived For', which begins with the magnificent declaration that 'At a certain season of our life we are accustomed to consider every spot as the possible site of a house' (Thoreau, 54)—a recognition of the need to take stock, and take root, and look round, and face up—Thoreau writes:

With this more substantial shelter about me, I had made some progress toward settling in the world. This frame, so slightly clad, was a sort of crystallization around me, and reacted on the builder. It was suggestive somewhat as a picture in outlines. I did not need to go out of doors to take the air, for the atmosphere within had lost none of its freshness. It was not so much within doors as behind a door where I sat, even in the rainiest weather. The Harivansa says, 'An abode without birds is like a meat without seasoning.' Such was not my abode, for I found myself suddenly neighbour to the birds; not by having imprisoned one, but having caged myself near them. (57–8)

According to Cavell any single passage of *Walden means* as deliberately as any other ('is isomorphic with every other'). To read it is to *wake up* to it, and to be *awake* to it is *to be alive*—not on Thoreau's terms but on yours, which become his only by being yours:

To realize where we are and what we are living for, the conditions of our present, the angle at which we stand to the world, the writer calls 'improving the time'...And our conditions are to be realized within each calling, whatever that happens to be. Each calling—what the writer means (and what anyone means, more or less) by a 'field' of action or labour—is isomorphic with every other. This is why building a house and

---

[13] Gaston Bachelard, *The Poetics of Space*, trans. Maria Jolas (1964; Boston, Beacon Press, 1994), 7.

hoeing and writing and reading ... are allegories and measures of one another. All and only true building is edifying. All and only edifying actions are fit for human habitation. Otherwise they do not earn life. If your action, in its field, cannot stand such measurement, it is a sign that the field is not yours. This is the writer's assurance that his writing is not a substitute for his life, but his way of prosecuting it. He writes because he is a writer.[14]

To write because one is a writer is the same as building because one is a builder, dwelling because one is a dweller, thinking because one is a thinker. In so far as one does them well, they are all isomorphic with one another. An almost identical point is made by the later Heidegger, in the essay 'Building Dwelling Thinking' (as the title alone suggests), written in the 1950s, when Heidegger had moved on, mollified, beyond what Bachelard called 'the hasty metaphysics' ushered in by *Being and Time*.

Where Cavell differs from both Heidegger and Bachelard, however, is in his express political emphasis—which is something that he seems to share with Arendt. One of his main purposes in the *The Senses of Walden* is to argue that Thoreau's retreat to a house of his own building, in the woods by Walden pond, is not a negation of politics, but a constructive political act, whose politics, he grants, seem at first to be obscure. But this is because, according to Cavell, politics begins with loss, begins with mourning.

In one of many passages on 'loss', Thoreau writes: 'Not till we are lost, in other words, not till we have lost the world, do we begin to find ourselves, and realize where we are and the infinite extent of our relations' (Thoreau, 115). Cavell glosses:

The writer comes to us from a sense of loss ... Everything he can list he is putting in his book; it is a record of losses. Not that he has failed to make some gains and have his finds; but they are gone now. He is not present to them now. Or, he is trying to put them behind him, to complete the crisis by writing his way out of it. It is a gain to grow, but humanly it is always a loss of something, a departure. Like any grownup, he has lost his childhood; like any American, he has lost a nation and with it the God of the fathers. He has lost Walden; call it Paradise; it is everything there is to lose. (*Senses of Walden*, 52)

In Cavell's forceful reading of Thoreau's celebrated image of ecstatic doubleness, it is *loss* that prepares the ground for being beside oneself, which in turn prepares the ground for politics. Cavell's debt to Freud, and to 'Mourning and Melancholia' (1917) in particular, is obvious.[15] Loss, that is to say mourning, is at one with reality-testing: it makes reality possible again. 'That was the point of the experiment; not to learn that life at Walden was marvellous, but to learn to leave it' (*Senses of Walden*, 45): to leave it because one had 'several more lives to

---

[14] Cavell, *Senses of Walden*, 61–2.
[15] For a detailed discussion of Cavell's indebtedness to Freud, also in relation to Thoreau, see Stephen Mulhall, *Stanley Cavell: Philosophy's Recounting of the Ordinary* (Oxford, Clarendon: 1994), esp. ch. 10.

live' (Thoreau, 213). Mourning is a kind of thinking, not death-loving but overcoming. 'With thinking'—with this thinking—'we may be beside ourselves in a sane sense' (Thoreau, 90). It is only when one has established this relationship to, or rather with, oneself, a relation of sane observation, that one can enter fully into the political life of the nation or community. Thoreau's ecstatic sanity of the doubled self is 'viewed not as a mutual absorption'—that is to say, as narcissism—'but as a perpetual nextness, an act of neighbouring or befriending' (*Senses of Walden*, 108). On this basis, on these conditions, '*Walden* is . . . a tract of political education, education for membership in the polis' (85). We can only befriend others when we have befriended ourselves. 'Education for citizenship is education for isolation' (85–6). Neighbourliness begins at home, politics—the art of being-with—in the isolate 'house of being'.

In what follows I will be arguing that much of what Cavell says about Thoreau could just as well be said of Dickinson. There we find an equally vivid sense of life lived as mourning or loss, which is in turn generative of an astonishing self-awareness, with the whole dynamic evoked through synecdoche of the house—figures of intimate space. But how could this be political, even in Cavell's sense? That is the question. The attempt to answer it will expose once again the great strength and the singular weakness of Arendt's political theory: the great strength consists in the originality of her developing argument that life is political in so far as appearance itself is political; the weakness, as we shall see, is in the way that that very argument enables her to elide the question of the political significance of privacy (gender, the socio-economic). And as we have seen, it is the feminist critique of Arendt, as set out by Benhabib, that has exposed this most clearly.

3.2 FROM CAVELL TO DICKINSON

3.2.1

We have to get the picture right. A woman so startling, so original, it would not be inappropriate to stand her next to Kierkegaard—that is, if it did not appear to be her fate somehow, no less than his, to wind up standing alone. Of course, they stand on opposite sides of the Atlantic. And she hasn't the advantages of his education. Nevertheless her ironical dialectical acumen is comparable to his, and so she represents as much as he, the acute point of nineteenth-century Protestantism, impatient of belief and disbelief alike. Despite her preference for solitude, she can be intensely, if selectively, sociable—every bit as much perhaps as Kierkegaard himself, but because she is a woman she hasn't half as much freedom as he has to test out where her sociability ends. In fact she will almost certainly find that limits are imposed on her, not by her. She will be left before she leaves—she will have to learn from early on the arts of mourning and self-befriending. To 'practice losing', as Elizabeth Bishop put it a century later.[16]

We are concerned, following Cavell, to trace a sequence of moments in Dickinson's poetry: first, the salience of the figure of the house; secondly, the centrality of the experience of losing or mourning as figured through the house; thirdly, the condition of being beside herself in a sane sense (again as so figured); and finally, as I've said, to ask in what sense, if any, this last could be interpreted as political.

3.2.2

In her book *Emily Dickinson and the Image of Home,* Jean McClure Mudge argues that if synecdoche might be called Dickinson's dominant trope, the house is perhaps her greatest fund of synecdoche: 'Dickinson's image of house or home ... is perhaps the most penetrating and comprehensive figure she employs'; her 'largest fund of expression, second only to a penchant for technological terminology, derives from the domestic scene she intimately knew'.[17] Drawing on a thorough acquaintance with her poems and letters, together with a sound knowledge of the Dickinsons' family history and the two Amherst houses in which Dickinson lived, Mudge provides a great deal of detailed evidence to back this claim up. She argues that what she calls Dickinson's *total concept of home* 'reflects her inner landscape, which may be called her *spatial inscape,* a sensitivity to space dependent on both personal and social factors'.[18]

We could say that Dickinson's consciousness is, so to speak, haunted by a house:

> One need not be a Chamber—to be Haunted—
> One need not be a House—
> The Brain has Corridors—surpassing
> Material Place
>
> (*Complete Poems,* 670)

Consciousness 'need not be a House', but it does find its shape there. 'Conscious am I in my Chamber': i.e. I take the shape of my chamber, whereas it is indicative of the unreliability of 'Immortality' that it is a 'shapeless friend' (679). This consciousness of shape, moulded by the house, also informs

---

[16] Elizabeth Bishop, 'One Art', *Complete Poems 1927–1979* (New York: Farrer, Straus and Giroux, 1983), 178.

[17] Jean McClure Mudge, *Emily Dickinson and the Image of Home* (Amherst: University of Massachusetts Press, 1975), 1. Mudge's instincts and conclusions seem to me to be very much on the right track, and the book manages a nice balance of objective cultural and historical knowledge on the one hand, and psychological and thematic interpretation on the other. Above all the contention that Dickinson's 'consciousness of space, especially enclosed space ... dominated her sensibility' is hard to contradict (3).

[18] Ibid. 1, emphasis in the original.

her imaginings of death and dying: 'The Shapes we buried, dwell about, | Familiar, in the Rooms—' (607). Likewise the house gives form to the death of others:

> There's been a Death, in the Opposite House,
> As lately as Today—
> I know it, by the numb look
> Such Houses have—alway—
>
> (389)

We could look at any number of poems, but 636 seems to be a perfect illustration of Bachelard's thesis that 'With the house image we are in possession of a veritable principle of psychological integration' and 'a *tool for analysis* of the human soul' (Bachelard, pp. xxxvi–xxxvii):

> The Way I read a Letter's—this—
> 'Tis first—I lock the Door—
> And push it with my fingers—next—
> For transport it be sure—
>
> And then I go the furthest off
> To counteract a knock—
> Then draw my little Letter forth
> And slowly pick the lock—
>
> Then—glancing narrow, at the Wall—
> And narrow at the floor
> For firm Conviction of a Mouse
> Not exorcised before—
>
> Peruse how infinite I am
> To no one that You—know—
> And sigh for lack of Heaven—but not
> The Heaven God bestow—

A letter in its seal, in the fingers of a woman, behind a door, in a room, in a house: inside, inside, inside . . . Having locked her door she doesn't open the letter immediately but first gets as far inside the room as possible—'To counteract a knock'. Her movement into the room will be complimented by the 'draw[ing] forth' of the letter—secret space unfolding into secret space. The 'lock[ed] door' encloses the letter that is to be unlocked—the letter too, then, is a room, contains space, infinitude, the possibility of 'transport'. The room is, as we have seen, an extensive figure for both body and consciousness, figuring one in the other. The speaker becomes narrow—she assumes the furtive, secretive shape of her room. The room has fingers; consciousness has walls and doors. Her alter ego, the poem half-jokes, is the mouse. Such 'polar privacy' (1695) feels illicit, feels like theft: 'slowly pick the lock'—as a mouse might pick at cheese. 'You', 'God', and 'Heaven' all get shut out in the final stanza, while she peruses 'how infinite

I am'. It is only when the confines are established that they get to be transcended: 'The Props assist the House I Until the House is built' (1142).

The paradox, with its play on infinity, figuring the illimitable through the strictly limited, is familiar from the Bible: 'In my Father's house are many mansions';[19] and then of course from Emerson: 'There is a property in the horizon which no man has but he whose eye can integrate all the parts, that is, the poet.'[20] Dickinson expresses it again when she writes, 'The Brain—is wider than the Sky—' (632). But where Emerson presents the paradox through a disembodied horizon, Dickinson conveys it through images of enclosed and inhabited space. She doesn't just *see* it—*she lives in it*, in the same way and to the same degree that she lives in a house. The confines are transcended in confined terms. Hegel would have pointed out that this is not logically the infinite at all—since what it excludes is, by definition, finite. But to the Kierkegaard-like Dickinson this is the only infinite possible—a lived infinite ('not I The Heaven God bestow'). It is 'Finite infinity' (1695), hemmed in so to speak by walls, doors, locks, windows; it is scarred, labyrinthine, internally differentiated. 'Angels rent the house next ours', she writes (punning, possibly, on *rent* and *rend*), 'Wherever we remove—' (1544). For Dickinson, nothing embodies this paradox in quite the way a poem does.

3.2.3

The definition of life as finite infinity brings us round to the theme of mourning. In 657, 'I dwell in Possibility— I A fairer House than Prose—',[21] the 'possibility' with which the poem is occupied is the possibility of life—the possibility that the poem lives ('Are you too deeply occupied to say if my Verse is alive?');[22] the possibility—which all life seems to share while it lives (Dickinson, her poem)— that it could go on indefinitely. Life may be visited upon the poem, as Dickinson felt that it was from time to time visited on her, coming in as it were through the poem's 'windows' and 'doors', contradicting it with that infinite which the poem in turn, being otherwise finite, contradicts ('My life closed twice before its close—').[23] For life is, as the poem is, a contradicted infinite—*narrow paradise*. Possibility is possibility lived from inside ('I dwell *in* Possibility'), it is immanent or nothing:

---

[19] John 14: 2. Dickinson singles out this biblical verse for typically sardonic treatment in poem 127.

[20] Emerson, 'Nature', *Essays and Lectures*, 9.

[21] Compare the punning 613: 'They *shut me up* in Prose' (my emphasis).

[22] Letter to T. W. Higginson, 15 April 1862, letter 260 of *The Letters of Emily Dickinson*, ed. Thomas H. Johnson, associate ed. Theodora Ward (1957; Cambridge, Mass.: The Belknap Press of the University of Harvard Press, 1986), 403.

[23] *Complete Poems*, 1732.

Of Visitors—the fairest—
For Occupation—This—
The spreading wide my narrow Hands
To gather paradise

(657)

Consider the almighty existential emphasis on 'This';[24] and that word 'narrow' again—the narrowness of hands, glances, rooms, lines (the narrow possibilities of verse). Because Dickinson's poems live, they can't just end. They die—and die again ('And finished knowing— | Then—').[25]

No. 640 is one of Dickinson's greatest poems of mourning, and the word *life*, as we might expect, is in the foreground.[26] Even by Dickinson's standards, the images and argument bespeak an atmosphere of intensive care. Judith Farr has written that in this poem 'there is no landscape at all and no real place', but it seems to me that the sense of lived space, the consciousness of life as *taking, requiring, necessitating, place*—the realization that the loss that is lived in time *expresses itself in space*—is inescapable:[27]

I cannot live with You—
It would be Life—
And Life is over there—
Behind the Shelf

The Sexton keeps the Key to—
Putting up
Our Life—His Porcelain—
Like a Cup—

Discarded of the Housewife—
Quaint—or Broke—
A newer Sevres pleases—
Old Ones crack—

I could not die—with You—
For One must wait
To shut the Other's Gaze down—
You—could not—

What we have here is an image of the space two people might have shared (it is all there, or not there, in that simple word *with*) and the several spaces into which

---

[24] Compare Thoreau: 'The present was my next experiment of this kind...' (57).

[25] *Complete Poems*, 280.

[26] Compare the pressure Thoreau puts on the words live and life in the extraordinary paragraph of the second chapter of *Walden* beginning, 'I went to the woods because I wished to live deliberately...' (61).

[27] Judith Farr, *The Passion of Emily Dickinson* (Cambridge, Mass.: Harvard University Press, 1992), 306.

they are severed. For Dickinson severs, line by line, 'Life' from 'live' (lines 2 and 1), and 'Life' from 'Life' (lines 3 and 2); the life that isn't, from the life that is. By the time we get to line 3, life is already split down the middle. Dickinson evokes space to evoke the emptiness involved: the spatiality of 'over there', 'Behind', 'up', 'with' or *not with*—the dimensions things have when you live alone, the space which must not only be faced but which will have to be filled or left. When we get to 'Our Life' (line 7) we already know it is semantically cracked, like the pun on 'Sevres', two words badly stuck together. Life is on the shelf: in the double sense that the poet is being left on the shelf (as poets are wont to be), and then in the opposing sense that Dickinson is *here* but life is out of reach. What is a shelf? A shelf is a small room—a room within a room—a room you *cannot live in.*

And just as shelf is a synecdoche of room, so is cup of life. It is the cup that is empty or full, the cup that runneth over, or the bitter cup that Christ asks may pass from him. But a cup is also importantly spatial: it is round and receptive— its business is circumference. It may stand, as here, for two lives joined together as one, but its being one is simultaneously redolent of solitude. (Bachelard quotes Van Gogh's proposition that 'Life is probably *round*'—which Emerson would have endorsed—before going on to observe that, 'when a thing becomes isolated, it becomes round'.)[28] A cup may learn in time to contain its own emptiness—on the other hand it might just crack with age.[29]

There are other household images, which I won't dwell upon. 'Key' recalls the locks and doors of 636.[30] Then there is the 'Housewife' (wondrously accustomed to *discard*, to handle damage and loss) and the 'homesick Eye' (line 26)—for home is preferred, it seems, to heaven and to hell. And then there is the close:

> So We must meet apart—
> You there—I—here—
> With just the Door ajar
> That oceans are—and Prayer—
> And that White Sustenance—
> Despair—

The pattern of severance we encountered in the opening stanzas is repeated still more explicitly here. To 'meet apart' ('Parting is all we know of heaven, | And all we need of hell'):[31] consciousness as the consciousness of division, conscious- ness not just as loss but as saying goodbye—what Cavell means by departure (compare 911: 'Each Consciousness must emigrate | And lose its neighbour

---

[28] Bachelard, 232, 239.

[29] In a letter approximately dated to late August 1858, Dickinson wrote to Samuel Bowles, to whom it is supposed that poem 640 may well have been addressed: 'I hope your cups are full. I hope your vintage is untouched. In such a porcelain life, one likes to be *sure* that all is well, lest one stumble upon one's hopes in a pile of broken crockery.' Letter 193, *Letters of Emily Dickinson*, 338.

[30] Dickinson's editor Thomas Johnson observes that 640 and 636 were collected in the same packet.

[31] *Complete Poems*, 1732.

once'). The only way of being together is not to be—this is the only form it takes, the contradicted infinite, the whole broken cup. And the figure Dickinson reaches for belongs again to the house, one of her favourite figures: 'the Door ajar'.[32] This repeats the poem's dominant spatial figure—an enclosed space *with an aperture somewhere* (room, shelf, cup, eye). Doors close like eyes in Dickinson's poetry ('One must wait I To shut the Other's Gaze down'): eyes open like doors. Just because there is a way in, it doesn't follow that you go in; just because there is a way out, it doesn't follow that you take it. Dickinson chooses to dwell in-between—in the very doorway. Bachelard calls it 'the dialectics of inside and outside' ('man', he writes, 'is half-open being')[33]—it is broken space reconstituted as 'sustenance'.

3.2.4

What Cavell calls departure, the process of loss and mourning, the extremes of living and dying, and living with dying, is one of the abiding subjects of this poet's work, for which the house functions as both mediating figure and control. In Dickinson being is always divided—even loss is 'Double' (departure 'Afflicts me with a Double loss— I 'Tis lost—And lost to me—').[34] Thus in 470 the startling assertion that, 'I am alive—because I I do not own a house', occasions the recognition that she is 'Alive—two-fold':

> I am alive—because
> I do not own a House—
> Entitled to myself—precise—
> And fitting no one else—
>
> And marked my Girlhood's name—
> So Visitors may know
> Which Door is mine—and not mistake—
> And try an other Key—
>
> How good—to be alive!
> How infinite—to be
> Alive—two-fold—The Birth I had—
> And this—besides, in—Thee!

We can argue, following Cavell, that the condition of *losing* or *not owning* a house, the *disowning* of it, this negation, is the precondition for the birthing of that second self. In the elegy she wrote for her mother some twenty years later, probably in the spring of 1883, these two ideas (i.e. living and dying, and really

---

[32] Mudge notes that the word 'door' occurs no less than eighty-two times in Dickinson's poetry (264 n. 14).
[33] Bachelard, 222.
[34] *Complete Poems*, 472.

living as the consciousness of really dying) are laconically joined in the biting description of 'existence' as being 'Homeless at home' (1573).

No. 470 is one of the most explicit examples of the way in which the speaker of Dickinson's poems bears witness to her self: 'I am alive—I guess'. Just as in Thoreau, the measure of what it really means to be lover, neighbour, friend (where we cannot know what it is like to be *with* until we have also been *without*), is our familiarity with the ecstatic arts of self-neighbouring and self-befriending. I find it hard to believe that the great poem 822 is not at some level a laconic rejoinder to Thoreau's *Walden*—which anticipates with preternatural accuracy Cavell's response to it:[35]

> This Consciousness that is aware
> Of Neighbours and the Sun
> Will be the one aware of Death
> And that itself alone
>
> Is traversing the interval
> Experience between
> And most profound experiment
> Appointed unto Men—
>
> How adequate unto itself
> Its properties shall be
> Itself unto itself and none
> Shall make discovery.
>
> Adventure most unto itself
> The Soul condemned to be—
> Attended by a single Hound
> Its own identity.

Here, with barely an adjective to mollify their starkness, are several of Thoreau's key terms, symbols, and concerns, as underlined for us by Cavell: the obsession with neighbours ('When I wrote the following pages, or rather the bulk of them, I lived alone, in the woods, a mile from any neighbour'); that awareness of seasonal, cyclical time that ensures that the book revolves like a literary planet round the sun ('The morning, which is the most memorable season of the day, is the awakening hour'); death ('happily conclude your mortal career') and life, i.e. consciousness ('To be awake is to be alive'); traversing ('I am a sojourner . . . I have travelled'); experience ('I am confined to this theme by the narrowness

---

[35] It is impossible to say with any certainty how far Dickinson was familiar with Thoreau's writing. She makes no mention of any specific part of it and there are just two references to him in the letters. On the other hand Jack Capps quotes Dickinson's cousin, Mrs Ellen E. Dickinson, to the effect that 'Thoreau was naturally one of [Emily's] favorite authors from his love of nature and power of description in that direction.' Jack L. Capps, *Emily Dickinson's Reading: 1836–1886* (Cambridge, Mass.: Harvard University Press, 1966), 118–19.

of my experience'); experiment ('The present was my next experiment of this kind, which I purpose to describe more at length');[36] and property, of course, in the punningly Emersonian sense. Above all, that 'single Hound' recalls the passage that Cavell describes as perhaps *Walden*'s 'most famously cryptic' (*Senses of Walden*, 51):

> I long ago lost a hound, a bay horse, and a turtle dove, and am still on their trail. Many are the travellers I have spoken to concerning them, describing their tracks and what calls they answered to. I have met one or two who had heard the hound, and the tramp of the horse, and even seen the dove disappear behind a cloud, and they seemed as anxious to recover them as if they had lost them themselves. (Thoreau, 11)

Cavell takes this to be a parable of the injunction to lose the world, what Dickinson in No. 341 calls 'letting go'. It's as if in 822 Dickinson is saying that the irony of Transcendental individualism is that it might get more than it bargained for. The pulverizing repetition of 'itself' (it occurs five times: in lines 4, 9, 11—twice—and 13), is both an assault on any notion of identity (each instance is another nail in its coffin), and a confirmation of it in its mortal inescapability. 'I should not talk so much about myself if there were any body else whom I knew as well,' Thoreau says (1). 'Unfortunately', he continues, 'I am confined to this theme by the narrowness of my experience'—lighting on a concept, *narrowness*, that Dickinson really makes her own. Here, then, in Dickinson, is being beside oneself all right, taken to a rare pitch.

3.2.5

Arendt argues that 'the space of appearance . . . predates and precedes all formal constitution of the public realm' (*HC*, 199). We can say in effect that people have, as one of what Arendt calls their *conditions*, an ontological disposition to public life. It's an argument that she set out most emphatically, perhaps, not in *The Human Condition*, but twenty years later in *The Life of the Mind*: 'To be alive means to be possessed by an urge toward self-display which answers the fact of one's own appearingness . . . It is indeed as though everything that is alive—in addition to the fact that its surface is made for appearance, fit to be seen and meant to appear to others—has an *urge to appear*' (1. 21, 29). But appearance is in turn founded on plurality: 'every appearance, its identity notwithstanding, is perceived by a plurality of spectators' (1. 21). Thus for Arendt plurality is political in itself—privacy, properly speaking, is not plural at all (it is our undifferentiated 'metabolism with nature'). For Benhabib, plurality becomes

---

[36] Thoreau, 1, 60, 66, 61, 1–2, 1, and 57. As regards the claim that 'The present was my next experiment of this kind', Cavell glosses this as follows: 'Of course he means that the building of his habitation (which is to say, the writing of his book) is his present experiment. He also means what his words say: that the present is his experiment, the discovery of the present, the meeting of two eternities' (*Senses of Walden*, 10).

political only in so far as it willingly embraces the socio-economic—i.e. only in so far we find within the socio-economic such 'principles, interests, values', as 'have a generalizable basis', and 'concern us as members of a collectivity'. Both positions have much to commend them—and as I've said, it is not my purpose to come down on one side or another, but to trace their implications as reflected in the works of the poets under consideration here, beginning with Dickinson.

Cavell's concept of neighbouring or nextness sounds very like Heidegger's concept of being as being-with, which in Arendt was revised and politicized as the space of appearances.[37] For Arendt, authentic being-with only occurs in public; in private, being-with is merely submersion in the life-process. In other words, Arendt makes being-with political by introducing a rigid distinction between public and private (a dramatic revision of Heidegger's concept of the worldhood of the world): Cavell makes it political by blurring any distinction. But the same criticism applies to Cavell's conception of 'neighbouring', 'next-ness', as applies to Arendt's *polis*; that neither is of itself political—they become political, as *The Senses of Walden* somewhat unwittingly demonstrates, only through contact with the socio-economic.

Cavell's interpretation of *Walden* as 'a tract of political education' only makes sense when it is seen as the constructive counterpart of Thoreau's breathtaking critique of society, a critique so astute in parts as to have begged comparison with Marx.[38] In other words it is the social criticism that makes Thoreau's polis political—and not Cavell's metaphysics of mourning, brilliant as that is. And this is true even when Cavell is being metaphysical about the socio-economic:

The opening visions of captivity and despair in *Walden* are traced full length in the language of the first chapter, the longest, which establishes the underlying vocabulary of the book as a whole. 'Economy' turns into a nightmare maze of terms about money and possessions and work, each turning toward and joining the others. No summary of this chapter will capture the number of economic terms the writer sets in motion in it . . .
The network or medium of economic terms serves the writer as an imitation of the horizon and strength both of our assessments of our position and of our connections with one another; in particular of our eternal activity in these assessments and connections, and of our blindness to them, to the fact that they are ours. The state of our society and the state of our minds are stamped upon one another. (*Senses of Walden*, 88–9)

It is precisely the juxtaposition with the socio-economic referred to in passages like this that puts politics into Thoreau's *polis*. For we can find the metaphysics of mourning worked out with comparable intensity and dialectical consistency in Dickinson—but there's nothing necessarily political about that. Dickinson's immersion in mourning may have prepared her for politics, but there is nowhere for that preparedness to go.

[37] See Heidegger *Being and Time*, division 1, ch. 4.
[38] See e.g. Michael T. Gilmore, 'Walden and the "Curse of Trade"', *American Romanticism and the Marketplace* (Chicago: University of Chicago Press, 1985), 35–51.

Dickinson demonstrates that the mastery of being beside oneself, in all its shapes and shades ('my self is something, apparently, toward which I can stand in various relations'),[39] does not bring about entry into the public domain. Meanwhile privacy left to itself ('itself unto itself', as Dickinson says) becomes cause for despair. Thoreau published his privacy. Dickinson famously did not. 'Publication', she wrote, 'is the Auction | Of the Mind of Man' (709). Her disdain for women publishing was common enough in the circle in which she moved, but it is her achievement as an artist that gives it the special force of a vocation.[40]

My criticism of the ambiguity of Cavell's concept of politics is not intended to suggest that I do not admire his concept of neighbouring as beginning with 'nextness to ourselves' (*Senses of Walden*, 109). On the contrary, it supports my argument that *people have, as one of what Arendt would call their conditions, an ontological disposition to public life*. But I am interested in what happens to us when, from this condition of primary nextness as it were, the momentous step over into the political or even into the space of appearance (the step Olive Chancellor takes at the conclusion of *The Bostonians*, from which James's narrator modestly averts his eye) is not taken.

I conclude this section by reflecting for a moment on what I referred to earlier as the exhaustion of privacy in Dickinson. The idea is that privacy's presentation of itself to itself—its twofold life, as Dickinson put it—is one of the preconditions, call it the intimate precondition, for the metamorphosis from private to public life—the graduation from one to the other. Here I agree with Cavell *and* Arendt. The doubled self's presentation of itself to itself anticipates, points toward, what Arendt called the space of appearance. We may call on further support for this idea from Jürgen Habermas, who argues, in *The Structural Transformation of the Public Sphere*, where he is clearly responding to Arendt, that rather than destroying the public domain, it was the virtue of the bourgeois family of the eighteenth and nineteenth century to nourish and extend it. It was inside the intimate sphere of the family, he argues, that the individual learned this whole business of appearing before others—learned to express and perform his or her personality; in other words acquired a personality.[41]

Nevertheless, admission into the space of appearance is something that Dickinson's (or Thoreau's or any other poet's) twofold self can never satisfactorily realize, precisely

[39] *Senses of Walden*, 53.
[40] Judith Farr discusses the obituary for Dickinson that was written by Susan Dickinson, her intimate friend and sister-in-law, in which the latter boldly linked the poet's '"worth" with her "work"', but was at the same time 'careful to emphasize that Emily Dickinson was a gentlewoman, who believed as a Victorian lady should that "a woman's hearthstone is her shrine"' (Farr, 11).
[41] See Jürgen Habermas, *The Structural Transformation of the Public Sphere: An Inquiry into a Category of Bourgeois Society*, trans. Thomas Burger with the assistance of Frederick Lawrence (1962; Cambridge: Polity Press, 1992). 'Subjectivity', writes Habermas, 'as the innermost core of the private, was always already oriented to an audience' (49): the 'intimate sphere of the conjugal family...and not the public sphere itself (as the Greek model would have it) was humanity's genuine site' (51). For 'Greek model', we may also read Arendtian model.

because the self cannot, by itself, sustain its dividedness long enough—sustain its dividedness *by itself.* This it seems to me is where Cavell's political education falls short, and Arendt's notion of the space of appearance as predicated on human plurality has rather more to offer. In the face of this dilemma Dickinson cuts an extraordinary figure, as she wrestles with the limitations of even the twofold self. The moment of departure in her work, the moment of parting, of closing, is also the point at which the self appears before itself: we might say that here Dickinson becomes her own public, rehearses her own being, is received by herself, and anticipates the public recognition of her work.[42]

In Section 3.4 of this chapter I shall look at a poet, Mina Loy, who, hard as it may be to believe, could be said to experience this paradox in still more aggravated form.

3.3 FOUR FACETS OF *UNHEIMLICHKEIT*: FREUD, HEIDEGGER, ADORNO, GILMAN

By the time Emily Dickinson's poetry began to be published during the early twentieth century the private world lay under intolerable suspicion. It was charged with compromising desire, labour, freedom, and identity. The charges can be categorized in terms of specific ideological standpoints, though in practice they overlapped: these are respectively the Freudian (the betrayal of desire); the Marxist (the betrayal of labour to property relations); the existentialist (the betrayal of one's calling to free authentic individuation); and the feminist (the betrayal of identity to arbitrary and historically determined gender roles). After its broad, inchoate, and eclectic fashion, modernism took succour from all sides of this critique—emerging in its turn as in part a critique of compromised *expression*, the most colourful form of hostility to the 'bourgeois'. Yet this widespread hostility to the private world, now dismissed as inauthentic or bourgeois, gathered momentum often without the slightest notion of a better public one—a negativity which became true in the end even of Western Marxism. Everywhere the benign coincidence of house, home, and spirit was found to be untenable. As Adorno put it, to find a way of not being at home in one's home, became, as we shall see, the morality of modernism.

Yet, according to Arendt, 'To have no private place of one's own . . . meant'— and means—'to be no longer human' (*HC*, 64): 'A life spent entirely in public, in the presence of others, becomes, as we would say, shallow. While it retains its

---

[42] Farr begins her book on Dickinson by relating that her physician, 'Dr Bigelow, was expected to diagnose her final illness by observing her fully dressed figure pass an open doorway, the face averted in shadow' (Farr, 1). Hardly a public appearance—but it is possible to imagine that in proportion as Dickinson failed to appear to the doctor, the more keenly she could feel what it might be like to appear.

visibility, it loses the quality of rising into sight from some darker ground which must remain hidden if it is not to lose its depth in a very real, non-subjective sense' (*HC*, 71). Like Thoreau's *Walden*, Gaston Bachelard's account of the 'house of being' is one of the most insightful and persuasive analyses we have of that authentic privacy which Arendt claims human beings are obliged, for the sake of their humanity, to cherish.

In *The Fate of Place*, Edward Casey argues convincingly that the more we think of Bachelard's account of 'psychic place', with its 'special kind of insideness and its own modalities of surface and depth',

the closer we come to Freud, who also proposes psychic depth and interiority and who, at the very end of his life, proclaimed the unconscious to be extended. Bachelard is well aware of the parallel course he is on with Freud—and with Jung as well. A relation of congenial competition with psychoanalysis is palpable from *The Psychoanalysis of Fire* (1938) to *The Poetics of Space* (1957), the two books that frame Bachelard's thinking about poetic imagery and the psyche. What is an exceptional comment in Freud, or an equally exceptional dream in Jung, becomes for Bachelard a region of research that deserves its own name: 'topoanalysis'. In topoanalysis, descriptive psychology, depth psychology, psychoanalysis, and phenomenology all come together in a common enterprise, one that can be defined as 'the systematic psychological study of the localities of our intimate lives' [Bachelard]. Less a method than an attitude, topoanalysis focuses on the placial properties of certain images, for instance the house: 'On whatever horizon we examine it, the house image would appear to have become the topography of our intimate being' [Bachelard].[43]

A little surprisingly perhaps, Casey does not discuss the work in which Freud himself draws most particularly upon the psychic profundity of the image of the house, the great essay on '*Das Unheimliche*' (1919). The title is of course usually translated into English as 'The "Uncanny"', but because the concept of *Heim* embedded in the *Unheimliche* is precisely what I am interested in, I shall tend to use the German terms in what follows. Freud attempted to explain what it is 'which allows us to distinguish as *unheimlich* [i.e. as 'uncanny'] certain things which lie within the field of what is frightening'.[44] He argued that 'the frightening element can be shown to be something repressed which *recurs*' (363). To summarize a long and elaborate discussion, what recurs is a memory of life in the womb. The fear of being buried alive, for instance, is an inverted fantasy of returning to the womb (367).

It is in other words a classic Freudian argument, with the usual repression and reversal at its heart, and the whole symptomatology of *Unheimlichkeit*, of 'uncanniness' (the double, repetition, déjà vu, the fear of losing eyes, organs, etc.) brilliantly adduced on the way. Not the least interesting part of the entire

---

[43] Edward S. Casey, *The Fate of Place: A Philosophical History* (Berkeley and Los Angeles: University of California Press, 1997), 288.
[44] 'The "Uncanny"', *Penguin Freud Library*, 14. 335–76 (339).

piece is the etymological discussion at the beginning, where Freud works through the shifting meanings of *heimlich* and *unheimlich* in the *Wörterbücher* of Daniel Sanders and the Brothers Grimm, with their quotations from Schelling, Schiller, and all. The adjective *heimlich* has two principal meanings: it designates, first, what *belongs to the house*, what is essentially intimate and familiar, not wild or strange, but 'arousing a sense of agreeable restfulness and security as in one within the four walls of his house' (342). The second designation builds on this: '*From the idea of "homelike", "belonging to the house", the further idea is developed of something withdrawn from the eyes of strangers, something concealed, secret*' (346, italics in the original). Freud also surveys the meaning of the negative compound *unheimlich*—eerie, weird, ghostly, arousing gruesome fear —and is particularly struck by a quotation from Schelling: '*"Unheimlich"* is the name for everything which ought to have remained . . . secret and hidden but has come to light' (345). This passage provides Freud with the basis for his own definition of the *Unheimliche* as 'something repressed which *recurs*'.

It is worth comparing Freud's account of the *Unheimliche* with Heidegger's account of it, just eight years later, in *Being and Time.*[45]

In anxiety one feels '*uncanny*'.[46] Here the peculiar indefiniteness of that which Dasein finds itself alongside in anxiety, comes proximally to expression: the "nothing and nowhere". But here "uncanniness" also means "not-being-at-home" [das Nicht-zu-hause-sein]. In our first indication of the phenomenal character of Dasein's basic state . . . Being-in was defined as "residing alongside . . .", "Being-familiar with . . ." This character of Being-in was then brought to view more concretely through the everyday publicness of the "they",[47] which brings tranquilized self-assurance—'Being-at-home', with all its obviousness—into the average everydayness of Dasein. On the other hand, as Dasein falls, anxiety brings it back from its absorption in the 'world'. Everyday familiarity collapses. Dasein has been individualized, but individualized *as* Being-in-the-world. Being-in enters into the existential 'mode' of the "*not-at-home*". Nothing else is meant by our talk about 'uncanniness'. (*Being and Time*, 233)

For Heidegger, the feeling of uncanniness is one of the characteristic ways in which we encounter the fundamental anxiety of *Dasein*. In not-being-at-home, *Dasein* is as it were true to itself—and likewise true to Being. For Being resides 'alongside . . . the "nothing and nowhere"'. What Heidegger shares with Freud, despite their very different philosophical orientations, is the belief that

---

[45] In order to avoid confusion, I should make it clear that in this and all subsequent extended quotations from *Being and Time* I have simply reproduced single and double quotation marks exactly as they appear in the translation by Macquarrie and Robinson, and I have also followed them in not italicizing the original German terms as and where they have seen fit to include them.

[46] The English translators of *Being and Time* observe in a footnote that while they have translated *unheimlich* 'as "uncanny", it means more literally "unhomelike", as [Heidegger] proceeds to point out' (233).

[47] *Das Man.*

susceptibility to the uncanny is part of what constitutes us as beings who are authentically disposed to their mortality—and thus to Being as such.

Thinking back again to Heidegger's former pupil Arendt, it is worth pausing over this passage from *Being and Time* for a moment longer to remark the dismissive concepts of 'everyday publicness' (*die alltägliche Öffentlichkeit*) and 'absorption in the "world"' (*das verfallende Aufgehen in der 'Welt'*).[48] For Heidegger, this everyday publicness of the 'world' is also a place where we can be *at home*, in what he sees as a state of 'tranquilized self-assurance' (*die beruhigte Selbstsicherheit*). When we are at home in the world we are forgetful of Being. But the uncanny calls us back—this is the fateful grace of anxiety. For Arendt by contrast the public and the world are the last places one could ever be *at home*—these realms are absolutely and necessarily distinct. We might well feel that Arendt shows up Heidegger's lack of conceptual variety and nuance here—as anti-bourgeois prejudice tricks him into what Adorno would call identity-thinking, the idealistic tendency to merge and simplify phenomena.

For the duration of the Second World War the German-Jewish philosopher and critic Adorno lived in the democratic sanctuary of the United States—first in New York, then Los Angeles.[49] It was there that he wrote *Minima Moralia*, as Gillian Rose says, his 'best-written book', and the one which of all his works seems to be the most saturated with the experience of exile—and therefore with the accompanying questions of place, belonging, home, who one is, and if and how and to whom it matters.[50] It is also the book in which Adorno formulates his own ethical version of *Unheimlichkeit*:

The predicament of private life today is shown by its arena. Dwelling, in the proper sense, is now impossible. The traditional residences we grew up in have grown intolerable: each trait of comfort in them is paid for with a betrayal of knowledge, each vestige of shelter with the musty pact of family interests. The functional modern habitations designed from a *tabula rasa*, are living-cases manufactured by experts for philistines, or factory sites that have strayed into the consumption sphere, devoid of all relation to the occupant: in them even the nostalgia for independent existence, defunct in any case, is sent packing ... The attempt to evade responsibility for one's residence by moving into a hotel or furnished rooms, makes the enforced conditions of emigration a wisely-chosen norm. The hardest hit, as everywhere, are those who have no choice. They live, if not in slums, in bungalows that by tomorrow may be leaf-huts, trailers, cars, camps, or the open air. The house is past. The bombing of European cities, as well as the labour and concentration camps, merely proceed as executors, with what the immanent development of technology had long decided was to be the fate of houses. These are now good only to be thrown away like old food cans ... The best mode of conduct, in face of all this, still seems an uncommitted, suspended one: to lead a private life, as far as the social order and one's own needs will

[48] Martin Heidegger, *Sein und Zeit* (1927; Tübingen: Max Niemeyer Verlag, 1993), 188–9.

[49] Gillian Rose, *The Melancholy Science: An Introduction to the Thought of Theodor W. Adorno* (London: Macmillan, 1978), 9.

[50] Ibid. 16.

tolerate nothing else, but not to attach weight to it as to something still socially substantial and individually appropriate. 'It is even part of my good fortune not to be a house-owner', Nietzsche already wrote in the *Gay Science.* Today we should have to add: *it is part of morality not to be at home in one's home.* This gives some indication of the difficult relationship in which the individual now stands to his property, as long as he still possesses anything at all. The trick is to keep in view, and to express, the fact that private property no longer belongs to one, in the sense that consumer goods have become potentially so abundant that no individual has the right to cling to the principle of their limitation; but that one must nevertheless have possessions, if one is not to sink into that dependence and need which serves the blind perpetuation of property relations. But the thesis of this paradox leads to destruction, a loveless disregard for things which necessarily turns against people too; and the antithesis, no sooner uttered, is an ideology for those wishing with a bad conscience to keep what they have. Wrong life cannot be lived rightly.[51]

Many of the questions central to this chapter are touched upon here in the terse drama of Adorno's prose. Above all the obsolescence of house and home as an expression and extension of the 'predicament of private life'. Private life is exhausted, hollow, expendable. 'Independent existence' is a fantasy. Houses are built to be flattened, flattened to be built: bombs and domestic architecture are made for each other. Emigration is one way of acknowledging this—another is by 'moving into a hotel or furnished rooms'. The last is also a kind of exile, an attempt to fashion an 'uncommitted' or 'suspended' existence, a way 'not to be at home in one's home'. Nevertheless, aside from the fact that many of those who 'choose' this way of life *have no choice*, this option, where it still appears to be one, is really an illusion—for when we reject possessions, when we reject homeowner-ship, we continue to serve as foot soldiers in the war games of supply and demand. We can turn our backs on the family home but not on the property market, which makes use of us anyway and behind our backs.

Yet while Adorno carefully demolishes the existential consolations of exile, there is one sort of homelessness, one sort of exile, whose provisional validity he still seems prepared to vouchsafe, albeit after the most tentative and ironical fashion. This is the homelessness, the not-being-at-home-in-one's-home, of writing. 'For a man who no longer has a homeland, writing becomes a place to live', he says. And he paints a Spartan picture of the writer, ensconced in the pigsty of his affections, obsessively fondling his leftovers, then hunted up and down by his aesthetic conscience, whose standards are pitiless, whose measure brings everything to book:

In his text, the writer sets up house. Just as he trundles papers, books, pencils, documents untidily from room to room, he creates the same disorder in his thoughts. They become pieces of furniture that he sinks into, content or irritable. He strokes them affectionately, wears them out, mixes them up, re-arranges, ruins them. For a man who no longer has a homeland, writing becomes a place to live. In it he inevitably produces, as his family once did, refuse and lumber. But now he lacks a store-room, and it is hard in any case to part from left-overs. So he pushes them along in front of him, in danger finally of filling his pages with them. The demand that one harden oneself against self-pity implies the technical necessity to counter any slackening of intellectual tension with the utmost alertness, and to eliminate anything that has begun to encrust the work or to drift along idly, which may at an earlier stage have served, as gossip, to generate the warm atmosphere conducive to growth, but is now left behind, flat and stale. In the end, the writer is not even allowed to live in his writing. (*Minima Moralia*, 87)

The writer is not allowed to live in his writing in the sense that the finished work cuts free of the junk on which it fed—it shuts the junk out and the writer with it. What part of the junk it keeps it changes; takes for itself, preserves on its own terms, barely recognizable. The finished work is finished: the writer has done all he can do for it. And he finds he has paid a high price for finishing the thing, for bringing it to this finish: he can no longer live there. He must take his mess elsewhere.

In some sense this reads like a more stringent version of Cavell's reading of Thoreau's writing as the practice of loss. But there is also an allegory here, among other allegories, of what Adorno sees as the guilt of art—guilt over its inhumanity. For art—and this means especially modernist art, the art of *Unheimlichkeit*—now has a share (as indeed it must have) in the greater inhumanity of the twentieth century. It too refuses to accommodate us, refuses to house us.

Yet so ubiquitous is modernity's obsession with *Unheimlichkeit* that it is no surprise to see Adorno, the caustic enemy of Heidegger and the jargon of authenticity, now entering the same neighbourhood as post-war Heidegger, who in the 1950s published his own brilliant ruminations on dwellings past and present: 'Bauen Wohnen Denken'. Lacking the other's swashbuckling dialectical style, Heidegger is in some ways even more ironical, even more contemptuous, for seeming less so:

Not every building is a dwelling. Bridges and hangars, stadiums and power stations are buildings but not dwellings; railways stations and highways, dams and market halls are built, but they are not dwelling places... These buildings house man. He inhabits them and yet does not dwell in them, when to dwell means merely that we take shelter in them. In today's housing shortage even this much is reassuring and to the good; residential buildings do indeed provide shelter; today's houses may even be well planned, easy to keep, attractively cheap, open to air, light, and sun, but—do the houses in themselves hold any guarantee that *dwelling* [*Wohnen*] occurs in them?[52]

[52] Martin Heidegger, 'Building Dwelling Thinking' (1954), *Poetry, Language, Thought*, trans. Alfred Hofstadter (New York: Harper & Row, 1975), 143–61 (145–6).

Or as Adorno says, 'Dwelling, in the proper sense, is now impossible.'[53]

The feminist concept of *Unheimlichkeit* was most forcefully articulated at the very end of the nineteenth century in Charlotte Perkins Gilman's *Women and Economics: A Study of the Economic Relation Between Men and Women as a Factor in Social Evolution*. Influenced by Marx, Darwin, and Thorstein Veblen, as well as nineteenth-century American feminism, Gilman was a political progressive, who believed that woman's development was thwarted by the sexual division of labour that confines her to the home. Women labour in the house as unpaid private servants, untrained and incompetent, while men flower, so to speak, in the civilizing world of work. 'The embryonic combination of cook-nurse-laun-dress-chambermaid-housekeeper-waitress-governess' makes a woman '"jack of all trades" and mistress of none'.[54] Gilman wanted to take the home, or all that was debilitating in it, out of the house entirely. 'Our general notion is that we have lifted and ennobled our eating and drinking by combining them with love. On the contrary, we have lowered and degraded our love by combining it with eating and drinking' (Gilman, 235). She describes the typical marriage as, in a memorable phrase, 'this Cupid-in-the-kitchen-arrangement' (236). She argues instead for 'the specializing of the industries practised in the home and for the proper mechanical provision for them' (243).

Without repudiating the idea of the home as the first seat of love, peace, privacy, and shelter, she scoffs at the cult of domesticity, where provision get lost in superstition. Home, she writes,

is the last stronghold. Solidly intrenched herein sits popular thought, safe in the sacred precincts of the home. 'Every man's home is his castle,' is the common saying. The windows are shut to keep out the air. The curtains are down to keep out the light. The doors are barred to keep out the stranger. Within are the hearth fire and its gentle priestess, the initial combination of human life,—the family in the home . . .

In homes we were all born. In homes we all die or hope to die. In homes we all live or want to live. For homes we all labor, in them or out of them. The home is the centre and circumference, the start and the finish, of most of our lives . . . We reverence it with the blind obeisance of those crouching centuries when its cult began . . .

Yet everywhere about us today this inner tower, this castle keep of vanishing tradition, is becoming more difficult to defend or even to keep in repair. We buttress it anew with every generation; we love its very cracks and crumbling corners; we hang and drape it with endless decorations; we hide the looming dangers overhead with fresh clouds of incense. (203–5)

---

[53] *Minima Moralia*, 38. '*Eigentlich kann man überhaupt nicht mehr wohnen.*' Theodor W. Adorno, *Minima Moralia: Reflexionen aus dem beschädigten Leben* (1951; Frankfurt am Main: Suhrkamp Verlag, 1997), 40.

[54] Charlotte Perkins Gilman, *Women and Economics: A Study of the Economic Relation Between Men and Women as a Factor in Social Evolution* (1898; Berkeley and Los Angeles: University of California Press, 1998), 155.

The home has become an obstacle to progress: not 'home life *per se*, but . . . the kind of home life based on the sexuo-economic relation. A home in which the rightly dominant feminine force is held at a primitive plane of development, and denied free participation in the swift, wide, upward movement of the world, reacts upon those who hold it down by holding them down in turn' (261). Gilman is as undeceived as Adorno was by what the latter would call 'the musty pact of family interests': 'The home is the one place on earth where no one of the component individuals can have any privacy. A family is a crude aggregate of persons of different ages, sizes, sexes, and temperaments, held together by sex-ties and economic necessity; and the affection which should exist between the members of a family is not increased in the least by the economic pressure, rather it is lessened. Such affection as is maintained by economic forces is not the kind which humanity most needs' (Gilman, 258–9).

Although she is vulnerable to the Arendtian criticism that she conceives of socialization purely in terms of what she calls the 'world's work', i.e. in terms of productive labour, and has no concept of communicative action, nevertheless, in her refusal to classify herself as a feminist, and in her consistent emphasis on what Virginia Woolf calls 'the common life which is the real life and not . . . the little separate lives which we live as individuals',[55] Gilman looks forward to Arendt's republican humanism:

The highest emotions of humanity arise and live outside the home and apart from it. While religion stayed at home, in dogma and ceremony, in spirit and expression, it was a low and narrow religion. It could never rise till it found a new spirit and a new expression in human life outside the home, until it found a common place of worship, a ceremonial and a morality *on a human basis, not a family basis. Science, art, government, education, industry,—the home is the cradle of them all, and their grave, if they stay in it. Only as we live, think, feel, and work outside the home, do we become humanly developed, civilized, socialized.* (Gilman, 222, my emphasis)

3.4 MINA LOY

The common tragedy is to have suffered
without having 'appeared.'

Mina Loy, 'Show Me a Saint
Who Suffered'[56]

---

[55] Virginia Woolf, *A Room of One's Own* (1929; London: Grafton, 1977), 108.
[56] Mina Loy, *The Last Lunar Baedeker*, ed. Roger L. Conover (Manchester: Carcanet, 1985), 223.

3.4.1

In this next section of the chapter I try to show how the four concepts of *Unheimlichkeit* exemplified and summarized above play out in the poetry of Mina Loy. For Loy, ambivalence toward the house is a function of her ambivalence toward identity itself, which is also expressed in her contempt for all forms of stability, settlement, or fixity. 'Most movements have a fixed concept towards which they advance', she wrote, in a piece called 'International Psycho-Democracy', 'we move away from all fixed concepts in order to advance'.[57] 'CONSCIOUSNESS', she wrote, in her 'Aphorisms on Futurism' (1914), 'has no climax'.[58] The dynamics of consciousness is the subject of one of her earliest published poems, 'There is no Life or Death' (3). The poem scorns these 'fixed concepts', these grand ideas—Life, Death, Love, Lust, First, Last, Space, Time— on the grounds that their fixity, their nominal grandeur, is an illusion: there is, the poem argues, only 'activity', movement, momentum, process. The championing of unconfined will or desire—the desire of the infinite for the infinite— over against the dead hand of possession, along with the prophetic tone, superficially recall Blake.[59] To possess is to try to fix in place, in other words, to reify; but the entity we grab hold of is, by definition, a 'nonentity', and the one who possesses it is accordingly no better. There are no entities—there is only activity. All *things* are 'tame things'. The problem for Loy, however, is that, having dismissed these nouns as illusions, what the poem offers instead, in the name of activity or process, are more nouns: *activity, propensity, intensity.* Here Loy differs markedly from Ernest Fenollosa and Ezra Pound, who at roughly the same moment in history were seeking to activate the substantive by putting emphasis on 'the sentence, in its naked anatomy of subject/verb/object, as the natural unit of poetic perception'.[60] This technical contradiction is not only characteristic of Loy's work, it is also, it should be said, extremely generative. Loy fights her war with the nominal from within the nominal, with the result that she puts her nouns and pronouns under tremendous pressure, as we shall see, in the effort to uncover the activity within them, the propensity, the instability.

[57] *The Last Lunar Baedeker*, 278.
[58] Mina Loy, *The Lost Lunar Baedeker*, ed. Roger L. Conover (New York: Noonday Press, 1997), 151. It should be noted that the two principal published editions of Loy's work are both edited by Roger L. Conover and have almost identical titles. I cite the later edition, *Lost Lunar Baedeker*, whenever possible.
[59] e.g.: 'The desire of Man being Infinite the possession is Infinite & himself Infinite.' William Blake, *The Complete Poetry and Prose*, ed. David Erdman (Berkeley and Los Angeles: University of California Press, 1982), 3.
[60] Donald Davie, *Poet as Sculptor* (London: Routledge & Kegan Paul, 1965), 43. Olson gives his own highly effective spin to the idea in 'Projective Verse', referring to 'what Fenollosa is so right about, in syntax, the sentence as first act of nature, as lightning, as passage of force from subject to object, quick'. Charles Olson, *Collected Prose*, ed. Donald Allen and Benjamin Friedlander (Berkeley and Los Angeles: University of California Press, 1997), 244.

She is dogged by an unanswerable question: to what can she entrust her sense of self in circumstances where identity, wherever it emerges, cannot be trusted? Circumstances in which the house has fallen, as we have said, under fourfold suspicion: Freudian, Marxist, existentialist, and feminist.

'For Mina, the metaphor of the house held ambivalent meanings', writes her biographer Carolyn Burke.[61] The ambivalence comes from the fact that the house stands for these different betrayals of identity and yet at the same time for the longing *for* identity—stands both for what is desired (authentic selfhood, authentic experience) and for the various ways in which desire is betrayed (by family, by gender roles, by political economy). It stands if you like for the false problem of identity—or rather, for that *real* problem which we have come to call, perhaps *falsely*, the problem of identity—as well as for all its false solutions. 'Wrong life cannot be lived rightly', as Adorno says (*'Es gibt kein richtiges Leben im falschen'*).[62]

Let us also keep in mind the larger argument, namely that the modernist dilemma of identity is the negative or shadow of a more overwhelming intuition: the Arendtian intuition that, contra Cavell, *privacy may not confer identity at all.* For identity is in the gift of the public domain; it manifests itself *with a seeming impersonality* within the space of appearances. In the absence of an authentic public domain, modernism directs its *ressentiment*, that is to say, its thwarted political longing, against privacy; blames it for not being able to confer what only the political can.

3.4.2

And I don't know which turning to take
Since you got home to yourself—first

Loy, 'Songs to Joannes'

Perhaps the most immediate evidence for the claim that Loy was unable or unwilling to get home to herself is the difficulty readers have in placing her: this 'mongrel-girl | of Noman's land'; 'this child of Exodus | with her heritage of emigration'.[63] Born in London, with a Hungarian Jew for a father, and a prim English rose for a mother ('trimmed with some travestied flesh | tinted with bloodless duties   dewed | with Lipton's teas'),[64] Loy had already lived in Paris and Florence when, at the age of 34, she turned up in New York. Marjorie Perloff writes that Loy would 'seem to be the prototype of the deracinated cosmopolite',

---

[61] Carolyn Burke, *Becoming Modern: The Life of Mina Loy* (New York: Farrar, Straus and Giroux, 1996), 205.
[62] *Minima Moralia: Reflexionen aus dem beschädigten Leben*, 42.
[63] 'Anglo-Mongrels and the Rose', *Last Lunar Baedeker*, 143, 170.
[64] Ibid. 121.

the sort who tramps through Eliot's *Waste Land*.[65] And she confronts one of the paradoxes of Loy's critical reception, from the heyday of modernism until now: 'Fluent in French, Italian, and German as well as in her own late Victorian English, she lived in New York for only one of her first fifty-four years. How, then, could Pound call her work a "distinctly nation product"—an oeuvre that couldn't "come out of any other country"? And how is it that Virginia Kouidis would call her book on Loy [the first book-length critical study] *Mina Loy: American Modernist Poet*?'[66] Despite these reservations Perloff argues that 'what does make Loy, like her friend Gertrude Stein, so curiously "American" . . . is her invention of an intricately polyglot language—a language that challenges the conventional national idiom of her British (as well as her French or Italian, or, paradoxically, even her American) contemporaries' (195). If Paris was the capital of the nineteenth century, as Walter Benjamin said, New York was quickly recognized, by the likes of Loy and Marcel Duchamp, as set fair to become the capital of the twentieth: it was a city of émigrés and exiles for what would become the century of exile—a city which corresponded to the incipient modernist demand to be somehow homeless at home.[67] Reflecting caustically on this spirit of homelessness, Loy's great contemporary the Russian poet Marina Tsvetaeva said that 'all poets   are Jews':[68] but for the half-Jewish Loy this is only half true, that is, it is a European truth; from the perspective of the modernism she championed, all poets are New Yorkers. Loy, as I say, recognized New York: and this recognition—which was reciprocal, apparently, for a time—was based on what Perloff calls the new phenomenon of an 'intricately polyglot language'.[69] 'It was inevitable', Loy wrote in 1925, 'that the renaissance of poetry should proceed out of America, where latterly a thousand languages have been born, and each one, for purposes of communication at least, English—English enriched and variegated with the grammatical structure and voice-inflection of many races, in novel alloy with the fundamental time-is-money idiom of the United States, discovered by the newspaper cartoonists.'[70]

[65] Marjorie Perloff, *Poetry On and Off the Page: Essays for Emergent Occasions* (Evanston, Ill.: Northwestern University Press, 1998), 194.

[66] Ibid.

[67] For a lively account of the period, see Steven Watson, *Strange Bedfellows: The First American Avant-Garde* (New York: Abbeville Press Publishers, 1991).

[68] Marina Tsvetaeva, 'Poem of the End', *Selected Poems*, trans. Elaine Feinstein (Oxford: Oxford University Press, 1993), 87. Tsvetaeva's desperately dramatic poem plays out a number of prescient variations on the theme of writing and homelessness found in Adorno: 'The whole world is suburb', she scoffs, 'Where   are the real towns?' Indeed she anticipates *Minima Moralia*'s most famous single aphorism: 'Life is a place', she writes, 'where it's forbidden I to live' (86).

[69] 'It is significant', Perloff notes, 'that, from the beginning, it was the United States, not England, whose little magazines—*Camera Work, Trend, Rogue, Blind Man, Others*, and *Dial*— were receptive to Mina Loy's writing' (195).

[70] *Lost Lunar Baedeker*, 158.

Loy explores the origins of her habitual homelessness, her satirical resistance to the home, in what is probably her most ambitious, if not perhaps her most successful poem, 'Anglo-Mongrels and the Rose' (1923–5). The poem scoffs at capitalism, imperialism, anti-Semitism, and, of course, class: finding in each of these the interminable obsession with images and securities. The poem's astringent sympathies lie not just with the mongrel daughter, Ova, the story of whose growth and development it relates, but also with Exodus, the Bloom-like wandering Jew of a father driven to security by *insecurity*. The poem is characterized by that tension between the sterile and the dynamic which is typical of Loy, though at times the tension can seem entrapped in the one frozen note of monotonous satirical protest.[71] Nevertheless, what does give the poem strength and interest is its innovative concern with childhood, environment, and perception: '(The drama of) | a human consciousness', as it 'gyrates | on the ego-axis';[72] that is, its concern with consciousness as drama: and with the question of growing up as the question of balancing, without thwarting, this drama, or dynamic, of consciousness. It is not by any means on the scale of *The Prelude*, but it is serious and substantial nonetheless, and in the poem's best passages Loy's various themes and virtues come together.

'Anglo-Mongrels' describes the family home as a 'marriage box', where people 'shut themselves up in hot boxes and breed', suffer their 'cruel privacy'.[73] The box is also a coffin, which extends 'from the nursery to the cemetery'.[74] Loy's ambivalence about marriage was in keeping with a lucid feminist critique of society to which she had already given expression in a series of poems which are haunted by the familiar image of the house. As her biographer remarks: 'In 1914 and 1915, while Mina was working out her ideas on "feminine politics," she was also writing a series of poems that critique the social, economic, and psychological control of women—and, through these poems on Italian women's destinies, making comparisons to her own.'[75] Burke calls them Loy's '"house" poems' (*Becoming Modern*, 199).

'Houses hold virgins | The door's on the chain': so begins Loy's poem 'Virgins Plus Curtains Minus Dots' (1915), a satire of the moral damage perpetrated by the cult of virginity and the related custom of marriage portions ('dots'): to be

---

[71] Carolyn Burke writes not unfairly that 'despite claims for "Anglo-Mongrels" as "one of the lost master-poems of the 20th century," it is of interest chiefly as one of Mina's most polished attempts to understand her background...The poem uses logopoeia as a battering ram—an approach that softens only in lines on Ova's spiritual yearnings' (*Becoming Modern*, 353).

[72] *Last Lunar Baedeker*, 152.

[73] Ibid. 143–4.

[74] Ibid. 156.

[75] Burke, *Becoming Modern*, 199. For further discussions of Loy and feminism see Linda A. Kinnahan, *Poetics of the Feminine: Authority and Literary Tradition in William Carlos Williams, Mina Loy, Denise Levertov, and Kathleen Fraser* (Cambridge: Cambridge University Press, 1994), and Rachel Potter, *Modernism and Democracy: Literary Culture 1900–1930* (Oxford: Oxford University Press, 2006).

dotted is in effect to lose one's virginity, whereas to be 'minus dots' is, we may suppose, to remain dotless, *spotless*, pure ('plus' and 'minus' point up the calculating, economic nature of the business). The sexual symbolism of houses, curtains, doors is obvious enough. More interesting perhaps is the way in which the virgins without dowries take so to speak the point of view of the house:

Virgins   without dots
Stare   beyond probability

See the men pass
Their hats are not ours
We   take a walk
They are going somewhere
And they   may look everywhere
Men's eyes   look into things
Our eyes   look out

(*Lost Lunar Baedeker*, 21)

The virgins are *in* looking out, while the men are *out* looking in: men's eyes are penetrative, though the meaning is also ironic, for there is a manifest failure here to 'look into' what all this virginal stuff is about. For the virgins, walking, like seeing, is tied to the house: to 'take a walk' is not the same as 'going somewhere', as it is for the men ('So much flesh in the world | Wanders at will')[76]—it is a chaste constitutional, to help pass the time ('There is so much   Time').[77]

One of Loy's tasks then in her early poetry will be to establish the freedom of her powers of observation—including her powers of observation as a woman (note by the way that there are no *women* in this poem, only virgins—the word *woman* is never used); to get them, as it were, out the house.

A more substantial poem, which dates from the same period, is 'The Effectual Marriage: or the Insipid Narrative of Gina and Miovanni' (1917), as dry a satire as the best of early Eliot or Pound's *Hugh Selwyn Mauberley*. Again the poem begins with the image of a door:

The door was an absurd thing
Yet it was passable
They quotidienly passed through it
It was this shape

(*Lost Lunar Baedeker*, 36)

The door is, once again, an image of virginity: 'an absurd thing' made 'passable'—i.e. not just penetrable, but acceptable, fitting, familiar, through sheer blind cultural practice. In this case, however, it represents a virginity

---

[76] *Lost Lunar Baedeker*, 22.
[77] Ibid. 21.

which the *two of them*, Gina *and* Miovanni, have to pass through—and Loy good-humouredly allows that it has its quotidian aspect, alongside the cultural pressure of the concept. Nevertheless, the concept and the physical actuality are different—or as Loy says, 'It was this shape'. The ambiguity is comprehensive and succinct. What was 'this shape'? Sex? His? Hers?

Once they get through the door they are ensconced in the house, where they remain for the duration of the poem ('She flowered in Empyrean | From which no well-mated woman ever returns').[78] As in 'Virgins Plus Curtains', there is a lot of looking through windows but no real venturing out. She 'marketed | With a Basket' (39), we are told at one point, but we don't see her at market—the basket is a sort of fake-bucolic extension to the kitchen:

> In the evening they looked out of their two windows
> Miovanni out of his library window
> Gina from the kitchen window
> From among his pots and pans
>
> (36)

The windows once again are like eyes—and the fact that there are only two of them also suggests the 'insipid' personality of the pair, to all appearances merged. At the same time, appearances are, as always, deceptive: each of them has a window, but she has '*his* pots and pans' (my emphasis)—with the alliterative coupling conveying the double nature of the injustice: he has a library, she has a kitchen; but what she has, is—like what he has—*his*!

Loy makes exact economical use of repetition, to get at the tautological foundations of the sexual division of labour: 'Gina had her use   Being useful' (36). Or to take a longer passage:

> So they   the wise ones   eat their suppers in peace
>
> Of what their peace consisted
> We cannot say
> Only that he was magnificently man
> She insignificantly a woman who understood
> Understanding   what is that
> To Each   his entity   to others
> their idiosyncrasies   to the free expansion
> to the annexed   their liberty
> To man his work
> To women her love
> Succulent meals   and an occasional caress
>   So be it
>   It so seldom is
>
> (37–8)

[78] Ibid. 37.

Alongside the exposure of ideological repetition, ideology as compulsive repetition ('peace', 'man', 'woman', 'understood | Understanding'), Loy lets loose a more disruptive syntax, breaking up the obstinate rhythms of cliché ('what is that'?), and sending repetition into reverse: 'So be it | It so seldom is'. Alongside its satirical impact, repetition is also being used to loosen up meaning, to mobilize it, to strip it of its identity, to encourage the reader, even, to misidentify it:

> Gina was a woman
> Who wanted everything
> To be everything in woman
> Everything everyway at once
> Diurnally variegate
> Miovanni always knew her
> She was Gina
> Gina who lent monogamy
> With her fluctuant aspirations
> A changeant consistency
> Unexpected intangibilities
>
> (38)

On the one hand, Miovanni sees through Gina's 'changeant consistency'—her 'fluctuant' eroticism: her polymorphous perversity is ultimately *all the same*. That is the nature of 'monogamy'. On the other hand, asks Loy, what is it that is all the same—if Gina is Gina, but Gina is a fake, a social manikin, then who else is she, who else could she be? ('She is **NOT!**' Loy declares, in her 'Feminist Manifesto').[79] 'The verbs *to be* and *to write* are hard to reconcile', writes Bachelard (*Poetics of Space*, 138). Loy doesn't try to reconcile them. On the contrary, language gets in the way of being, and she encourages it to get in the way: for what isn't true of Gina as such may turn out, in the end, to be true of language.

One of the discoveries that Loy is constantly making in her work is that language too, if we do not recover its mobility, functions like a marriage box— identity is housed, that is to say, stifled there. We could say that *language is a house which must be made to move.* The point is well put in 'The Black Virginity' (1918), with its acerbic portrait of Catholic novices ('babies' begotten of what 'they' think of as 'world flesh and devil'), as 'Ebony statues training for immobility':

> It is an old religion that put us in our places
> Here am I in lilac print
> Preposterously no less than the world flesh and devil

---

[79] *Lost Lunar Baedeker*, 153.

Having no more idea what those are
What I am
Than Baby Priests of what 'He' is
or they are—

(*Lost Lunar Baedeker*, 42–3)

'It is an old religion that put us in our places': the nostalgic, loosely iambic
rhythm of this, which Loy's American contemporary Wallace Stevens also
exploited in his poem 'Sunday Morning' (1915), is itself part of that 'old reli-
gion'—inseparable from what Whitman called feudalism—which would put us
and our words and our poems in our places. But how different the ensuing is from
Stevens! Stevens reasons against the Old World in the rhythms of the Old World:
Loy cuts loose. 'Here I am in lilac print', she jokes—i.e. wrapped in the florid
words given women. And off she goes, with a series of sceptical assertions, all fired
off at point-blank range, reminiscent in a way of Shakespeare's Cressida—as
undeceived, as given to misgivings ('What I am | ... what "He" is | or they are').

'And how many doors were doors of hesitation!' writes Bachelard. 'If one were
to give an account of all the doors one has closed and opened, of all the doors one
would like to re-open, one would have to tell the story of one's entire life' (*Poetics
of Space*, 223-4). In the magnificently evocative 'At the Door of the House'—a
poem which almost certainly evoked, *gave voice to*, unacknowledged, the
Madame Sosostris passage of Eliot's *The Waste Land* (surely one of the most
fastidious bits of plundering in twentieth-century poetry),[80] and quite possibly
inspired the ornate play of exotic names which is part of the characteristic music
of both that poem and 'Gerontion'—Loy paints an ironical picture of female
trepidation, caught between 'an inconducive bed-room' and a mysterious 'jour-
ney'.[81] A house ruled by superstition and anxiety is a house of cards—'Tauro
cards'. In one of those links that are never made directly and which for that very
reason cement a composition with all the more force (discoveries that the poem is
in the act of making, and which act like bonds), the cards are like doors, opening
or closing on the future or the past:

A man cut in half
Means a deception
And the nude woman
Stands for the world

(*Lost Lunar Baedeker*, 34)

---

[80] Loy contributed three poems, including this one, to the *Others Anthology* for 1917, which was
reviewed in the *Egoist* the following year by Eliot under the pseudonym T. S. Apteryx. He doesn't
refer to the poem, but as Virginia Kouidis observes, in *Mina Loy: American Modernist Poet* (Baton
Rouge: Louisiana State University Press, 1980), 34, 'the tone, phrasing and imagery . . . foreshadow
the Tarot passage in . . . *The Waste Land*'.
[81] *Lost Lunar Baedeker*, 33.

To be 'at the door of the house', which is where the last line leaves us, is to be on the edge of being, on the very edge of venturing out. Or, as Loy put it, in parenthesis, in 'The Effectual Marriage', anticipating Gilbert and Gubar by light years: '(This narrative halted when I learned that the house which inspired it was the home of a mad woman.)' (39). Here the very brackets seem to act like a restraining order or a padded cell.

3.4.3

In the discussion of Dickinson it was suggested that the house represents the way in which the mind haunts or inhabits the body, is diffused through the body, as the body is diffused through the mind—the way then that these two haunt each other. Houses, rooms, chambers in Dickinson's poems echo that intimate embodied relationship—they are the rooms wherein it echoes—as the rooms are then poems. But what we also note in Dickinson is the extraordinary stillness of the poems—their sitting (not kneeling) posture. They are as it were at church in themselves. Thus even where Dickinson abjures the home, she abjures it for a house of words, the home she makes for her words with poems. Her refuge, that is, is still modelled on the house—it is all about being 'Homeless at home' (a characteristic dialectical reversal, just as her disputes with Christianity have the ironical dialectical fanaticism of the best Protestant theology). The house has a similar function in Loy—up to a point. The house resonates with the relationship of body and consciousness—stands as it were for their curious integrity (rather in the way that Benjamin described the Paris arcades as integrating inside and outside, subject and object). The difference is that by the time we get to Loy this integrity feels bought at too high a price—so that Loy is always on the run. On the run from the very image of identity at which she seemed to have arrived. And this sense of being on the run, this sense of the self on the run from identity in the quest for identity—or rather not just for identity but for something better —is communicated through the jostling momentum of a language, a train of words, that is meant to unsettle one at every turn: in its syntax, rhythms, vocabulary, images, and subject matter. It all adds up to what Loy called— revolving again round the idea that 'consciousness has no climax'—'the gait of a mentality'; that is to say, the way a given mind walks or moves: 'The structure of all poetry is the movement that an active individuality makes in expressing itself. Poetic rhythm . . . is the chart of a temperament . . . It will be found that one can recognize each of the modern poets' work by the gait of their mentality.'[82]

Two of the best of Loy's poems exploring 'an active individuality expressing itself'—that is, consciousness as *gait*, as *movement*—are 'Parturition' (1914) and 'Der Blinde Junge' (1922). The later poem paints a grotesque picture of a blind

---

[82] 'Modern Poetry', *Lost Lunar Baedeker*, 157.

youth busking on the pavements of Vienna. It is one of Loy's most striking studies in ambivalence, a significant element of which is trained, gun-like, on the artist's unequal and unstable relationship to his or her public. Thom Gunn remarks that Loy's 'overt feeling' in 'Der Blinde Junge' is one of 'contempt, turned upon the rest of us, the illuminati reading her poem, complacently assuming that we are heirs to culture'.[83] But the contempt is complicated. The speaker of the poem cannot take her eyes off the boy, by whom she is both fascinated and repelled. There is a marked sense of identification:

> this slow blind face
> pushing
> its virginal nonentity
> against the light
>
>   .   .   .   .
>
> Void and extinct
> this planet of the soul
> strains from the craving throat
> in static flight upslanting
>
> A downy youth's snout
> nozzling the sun
> drowned in dumbfounded instinct
>
> Listen!
> illuminati of the coloured earth
> How this expressionless 'thing'
> blows out damnation and concussive dark
>
> Upon a mouth-organ
>
>   (*Lost Lunar Baedeker*, 83–4)

What Loy identifies with is not the boy's situation obviously (a war veteran, perhaps, and a beggar) but with his frustrated movements, with his having and inhabiting a body, and a body whose limitations are getting in his way. The language anticipates the description of the baby Ova in 'Anglo-Mongrels and the Rose'.[84] Loy also examines the relationship between movement and expression: 'this expressionless "thing"', she calls the youth in the end, as if to suggest that you cannot express yourself—become who you are—without moving. Reification is rigor mortis. As in her explicitly feminist poems, she also puzzles once again over the relationship between identity and virginity: virginity as a stage, so

---

[83] Thom Gunn, 'Three Hard Women: HD, Marianne Moore, Mina Loy' in Vereen Bell and Laurence Lerner (eds.), *On Modern Poetry: Essays Presented to Donald Davie* (Nashville: Vanderbilt University Press, 1988), 37–52 (51).
[84] 'The isolate consciousness | projected from back of time and space | pacing its padded cell': 'A faggot of instincts' (*Last Lunar Baedeker*, 131, 135).

to speak, of pre-identity—which the artist must re-enter in order to be artist, and somehow, god knows, overcome.

But the overwhelming source of her identification is revealed when she invites the audience not to look but to 'listen!' To listen to what?—to the mouth-organ, or to the poem? To both surely. 'You might, at least, keep quiet while I am talking', she had written in 1917, in a short text on 'The Artist and the Public'.[85] Part of the joke is after all that the boy is an artist—a shocking one at that, like Loy or her lover, the poet and Dadaist Arthur Cravan. And like any modern artist he cannot hope to count on the recognition of the public. We might compare the poem to the earlier 'Sketch of a Man on a Platform' (1915), where, right up until the point at which he 'Stings the face of the public', the artist is imagined in terms of the actual gait or *physique* of his personality: 'Your genius | So much less in your brain || Than in your body'.[86] But as always ambivalence holds sway. If the boy is a portrait of the Dadaist inherent in the modernist artist, the sting he carries in his tail, his blindness also identifies him, metaphorically, with the public's ignorance. He embodies the incapacity for recognition like a kind of stigmata, and turns on them the blind gaze they already turn on him.

As well as recalling the opening poem of 'Songs to Joannes', with its combination of virginal 'I' and unseeing phallic 'snout',[87] 'Der Blinde Junge' also recalls 'Parturition', with its extravagant description of centripetal pain:

> I am the centre
> Of a circle of pain
> Exceeding its boundaries in every direction
>
> The business of the bland sun
> Has no affair with me
> In my congested cosmos of agony
> From which there is no escape
> On infinitely prolonged nerve-vibrations
> Or in contraction
> To the pin-point nucleus of being
>
> (*Lost Lunar Baedeker*, 4)

In this poem Loy seems to be playing with Donne's 'Busy old fool, unruly sun'—and playing, we might add, with the biological consequences of Donne's playing . . . But the point about pain is also the same one Emily Dickinson made (presumably another reader of Donne—or is the line 'Done with the Compass' mere coincidence?),[88] and both of them make it half-jokingly: pain as a clue to eternity, to what Dickinson called 'Infinite contain'.[89] Loy plays, Proust-like

[85] *Last Lunar Baedeker*, 285.   [86] *Lost Lunar Baedeker*, 19.
[87] Ibid. 53.   [88] Dickinson, *Complete Poems*, 249.
[89] Ibid. 650. The theme is also explored in the less memorable 967.

(another connoisseur of pain, as it happens), with her own egotism, as Donne played with his: 'I am the centre'.

But the poem also uses the pain of giving birth to beget a meditation on what it is to have a body—on the limits of the body, the question of where it begins and ends, and the question of whether one has it *inside* or *outside*:

> Locate an irritation   without
> It is   within
>   Within
>
> It is without

(*Lost Lunar Baedeker*, 4)

The writing breaks into two overlapping columns, a diagram of restless dualism. The pregnant woman's body is proving to be the real scene of what Bachelard calls the 'dialectics of outside and inside'. Like Dickinson, and with no less wit, Loy anticipates those twentieth-century philosophical debates, particularly in Anglo-American circles, which take pain as the critical instance of what is called incorrigibility in respect of the mind–body problem: 'I like a look of Agony, | Because I know it's true', says Dickinson (241), sounding for a moment like Gilbert Ryle.

The speaker of the poem seems to trace the question of her identity to this diagrammed space between the two inseparable columns of words. She continues:

> I am the false quantity
> In the harmony of physiological potentiality
> To which
> Gaining self-control
> I should be consonant
> In time

(*Lost Lunar Baedeker*, 4)

Identity is the 'false quantity | In the harmony', the difference between what is there and what 'should be', the ghost in the musical machine . . . Whenever the 'I' appears it seems to fall through the floor into the word 'In' beneath it. What is meant by 'I'? The illusion of our singularity can run on ecstasy, can run on pain. But the self that is alone with pain is obliterated by it 'in time'. The self might think it has arrived, 'Gaining self-control'—only to see the question of identity revert to the unspecified quantity *between* what gains control and what doesn't; what is controlled and what isn't. It reverts, as Loy says, to the false.

Loy's response to this fluid differential is to imagine identity as permanently in process:

> The irresponsibility of the male
> Leaves woman her superior Inferiority
> He is running up-stairs

I am climbing a distorted mountain of agony
Incidentally with the exhaustion of control
I reach the summit
And gradually subside into anticipation of
Repose
Which never comes
For another mountain is growing up
Which   goaded by the unavoidable
I must traverse
Traversing myself

(5)

The image of the man running, as of the woman climbing—the woman as tortoise to the man's hare—is not just a satire of male irresponsibility, but an image of the body moving (rather like her friend Marcel Duchamp's painting, *Nude Descending a Staircase*); an image of becoming, of the crazy motion of reproducing; and of verse 'traversing'. One sees why Loy naturally preferred the word individuality to individual in the essay on 'Modern Poetry'—suggesting not a fixed person, but consciousness projected through the process of a word: 'Which ... | I must traverse | Traversing myself'.

The title of the poem, 'Parturition', refers not just to the act of giving birth to an infant, but, more importantly, since children barely figure in it, to the act of giving birth to the self: the begetting of identity. And here is the clue again to the modernist crisis to which the poem bears witness: for it can be taken to demonstrate the justice of what I called the Arendtian intuition that privacy— the self by itself—may not confer identity at all. The self is a vicious circle: 'I am the centre | Of a circle of pain'. What is missing from Loy's picture of natality, ecstatic as it is, is precisely the recognition and celebration of the beginning of the other—which becomes the very paradigm, for Arendt, of the political life. 'Birth', as Julia Kristeva says, 'as a constant succession of new beginnings ... Our freedom is not ... a psychic construction, but the result of our ... being born'. Loy's whole problem, modernism's problem, is that it inherits the idea of freedom as a 'psychic construction'. On the contrary, it is the appearance of others among us which is the basis of political life—and without political life, where we ourselves can be recognized by others, freedom and identity are phantoms. As Loy herself put it in a late poem: 'The common tragedy is to have suffered | without having "appeared"' ('Show Me a Saint Who Suffered').[90]

---

[90] Speaking of Loy's pamphlet 'International Psycho–Democracy', Rachel Potter argues that Loy's 'psychologism ... is a kind of radical individualism in which the form and content of politics is fused on the level of the individual' (*Modernism and Democracy*, 182). But this fusion is just what the poetry itself, by contrast, is unable to bring off. As Potter herself writes suggestively: Loy's 'poems are at their most powerful when they make for slightly uncomfortable reading—when they

3.4.4

In Loy's masterpiece, 'Songs to Joannes', one of the most spectacular poetic sequences to appear in English in the first half of the twentieth century, childbirth has become unnatural ('We might have given birth to a butterfly | With the daily news | Printed in blood on its wings'), or terminal ('Bird-like abortions | With human throats'), or merely the stuff of evolutionary farce ('Foetal buffoons').[91] What she calls 'The procreative truth of Me | Peter[s] out' (XXIV). It is very much in keeping with the fact that for her, as for Charlotte Perkins Gilman, the house has become 'untenable ground': 'And I don't know which turning to take', she writes, 'Since you got home to yourself—first' (V). For Loy, *getting home to herself* was not a possibility. There is in her work a resistance to any expression of settled, fixed or domesticated identity. It is always some other, like the composite lover Joannes, who seems to be at home in the house of being:

> My finger-tips are numb from fretting your hair
> A God's doormat
> > On the threshold of your mind
> > > (II)

The lover is a house from which the speaker is shut out—though, we may add, not unwillingly: 'Don't realise me', she tells him (XIII). Resistance to fixed identity becomes hostility to stability per se, which commingles nonetheless with consciousness of a certain inescapable attraction—sometimes on the periphery of vision: 'Unthinkable   that white over there/— — — Is smoke from your house' (XXVIII). It is striking that it is the male lover, Joannes, who is associated with the house, the homely, rather than the presumably female speaker. Only once does she use the word with reference to herself: 'I am the jealous store-house of the candle-ends | That lit your adolescent learning' (VIII). The phallic nature of the candle-ends is hidden behind the arch maternal image of worshipful cherishing and nurture—as *adolescent yearning* is hidden behind 'learning'. There is a hint of theatrical bravado about it—but she is not fooled by being fooled:

capture something of the raw mental spaces which one feels might be better left uncovered. Loy focuses on such spaces, it seems, because they tell us something about the clash between convention and those aspects of naked self-interest which constitute our drives and desires' (166). By 'raw mental spaces', Potter means, I take it, unidentified mental spaces, where the self is hard to name or designate. I would prefer to say that the poems don't focus on such spaces so much as they end up in them, and they are, I agree, uncomfortable. On my reading the discomfort arises because the individual is no solution to the political problem of individuality—or as the poems keep discovering, identity cannot sustain itself, by itself, indefinitely.

[91] 'Songs to Joannes', *Lost Lunar Baedeker*, 53–68, III, IV, and XXX. Here and in the discussion that follows I refer to the poems by Roman numerals according to their number in the sequence.

Behind God's eyes
There might
Be other lights
(VIII)

Later on in the sequence she recalls us to the finale of section V:

In ways without you
I go
Gracelessly
As things go
(XXII)

Alongside the elegant pathos of this, the insistent longing, Loy underlines her unwillingness to pretend she can merge with her lover, that they have tumbled 'Depersonalized I Identical I Into the terrific Nirvana' (XIII). Instead of going home, to her own house or to his, Loy goes 'As things go': i.e. *she is* as she goes—because, and only in so far as, she goes. 'It is true', she says, 'That I have set you apart' (XII): she has not only set him apart from the 'crowd' (ibid.), but apart from herself. It is, she knows, graceless of her. But like Dickinson in 'I cannot live with You', she has the courage to go gracelessly. It is her eye in fact for the thingliness of things—for their ungraced materiality—their unreality—that saves her. The only acceptable things are uncanny or *unheimlich* things. Here Loy can seem to draw close to surrealism, to the surrealist object, something touched with a kind of animism. She has a gift not for what will come to be called Objectivism, but for something altogether more irrational than that—a gift for *radical objectification*: people, like things, turn into *things*—alienated fetishized objects, all the more attractive for being alien, but alien nonetheless. As in XXV: 'We twiddle to it I . . . I And turn into machines'; or as below:

Something the shape of a man
To the casual vulgarity of the merely observant
More of a clock-work mechanism
Running down against time
To which I am not paced
    My finger-tips are numb from fretting your hair
A God's door-mat
                        On the threshold of your mind
(II)

Despite the tenderness, there is, coextensive with the self-consciously Nietzschean grandeur of the image of 'God's door-mat', a suggestion of personal estrangement from the intimacies of the hearth. Confronted with what is human-all-too-human, Loy's imagery responds by going over-the-top ('I had to be caught in the weak eddy I Of your drivelling humanity I To love you most', she says, in XV). But the image oscillates. 'Something the shape of a man' may conceal a *god*, but also, equally, a lifeless *thing*: 'a clockwork mechanism'. Yet what both images have in common is that they keep the speaker at a distance— unsolved, unmerged, outside: 'On the threshold of your mind'. The *heimlich* must be rendered *unheimlich*—the furniture must be seen to move. 'But for the abominable shadows', she writes, 'I would have lived | Among their fearful furniture' (IV). And then:

> I don't care
> Where the legs of the legs of the furniture are walking to
> Or what is hidden in the shadows they stride
> Or what would look at me
> If the shutters were not shut

(XVII)

It's not just the legs of this 'fearful furniture' that are walking, but the legs of the legs, as if they have been dismembered, or even have the power to reproduce, to multiply—than which nothing for Loy could be more uncanny (see for instance, in 'Parturition', the 'dead white feathered moth' *still* 'Laying eggs' or the cat 'With blind kittens | Among her legs'). The question is not *who* would 'look at me' (i.e. a person) but '*what would*' (i.e. a thing). In his essay on 'The "Uncanny"', Freud writes: 'Dismembered limbs, a severed head, a hand cut off at the wrist . . . feet which dance by themselves . . . all these have something peculiarly *unheimlich* about them, especially when, as in the last instance, they prove capable of independent activity in addition' (366).

If Loy's poetry presents us with a composite or amalgam of the four facets of *Unheimlichkeit*, culminating in the *unheimlich* house itself, Lorine Niedecker, whom I shall be looking at in the final section of this chapter, presents us, by contrast, with an insistent homeliness, proofs of a willingness to live undeceived in the world. Where Loy suggests that freedom is a psychological or emotional absolute, towards or in the face of which one flies, but by definition 'Never reaching — — — — — —' (VII)—and note how the 'flight' is mimicked in those seven dashes—Niedecker proposes that freedom is qualified and material. And her poetry lives out, or makes itself at home in these material qualifications. In her concreteness she recalls Thoreau, but with a still stronger sense of the real material cost of the life exemplified in *Walden*. She is arguably the quietest, dare one say the subtlest, of the great American poets.[92]

---

[92] Despite her neglect, this pithiest of poets had the good fortune to attract the pithiest of critics, Kenneth Cox, who also notes the poems' 'immediate human context, the attachments and irritations of domesticity', confirming their occupation or preoccupation with the cost of living: 'The poems gather together a sense of kinship and house, the biological and economic axes of society, with a scope and sense of proportion more often found writ large among the novelists.' Kenneth Cox, 'The Poems of Lorine Niedecker', *Cambridge Quarterly*, 4/2 (1969), rpt. Kenneth Cox, *Collected Studies in the Use of English* (London: Agenda Editions, 2001), 158, 161.

3.5 LORINE NIEDECKER

For Niedecker, economics is part of the concrete of reality. It is not poetry's
business to transcend economics but to apprehend it, to apprehend this life of
which economics is a part. She describes the economic conditions at any given
moment much as she describes the action of the seasons on the leaves of the trees.
The effect is not to naturalize the unnatural, but to particularize it. It's hard to
think of a twentieth-century English-language poet who is more alive to the way
in which exchange-values muddy use-values, who registers more exactly this gross
and insidious mediation, the price on every aspect of one's basic domestic lot:

> I am sick with the Time's buying sickness.
> The overdear oil drum now flanged to my house
> serves a stove costing as much.
> I need a piano.
>
> Then I'd sing 'When to the sessions
> of sweet silent thought'
> true value expands
> it warms.
>
> •
>
> The death of my poor father
> leaves debts
> and two small houses.
>
> To settle this estate
> a thousand fees arise—
> I enrich the law.[93]

The house has its price—and everything in it. The first of these poems articulates
beautifully the dilemma of trying to ascertain any longer what 'true value' is when
everything one values must be bought and sold: the oil drum, the stove, a piano;
everything that warms the body or the soul. One feels compromised at heart; in a
world of mediations 'half sick of shadows' ('The Lady of Shalott'). If the opening
line recalls Keats and Tennyson, the capitalizing of 'Time' seems to be another nod
to Shakespeare, whose authority on time and money anticipates that of Ben
Franklin and Karl Marx: time is money; 'Time hath, my lord, a wallet at his back'.[94]
    In the second poem Niedecker's wonderful facility with oblique puns is again
quietly in evidence: debt doesn't just sound like death, it is one of its meanings;
'poor father' is not just an endearment, it alludes to her father's 'notoriously

[93] Lorine Niedecker, *Collected Works*, ed. Jenny Penberthy (Berkeley and Los Angeles: University of
California Press, 2002), 157. As Penberthy makes clear, the poet gave minute consideration, in the sad
absence of any like interest from publishers, to the sequence in which her poems would appear.
[94] *Troilus and Cressida*, 3.3.145.

reckless' management of his once considerable property on Black Hawk Island in Wisconsin and to the failure, in the 1930s, of his carp-fishing business.[95] There is a satisfying irony in the feudalistic—or Shakespearean—resonance of words like 'houses' (as in 'a plague o' both your houses'), 'estate', 'arise', 'enrich', all of which suggest an ancient landed class. To 'enrich the law' is not just to pay money to it, which would hardly be enough to make it rich, but to be an instance of its comprehensive and elaborate action.

In several poems which explicitly identify property with prose, Niedecker's diction recalls Emily Dickinson's stark distinction between the prosaic and the poetic, which for the earlier poet was another manifestation of the difference between the public and the private, the worldly and the unworldly, the visible and the invisible, as well as recalling, as Dickinson herself did, Emerson's intuition that 'there is a property in the horizon which no man has but . . . the poet'. Here are three short instances:

> Property is poverty—
> I've foreclosed.
> I own again
>
> these walls thin
> as the back
> of my writing tablet.
>
> (Niedecker, 194)

> To foreclose
> or not
> on property
> and prose
>
> or care a kite
> if the p-p
> be yellow, black
> or white
>
> (Niedecker, 197)

> *Foreclosure*
>
> Tell em to take my bare walls down
> my cement abutments
> their parties thereof
> and clause of claws
>
> Leave me the land
> Scratch out: the land
>
> May prose and property both die out
> and leave me peace
>
> (Niedecker, 291)

[95] Penberthy, 'Life and Writing', in Niedecker, 6.

Niedecker lives out the dilemma described by Adorno, that despite one's moral and political contempt for the concept of property, to which Niedecker even adds a certain practical contempt, a loathing for the trouble it causes one, this having, as the Heidegger of *Being and Time* would say, to take care of it, to bother with it; despite all this, she concedes that 'one must nevertheless have possessions, if one is not to sink into that dependence and need which serves the blind perpetuation of property relations' (Adorno). The paradox that makes possible Emerson's idealism is only felt more acutely, concretely. 'Leave me the land I Scratch out: the land'. For Niedecker, the existential apprehension of one's presence to oneself ('I own again') is not finally separable, as for Dickinson the privacy of home ultimately was, from the economic conditions that both secure and yet aggravate each moment of apprehension. In the twentieth century at least apprehension is inherently apprehensive. Niedecker puns on the hidden affinity of owning and being on one's own, sees that security is also economic, even when it seems purely existential. As she says elsewhere: 'I sit in my own house I secure' (167): security feels insecurity pressing up against it—making it secure.

> *On a row of cabins*
> *next my home*
>
> Instead of shaded here
> birds flying through leaves
> I face this loud uncovering
> of griefs.
>
> (Niedecker, 134)

The terse italicized title leaves us measuring the distance between those 'cabins' and her 'home', which is presumably not a cabin, and invites us to ask whether a cabin can be a home—or why on earth it can't be. Her use of the word 'next' reminds us of the harsh economic truths that give colour to what Cavell calls, writing of Thoreau, the condition of nextness or neighbouring. The poet's 'leaves' are trenchantly offset by the brutal half-rhyme with the shorter, *louder* 'griefs'. 'Uncovering' suggests both a revelation (a Heideggerian disclosing) and a divesting of all shelter, of all cover: meanwhile the poet catches herself in the act of merely *facing* (as we might say of a house, that it *faces onto*) her wretched neighbours—in an epitome of ironic bourgeois nextness.

Another poem dryly instances what Heidegger and Adorno see as the obsolescence of the house: 'The hardest hit, as everywhere, are those who have no choice. They live, if not in slums, in bungalows that by tomorrow may be leaf-huts, trailers, cars, camps, or the open air. The house is past' (Adorno).

> Terrible things coming up,
> these trailer houses.
> People want to live in em,

> park all over,
> set out for somewhere,
> never come home.
>
> Nice!—
> needn't clean anything,
> just throw it out the window
> onto somebody else.
> Shiftless life!
>
> (Niedecker, 119)

No guarantee that dwelling occurs here, then! Nevertheless, the strength of this poem is not in its disabused picture of the squalor of the migrant, but in its fine sense of the paradoxical longing to make a home that also drives the homeless: 'People want to live in em'; want, as Heidegger would say, to dwell. People may be at home by not being at home—but a home it still is. The pun on 'shiftless' sums it up: it ordinarily means lazy, careless, not resourceful, but here it also means immobile, fixed, reluctant to shift, in other words settled—at home. As another poem puts it, in words that might speak to the exile of Adorno himself, 'International loneliness | is homed' (Niedecker, 171).

Niedecker also addresses herself frankly to the most notorious manifestation of the phenomenon of American nextness, the colour-line. The problem may not begin at home, but that is where it ends up:

> When brown folk lived a distance
> from my cottages my hand full of lilies
> went out to them
> from potted progressive principles.
>
> Now no one of my own hue will rent.
> I'll lose my horticultural bent.
>
> I'll lose more—how dark
> if to fight to keep my livelihood
> is to bleach brotherhood.
>
> (Niedecker, 136)

What is impressive about this is the poet's clear-eyed portrait of her tentative progressiveness, as her democratic values (*folk* for Niedecker is a positive term not a patronizing one)[96] clash with economic and political realities, all beautifully adumbrated in terms of the somewhat precious delicacies of space and gardening.

What we find then in Niedecker is not the sense of *Unheimlichkeit* so characteristic of Loy, but rather a sense of rootedness, of being and having to

---

[96] See Peter Middleton, 'Lorine Niedecker's "Folk Base" and Her Challenge to the American Avant-Garde', in Rachel Blau DuPlessis and Peter Quartermain (eds.) *The Objectivist Nexus: Essays in Cultural Poetics* (Tuscaloo: University of Alabama Press, 1999), 160–88.

be at home, despite the trouble or difficulty this brings with it. Where Loy is apt to mock, negate or transcend, Niedecker accurately and uncomfortably *accommodates*. Above all, *she accommodates herself* ('I own again'). And part of the process of accommodating oneself, and accommodating oneself to one's surroundings, is, she recognizes, to protest their injustice. Her feminism is not transcendent, like Loy's ('She is **NOT!**'), but deeply, amusedly, immanent. As for instance in the following poem, which is, we may suppose, a supremely laconic ballad of her parents' marriage:

> She grew where every spring
> water overflows the land,
> married mild Henry
> and then her life was sand.
>
> Tall, thin, took cold on her nerves,
> chopped wood, kept the fire,
> burned the house, helped build it again,
> advance, attack, retire.
>
> Gave birth, frail warrior—gave boat
> for it was mid-spring—
> to Henry's daughter who stayed
> on the stream listening
>
> to Daisy: 'Hatch, patch and scratch,
> that's all a woman's for
> but I didn't sink, I sewed and saved
> and now I'm on second floor.'

> (Niedecker, 166–7)

Among the many felicities here is that deadpan fourth line. To say one's life is sand is, obviously, to let it sound barren and monotonous. But the poem complicates this by acknowledging, in contrast to the constant threat of flood ('every spring | water overflows the land'), and in a world where it's perilously easy to sink ('I didn't sink', Daisy declares), that marriage might have seemed to offer the relative safety of dry land. As the third stanza suggests, Niedecker would live to identify herself through her proximity to water. 'My Life by Water' she calls perhaps her best-known poem (Niedecker, 237)—which as an epitaph goes one better, I think, than that of Keats (the name written not *in* water but *by* it, that is to say, authored by it), and as Keats would have appreciated, does it in fewer words. The final stanza, where Niedecker skilfully brings domestic reality to bear on the child's suspended 'listening', depicts the mother's determination to make a home as the constant, almost crazy struggle to survive. The woman here is not the man's passive helpmeet but his fellow combatant. The final line echoes the mixed emotions of the fourth—'second floor' is hardly seventh heaven, but of what else, it asks, is victory made? Life, the poem notes, is all mixed feelings, all accommodation—which is a critical process, not a submissive one. 'But what vitality!':

> I heard their rehashed radio barbs—
> more barbarous among hirelings
> as higher-ups grow more corrupt.
> But what vitality! The women hold jobs—
> clean house, cook, raise children, bowl
> and go to church.
>
> What would they say if they knew
> I sit for two months on six lines
> of poetry?

> (Niedecker, 143)

Niedecker describes here something like that 'embryonic combination of cook-nurse-laundress-chambermaid-housekeeper-waitress-governess', in Gilman's apt words, that makes a woman '"jack of all trades" and mistress of none'. But she brings a different kind of wit to it, best illustrated by that wonderfully surprising, perfectly timed reference to going bowling! There is the implication that woman's *vitality* is taking her, slowly but steadily, out of the house.

The last three lines seem to underline the idea of a world beyond both the household and the labour that sustains it, reminding us that art aims, as Arendt says, at permanency. It is to that extent world-making. Art and artifice give shelter to the fragile space of appearance, making 'a place fit for action and speech' (*HC*, 173). But these fine distinctions take on a certain irony because of the implicit sense of Niedecker's isolation in that world, the sense that she is by and large unknown to it. 'What would they say if they knew?' Niedecker asks, of these women. Could 'they' make such a world? What recognition could they give her?

If Niedecker evokes that classical opposition between the world and the household, she also breaks it down. She mockingly explores the parallels between the housewife's intermittent sense of what Arendt would call the futility or nothingness of her labour and the poet's intuition that without recognition, without readers, she too might seem to have spent her life on nothing. Here poetry emerges as another kind of housework:

> I'm pillowed and padded, pale and puffing
> lifting household stuffing—
>   carpets, dishes,
>   benches, fishes
> I've spent my life in nothing.

> (Niedecker, 148)

Similarly, in the poem I looked at a moment ago, the sardonic image of her sitting 'for two months on six lines | of poetry' (note the muted pun on 'on') is,

whatever else it is, also *homely:* quiescent and maternal—she is like a nesting
water-bird sitting on eggs.

Niedecker frequently identifies with water-birds, such as the sora rail—as for
instance in the three opening poems of *For Paul and Other Poems,* the
second of which constructs, once again with exquisite economy, the paradox of
activity within stillness, stillness within activity, central to her vision of what
a poem is.

> What bird would light
> in a moving tree
> the tree I carry
> for privacy?
>
> Down in the grass
> the question's inept;
> sora's eyes . . .
> stillness steps.

(Niedecker, 137)

Here she brings off a conceit of astonishing delicacy and tact: the 'moving
tree' is poetry, poe-*tree,* itself—the tree she carries, in other words, the laurel—
though in spelling things out like this one only underlines what Niedecker
achieves by not spelling them out. Such restraint, such taciturnity, is part of the
vision of *privacy* the poem affirms. We might think again of Dickinson, and,
equally, of Arendt. 'A life spent entirely in public, in the presence of others, becomes,
as we would say, shallow. While it retains its visibility, it loses the quality of rising
into sight from some darker ground which must remain hidden if it is not to lose
its depth in a very real, non-subjective sense.' And what applies to life applies to
meaning. Or as Heidegger says, 'The light of the public obscures everything.'

Privacy can be excessive, as we saw with Dickinson—and until almost the end
of her life there seemed little chance of Niedecker's finding that her achievement
was being obscured by the light of publicity. The poems deal gracefully with her
creative and emotional isolation. In another poem from *For Paul* she inadvertent-
ly and uncannily echoes Loy's use of the image of the house in 'Songs to Joannes',
to communicate the pathos of solitude, and the pathos of admitting likewise the
separateness of someone else—the fact of another person's having other fish to fry:

> I've been away from poetry
> many months
>
> and now I must rake leaves
> with nothing blowing
>
> between your house
> and mine

(Niedecker, 157)

Niedecker here is more stoical than Loy; drier, dare one say, and that is in part an effect of the reminder, in the final line, that she has (in contrast to Loy) her own house; which is to say, her own firm if not inviolable sense of self. She has come through the modernist crisis of identity, which as we saw was the product of the unsatisfactory notion that freedom might be a purely psychic construction. However, she has done this not by being admitted into the Arendtian *polis*—or at least not on Arendt's terms—but by wresting (her) identity from in among the realities of the socio-economic, where the great philosopher declined to look for it.

It is worth bearing in mind that in Loy's poetry even parturition, as she calls it, is uncanny—the stuff of 'bird-like abortions', whereas the childless Niedecker's celebration, or poetic adoption, of her friend and former lover Louis Zukofsky's child, the Paul of *For Paul and Other Poems*,[97] can be seen as a luminous example of what the childless Arendt meant by natality, i.e. the admittance of the new into the space of appearance: 'The child, this in-between to which the lovers now are related and which they hold in common, is representative of the world in that it also separates them; it is an indication that they will insert a new world into the existing world.' Niedecker gives another twist to this idea, as the poet recognizes in Paul what the world has failed to recognize in her.

I want to end this discussion of Niedecker by looking very briefly at two more instances of how the image of the house reflects her remarkable sense of self, which is, in its rootedness and resilience, in stark contrast, as I have said, to the *unheimlich* self of existentialism and psychoanalysis.

> In moonlight lies
>   the river passing—
> it's not quiet
>   and it's not laughing.
>
> I'm not young
>   and I'm not free
> but I've a house of my own
>   by a willow tree.

(Niedecker, 135)

Once again Niedecker acknowledges the limitations of the house, which are the limitations, as Arendt would say, of the pre-political—'I'm not free'—even as she recognizes there the privacy which shelters the self from the shallowness of undying exposure. Freedom is not in the gift of the subject alone—it is not something the subject can simply go ahead and grant itself: for it is also in the gift of the other, the *polis*, the space of appearance. As Arendt has it, I can only be free among others, my peers, in the space of speech and action. However, as we saw at

[97] Penberthy, 'Life and Writing', 4, 7.

the beginning of the chapter, it is the burden of most of the important criticism of Arendt's thought that things are never quite so clear-cut. We are never simply free or unfree (which is not to say that we aren't free at all); never wholly and purely ourselves (which is not to say that we aren't ourselves, or some part of ourselves, sometimes); and never quite shot of the socio-economic (which is not to say that we are completely in thrall to it).

It is right here that the example of Niedecker is so compelling, for she differs crucially from Arendt in her thought that who we are is not separate from the socio-economic but is born out of a deliberate confrontation with it. Denied a place in the space of appearance—as Dickinson and Loy, in different circumstances, also were—Niedecker strives to imagine that space, to catch some flicker of the light, not in spite of the socio-economic but by way of it. In the absence of the *polis*, the socio-economic becomes a clue to the larger life of mankind.

Meanwhile the self that is not present to others lives under tremendous moral and psychological pressure, as we have seen when looking at all three poets. In the absence of public recognition, it has somehow to recognize itself—to act and see itself acting. It has, in a word, to double its work.

> Don't tell me property is sacred!
> Things that move, yes!—
> cars out rolling thru the country
> how they like to rest
>
> on me—beer cans and cellophane
> on my clean-mowed grounds.
> Whereas I'm quiet . . . I was born
> with eyes and a house.

(Niedecker, 172)

This poem begins with another acknowledgement of the limitations of private property. But it is exuberant this time—and the second line extends the mood, with what seems to be an ironical reference to the glib ascendancy of metaphysical notions of transience and the ephemeral, loosely derived from the likes of Heraclitus and Lao Tzu. Niedecker brings it all back down to earth: the celebration of flux is an excuse for 'shiftless' souls not to take their rubbish home. In the previous poem ('In moonlight lies'), the fact that the surrounding world is 'not quiet' is what draws our attention to the quietness of the house. But in this poem, Niedecker names her quietness directly. And the stroke of genius is in the contained surrealism of that final composite image: 'I was born | with eyes and a house.' In a way it's a description of a face: *I was born with eyes and a mouth.* The doors and windows of a house seem to give it a face—as children show us when they draw them. (Childhood is to the point—'I was born', writes Niedecker.) House and mouth have the same vowel sound—so that the word she uses rhymes, or half-rhymes (an effect she prefers) with the word she implies.

Meanwhile the fact that, to all appearances, *she has no mouth* (it as if she wasn't born with one) evokes her silence as an artist (and we might add, her neglect). It's a self-portrait—but a reticent, secret, *heimlich* one.

I will give the final word in this chapter to the larger argument with Arendt. As we have seen, Dickinson and Loy demonstrate the limitations of privacy as Arendt understands it, and they can be used to show how even the most extreme kind of privacy, in so far as it expresses itself in writing, grows towards the light or oxygen of publicity; meanwhile Dickinson especially shows up the problems inherent in a Cavellian reading of privacy as giving birth to the political, individually and autonomously, by cultivating double-consciousness. However, while both these poets could be said to vindicate Arendt's strict separation of public and private, despite the feminist critique of it with which this chapter began, it is Niedecker who answers Benhabib's corrective reading of Arendt by repeatedly recognizing in her poetry the abiding interconnectedness, or better, the entangledness, of the public, the private, and the socio-economic. Yet there is still an Arendtian rejoinder to be made to those who would argue that it is only by incorporating the socio-economic or by acknowledging the political claims of privacy that the space of appearance becomes political: for if there were no public domain, no space of appearance, then neither the socio-economic nor privacy in general could acquire political significance. That is to say, the space of appearance must somehow pre-exist the private or the socio-economic if either of these is to appear there. It is to this distinction that Arendt directs her thought. Of what does this space of appearance consist? What makes appearances appear? The answer for Arendt is inseparable from the recognition of our plurality—and the plurality therefore of our recognitions. In the next chapter I shall try to increase the dialectical pressure on this question of the relationship between the political and the socio-economic.

4

Williams Stevens Williams . . .
Continuing Revolution

In this chapter 1 begin by looking at how American revolutionary values are picked up in the work of William Carlos Williams and within the greater American experimental tradition. I then proceed to show how a contrasting set of values, the values espoused by those who brought about the stern appraisal and transformation of the American Revolution within twelve years of its occurrence, are at work in the critique of Williams's aesthetics elaborately set out by his contemporary Wallace Stevens. In the process I also attempt to show how the argument over revolution dovetails with a distinction between values in use and values in exchange which runs through all economic thinking from Aristotle to Marx. It is important to emphasize that, as regards both the Revolution and its critics, I am arguing not *for* one and *against* another, but *for and against both*. That is, I am arguing above all for the overarching significance of the American revolutionary dialogue—the dialogue between revolution and constitution which was at the heart of the creation of the American Republic. As Michael Kammen has written, 'Insofar as we have had a feeling for tradition at all . . . I am prepared to argue that the American Revolution has been at its core. The Revolution is the one component of our past that we have not, at some point or other, explicitly repudiated.'[1] It is this historic American dialogue which gives body and political resonance to the no less American dialogue between William Carlos Williams and Wallace Stevens—which is, I think, with all due respect to Eliot and Pound, the central dialogue of the American experimental tradition. As we saw in Chapter 2, the American Revolution was of major significance for Pound, but he betrayed its essential character, which was to be unstable, participatory, and dialogical. And he did this even as his own experiments in poetic form revealed the dynamic potential of an inclusive dialogical technique. The poetry is at odds with the poet as philosopher-king, but the philosopher-king is still there, haunting the wreckage. If *The Cantos* is a republic, it is an ambivalent one. There is no such ambivalence about Williams Carlos William's grasp of what the Revolution was about, his sympathy with its defining values is uncompromising

---

[1] Michael Kammen, *A Season of Youth: The American Revolution and the Historical Imagination* (1978; Ithaca, NY: Cornell University Press, 1988), 15.

and unambiguous. Moreover these values infuse William's sense of form in astonishing ways. For that very reason it takes another poet, whose values are in some respects counter-revolutionary, to set them off to full effect. Wallace Stevens, as we shall see, was just such a poet.

The two poets were always aware of one another. When, in November 1945, Williams read Stevens's poem, 'Description Without Place', in the *Swanee Review*, he interpreted it as being addressed to him—'as it probably was'.[2] In the final section of the poem Stevens summons the ghosts of place, his Spanish-speaking friend's Latin ancestry, in order to evoke him; to describe him as it were without quite placing him. And the poem's emphasis on the unreality of place as against the high reality of the poet's description, his pleasure in propounding the 'theory of description', is a flagrant contradiction of Williams's lifelong emphasis on the purely local, the American grain: 'A seeming of the Spaniard, a style of life, | The invention of a nation in a phrase'.[3] Williams would still have been working on his long poem *Paterson* when he read this, where the man is the poem is the place. He wrote privately that he 'didn't like [it] at all'.[4] And it mattered, as Stevens knew it mattered, but for different reasons:

> It matters, because everything we say
> Of the past is description without place, a cast
>
> Of the imagination, made in sound[5]

Williams's response, when it came, was dazzling. If Stevens wanted something 'made in sound', then Williams would give it to him all right. In her biography of Stevens, Joan Richardson writes of 'Stevens' brilliant use of language' throughout 'Description Without Place', instancing in the fourth section the 'procession of sounds from "swarms" to "swans" to "suavest" to "suited" to "silences"'.[6] In the poem he writes in reply, Williams squeezes a poem's worth of sounds into the mere title—'A Place (Any Place) to Transcend All Places'—eating Stevens's words and inviting Stevens to eat them.

In fact some of Stevens's most ardent admirers have found the wordplay of Stevens's 'Description' to be unusually barren.[7] Williams is anything but barren, as for instance in the following passage:

---

[2] Mariani, *William Carlos Williams*, 517.

[3] Wallace Stevens, 'Description Without Place', *Collected Poems* (1954; London: Faber and Faber, 1984), 345.

[4] Alan Filreis, *Wallace Stevens and the Actual World* (Princeton: Princeton University Press, 1991), 181.

[5] Stevens, *Collected Poems*, 345–6.

[6] Joan Richardson, *Wallace Stevens: The Later Years, 1923–1955* (New York: William Morrow, 1986), 255.

[7] Joseph Riddel speaks of a 'dangerous aridity' in *The Clairvoyant Eye: The Poetry and Poetics of Wallace Stevens* (Baton Rouge: Louisiana State University Press, 1965), 198; and Harold Bloom refers to 'Stevens at his most arid' in *Wallace Stevens: The Poems of Our Climate* (Ithaca, NY: Cornell University Press, 1977), 239.

> leaves filling,
> making, a tree (but
> wait) not just leaves,
> leaves of one design that
> make a certain design,
> no two alike, not like
> the locust either, next in line,
> nor the Rose of Sharon, in
> the pod-stage, near it—a
> tree! Imagine it! Pears
> philosophically hard.[8]

Williams does here what he already did in the title: he shows that 'no two' words, not even if they are the same word ('not just leaves, | leaves of one design') are 'alike': their *placement* in the line *changes* them. And 'Pears | philosophically hard' is a wonderfully witty way of restating his great axiom (from the original shorter 'Paterson'), 'No ideas but in things', while simultaneously alluding, first, to the Fall of Man, which becomes in turn the Fortunate Fall, that is, the cultural myth of the American Adam—belied by the grimmer realities of the American scene described elsewhere in the poem—and secondly to Stevens's fruitiness (his 'Study of Two Pears', for example), the epicurean connoisseurship of his poetry. And all this in three words.

But Stevens's 'procession' of sounds in 'Description' has another function besides transcending or abstracting from place. Among other figures in the poem are the arch individualist Nietzsche and the arch collectivist Lenin; and in the section in which they feature, which is the same section Richardson singles out for special praise, sound is used to disperse, reconfigure, and contain the revolutionary impulse in the Eternal Return: 'In perpetual revolution, round and round . . .' (*Collected Poems*, 342); but in the Eternal Return itself reconfigured as the return or repetition of mere empty sound, 'hollow-bright': 'Like rubies reddened by rubies reddening' (345–6). Thus in this the final line of the poem, proletarian red, the colour of Williams's wheelbarrow and the red scare, is disarmed. It is merely red after all, description without place.

Williams and Stevens were friends and rivals, warmly and warily observing one another's lives and careers. From 1918, when Stevens published his 'Nuances of a Theme by Williams', through Williams's Prologue to *Kora in Hell*, Stevens's Preface to Williams's *Collected Poems* (1934), to Williams's appreciation of Stevens in *Poetry* following his death in 1955, they acknowledged, provoked, lampooned, and critiqued one another, in poetry and prose, sometimes explicitly, sometimes not, in private and in public. Paul Mariani's testimony says a great

---

[8] William Carlos Williams, 'A Place (Any Place) to Transcend All Places', *The Collected Poems*, 2. *1939–1962*, ed. Christopher MacGowan (Manchester: Carcanet, 1988), 164. Hereafter cited as *WCW2*.

deal: 'It was really only when I began teaching modern poetry at the University of Massachusetts with my fresh Ph.D. in the fall of '68 that I finally realized what I had been missing in not paying more attention to William Carlos Williams, who by that point had already been dead a full five years...I argued with Williams, fought with him, wrestled, despaired. And in a remarkably short time he became the single most important American poet of the twentieth century for me, with Stevens right behind him.'[9] With Stevens right behind him! The proximity of these two poets, the dialogue between them, changes the meaning of their poetry and from time to time discovers it.

Before we can go any further, however, it is necessary to review, in quite elementary terms, some of the main issues at the heart of the American Revolution and the Federalist critique of it.

4.1 REVOLUTION

The main ideological thrust of the Revolution can be summarized under three headings: representation, sovereignty, and equality.

4.1.1 Representation

'No political conception was more important to Americans in the entire Revolutionary era', Gordon Wood concludes, than 'the great English discovery of representation', the principle, in a phrase of the time, of 'substituting the few in the room of the many'.[10] Yet part of the Revolution was a revolution in the notion of what representation meant. Since the English Parliament believed that the English people 'were essentially a unitary homogeneous order with a fundamental common interest' (Wood, 174), every representative was assumed to speak not just for his constituency's best interest but for that of the whole: representation was *virtual* rather than *actual* (182–4). In keeping with this doctrine the English Parliament took the view that America was also virtually represented and it could tax the colonies as it saw fit. But as the terms of American trade and manufacture were dictated by the British Empire, this assumption of 'mutuality of interest' became more and more untenable and provocative. The consequences for the theory of representation were dramatic. 'Once the mutuality of interests between representatives and people that made representation what it was to most eighteenth-century Englishmen was broken down...the only criterion of representation left was election, which helps explain the Americans' increasing concern with the right to vote as a measure of representation' (387–8). The

---

[9] Mariani, pp. ix–x.
[10] Gordon S. Wood, *The Creation of the American Republic 1776–1787* (1969; Chapel Hill: University of North Carolina Press, 1998), 164.

revolutionaries wanted direct or actual rather than virtual representation, and when, in 1776, at the bidding of the Continental Congress, the independent state legislatures began to draw up their separate constitutions, this overwhelming demand was reflected in the greater number of their members, the frequency of elections, the limits set to the number of years a man could hold office, the low property qualifications for holding office, and the minute and ardent localism of the legislation that was passed. Even so, there was in the commitment to direct representation a straining for perfect representation which could never be fully satisfied: in other words, it was part of the intentional structure—that is, the effective intention—of direct representation that it wanted to do away with representation altogether.

4.1.2 Sovereignty

The colonists came face to face with the problem of sovereignty in the form of the unchecked authority of the royal governors and the defencelessness of the colonial legislatures and judiciaries to gubernatorial manipulation. The governor, it was observed, 'calls, dissolves, prorogues, adjourns, removes, and other ways harasses the General Assembly at Pleasure' (Wood, 166). As a matter of fact, with their extensive powers of appointment, the governors enjoyed more formal power than the king of England (157). Under the sway of revolution, however, supreme authority was given over to the elective state legislatures and the magistracy was more or less reduced to an administrative role. The most radical of all the state constitutions, the Pennsylvania Constitution, did away with the chief magistrate altogether: the people reasoned that since they would be represented by the state legislatures, they had no need now for a representative of the king (137–8). There was no separation of powers. Where before the state governor had been allowed to reign unchecked, now it was the independent state legislatures that did so. This perhaps more than any other effect of the Revolution would provoke the critical ire of the Federalists.

4.1.3 Equality

The third and possibly most diffuse issue comprises the momentous notions of equality and rights—'that all men are equal in their rights', as Joel Barlow put it (Wood, p. xv). As Edward Countryman has said, the 'colonists confronted political life in terms of a language that stressed rights'—those 'certain inalienable rights' of the Declaration of Independence—rather than feudal obligations or *noblesse oblige*.[11] As the English philosopher John Locke saw it, society was, first and foremost, a compact of individuals with a right to property and privacy, jealously

---

[11] Edward Countryman, *The American Revolution* (London: I. B. Tauris & Co. Ltd, 1986), 17–18.

guarding their liberty against the usurpations, in Jefferson's word, of the state. Add to these rights the notion of equality, and the result was that state legislation, where it did interfere, betrayed an unmistakeable tendency toward the redistribution of property.[12]

4.2 THE FEDERALIST CRITIQUE

The American Constitution, for which the Federalists campaigned, and which was ratified in 1788, refined, qualified, or overhauled, depending on how you see it, each of these revolutionary positions.

4.2.1

The first challenge was to unseat the revolutionary pre-eminence of direct representation. The advocates of this last held that the state legislatures should be 'an exact miniature of their constituents ... The whole body politic ... reduced to a smaller scale'; or as Melancton Smith put it, representatives must 'resemble those they represent. They should be a true picture of the people.'[13] The legislature was the people in microcosm: a direct reflection of their lives and their will. To keep the legislatures as close to the people as possible, constituencies should be small, representatives many, and terms of office short.

The Federalists argued that this kind of 'pure democracy', as James Madison called it, produced hasty and unstable legislation crippled by a minutely localist bias and apt to be changed at the next rotation of delegates. Far from being the

---

[12] The ambiguity of property relations in Revolutionary America is powerfully expressed in Locke's political thought, which, primarily as set out in his *Two Treatises of Civil Government*, a defence of the English Revolution of 1688, influenced the American Revolution as much as any man's—a point vigorously argued by Louis Hartz for instance in his *The Liberal Tradition in America* (1953). Yet, there is an unacknowledged conflict in Locke between his democratic defence of majority rule and his insistence on the natural right to property. See Alasdair MacIntyre, *A Short History of Ethics* (London: Routledge & Kegan Paul, 1967), 158–9: 'A man's initial right is only to such property as his labor has created; but with the wealth derived therefrom he may acquire the property of others and he may acquire servants. If he does, *their* labour creates property for *him*. Therefore, gross inequality in property is consistent with Locke's doctrine of a natural right to property. Not only this, but Locke seems to have been aware of the fact that more than half the population of England was effectively propertyless. How, then, is he able to reconcile his view of the right of the majority to rule with his view of the natural right to property? ... Might it not be argued that to give the rule to the majority will be to give the rule to the many whose interest lies in the abolition of the right of the few to the property which they have acquired? This problem is raised nowhere explicitly in Locke.' The inescapable centrality of this dilemma was amply demonstrated in America by the newly independent state legislatures. Among historians there seems little doubt that the Constitution was deliberately and successfully conceived partly to put a stop to the Revolution's redistributive momentum.
[13] Isaac Kramnick, Introduction, in James Madison, Alexander Hamilton, and John Jay, *The Federalist Papers*, ed. Isaac Kramnick (1788; Harmondsworth: Penguin, 1987), 44.

most immediate possible expression of the people, Madison argued, it was the function of government to *mediate*—to act not as the people but as the people's chosen medium; to determine what is good for the country as a whole and serve the people to that end. It was government's task, he wrote, in *Federalist* No.10:

> to refine and enlarge the public views by passing them through the medium of a chosen body of citizens, whose wisdom may best discern the true interest of their country and whose patriotism and love of justice will be least likely to sacrifice it to temporary or partial considerations. Under such a regulation it may well happen that the public voice, pronounced by the representatives of the people, will be more consonant to the public good than if pronounced by the people themselves, convened for the purpose.[14]

Contrary to accepted revolutionary beliefs, tenure of office should be long and the number of representatives few—and contrary to traditional republican theory, as expressed above all in Montesquieu's *Spirit of the Laws*, a constituency might properly contain a great many citizens spread across a great deal of country.[15]

4.2.2

The Federalists had been principally provoked by what was widely criticized as the unrestrained tyranny of the state legislatures. In Jefferson's famous words: 'An *elective despotism* was not the government we fought for' (Wood, 452). The first priority then was to take absolute power away from the states and invest it in a central federal government. Since the Federalists believed furthermore that, as Madison summed it up in *Federalist* No. 47, 'The accumulation of all powers, legislative, executive, and judiciary, in the same hands'—which had been the case often enough under the state governments—was 'the very definition of tyranny', the Constitution tried to keep these three powers separate (*Federalist Papers*, 303). With a view to this the Federalists even reintroduced the obscurely monarchical figure of the chief executive or magistrate: the president.

---

[14] *Federalist Papers*, 126.

[15] See Montesquieu, *The Spirit of the Laws*, qtd. in Bernard Bailyn, *The Ideological Origins of the American Revolution*, enlarged edn. (Cambridge, Mass.: The Belknap Press of the University of Harvard Press, 1992), 347: 'It is natural to a republic to have only a small territory, otherwise it cannot long subsist. In a large republic there are men of large fortunes, and consequently of less moderation . . . he has interest of his own; he soon begins to think that he may be happy, great and glorious by oppressing his fellow citizens, and that he may raise himself to grandeur on the ruins of his country. In a large republic, the public good is sacrificed to a thousand views . . . In a small one, the interest of the public is easier perceived, better understood, and more within the reach of every citizen; abuses are of less extent, and of course are less protected.' As Bailyn comments, 'The logic of this process was variously expounded, variously phrased, but the conclusion was everywhere the same and always derived from the same received tradition of pre-Revolutionary thought' (ibid.).

4.2.3

While the Anti-Federalists like the Revolutionaries before them tended to take equality for granted, as the Declaration of Independence ringingly declared, the Federalists insisted on fundamental inequality. 'All men are created equal', wrote Jefferson, but in *Federalist* No.10 Madison contradicts this tersely: 'Theoretic politicians . . . have erroneously supposed that by reducing mankind to a perfect equality in their political rights, they would at the same time be perfectly equalized and assimilated in their possessions, their opinions, and their passions' (*Federalist Papers*, 126). But equality is at best political and in no sense fundamental:

The diversity in the faculties of men, from which the rights of property originate, is not less an insuperable obstacle to a uniformity of interests. The protection of these faculties is the first object of government. From the protection of *different and unequal faculties of acquiring property*, the possession of different degrees and kinds of property immediately results; and from the influence of these on the sentiments and views of the respective proprietors ensues a division of the society into different interests and parties. (*Federalist* No.10)[16]

To summarize then: Madison's mentor Jefferson tried to build a politics on *nature*, but his nature unfortunately was *politics* all along. Madison, by contrast, tries to naturalize inequality—'different and unequal faculties of acquiring property'—but ends up by defending it. He wants to give a neutral description of the order of things, in the interest of disinterest, but disinterestedness turns out to be *interested in property* ('the first object of government').

In order to circumvent the authority of the States, the Federalists played a remarkably double game. When the draft Constitution was presented to the state conventions for ratification in 1788, the Anti-Federalist Patrick Henry picked on the resonant preamble beginning, 'We, the people . . . '. For the fact was that the Philadelphia Convention which drafted the Constitution had not been authorized to speak for the people, but simply for the States. 'What right had they', asked Henry, 'to say, We, the people? . . . Who authorized them to speak the language of We, the people?'[17] Invoking 'the sovereignty of the people', the people-out-of-doors, was a brilliant device. It suggested that the ex-colonists had something more fundamental in common than the revolutionary cause— implied in fact a deeper homogeneity. But as Madison never tired of pointing out, homogeneity of interest was an illusion. As the whole revolutionary and federal turmoil demonstrates, it had become increasingly difficult to speak for the people, if it had ever been possible at all.[18]

---

[16] *Federalist Papers*, 124, my emphasis.

[17] Kramnick, Introduction, *Federalist Papers*, 32.

[18] In his *Political Disquisitions* (1774), James Burgh wrote: 'In planning a government by representation, the people ought to provide against their own *annihilation*. They ought to establish a regular and constitutional method of acting by and from *themselves*, without, or even

It was, after all, just this unsettling realization that had radicalized the original state constitutions, where the very notion of representation can be seen to be bursting at the seams: 'The radicals in Pennsylvania actually carried this right of the people-at-large to legislate into constitutional form. In the 1776 Constitution the representative assembly became a kind of upper house, while the people "out-of-doors" retained all their original power of legislation' (Wood, 366). As Wood's work effectively shows, Anti-Federalist conceptualization of representation as a mirror during the debates over ratification actually undersold the revolutionary conception of participatory democracy—which was an altogether more unstable conception. *For the effectual thrust of revolutionary thinking was to ask whether representation were possible at all.* The radical alternative to representation was of course outright participation—what Madison dismissed as pure democracy.

With considerable dialectical genius the Federalists turned the widespread insight into the inadequacy of representative government into an argument for it rather than against it. The defence of representative government with its built-in checks and controls comes to be founded on a full knowledge of its inadequacy: it doesn't seek perfection but to make the best of imperfection. This was the Whig suspicion of power doubling back on itself—conscious now of what mere suspicion, if it were left unchecked, could and couldn't achieve. It couldn't at any rate make a case for perfection. And the person who best spoke for the qualified perfection, which is to say the political perfection, *perfect as far as politics goes,* of a properly cognizant imperfection, was James Madison:

Ambition must be made to counteract ambition. The interest of the man must be connected with the constitutional rights of the place. It may be a reflection on human nature that such devices should be necessary to control the abuses of government. But what is government itself but the greatest of all reflections on human nature? If men were angels, no government would be necessary. If angels were to govern men, neither external nor internals controls on government would be necessary. In framing a government which is to be administered by men over men, the great difficulty lies in this: you must first enable the government to control the governed; and in the next place oblige it to control itself. (*Federalist* No. 51)[19]

As Wallace Stevens wrote 150 years later, 'The imperfect is our paradise.'[20]

---

in opposition to their *representatives*' (qtd. in Wood, 323). As Wood comments, this was 'surely the most disruptive yet the most creative idea expressed in the entire Revolutionary era, since it meant that the final and full embodiment of the people in the government was impossible' (323).

[19]   *Federalist Papers,* 319–20. See also *Federalist* No. 38: 'It is not necessary that the former [the new Constitution] should be perfect; it is sufficient that the latter [the old constitution or Articles of Confederation] is more imperfect' (*Federalist Papers,* 252).

[20]   Stevens, 'The Poems of Our Climate', *Collected Poems,* 194.

4.3 *IN THE AMERICAN GRAIN*

4.3.1

What the major studies of the journey through Revolution to Constitution tend in their different ways to suggest is that there can hardly have been a more luminous example anywhere in Western history of the efficacy, the practical influence at the heart of events, of what Jürgen Habermas calls communicative reason. One historian writes of 'the sheer wordiness of the Revolution', which through pamphlets, broadsides, poems, plays, songs, sermons, and 'a press that was as free as any in the eighteenth-century world' (Countryman, 57), seemed to insist that 'men became most fully human in public life' (18). Although the Federalists won the day, the arguments themselves are unresolved: they are open-ended; constructed on shifting ground; and they share or appropriate each other's assumptions and conclusions in a way that can seem truly dialectical. But the Constitution is no moment of speculative synthesis—and history teaches us to see the arguments of the period as arguments in process, arguments in need of each other, that break down and add up, add up and break down, but do not resolve into a single overwhelming idea. These arguments need each other now in the sense that they got each other then—so that together becomes the only to see them, dissolving into context.

Writing in the wake of Charles A. Beard's influential *An Economic Interpretation of the Constitution of the United States* (1913), which argued, albeit in terms that were to prove unconvincing, that the Constitution 'marked the triumph . . . of self-seeking speculators' (Countryman, 247), the poet William Carlos Williams offered a more general and durable insight: 'If there is agreement on one point in history, be sure there's interest there to have it so and that's not truth.'[21] Significantly, it is as *disagreement*, which is to say, as *dialogue*, that Williams presents his own thoughts about the contested heart of the early American Republic, in the chapter 'The Virtue of History' from *In the American Grain* (1925), which begins with some of the most brilliant writing on the life of history anywhere in American letters: 'History follows governments and never men. It portrays us in generic patterns, like effigies or the carvings on sarcophagi, which say nothing save, of such and such a man, that he is dead. That's history. It is concerned only with the one thing: to say everything is dead. Then it fixes up the effigy: there that's finished. Not at all. History must stay open, it is all humanity' (188–9). Williams builds his chapter around the figure of Aaron Burr, Thomas Jefferson's Republican running mate in the 1800 presidential election. When Jefferson was finally elected to office, the Republicans began to chip away at the legacy of the Federalists, who had done all they could to concentrate power

---

[21] William Carlos Williams, *In the American Grain*, 188.

in central government. Jefferson began this revolution within a revolution, as it is sometimes called, by demurring at the Federalists' deliberately monarchical conception of presidential sovereignty.[22] Williams, however, bypasses the man who is traditionally regarded as the embodiment of American democracy, and focuses, with cavalier audacity, on the more disreputable figure of Burr. And what he does with 'him' is ingenious. Burr is given to us not as the treacherous adventurer of the history books but as a figure of unfinished imaginative freedom. Throughout the dialogue it is he who is identified with what the Revolution stood for: 'Perhaps Burr carried into politics an element of democratic government, even a major element, those times were slighting' (*In the American Grain*, 190). Meanwhile Alexander Hamilton, the former Secretary of the Treasury, co-author, with Madison and Jay, of *The Federalist Papers*, the man Burr killed in a duel in 1804, is, as we might expect, identified with Federal aggrandizement:

So you have raised the point that once the Revolution was over the New World instead of being freed slipped into a tyranny as bad as or worse than the one it left behind; that, of this tyranny, Hamilton was the agent; and that—perhaps—in Burr reposed the true element, liberty, which a party in power tried to smother. What basis, other than the one adopted under the Constitution, could the new Government have taken firmer? Burr proposed none. This is the charge against him. (195–6)

This last charge was also made by Madison against the Anti-Federalists (as for example in *Federalist* No. 38): that their criticisms were incoherent and they proposed no alternative. Burr, then, is deliberately identified with the Revolution —but with a Revolution that is thereby opened up, like Burr himself, from death to humanity—and in a way that also *leaves things open*. When speaking of Burr's contribution to democracy both interlocutors use the word 'perhaps'. Nothing is certain, least of all history.

Williams's dialogue on Burr acts out the same basic question of signification that motivates the more or less contemporaneous poetry and prose of *Spring and All* (1923) and the later long poem *Paterson*: that is to say, the question of the relation between the name, sign, word, or acoustic image, in this instance 'Aaron

---

[22] From the beginning Jefferson 'purposefully set a new tone of republican simplicity that was in sharp contrast to the stiff formality and regal ceremony with which the Federalists, in imitation of European court life, had surrounded the presidency. The Federalist presidents, like the English monarchs, had personally delivered their addresses to the legislature "from the throne," but Jefferson chose to submit his in writing. Unlike Washington and Adams, he made himself easily accessible to visitors, all of whom, no matter how distinguished, the British government's representative to the United States reported, he received "with a perfect disregard to ceremony both in his dress and manner." Much to the shock of foreign dignitaries, at American state occasions Jefferson replaced the protocol and distinctions of European court life with the egalitarian rules of what he called "pell-mell."' Bernard Bailyn, Robert Dallek, David Brion Davis, David Herbert Donald, John L. Thomas, Gordon S. Wood, *The Great Republic: A History of the American People*, vol. 1 (1977; Lexington, Ky.: D. C. Heath, 1992), 337.

Burr', and the historical phenomenon—also Aaron Burr (1756–1836)—who is fixed, finished, dead. For Williams wants to represent history without holding a mirror up to it: he wants to represent it but not reflect it; he wants to present it more than represent it; he wants it to live. Burr is not mirrored or reflected by Williams's imaging of him but on the contrary imagined, moved, brought to life. It is the unreliability—the riskiness of representation—in the impossibility of it the mere *possibility*, that Williams evokes. Signification is all about imagination —that seems to be the rule. If y is the stuff of history, the signified, it is not by insisting that x reflects, represents, or signifies y that history, that is y, is opened up, unfixed—but by imagining x as a possibility of y. Y is not left alone by the dance of x, but left to dance or not, according to history. To adapt the terms of *Spring and All*, it is not by accurately reflecting history that we shall let it be—but by *accurately tuning* to it, playing a tune upon it—'thus freeing it and dynamizing it at the same time'.[23]

It is worth quoting at length that last burst of prose from *Spring and All*, with Williams straining at the limits of articulacy, laughing at himself in the process, and yet producing for all that one of his most spectacular attempts to tell us how the imagination works:

The imagination uses the phraseology of science. It attacks, stirs, animates, is radio-active in all that can be touched by action. Words occur in liberation by virtue of its processes.

In description words adhere to certain objects, and have the effect on the sense of oysters, or barnacles.

But the imagination is wrongly understood when it is supposed to be a removal from reality in the sense of John of Gaunt's speech in Richard the Second: to imagine possession of that which is lost. It is rightly understood when John of Gaunt's words are related not to their sense as objects adherent to his son's welfare or otherwise but as a dance over the body of his condition accurately accompanying it. By this means of the understanding, the play written to be understood as a play, the author and reader are liberated to pirouette with the words which have sprung from the old facts of history, reunited in present passion.

To understand the words as so liberated is to understand poetry. That they move independently when set free is the mark of their value.

Imagination is not to avoid reality, nor is it description nor an evocation of objects or situations, it is to say that poetry does not tamper with the world but moves it—It affirms reality most powerfully and therefore, since reality needs no personal support but exists free from human action, as proven by science in the indestructibility of matter and of force, it creates a new object, a play, a dance which is not a mirror up to nature but—

As birds' wings beat the solid air without which none could fly so words freed by the imagination affirm reality by their flight . . .

According to my present theme the writer of imagination would attain closest to the conditions of music not when his words are disassociated from natural objects and

[23] William Carlos Williams, *The Collected Poems*, 1. *1909–1939*, ed. A. Walton Litz and Christopher MacGowan (Manchester: Carcanet, 1987), 235. Hereafter cited as *WCW1*.

specified meanings but when they are liberated from the usual quality of that meaning by transposition into another medium, the imagination.

Sometimes I speak of imagination as a force, an electricity or a medium, a place. It is immaterial which: for whether it is the condition of a place or a dynamization its effect is the same: to free the world of fact from the impositions of 'art' . . . and to liberate the man to act in whatever direction his disposition leads.

The word is not liberated, therefore able to communicate release from the fixities which destroy it until it is accurately tuned to the fact which giving it reality, by its own reality establishes its own freedom from the necessity of a word, thus freeing it and dynamizing it at the same time.[24]

Note the concern with liberation, freedom. The parallels with *In the American Grain* are inescapable. Words dance not when they deny history/facts/reality; not when they mirror it, avoid it, describe it or evoke it, but when they 'have sprung' from it: that is to say, when they name it and move or fly on. In the same way Williams is dancing (or flying) with Burr—dancing with history. And he is dancing because he wants, impossible as it may seem, to open up the history book around the man and let him live for a moment again in his freedom. He means 'to liberate the man'—to liberate him from 'the old facts of history'—so that he will be free again, in imagination, 'to act in whatever direction his disposition leads'; so that we might imagine him, in other words, not as *fixed, finished, dead*, but as independent, active, and alive.

For in so far as it has failed to represent the life, history has failed to represent Burr. Representation has failed him.[25] The alternative is to imagine him; to open up the field, to join in. Such is the emphasis on phenomenal particularity in Williams that the representation of it becomes suspicious, dubious: it is at best something else. The only way to represent is to participate, to revolutionize, to dance.

---

[24] *WCW1*, 234–5.

[25] See Bryce Conrad, *Refiguring America: A Study of William Carlos Williams'* In the American Grain (Urbana: University of Illinois Press, 1990), 127: 'Williams's plea for an "open history" forms the preface to his creation of an "open" Burr', writes Conrad. 'Burr's life, Williams contends, has been "twisted" to fit the "tyrannous designs" of history, the man "stifled", the true marks of his character purged from memory' (ibid.). While I agree of course about the openness, I differ in point of emphasis. For as Conrad concedes, it doesn't follow that Williams pretends, in his dialogue, to be recovering 'the true marks' of Burr's character (Conrad, 131). So what is Williams's purpose? It is, as I see it, an act of imaginative provocation—a way of pointedly enacting the fact that we cannot know exactly what Burr was really like, just as we've no way of knowing that the heroic portrait hazarded is absolutely wrong. In other words, what remains at issue are the liberties history takes—in every sense. 'If we cannot make a man live again when he is gone, it is boorish to imprison him dead within some narrow definition' (*In the American Grain*, 190). That representation, history, was apt to fail Burr is also a point made by Gore Vidal at the beginning of his historical fiction of that name, as the narrator, 'a none-too-efficient law clerk', a mere scrivener in other words, attempts to describe this larger-than-life personality, that is to say, *this personality who had been as large as life*: 'I don't seem to be able to catch the right tone', he says. Burr is a 'monster', who 'makes even a trip to the barber seem like a plot to overthrow the state'. He 'resemble[s] the devil . . . He is a labyrinth'. Gore Vidal, *Burr: A Novel* (New York: Random House, 1973), 3–7.

This same realization guided the most radical constitutions of the Revolution: the revulsion from representation in favour of participation. It was a feeling that nothing could stand and do justice in one's place. But is it going too far, even so, to contend that Williams's poetics of representation by participation is significantly and intelligently continuous with Revolutionary ideology—democratic, localist, anti-centrist? Surely not. For this is what Williams was discussing: the poetics of historiography, the poetics of Federal historiography in fact: 'if there is agreement on one point in history, be sure there's interest there to have it so and that's not truth'. It is against that interestedness that Williams is writing. Not because what he has to say is more true but because discord is a sign of life. The larger aim is not to represent the truth but to let it be.

4.3.2

Burr is not just identified with the Revolution, there was something, some 'aristocratic strain' in him—'straight out of the ground'—which was ripe with the values of Williams's poetry, as he already declared them in *Kora in Hell* and *Spring and All*. Williams has in mind: 'Its immediacy, its sensual quality, a pure observation, its lack of irritation, its lack of pretense, its playful exaggeration, its repose, its sense of design, its openness, its gayety, its unconstraint. It frees, it creates relief. In the great it is the same, or would be if ever it existed, a delicious sincerity (in greater things of course) not a scheme, nor a system of procedure— but careless truth' (*In the American Grain*, 206). This is how Williams writes of Burr's 'directness' and 'sincerity' (ibid.). Not only is Burr identified with Williams's poetic values, he is robed with the very imagery of *Spring and All*— in particular with the motifs of the season and the New World: 'A new world, that's what we were. It was a springtime that the colonists, at their most impassioned, were attempting' (196). He is as much a figure of imaginative freedom ('Burr saw America in his imagination, free'),[26] as, ten pages later, Edgar Allen Poe will be, whom he prefigures, and in whom Williams recognizes the same principle of unyielding locality—emerging in Poe's case as method, formal pressure.[27] Deeper than Poe's overtly undemocratic politics, the style of both men 'asserts their aristocratic origin, or their democratic origin, the same, . . . since an aristocracy is the flower of a locality and so the *full* expression of a democracy' (231). The cadence there, the weight specifically of 'the same', is pure Whitman—which is as appropriate as it is unconscious.[28]

---

[26] *In the American Grain*, 197.

[27] See ibid. 216–33, where it is argued that Poe's technique as an artist was a means of discovering 'points of firmness by which to STAND and grasp, against the slipping way they had of holding on in his locality' (219).

[28] See Whitman, 'Song of Myself', *Leaves of Grass*, p. 29, line 7: 'born here from parents the same, and their parents the same'.

The key term, however, is locality. In keeping with which, Williams writes repeatedly of 'digging', of standing, and of 'ground'.[29] Locality is the only thing that gives a man authority, authenticity. This is Williams's version of Jeffersonian Republicanism, the proper organic relation between power and specific place. As Richard Hofstadter illustrates it: 'In 1776 Jefferson proposed that Virginia grant fifty acres of land to every white of full age who had less than that amount. This would have made suffrage practically universal. It also illustrates his belief in broadening economic opportunities where free land made the policy possible, as well as the vital linkage in his mind between landed property and democracy.'[30] That human imperfection which was, for Madison, ground for caution, was for Jefferson ground for hope. The local is opposed to the Federalist position that, in the words of Williams's fictive interlocutor, 'central power is strength' (*In the American Grain*, 197). The larger meaning Williams invested in the local is expressed with sinuous clarity in a later essay, 'Against the Weather' (1939):

If I succeed in keeping myself objective enough, sensual enough, I can produce the factors, the concretions of materials by which others shall understand and so be led to use —that they may the better see, touch, taste, enjoy—their own world *differing as it may* from mine. By mine, they, different, can be discovered to be the same as I, and, thrown into contrast, will see the implications of a general enjoyment through me.

That—all my life I have striven to emphasize it—is what is meant by the universality of the local. From me where I stand to them where they stand in their here and now—where I cannot be—I do in spite of that arrive! through their work which complements my own, each sensually local.[31]

There is no happier formulation anywhere in Williams's prose of his sense of those incorrigible, virtually unrepresentable differences whose local contiguity drives the lifeblood of democracy. The poet insists that his conception of the artist's local base is a political conception: 'His work might and finally must be expanded—holds the power of expansion at any time—into new conceptions of government' (*Selected Essays*, 197). Its ideological significance cannot be over-stated: it is his take on the whole constitutional question of sovereignty and power. But if Williams emphasizes the local, so indeed, for entirely opposite reasons, do Madison and Hamilton. For 'the spirit of locality', as Madison called it, was precisely what the Federalists had been determined to expel from politics altogether. See in particular *Federalist* No. 46:

---

[29] Charles Olson, whose quirky syntactical invention is hugely indebted to that of Williams, recalls this imagery at the beginning of *Call Me Ishmael* (1947)—an attempt to pick up where *In the American Grain* left off—when he writes that 'Poe dug in' (*Collected Prose*, 17).

[30] Richard Hofstadter, *The American Political Tradition* (1948; New York: Vintage Books, 1989) 41 n. 6. Conrad notes in *Refiguring America* that Williams's 'planned sequel to *In the American Grain* was to begin with Jefferson' (149 n. 22).

[31] William Carlos Williams, *Selected Essays* (1954; New York: New Directions, 1969), 197–8.

What is the spirit that has in general characterized the proceedings of [the Continental] Congress? A perusal of their journals, as well as the candid acknowledgement of such as have had a seat in that assembly, will inform us that the members have but too frequently displayed the character rather of partisans of their respective States than of impartial guardians of a common interest; that where on one occasion improper sacrifices have been made of local considerations to the aggrandizement of the federal government, the great interests of the nation have suffered on a hundred from an undue attention to the local prejudices, interests, and views of the particular States. (*Federalist Papers,* 299)

4.3.3

I shall be discussing this most diffuse of all democratic ideas (representation and local difference) at greater length in the next section. For now I want just to indicate very briefly that while Williams may not always hear the crackle of electricity Whitman heard in words like democracy and equality, there can be no question but that he shares the earlier poet's general sense of the nostalgic, romantic redundancy of the old feudal aristocracy, of inherited privilege. Williams's aristocrats are 'the flower...of a democracy'. They are elected by their work. It is the meritocracy of art.

Tocqueville wrote prophetically of the democratic excitement Whitman would be the first to capture in poetry—people excited by themselves and their conditions. At the same time he explains why 'aristocracy is much more favourable to poetry than is democracy':

There are some privileged people in aristocracies whose existence is, so to say, beyond and above man's lot; power, wealth, renown, wit, refinement, and distinction in all things seem their natural prerogative. The crowd neither sees them very close nor follows them in detail. It is not hard to represent such men in poetic terms...

When skepticism had depopulated heaven, and equality had cut each man to a smaller and better known size, the poets, wondering what to substitute for the great themes lost with the aristocracy, first turned their eyes to inanimate nature. Gods and heroes gone, they began by painting rivers and mountains...

[I regard this] as a transitional phenomenon...

Democratic peoples may amuse themselves momentarily by looking at nature, but it is about themselves that they are really excited. (*Democracy in America,* 484)

The following passage from 'The Poem as a Field of Action' (1948) essentially develops Tocqueville's point. And Williams brags as bravely as Whitman did:

Shakespeare—the butcher's son dreaming of Caesar and Wolsey. No need to go on through Keats, Shelley to Tennyson. It is all, the subject matter, a wish for aristocratic attainment—a 'spiritual' bureaucracy of the 'soul' or what you will.

There was then a subject matter that was 'poetic' and in many minds that is still poetry —and exclusively so—the 'beautiful' or pious (and so beautiful) wish expressed in beautiful language—a dream. That is still poetry: full stop. Well, that was the world to be desired and the poets merely expressed a general wish and so were useful each in his day.

But with the industrial revolution, and steadily since then, a new spirit—a new *Zeitgeist* has possessed the world, and as a consequence new values have replaced the old, aristocratic concepts—which had a pretty seamy side if you looked at them like a Christian. A new subject matter began to be manifest. It began to be noticed that there could be a new subject matter and that that was not in fact the poem at all. Briefly then, money talks, and the poet, the modern poet has admitted new subject matter to his dreams—that is, the serious poet has admitted the whole armamentarium of the industrial age to his poems. (*Selected Essays*, 282)[32]

We are familiar with this now. Everything that people get excited about, when they get excited about themselves, is properly the province of the poem. 'The whole armamentarium': that is the *all* in *Spring and All.*

4.4 USE AND USE-VALUE

In the beginning all the world was America, and more so than it is now; for no such thing as money was anywhere known.

· John Locke, *Second Treatise of Civil Government*

4.4.1

By highlighting the converging emphases on particularity, usefulness, and locality in American experimental poetry, the idea, in brief, that the use-value of the particular is bound up with a specific place—'the realization of the qualities of a place in relation to the life which occupies it', as Williams puts it[33]—I mean now to draw attention to the way in which American modernist poets circled compulsively around a distinction conceptualized by, among others, Aristotle, Adam Smith, Karl Marx, and Theodor Adorno, and which was given special resonance by American pragmatism; to argue that like the American Revolutionaries before them they were arguing for *the use-value of America itself*;[34] to suggest that they

---

[32] The passage occurs in an essay which is very much about the New World and the Old—about achieving distinction from within the crowd—as against aligning oneself with ancient distinction, borrowed finery: 'We seek profusion—the Mass—heterogeneous—ill-assorted—quite breathless—grasping at all kinds of things . . . Now when Mr. Eliot came along he had a choice: 1. Join the crowd, adding his blackbird's voice to the flock, contributing to the conglomerate . . . or 2. To go where there was already a mass of more ready distinction (to turn his back on the first), already an established literature . . . [to go where there was] an already established place in world literature—a short cut, in short' (*Selected Essays*, 284–5).

[33] Ibid. 157.

[34] See William Carlos Williams, *The Embodiment of Knowledge*, ed. Ron Loewinsohn (New York: New Directions, 1974), where it is argued that the *act of writing* is the *act of realizing* the use-value of America (73): 'poetry is all of a piece, knowledge presented in the form of pure writing

intuited, without necessarily conceptualizing, a certain common ground between the failure of government to represent the local, the failure of exchange to represent use, and the failure of language to signify a world—intuited in other words an identical abstraction; and to point out that where avant-garde poets in Europe since Baudelaire and Mallarmé have reacted to the domination of instrumental reason by sanctifying the uselessness of art, poets in America reacted against the banalizing influence of the commodity form (which they didn't always see as the commodity form but more often as the undifferentiated veneer of modernity) by championing specific and resistant use. As Williams writes: 'The purpose of art IS to be useful . . . Poetry is a rival government always in opposition to its cruder replicas' (*Selected Essays*, 179–80). In order to spell out the full significance of this we shall have to rehearse the meaning of certain familiar terms.

It was Aristotle who 'laid the foundation of the distinction between use-value and exchange-value, which has remained a part of economic thought to the present day'.[35] The distinction was adopted by Adam Smith in *The Wealth of Nations*, published in 1776, the same year as the Declaration of Independence and as that other defence of revolution and free trade, Tom Paine's *Common Sense*. In *The Politics* Aristotle wrote: 'Every piece of property has a double use; both uses are uses of the thing itself, but they are not similar uses; for one is the proper use of the article in question, the other is not. For example a shoe may be used either to put on your foot or to offer in exchange. Both are uses of the shoe.'[36] Although exchanging the shoe for something else is 'not the use proper to it', still it is, says Aristotle, natural enough, provided we are really trying to make the best of the perfectly natural fact that men have 'too much of this and not enough of that':

Such a technique of exchange is not contrary to nature and is not a form of money-making: for it keeps to its original purpose: to re-establish nature's own equilibrium of self-sufficiency. All the same it was out of it that money-making arose, predictably enough —for as soon as the import of necessities and the export of surplus goods began to

---

which is made of the writing itself'. Such writing, he claims, will 'embody America and myself in it' (47). Writing *embodies* and *makes use* precisely to the extent that it doesn't merely replicate the past: 'Why not write sonnets? Because, unless the idea implied in the configuration can be de-formed it has not been *used* but copied' (17). Writing as using is acting—the doing of a properly American deed: 'But now we will say, and mark it, that knowledge has no absolute value and all the value it has exists in the deed' (189). Elisa New suggests that the 'Five Philosophical Essays' at the end of this extravagantly fragmentary book 'may in fact amount to the most cogent and provocative poetics of pragmatism written since World War II' (*The Line's Eye*, 315 n. 2)—a claim that would need to be measured against the rival claims of Muriel Rukeyser's *The Life of Poetry* (1949) or the prose of Williams's follower, Charles Olson.

[35] Eric Roll, *A History of Economic Thought* (1938; London and Boston: Faber and Faber, 1992), 21–2.

[36] Aristotle, *The Politics*, trans. T. A. Sinclair, rev. Trevor J. Saunders (Harmondsworth: Penguin, 1992), 81.

facilitate the satisfaction of needs beyond national frontiers, men inevitably resorted to the use of coined money. (*The Politics*, 82)

Nature is Aristotle's measure. And it is the ascendancy of what Adam Smith will call 'value in exchange', beyond the immediate local environment in which use-values remain transparent, which Aristotle finds *unnatural*:

The acquisition of goods is then, as we have said, of two kinds; one, which is necessary and approved of, is to do with household-management; the other, which is to do with trade and depends on exchange, is justly regarded with disapproval, since it arises not from nature but from men's gaining from each other. Very much disliked also is the practice of charging interest; and the dislike is fully justified, for the gain arises out of currency itself, not as a product of that for which currency was provided. Currency was intended to be a means of exchange, whereas interest represents an increase in the currency itself. Hence its name [*Tokos*, 'offspring'], for each animal produces its like, and interest is currency born of currency. And so of all types of business this is the most contrary to nature. (*The Politics*, 87)

Here Aristotle anticipates Marx's analysis of the abstract and autonomous nature of exchange. 'The utility of a thing makes it a use-value', Marx writes, in his account of the commodity form.[37] It is limited by the physical properties of the commodity and has no existence apart from that commodity. Exchange-value, however, 'appears to be something accidental and purely relative, and consequently an intrinsic value, i.e. an exchange-value that is inseparably connected with, inherent in, commodities, seems a contradiction in terms... The exchange of commodities is evidently an act characterized by a total abstraction from use-value' (Marx, 422).

In the twentieth century, Marx's critique of exchange-value becomes the basis of Theodor Adorno's critique of social and cultural *reification* (*Verdinglichung*): the saturation of everyday life by the abstract glamour of the commodity form.[38] Marx upheld the distinction first laid down by Aristotle, but he asserted that 'exchange-value is the only form in which the value of commodities can manifest itself or be expressed' (Marx, 423). In other words, we are no longer in the presence of simple use-values, we only encounter them by way of exchange. Nearly a century later Adorno detected a still sharper twist of the historical knife. Exchange-values have now become entirely dominant and present themselves to us as enjoyable for their own sake: *exchange-values manifest themselves as use-values.*

For present purposes the work that best illustrates how Adorno applied the distinction between exchange-values and use-values in the realm of philosophical aesthetics is 'On the Fetish Character in Music and the Regression of Listening',

[37] Marx, *Selected Writings*, 421.
[38] On the history of the term *Verdinglichung* and Adorno's debts to and differences from Georg Lukács in respect of this concept, see Rose, *Melancholy Science*, esp. ch. 3.

the razor-sharp polemic of 1938 which he wrote in response to what has remained till this day a much more celebrated piece, Walter Benjamin's ambivalent exercise in surreal dialectics 'The Work of Art in an Age of Mechanical Reproduction' (1936). While he rubbishes Benjamin's notion of the emancipatory potential of popular art, Adorno insists that the satisfactions of so-called higher culture are no more likely to enlighten or liberate. 'The differences in the reception of official "classical" music and light music no longer have any real significance . . . All contemporary musical life is dominated by the commodity form.'[39] Adorno's essay is laced with stinging illustrative insights: 'the familiarity of the piece is a surrogate for the quality ascribed to it' (*Culture Industry*, 26); music 'serves in America today as an advertisement for commodities which one must acquire in order to be able to hear music' (33); the classical concert-goer is 'really worshipping the money that he himself has paid for the ticket to the Toscanini concert' (34). The pleasure is all in the buying. Payment creates 'the appearance of immediacy at the same time as the absence of a relation to the object belies it' (34). Such ersatz enjoyment brings about 'the liquidation of the individual' (31) at the same time as it evokes a fake togetherness: 'In American conventional speech, having a good time means being present at the enjoyment of others, which in its turn has as its only content being present' (34). America has been uniquely adept, Adorno thinks, at blazing trails for the commodity form.[40]

It is by way of *the appearance of immediacy*, then, that exchange-values pass themselves off as use-values:

To be sure, exchange value exerts its power in a special way in the realm of cultural goods. For in the world of commodities this realm appears to be exempted from the power of exchange, to be in an immediate relationship with the goods, and it is this appearance in turn which alone gives cultural goods their exchange value. But they nevertheless simultaneously fall completely into the world of commodities, are produced for the market, and are aimed at the market. The appearance of immediacy is as strong as the compulsion of exchange value is inexorable. (34)

We might say that a commodity is an object which appears to be useful, but is useful mainly to be bought and sold. Adorno thinks that it is the business of

---

[39] Theodor W. Adorno, 'On the Fetish Character of Music and the Regression of Listening', *The Culture Industry: Selected Essays on Mass Culture*, ed. J. M. Bernstein (London: Routledge, 1991), 26–52 (31, 33).
[40] I count four specific references to America in the first nine pages of 'On the Fetish Character in Music and the Regression of Listening': 'An American specialist in radio advertising' (27); 'In America, Beethoven's Fourth Symphony' (32); 'Music . . . in America today' (33); 'In American conventional speech' (34). Although he cites an assortment of Germans, Austrians, Russians, Italians, etc., American is the only *national type* he mentions, 'Greek thinkers' apart (29). Adorno's attitude to America appears to carry over into his essay on Thorstein Veblen and the latter's celebrated critique of consumer culture, collected and translated in *Prisms*, trans. Samuel and Shierry Weber (Cambridge, Mass.: MIT Press, 1994).

properly modern art, therefore, to awaken, in such audience as it has, a genuinely critical 'resistance' to that merely 'acquiescent' reception, in other words purchasing, consuming, which takes the illusion of happiness, the illusion of the social whole, for that happiness or wholeness which art had once promised (29). 'If in nothing else', remarks Adorno dryly, 'Schoenberg's music resembles popular songs in refusing to be enjoyed' (30).

There are fundamental differences between avant-garde or modernist art as it is conceptualized by Adorno and American experimental poetry. Nevertheless, in this respect at least, its dedication to specific use-values, the poetry appears to support Adorno's sense of modern art as 'resistance' to the domination of the commodity form: that is to say, the experimental tradition emerges as an attempt to salvage experience, the unadorned use-value of the particular, from the beguiling clutter of reification. There is a theoretical problem for Adorno, in as much as he has somehow to square his redemption of use-values with his famous critique of instrumental reason as the downside of the dialectic of Enlightenment. For the Americans, however, in a culture more receptive to pragmatic accommodation, there was no such problem.

4.4.2

Before we return to Williams it will help to establish the justice of the argument I am pursuing if we look at the valuation placed on usefulness in the writing of some of the poet's contemporaries from within the American experimental tradition. Consider, first, Muriel Rukeyser, a poet who expressly aligns herself with Whitman, and, secondly, Charles Olson, who is explicitly aligned—his whole linguistic demeanour declares it—with Williams.

Rukeyser's *The Life of Poetry*, published in 1949, is a book about use: the 'use' we fail to make of poetry, as index of the use we fail to make of the larger 'possibilities' of life itself.[41] 'We are a people tending toward democracy at the level of hope', she writes.[42] Democracy realized would mean people making full use of their resources—including poetry. Meanwhile we exist at quite another level, which is defined by 'the economy of the nation, the empire of business within the republic', which thrives on 'perpetual warfare'.[43] Rukeyser even scoffs at the superficiality of American pragmatism, not because she finds the notion of use inadequate, but because she thinks we don't use *enough*:

Everywhere we are told that our human resources are all *to be used*, that our civilization itself means the uses of everything it has—the inventions, the histories, every scrap of fact. But there is one *kind* of knowledge—infinitely precious, time-resistant more than

---

[41] Muriel Rukeyser, *The Life of Poetry* (1949; Ashfield: Paris Press, 1996), 83.
[42] Ibid. 61.
[43] Ibid.

monuments, here to be passed between the generations in any way it may be: never to be used. And that is poetry.

It seems to me that we cut ourselves off, that we impoverish ourselves, just here. I think that we are ruling out one source of power, one that is precisely what we need . . .

What help is there here?

Poetry is, above all, an approach to the truth of feeling, and what is the use of truth?

How do we use feeling?

How do we use truth? (*Life of Poetry*, 7–8)

She makes the point again barely half-a-dozen pages later:

In our schools, we are told that our education is pragmatic, that the body of knowledge is divided into various 'subjects,' that all of these subjects on which we pour our youth are valuable and useful to us in later life. We are told that our civilization depends on further and new uses for everything it has, the development and exploitation of these. We may go ahead and specialize in any of these usable fields.

Except for one . . .

This is here, to be passed on. But not to be used. Among all this pragmatic training, never to come into the real and active life.

This is what we learn about poetry. (13–14)

Rukeyser takes from Melville the phrase 'usable truth' (27): 'The use of truth', she argues, 'is its communication' (27). Part Three of the book is entitled 'The "Uses" of Poetry', and looks at 'popular arts', at for example cinema and blues, while Part Four insists on a *useful* relation between poetry and science. Rukeyser is against the critical isolation of rhythm, metre, metaphor, etc.: the critics' 'treatment of language gives away their habit of expecting units (words, images, arguments) in which, originating from certain premises, the conclusion is inevitable' (166). What she insists on is *relation*: 'In poetry, the relations are not formed like crystals on a lattice of words, although the old criticism . . . would have us believe it [is] so' (ibid.). The poem is an organic complex of dynamic lived relations; relations between 'clusters', 'constellations' (19), as against static perfectionism (83). 'It will simplify the amending of these ideas . . . if we dismiss every static pronouncement and every verdict which treats poetry as static' (167). Rukeyser even claims that the American Constitution itself is a reactive product of mechanistic thinking (63–4). Like a poem a constitution should be an expression of life, facilitating more life: 'The arrangement is the life' (167). Life is dynamic, which is to say it changes. The measure of it all is *use*: 'The usable truth here deals with change' (187).

Charles Olson, writing at roughly the same time as Rukeyser, in his manifesto 'Projective Verse' (1950), also makes use the measure of the truly natural, which is to say—for Olson—of the truly human. It is apparent from the first in his conception of what the poet should 'USE USE USE':[44]

---

[44] Olson, 'Projective Verse', *Collected Prose*, 239–499 (240).

What seems to me a more valid formulation for present use is 'objectism,' a word taken to stand for the kind of relation of man to experience which a poet may state as the necessity of a line or a work to be as wood is, to be as clean as wood is as it issues from the hand of nature, to be as shaped as wood can be when a man has had his hand to it. Objectism is the getting rid of the lyrical interference of the individual as ego, of the 'subject' and his soul, that peculiar presumption by which western man has interposed himself between what he is as a creature of nature (with certain instructions to carry out) and those other creations of nature which we may, with no derogation, call objects. For a man is himself an object, whatever he may take to be his advantages, the more likely to recognize himself as such the greater his advantages, particularly at that moment that he achieves an humilitas sufficient to make him of use.

It comes to this: the use of a man, by himself and thus by others, lies in how he conceives his relation to nature, that force to which he owes his somewhat small existence. If he sprawl, he shall find little to sing but himself... But if he stays inside himself, if he is contained within his nature as he is participant in the larger force, he will be able to listen, and his hearing through himself will give him secrets objects share.[45]

The concept of use is inseparable from the concept of particularism: and 'particularism', he tells us elsewhere, in language deliberately redolent of Pound, Williams, and Zukofsky, 'has to be fought for, anew'.[46] Particularism is also by definition local: we must not 'sprawl', we must realize our 'small existence'.

Now it is obvious that Olson's call for a 'clean' use of words ('as clean as wood is') echoes Pound's Imagist axioms of the 1910s ('To use absolutely no word that does not contribute to the presentation... The natural object is always the *adequate* symbol'), and their casual reiteration and development by Williams, who, in 'A Critical Sketch' of 1931 praised Pound's 'dry, clean use of words'.[47] Here is Williams, first from the Prologue to *Kora in Hell* (1918), and then from *Spring and All*:

The true value is that peculiarity which gives an object a character by itself. The associational or sentimental value is the false. Its imposition is due to lack of imagination, to an easy lateral sliding.[48]

Crude symbolism is to associate emotions with natural phenomena, such as anger with lightning, flowers with love it goes further and associates certain texts with...

It is typified by the use of the word 'like' or that 'evocation' of the 'image' which served us for a time. Its abuse [*sic*] is apparent...

What I put down of value will have this value: an escape from crude symbolism, the annihilation of strained associations, complicated ritualistic forms designed to separate

---

[45] Olson, 'Projective Verse', *Collected Prose*, 239–49 (247).

[46] Olson, 'Human Universe', *Collected Prose*, 156.

[47] Williams, *Selected Essays*, 111.

[48] William Carlos Williams, Prologue to *Kora in Hell, Imaginations*, ed. Webster Schott (New York: New Directions, 1971), 6–28 (14).

the work from 'reality'—such as rhyme, meter as meter and not as the essential of the work, one of its words. (*WCW1*, 188–9)

We see that, for Williams, *value* ('that peculiarity which gives an object a character by itself') means use-values: 'With decent knowledge to hand we can tell what things are for' (*WCW1*, 226). The language of poetry must not permit itself to 'slide' (or as Olson says 'sprawl') from these values. Louis Zukofsky, a close reader of Marx, will call it 'thinking with the things as they exist'.[49]

All four of these poets, Pound, Williams, Zukofsky and Olson, will seem, at various points, to entertain an analogy between the improper use of language and the improper use of money: between language that begets language, as opposed to *language that begets things*, and money that begets money ('currency born of currency', as Aristotle calls it), as opposed to *money that begets, is exchanged for, things*. In the essay 'Waste and Use' from *The Embodiment of Knowledge*, Williams writes of the economist as if he were a poet—writes, one might almost say, like Pound.[50] The language–money analogy is at its clearest in Pound's canto 45, 'With Usura', which is then evoked by Williams in *Paterson*, Book Two, Part One, in the passage beginning 'Without invention'.[51] But it is not without problematical implications, as we shall see.

Between *Kora in Hell* and *Spring and All*, however, Williams was on his way to a brilliant intuitive synthesis—one that enabled him to leap quite clear of Poundian Imagism. And it turns again on his paradoxical understanding of representation: whose necessity is of a piece with its 'virtual impossibility': 'But the thing which stands eternally in the way of really good writing is always one: the virtual impossibility of lifting to the imagination those things which lie under the direct scrutiny of the senses, close to the nose.'[52] Williams's solution—and perhaps we might refer to it as a native solution, the moment when he chances on the American grain—is that attention must be *loose, casual, improvisatory*; it must be indirect and oblique. Wallace Stevens will complain that Williams's poems are 'casual'. But the casual is necessarily their only mode—the only way to bring us within a whiff of reality. You cannot represent the thing by concentrating on it: the attention must follow 'a more flexible, jagged resort' (*Imaginations*, 14). Association is just as bad. The thing will only be if you let it be; if you leave go

---

[49] Louis Zukofsky, 'Sincerity and Objectification: With Special Reference to the Work of Charles Reznikoff' (1931), *Prepositions+*, 193–202 (194). In the same essay Zukofsky cites with approval Williams's attack on 'crude symbolism' from *Spring and All* quoted above (ibid. 198).

[50] 'Ignorance . . . is always poor economy . . . All excess is plainly poor economy . . . And fullest energy cannot be anything but fullest economy; neither under nor over use': 'Economy' and 'beauty' exist together in the 'deed'—in the 'perfection' which is 'the object of our activity' (*Embodiment of Knowledge*, 186–9).

[51] William Carlos Williams, *Paterson*, ed. Christopher MacGowan (1992; New York: New Directions, 1995), 50.

[52] Prologue to *Kora in Hell*, *Imaginations*, 14.

and move off: 'The imagination goes from one thing to another' (ibid.). Truth, as Williams says of Burr, must be 'careless' (*In the American Grain*, 206).

Here, then, is Williams's simple and decisive break from Imagism as Pound had defined it—and it was so lightly and delicately done that it has still not been properly acknowledged. What Pound advocated as 'Direct treatment of the "thing" whether subjective or objective',[53] is best achieved, Williams argues, indirectly: that is, casually, quickly, jaggedly, by going to another thing. Trust the things to invoke each other: let representation be.[54]

Meanwhile, 'that peculiarity which gives a thing a character by itself' will be acknowledged line by line, by and of itself—the more so in so far as we cannot dwell on it. Olson makes the same point in 'Projective Verse'—'keep it moving as fast as you can, citizen' (*Collected Prose*, 240)—while following Whitman, Pound, and Williams in implying that the theory of poetics is a theory of citizenship. The differentiated liberated individuated line (without superfluous ornament, metre or rhyme) symbolizes *and* enacts the uniqueness, the non-identity, of the use-value of each thing. Williams's conception of radical mimesis answers to the paradox of representation, as he understands it: in the impossibility of it the mere possibility. It is—as indeed it was—the very origin of the need for a revolution of the local.

We can illustrate some of the ways in which this manifests itself by having a brief look at two of the most famous poems from *Spring and All*. As Bram Dijkstra observes in what remains one of the best introductions to Williams, the first of these, 'To Elsie', is about what happens to people when there is no regional tradition to root them in their locality and then, via their locality, in nature: i.e. 'The pure products of America | go crazy' (*WCW1*, 217–19).[55] But that doesn't tell us what makes it a great poem—which is the wit and speed with which it skims the surface of what it evokes, refusing to dwell on the deprivations that it name-checks, declining to pretend that it can 'witness | and adjust', sympathize and compensate. It refuses to put words into the mouths of the people: it won't express what Elsie can't express, won't say what she can't say, mirror or represent what she herself can't present. It refuses to patronize. Either

---

[53] Pound, *Literary Essays*, 3.

[54] Among Williams's critics, none seems to have understood this better than Bernard Duffey, who emphasizes again and again how for Williams what is at issue is 'radical presence', and 'reference or bearing is of small account'; in other words, you refer by not making the mistake of trying to. Presence begets presence: the presence of language; but language that leaves 'open' the possibility of referring without the certainty of it. Moreover, such openness is more 'open' than bare 'indeterminacy'. Or as Duffey says: 'If Williams is indeed a poet of "indeterminacy" ... What has been felt to be "indeterminate" in [his] poetry may thus be linked to the universality and unalterability of immediate presence that his whole approach postulates.' Bernard Duffey, *A Poetry of Presence: The Writing of William Carlos Williams* (Madison: University of Wisconsin Press, 1986), 184, 15, 26.

[55] Bram Dijkstra, *Cubism, Stieglitz and the Early Poetry of William Carlos Williams* (Princeton: Princeton University Press, 1969), 176–80.

you know what the poem is talking about or you don't—and if you do, then you had better not dwell on it, for that would only result in sentimentality and bathos. As Williams puts it: 'If I succeed in keeping myself objective enough, sensual enough, I can produce the factors, the concretions of materials by which others shall understand and so be led to use—that they may the better see, touch, taste, enjoy—their own world *differing as it may* from mine.' So the poem moves by 'isolate flecks' that nonetheless connect up. The connections are not empathetic but formal. They seem to say somehow that things *are* connected—but except by dancing they don't say how. All connections are local, specific to the place where they are made. Williams drives *his* car, not theirs. 'That—all my life I have striven to emphasize it—is what is meant by the universality of the local. From me where I stand to them where they stand in their here and now—where I cannot be—I do in spite of that arrive!'

'The Red Wheelbarrow' also confronts what Williams calls 'the virtual impossibility of lifting to the imagination' ordinary everyday things—the impossibility of representation:

> so much depends
> upon
>
> a red wheel
> barrow
>
> glazed with rain
> water
>
> beside the white
> chickens
>
> (*WCW1*, 224)

A whole working environment depends upon the utility of the wheelbarrow. But how on earth do you represent it?[56] Where does that environment end? 'So much' of the national economy depends on each regional economy, which depends on the local economy, which depends on the family and the farm, which depend on the wheelbarrow—but not just on the wheelbarrow, also on the chickens and rain. The poem also 'depends I upon I I a red wheel I barrow'—but again *how much*? And which red wheelbarrow? A real one? One we've only *read* about? A picture of one? Our willingness to imagine such a picture? But doesn't that presume a real one somewhere? (It is just about possible to perceive the word *real* secreted in the words 'red wheel'.) How much depends on the barrow's being red, and how much does the red depend upon the white (the pun is inescapable: read against white, as words are read on a page), or for that matter the glaze? And

---

[56] Dijkstra's reading of this poem tends to oversimplify the mimetic gesture, ignoring the way in which the poem flagrantly exposes, in its abstract patterning alone, the inherent uncertainty of representation (168–9).

what part does the poem's formal structure play in all this (four pairs of lines comprising three words followed by one word)? Does anything depend on that? The poem works by provoking this dynamic complex of relationships, this question of relationships. If it works it works as the barrow works (if one works the other will)—immediately, locally, as Williams says, 'close to the nose'. It was this poet's great innovation to get his words to refer by freely acknowledging that they need not refer. They needn't but they might. 'So much depends.'

The claim that is being made here is in effect that through its insistence on particularity and locality, the use-value or particular in its place, experimental American poetry inherited the redistributive propensity within American revolutionary politics—without necessarily having in mind, any more than the American Revolution itself had, anything we might think of as utopian communism.[57] Why should the premium on use-values have a redistributive potential? Because use-value implies that what is useful is necessarily, and for the duration of its use, the property of the user, that it becomes mine through my labour—which is the only time that it is property, properly, at all. It implies equally a local context: what I use I use as and where I use it, perhaps only for the moment that I use it, and necessarily in a specific place. This is what Olson means when he speaks of 'the kind of relation of man to experience which a poet may state as the necessity of a line or a work to be as wood is, to be as clean as wood is as it issues from the hand of nature, to be as shaped as wood can be when a man has had his hand to it'. The claim is that a world governed by the commodity form, wherein property is also a commodity form, something we buy or sell rather than use, cannot understand what a thing in fact is. Use-value by contrast insists on the transience of all property relations: it comes *before* property. Though it by no means confronts the full ideological implications of its stance to reality, it is incontestable that the thingliness of American experimental poetry deliberately strips the thing of its place within the wider network of property relations and reveals again its specific use-value. We might as well say that like the unfulfilled Marxian dialectic itself, both these revolutions were, in Clive Bush's marvellous phrase, '*halfway* to revolution'.[58]

---

[57] 'Williams was never a Communist, finally,' writes Mariani, 'because he distrusted all orthodoxies, all ideologies. He was far too radical' (344).

[58] We might underline the argument again by citing another poet, who despite her formal ingenuity shares none of the overt political radicalism of Rukeyser, Olson or Williams, namely Marianne Moore. Moore actually has a poem called 'Values in Use', and in the original version of her most famous poem, 'Poetry' (1935), she identified the life of poetry with the usefulness of life itself. If poetry is or ought to be a hair-raising experience, then let it be so. She even appears to pun, if that notion can be ascribed to a writer who is always so inscrutably poised, on *use* and *us*. See Marianne Moore, *Complete Poems* (New York: Macmillan Company; Viking Press, 1967), 266–7:

> I, too, dislike it: there are things that are important beyond all
>   this fiddle.
> Reading it, however, with a perfect contempt for it, one

It is just this revolutionary momentum that disturbs Wallace Stevens—disturbs him much more profoundly, for example, than Williams's reputation for left-wing politics. The argument is, in a word, that what Stevens confronts, with some dismay, in Williams's experimental verse form is use-values without exchange or property relations—use-values seemingly running riot, running free. His response is critical and comprehensive and it runs the length of his career.

4.5 REPRESENTATIONS: FROM MADISON TO KANT

There is a fair amount of Lockean empiricism about Williams's notion of what constitutes knowledge. 'No ideas but in things' leaves no room for reflective judgement, the constitutive action of the mind. But where Locke's empiricism was a sitting duck, whose self-imposed inertia made it an obvious target for metaphysical critique ('knowledge, | undispersed, its own undoing | . . . | Minds like beds always made up'), Williams keeps his *ideas and things* moving.[59] There is still no scope for meditative judgement: but there is an extraordinary dynamism. For Williams, we might say, *movement serves instead of metaphysics.* For Stevens, however, with his intellectual base in romanticism, Transcendentalism, and Symbolism, that is, in a metaphysically inflected world that had been authorized supremely by

> discovers in
> it after all, a place for the genuine.
> Hands that can grasp, eyes
> that can dilate, hair that can rise
> if it must, these things are important not because a
>
> high-sounding interpretation can be put upon them but because
> they are
> useful. When they become so derivative as to become
> unintelligible,
> the same thing may be said for all of us, that we
> do not admire what
> we cannot understand

If poetry has a life, it is a useful life; it encourages or enables things to become what they are, to observe their calling, as Elisa New puts it, who describes Moore, very justly, as 'a Christian "rigorist" of work' (259). And when New writes that 'Moore's immersion in and fascination with procedures of all kinds makes her shrewder than perhaps any other American poet about the way processes become fetishes, about how expedient means ossify into ends, and how discourses—linguistic, technical, social—become self-authorizing' (254), it appears that she is not only deliberately glossing the verse quoted above—and doing so all the more effectively because at the moment in question she does not specifically cite it—she is drawing on Marxist terms and concepts to get at the distinction between values in use and values in exchange, a distinction that Marx has been permitted to make his own. 'Sealed against *experience*, our processes, whether verbal or mechanical, quickly go dead to ethical considerations', she writes (254). Stevens and Williams both admired Moore immensely of course: but as far as my overall argument is concerned, it says a great deal that for all his admiration of her Stevens never attempted anything like the high-wire balancing act of her syllabic lines, in which form and content use each other to such consummate effect.

[59] Williams, *Paterson*, 4–5.

Kant's critique of Locke, there is nothing without ideas—and then again not even nothing. Indeed from this point of view Williams's empiricism is also an idea: the constitutive action of the mind trying to pass itself off as passive and receptive.

If we leave aside the formal differences, which I shall attend to shortly, we can briefly illustrate these epistemological differences, by pausing over two parallel moments, where the poets use *more or less the same terms at more or less the same time to describe more or less the same thing.* In 1946, at the beginning of his most ambitious poem, *Paterson,* Williams elaborates beautifully on the meaning of 'No ideas but in things':

> In ignorance
> a certain knowledge and knowledge,
> undispersed, its own undoing.
>
> (4)

Knowledge is knowledge provided it moves or as the poem says *rolls*— provided one doesn't let it go 'stale' (4). The point is made concretely in a striking image of the sun:

> It is the ignorant sun
> rising in the slot of
> hollow suns risen, so that never in this
> world will a man live well in his body
> save dying
>
> (4)

The sun is ignorant because it has no idea of itself, an ignorance it shares with the poet, who has no real idea of it either (only stale preconceptions), *except* when he sees it —really sees it—rising. Williams returns to the image in Book Three of *Paterson.*

> When the sun rises, it rises in the poem
> and when it sets darkness comes down
> and the poem is dark
>
> (100)

The mind like the poem takes its light from the sun.

During the same decade, the 1940s, Stevens began one of his own most ambitious poems, 'Notes Toward a Supreme Fiction' (1942), by conjuring this same conjunction of sun, ignorance, and man, all there at the beginning. It is instructive to see how, even in a few lines, Stevens seems to stand the empiricism of Williams on its head, then on its feet, then on its head again:

> You must become an ignorant man again
> And see the sun again with an ignorant eye
> And see it clearly in the idea of it.
>
> (*Collected Poems,* 380)

The attempt to become an ignorant man again, seeing things without ideas getting in the way, is self-defeating—even if it remains, all the same, a wonderful idea. Things bring ideas with them. And ideas bring things. One is as much a revelation as the other—or one is a revelation *because* of the other. Stevens plays after this fashion for several stanzas, his ironical metaphysical circuitousness in stark contrast to Williams's controlled but momentous tumbling.[60]

We are bound, says Stevens, to think about things, which is not to say of course that things are what we think—or wholly independent of what we think, for then their very independence would appear to depend upon our thinking wrongly:

> There is a project for the sun. The sun
> Must bear no name, gold flourisher, but be
> In the difficulty of what it is to be.
>
> (*Collected Poems*, 381)

To be 'in the difficulty of what it is to be': to bear no name, even as Stevens promptly gives it another name ('gold flourisher').

Now in order to find in Stevens's argument with Williams—with the poet himself and with the experimental tradition of which he becomes in the end the representative figure—the wider significance that I am claiming for it, we need, first of all, to reprise the Federalist critique of American revolutionary government, particularly as set out by James Madison; and then to take a look at the broad philosophical basis of Stevens's poetics.

Government for Madison is evidence of human imperfection. 'It is', he writes, 'a matter both of wonder and regret that those who raise so many objections against the new Constitution should never call to mind the defects of that which is to be exchanged for it. It is not necessary that the former should be perfect: it is sufficient that the latter is more imperfect' (*Federalist* No. 38). A Republican government is one 'in which the scheme of representation takes place'. If men are to govern themselves, and not be ruled by a tyrant or a king, then they are stuck with representation: for if all men governed, no one would be subject. However, it is not just that men must be governed: government itself must be restrained. In these circumstances the best system would be one built on a systematic recognition

---

[60] Stevens's poem was first published in 1942 in a limited edition, pre-dating by a few years Book One of *Paterson*. The notes to the MacGowan edition of Williams's poem state that he 'told his friend Fred Miller in 1945 that the lines included a reference to the view from the back window' at his home (*Paterson*, 253). But there had also been plenty of time for Williams to have come across, and ruminated over, the passage from 'Notes Toward a Supreme Fiction'. The image of the sun does not appear, for instance, in the short poem 'Paterson' from 1927 (*WCW1*, 263–6), much of which is, as the editors say, 'reworked into Book One of *Paterson*' (512). In any case, whether Williams was thinking of Stevens's poem or not—and even more so if he was—Stevens's thought process seems to run rings round that of Williams. Nevertheless, when Stevens returned to this exemplary image of the sun at the beginning of 'Description Without Place', Williams, as we've seen, ran rings round him in turn.

of the inherent imperfection of this or any other political system. This requires the state to have a system of representation which seeks not to deny itself—to absolve itself of the burden of mediation, which for Madison is the inevitable burden of government—but which allows mediation, within certain limits or controls, to come into its own, to enact its part. Representation must not be overwhelmed or resisted but embraced. We could describe Madison's role as limiting representation, *in order to make room for representation*, limiting government, in order to make room for government.

The last sentence proposes what Stevens would call an 'unofficial' analogy—but more than an analogy, a striking historical conjunction. In 1781 Kant published his *Critique of Pure Reason*, the purpose of which was, as he subsequently said (in the Second Preface, of 1787), to 'deny knowledge in order to make room for faith'.[61] By knowledge Kant means here unconditioned knowledge of unconditioned truth—absolute knowledge. By denying (*verneinen*) knowledge Kant means to say that knowledge, *as human beings know it*, is not absolute but limited. As one Kant scholar put it: 'When the nature and scope of our experience of sensuous objects is examined according to this criterion of absolute completeness, its limitation is at once apparent.'[62] This is where the essentially negative concept of 'ultimate or noumenal reality',[63] or of things in themselves (Kant's notorious shorthand for unconditioned knowledge of the unconditioned, invoked by Stevens in poem after poem), comes into play. As Paul Guyer and Allen W. Wood summarize it, in their authoritative English edition of the *Critique*:

Kant says it is legitimate for us to speak of noumena only 'in a negative sense,' meaning things as they may be in themselves independently of our representation of them, but not noumena 'in a positive sense,' which would be things known through pure reason alone. A fundamental point of the *Critique* is to deny that we ever have knowledge of things through pure reason alone, but only by applying the categories to pure or empirical data structured by the forms of intuition. (13)

Kant is arguing that the only real knowledge humans have is partial knowledge, the knowledge not of ultimate reality (noumena) but of appearances, phenomena. Knowledge consists of representations (*Vorstellungen*). But if our knowledge is only partial, how is it knowledge at all? Why should we believe it? Why shouldn't we become outright sceptics? Kant's answer is to argue that the mind's faculty of synthesizing the objects of experience is prior to experience: 'experience itself is a kind of cognition requiring the understanding, whose rule I have to presuppose in myself before any object is given to me, hence *a priori*'

---

[61] Immanuel Kant, *Critique of Pure Reason*, trans. and ed. Paul Guyer and Allen W. Wood (1781; 1787; Cambridge: Cambridge University Press, 1999), 117.

[62] Theodore Meyer Greene, Introduction, *Kant: Selections*, ed. Theodore Meyer Greene (London: Charles Scribner's Sons, 1929), p. xlvii.

[63] Ibid., p. xlviii.

(111): so the world conforms to the representational faculty of the mind rather than the other way round. Historians of philosophy have come to call this, following Kant, his Copernican Turn: 'If intuition has to conform to the constitution of the objects, then I do not see how we can know anything of them *a priori;* but if the object (as an object of the senses) conforms to the constitution of our faculty of intuition, then I can very well represent this possibility to myself' (110). Stevens and Williams follow Kant, and follow Copernicus, in imaging the dawning of knowledge based on ignorance—and ignorance based on knowledge—in this same primordial context of the relative movement of the heavens and the earth.

There are three aspects to the dramatic historical conjunction I'm describing. The first is that at the very same time (to a decade in fact) that Madison, Hamilton, and the other Federalists were making a case for political representation based on an acceptance of its limiting and limited nature, Kant was arguing for the representative nature of knowledge. Secondly, while the Federalists were arguing that America had the opportunity to begin, for the first time in history, with a precise determination of the nature of the Constitution on which government should rest—in other words, with an explicit declaration of powers and limits, and powers *based on limits*—Kant was giving philosophy its critical Copernican Turn; arguing that with the *Critique of Pure Reason* philosophy had begun, for the first time in *its* history, to investigate the *constitution* (the scope and the limits) of its own critical faculty, the mind. Let us suppose, however, that the language (in translation after all) is just a coincidence and the structural similarity, so far, merely that. The third point then is more general. Kant's idea of the 'thing in itself' was a way to say, in Stanley Cavell's words, that

'the whole of things' *cannot* be known by human creatures, not because we are limited in the extent of our experience, but, as we might say, because we are limited *to* experience, however extensive... To know the world as a whole, or the world as it is in itself, would require us to have God's knowledge, to know the world the way we more or less picture God to know the world, with every event and all its possibilities directly present.[64]

Kant was making a case for the soundness, the reliability if you prefer, of partial knowledge; for the legitimacy of limitation. Madison was making a parallel case. The bridge from the assumption of the sovereignty of the people as a whole ('We the people') to the reinstitution of government by the few was an attempt to bring about *a workable concept of the whole*: not government by the people, man to man, face to face, not the thing in itself, the perfect state, but *real but limited* government: granted by the whole 'during good behaviour', it would have a conditioned relation to the whole, whose conditions could and must be clarified. (Similarly, the shift from the Revolutionary and then Anti-Federalist

---

[64] Stanley Cavell, *Pursuits of Happiness: The Hollywood Comedy of Remarriage* (Cambridge, Mass.: Harvard University Press, 1981), 75–6.

conception of representation as a mirror to the Federalist conception of representation as filtration or mediation finds a further analogue in the expanded meaning of the philosophical term *reflection*: the Lockean empirical mind reflects in that it mirrors; but Kant and Hegel expand the notion of reflection to mean, in Coleridge's happy phrase, 'reflection on the acts of the mind itself'. The Kantian mind is a bicameral mind: reflecting on reflection; representing representation.)

What is the purpose of thus presenting what I am calling this dramatic historical conjunction? The point is that these men, Kant and Madison, were contemporaries who in their very different spheres were trying to understand the nature of man's apparent but conditional centrality. Distrusting fanaticism as well as despair, they attempted to come to terms with the conditioned, limited, partial—the just plain ungodly nature—of man's way of being in the world. If Protestantism had isolated man at the heart of the universe, as Max Weber was to say, leaving nothing to intercede between himself and God, then the Enlightenment was, as Kant had already said, an invitation for man to stand up—to come out of mourning for his partial view of things and make the best partial job of it.[65] Not to be able to call on any ultimate authority is to have no authority except our own. It was Protestantism's coming of age.[66]

Stevens inherits, not uncritically, from Emerson and Anglo-American romanticism the Kantian distinction between experience and reality: we do not know the world as it is in itself, what we know are its representations (experience); and we can trust these representations because they correspond to a constitutive faculty of the mind. The priority that Kant gives to the mind, the active power he gives it, even as he hems it in with limits, account for his immeasurable influence on progressive liberal rationalism. It is a defence of freedom, of the individual, of common sense, and yet at the same time a defence of reason. Thus, although it was conceived apart from politics, Kantian epistemology is not politically neutral: it justifies our inexact knowledge of the whole, legitimizes representation, explains what Madison called 'the spirit of moderation', and its very optimism is wrought out of pessimism. The Kantian edifice may be, to adapt Cavell again, the greatest of all intellectual settlements with the terms of ordinary life. For all his inevitable differences from Kant, Stevens—who is, after all, only an *unofficial* philosopher—takes for granted the Kantian epistemological distinction between experience and reality and the corresponding inevitability of representation. The vicissitudes of representation and imagination are the very

---

[65] 'A feeling of unprecedented inner loneliness of the single individual', is how Max Weber describes the overwhelming consequence of the Calvinist doctrine of predestination. Max Weber, *The Protestant Ethic and the Spirit of Capitalism*, trans. Talcott Parsons (1930; London: Routledge, 1992), 104. Kant famously describes Enlightenment as 'man's emergence from his self-incurred immaturity', in his short essay, 'What is Enlightenment?' See *Kant's Political Writings*, ed. Hans Reiss, trans. H. B. Nisbet (Cambridge: Cambridge University Press, 1970), 54–60 (54).

[66] For an excellent discussion of this coming of age see Charles Taylor, *Sources of the Self: The Making of the Modern Identity* (Cambridge: Cambridge University Press, 1992), esp. 363–7.

stuff of poetry—yet they are nothing without reality, which is in turn nothing without them.

I am trying to be guided by the dialectical imperative which requires us to see the writer's work as all of a piece: to see one part in terms of another, or to convict one part of another. Sometimes this can involve treating the work as ideology, but as often as not it is to treat it as thought. Thus there is a politics to what Stevens takes for granted and works out in his poetics. And just as Williams's poetics seems to bear secreted within it the radical democratic values of the American Revolution, so Stevens's critique of his poetics may be seen as a critique of *revolutionary pretensions* and a defence of 'things as they are'. Stevens's differences from Williams as they emerge within the poetry can be grouped under two headings: representation and the question of the primacy or otherwise of form. It is to these I now turn.

4.6 FROM REPRESENTATION TO EXCHANGE-RELATIONS

'Nothing is itself taken alone. Things are because of interrelations or interactions', Stevens writes in his *Adagia*.[67] For Williams there are no ideas but in things: for Stevens there are things only as there are perspectives on things. In his reprise of Williams's thinking on poetics, Charles Olson will repeatedly defend the particularity of objects against what he calls 'the lyrical interference of the individual as ego', but for Stevens there is no way not to interfere. Interference is just one of the many forms of our attention: of interrelation, interaction, representation. As the phenomenologists would say: we always already interfere. And interference is the right word. Stevens is not a sceptic, though he understands scepticism: for him as for Kant there is a world out there, and for the lyric ego which tries to make song of it 'There is a conflict, there is a resistance involved'.[68] We interfere even as we register the world. In 'The Course of a Particular', 'The leaves cry' because we interfere in the specific instance—*and because we interfere as a general rule*. We can never be sure of touching what Olson called the bare wood, because we are never really 'naked', as Adam and Eve were naked—naked of clothes but also of ideas. ('And in what covert may we, naked, be | Beyond the knowledge of nakedness . . . ?' Stevens asks, in 'Extracts from Addresses to the Academy of Fine Ideas'. To which the answer is: only in 'a land beyond the mind'; for knowledge of nakedness interferes with our nakedness, it dresses it up.)[69]

---

[67] Wallace Stevens, *Opus Posthumous*, revised, enlarged, and corrected edn., ed. Milton J. Bates (1957; New York: Alfred A. Knopf, 1989), 189.
[68] 'The Course of a Particular', *Opus Posthumous*, 123–4 (123).
[69] *Collected Poems*, 252.

But the ambiguity Stevens relishes creates another. For it is Stevens's belief that poetry has a special claim, which it used to share with metaphysics, on the paradoxes of representation. The trouble is that this post-metaphysical acceptance of the inevitability of representation seems to run headlong into the Marxist critique of the same, already discussed above with reference to Adorno. The latter begins by making central the distinction between values in use and values in exchange, and then argues that the world today is represented first and foremost not by the imagination but by exchange-relations: it is exchange-values which mediate the world. In respect of Stevens specifically, the critical question that emerges may be expressed as follows: how far do the poetics of (imaginative) representation and the principles of capitalist exchange relations appear to coincide, and how far was Stevens aware of the coincidence? In other words, to what extent ought what Stevens calls 'Imagination as Value' to read *value as exchange*?

Almost any of Stevens's poems would serve for a discussion of representation, but I shall take 'The Man with the Blue Guitar', one of his major poems of the 1930s, which avows the 'universal intercourse' between poetry and reality during what was probably the most ideologically conflicted decade of the twentieth century. The whole poem is, if you like, about representation. It is a series of variations, which are themselves a coming to terms with the paradoxical state of affairs (one hesitates to call it *truth*, as Stevens says: 'The the'),[70] wherein the only way we can represent 'things as they are' is, indeed, by *representing* them. In other words the only way we can 'play things as they are' is by changing them—and this fact that they are changed when we play them is *how they are*; it is the condition of things. It is the fate of things to be represented: by playing on this truth the poem would help us to accept it. But it is not just the fate of things to be represented, it is the fate, if you will, of humanity, of what were known in the 1930s as the masses:

> So that's life, then: things as they are?
> It picks its way on the blue guitar.
>
> A million people on one string?
>
>   .   .   .   .   .   .
>
> The feelings crazily, craftily call,
> Like a buzzing of flies in autumn air,
>
> And that's life, then: things as they are,
> This buzzing of the blue guitar.
>
>   (*Collected Poems*, 166–7)

The consolation for the absurdity of being thus represented, whether by artists or politicians, is that it is a fate we all share—with each other and with things.

---

[70] 'The Man on the Dump', *Collected Poems*, 203.

I cannot bring a world quite round,
Although I patch it as I can.

I sing a hero's head, large eye
And bearded bronze, but not a man,

Although I patch him as I can
And reach through him almost to man.

If to serenade almost to man
Is to miss, by that, things as they are,

Say that it is the serenade
Of a man that plays a blue guitar.

(165–6)

The meaning here is carried by the pun on patch: Stevens's artist doesn't just patch the world together, shoring fragments as *The Waste Land* said, he sees it through and by way of an *eye patch* ('I patch')—an ambiguous Cyclopean figure of both blindness and focus as well as partiality. We all have our little patch, our limited place, our particular point of view—which is, once again, a sign of the fact that we *share the world* as well as occupy it. Here then is a more ironic take on that sense of locality championed by Williams.

Critics like James Longenbach and Frank Lentricchia paint a vivid picture of Stevens's struggle to get both feet securely on the economic ladder. He was a man who had to make himself vice president of the company 'before he could allow himself the pleasure of writing poetry'.[71] In an episode reminiscent of *The Autobiography of Benjamin Franklin*, it was Stevens's father who had inducted him in the brutalizing process of becoming self-reliant. When the young Stevens, fresh out of Harvard, asked for financial support while he attempted to establish himself as a writer, his father turned him down, taking the opportunity instead to give him a piece of his hard-earned wisdom. In so doing, he was, as Lentricchia says, 'passing on the wisdom of Poor Richard and Horatio Alger', that in America a man must 'start with nothing', that that after all is what America is about: 'your father cannot be your patron'.[72] But even before he found a niche for himself in the world of free-market property relations, Stevens's compassionate, even populist democratic politics had no real truck with the radical redistribution of property.[73] Capitalist property relations are a given, and business owns the means of production.

---

[71] James Longenbach, *Wallace Stevens: The Plain Sense of Things* (New York: Oxford University Press, 1991), 131.

[72] Frank Lentricchia, *Modernist Quartet* (Cambridge: Cambridge University Press, 1994), 127–8.

[73] Filreis, Longenbach, and Lentricchia are only the most prominent figures in what has been a glut of critical writing attempting to give a hard-headed cultural materialist account of the way Stevens's poetry is saturated in the economic and ideological conditions of its time and place. Other examples include Michael Szalay's *New Deal Modernism: American Literature and the Invention of*

I want to quote now the twenty-second section of 'The Man with the Blue
Guitar', followed by Longenbach's commentary on it:

> Poetry is the subject of the poem,
> From this the poem issues and
>
> To this returns. Between the two,
> Between issue and return, there is
>
> An absence in reality,
> Things as they are. Or so we say.
>
> But are these separate? Is it
> An absence for the poem, which acquires
>
> Its true appearances there, sun's green,
> Cloud's red, earth feeling, sky that thinks?
>
> From these it takes. Perhaps it gives,
> In the universal intercourse.
>
> (*Collected Poems*, 176–7)

Longenbach writes:

That opening line is not an aesthete's credo but a recognition of the limited scope of
poetry in a time when great demands were placed on literature. Building on 'Mr. Burnshaw
and the Statue' (where a poet's politics cannot suffice outside of poetry) and on 'The
Irrational Element' (where the poet cannot escape the world outside the poem), this passage
insists on a dialectical relationship between the 'poetry' of the poem and the 'reality' to which
it refers. As Stevens paraphrased the passage [in a letter to Hi Simons from 1940],
'imagination has no source except in reality, and ceases to have any value when it departs
from reality . . . There is nothing that exists exclusively by reason of the imagination, or that
does not exist in some form in reality . . . Imagination gives, but gives in relation.' To apply
this insight to the poem of which it is a paraphrase is to remember that despite its self-
referential and theoretical nature, the 'Blue Guitar' drew from Stevens's engagement with the
political and aesthetic questions the Depression threw into high relief. As Stevens explained
in 'Insurance and Social Change' (1937), an essay that follows the 'Blue Guitar' as 'The
Irrational Element' follows 'Owl's Clover': 'It helps us to see the actual world to visualize a
fantastic world. Thus, when Mr Wells creates a world of machines, a matter-of-fact truth
about the world in which we live becomes clear for all the fiction. When he passes from the
international to the interstellar, we hug the purely local.'[74]

Longenbach's interpretation—'this passage insists on a dialectical relationship
between the "poetry" of the poem and the "reality" to which it refers'—is in
keeping with the Kantian reading of reality that has been set out above. But

---

the *Welfare State* (2000), and Joseph Harrington, *Poetry and the Public: The Social Form of Modern
U.S. Poetics* (2002).

[74] Longenbach, *Plain Sense of Things*, 171–2.

consider: from the point of view of the critique articulated by Adorno, how dialectical is this dialectic? What if Stevens's understanding of change, of the dynamic rapport between appearance and reality, is subliminally modelled on the exchange-relation—which fundamentally doesn't change at all? In other words, what if the dialectic is flagrantly half-hearted? Then what changes in Stevens is just the gaudy surface of things as they are ('sun's green, | Cloud's red', etc.)—which is, for him, as we said, the one sure sign that they are there at all, a type of reciprocal *interference*. But what does not change is the principle of change: which is to say, the underlying principle of exchange-relations.

From this point of view, then, Longenbach is right to quote 'Insurance and Social Change', but he underestimates its significance. For there is a case for arguing that Stevens's underlying model of change, social or metaphysical change, is the exchange-relation itself—the money relation. For money changes things without changing them at all; that is to say without dislodging the centrality of the marketplace. So money represents things in the same way poetry does. Or in a different way, but to the same effect. This then is at the bottom of Stevens's charming and only superficially mysterious suggestion, in his *Adagia*, that money too is 'a kind of poetry' (*Opus Posthumous*, 191).

This last aphorism helps to particularize the sometimes striking parallels between Stevens and his fictional contemporary Jay Gatsby, taking Gatsby as a figure for, as it were, supercultural imagination. I'm thinking of Longenbach's accurate and poignant description of Stevens's original economic insecurity, his Franklinesque Protestantism; I'm thinking of their shared attraction to 'essential gaudiness' (the phrase Fitzgerald uses is 'ineffable gaudiness'), their acknowledged dandyism and social aloofness; I'm thinking of their broad Platonism, of how poetry for Stevens, springs, as Nick says of Gatsby, from its 'Platonic conception of [itself]'; and I'm thinking of how money is for each of them a delicious, sublimely fetishistic reference point, for Daisy's voice, we remember is —like poetry—like money.[75] And I'm thinking of 'Mr Nobody from Nowhere', as a kind of equivalent to Stevens's Snow Man, aiming 'above the hot struggles of the poor'.[76]

Such a reading can be supported first of all, by way of the general principle that, wars apart, the dynamism of a capitalist society—what makes it look as though it's always changing, renewing itself—is contained by the exchange-relation, the money relation, in any of its superficially different forms. Yet no matter how dynamic these changes are, the dialectical transformation that Marx

---

[75] F. Scott Fitzgerald, *The Great Gatsby* (1926; Harmondsworth: Penguin, 1990), 95, 115. Longenbach describes Stevens as 'someone who desperately needed to feel successful, someone who had to overcome the fear of necessity and the threat of poverty', and yet at the same time 'someone deeply uncomfortable with the success he achieved, someone who needed to deny himself whatever he desired most of all, someone who found the true subject of poetry in a recognition of the power of necessity and the threat of poverty' (131).

[76] Fitzgerald, 123, 142.

had in mind does not occur: the rule of private property (accordingly, of competition and the profit motive) remains intact; the dialectic stops halfway.

The aspect of explicit exchange-relations closest to Stevens was, naturally, given his job, the insurance claim. And his accounts of the insurance business illustrate perfectly how capitalism seems to give to reality an almost infinite variety without fundamentally varying it at all. What is given for Stevens, first of all (as it was for Locke and Madison), is the priority of private property—indeed that is where insurance might be said to begin. Stevens writes in 1937 in 'Insurance and Social Change': 'It helps us to see insurance in the midst of social change to imagine a world in which insurance had been made perfect. In such a world we should be certain of an income. Out of the income we should be able, by the payment of a trivial premium, to protect ourselves, our families and our property against everything' (*Opus Posthumous*, 234). Even here, where Stevens was prepared to consider insurance under Communism, it does not occur to him to imagine a world, even a 'perfect' world, that is not based on private property. And as natural as property is profit: 'It is all a question of remaining solvent, a question of making a reasonable profit. Agents have as much at stake as any group in the making of a reasonable profit' (236). Whatever changes, the profit motive stays: 'Yet the greater these activities are: that is to say, the more they are adapted to the changing needs of changing times (provided they are conducted at a profit) the more certain they are to endure on the existing basis' (237). Now there is a stable notion of change!

As for variety, as the essay 'Surety and Fidelity Claims', written less than six months later, makes clear, no two insurance claims are the same: 'you adapt yourself to each case' (*Opus Posthumous*, 238)—and Stevens gives some splendid illustrations of the *particular* complexities involved. Thus the question of particularity, what Williams called 'that peculiarity which gives an object a character by itself', becomes a question rather of the particular instance of the overall exchange-relation of which it is a part. The particular is, or comes to be, only as it is represented—in other words, it is the representation itself which is particular. The insurance man, like the poet, is a mediator ('The poet is the intermediary between people and the world in which they live and, also, between people as between themselves'),[77] evaluating the claims of reality, and given over for his pains to abstraction, that is, to 'an absence in reality' ('The Man with the Blue Guitar'). He sees, as was said earlier, the nothing that is not there and the nothing that is:

People suppose, since there is so much human interest in selling Fuller brushes or sorting postcards in a post office, that the same thing must be true of handling fidelity and surety claims. After all, over a period of time, you spend an immense amount of money, millions.

[77] Wallace Stevens, 'Materia Poetica', *Collected Poetry and Prose*, ed. Frank Kermode and Joan Richardson (New York: Library of America, 1997), 919.

But, actually, you never see a dollar. You sign a lot of drafts. You see surprisingly few people. You do the greater part of your work either in your own office or in lawyer's offices. You don't even see the country.[78]

It is a most affecting image of seeming emptiness that Stevens shows us here, in his droll snowman-like way: the lack of contact, the absence of real people, which feels like an absence of relation as such. It even feels like the absence of money ('actually, you never see a dollar')—as if one were even deprived of exchange-relations. At which point we may recall that it is the exchange-relation itself which Stevens is describing— for the exchange-relation goes deeper than money. It is what relation amounts to.

We can consolidate this interpretation of Stevens by looking back at the specific imagery of section 22 of 'The Man with the Blue Guitar'. For here Stevens clearly images poetry—to reverse the terms of his aphorism—as a kind of money. The poem *issues and returns*: the very words have, like some other of Stevens's favourite terms, *poverty* for instance—a great favourite this, and only a letter away from *poetry*—a distinct pecuniary resonance: issue in the sense of *fiduciary issue*, return in the sense of *profit*:

> Between the two,
> Between issue and return, there is
>
> An absence in reality,
> Things as they are. Or so we say.[79]

Once the use-value of a thing (things as they are—as what they are used for) gives place to its exchange-value, to what the world of exchange-relations represents its value as, there is indeed an 'absence in reality'. Use-values lie around shorn of their use-values (the poet is 'a shearsman of sorts'). It is in this sense that poetry—like money, issuing and returning from itself to itself—is 'a purging of the world's poverty and change and evil and death. It is a present perfecting, a satisfaction in the irremediable poverty of life' (*Opus Posthumous*, 193). Poetry and money are like the weather or the clouds: things that 'go round and again go round'. For revolution read change, or rather *exchange*; read 'the pleasures of merely circulating' (*Collected Poems*, 149).

4.7 THE ENIGMA OF FORM

> So I cradle this average violin that knows
> Only forgotten showtunes, but argues
> The possibility of free declamation anchored
> To a dull refrain
>
> John Ashbery, 'Street Musicians'

---

[78] Stevens, 'Surety and Fidelity Claims', *Opus Posthumous*, 237.
[79] Compare 'The Comedian as the Letter C', where Stevens writes of the quotidian that, 'For all it takes it gives a humped return | Exchequering from piebald fiscs unkeyed' (*Collected Poems*, 43).

4.7.1

The fact that we can map Williams's and Stevens's attitudes to matter, to things, on to what becomes the Marxist distinction between use-value and exchange-value finds supreme expression in Stevens's attitude—and Williams's attitude to Stevens's attitude—to form. The verse line in Williams, remember, exemplifies what we might call his formal idealism, his conception of radical mimesis, according to which, as I said, *the differentiated liberated individuated line (without superfluous ornament, metre, or rhyme) symbolizes and enacts the uniqueness, the non-identity, of the use-value of each thing.*

For Stevens, however, form is mere currency. It is what brings 'things as they are' into circulation—it is an abstraction from content, not an extension of it. Without that element of abstraction, however (which testifies to the poverty of things, their dependence on us) we shouldn't know them at all. The formal keynote of Stevens's verse, then, is not individuation but repetition, or better still sameness, what Stevens himself calls 'a banality of form'. Ornament, metre, and rhyme are not only not integral to the apparent subject, they could be exchanged for other ornaments or rhymes without much loss to meaning or difference to metre. Wilfully abstract, they foreground the abstract tendency which unites all appearances. Wilfully gaudy, they admit to a fateful superfluity, without which, however, we should barely apprehend them.

The beginning of 'The Man with the Blue Guitar' perfectly illustrates Stevens's handling of form. The facile rhyme *guitar/ are* is repeated three times and then at intervals throughout the poem. Nor does Stevens shy away from the sort of plain filling ('And they said then') or pompous inversion ('But play, you must') that adds nothing to meaning but at least keeps the rhythm going.[80]

The same formal principles can be shown to be at work in almost any of Stevens's poems, from any period of his writing. In 'To the One of Fictive Muse', for example, there is the play of *near, clear,* and *dear,* the archaic inversion 'out of our imperfections wrought', the deadly banality of the concluding rhyme, 'gave'/ 'crave'—nothing is allowed to disturb the almost somnolent pentameter (*Collected Poems,* 87–8). In 'The Idea of Order at Key West' the play of 'she', 'sea', 'sang', and 'self' never plays enough actually to unsettle the iambic rhythm, consolidated as usual by intermittent undistinguished rhymes, such as 'heard'/ 'word by word'/'stirred' (*Collected Poems* 128–30). The most significant of these is perhaps 'word by word'—which means little in the context but exemplifies the interchangeableness of words—there is a sense, an abstract sense, in which they are all one to Stevens. The sparest of the late poems, which must rate among his very greatest, still depend, like the earliest, on spoonfuls of alliterative honey. 'Not Ideas About the Thing But the Thing Itself' begins with the 'earliest ending

---

[80] See Mariani, 479: 'The trouble with using the old line, Williams had quipped, was that Stevens thought he had to keep sounding important when he used it.'

of winter' (like 'the final finding of the ear' in 'The Course of a Particular'),
before rising to a crescendo straight out of 'The Comedian as the Letter C':

> That scrawny cry—it was
> A chorister whose c preceded the choir.
> It was part of the colossal sun,
>
> Surrounded by its choral rings,
> Still far away. It was like
> A new knowledge of reality.

(Collected Poems, 534)

Of course the poem is still testament to the somewhat ironical fact that
Stevens's greatest formal effects are achieved by contrast—above all by the
sudden plain departure from the dominant alliterative current. Here for instance
it is the bathos of the revelation (hanging as it ingeniously does on what Williams
saw as the weakest word in the poet's whole armoury—'like'), which makes it a
revelation. Though the poet cannot resist a little bit of alliterative honey—'new
knowledge'—the modesty of which fits in, as luck would have it, with the
bathetic final note.

From Williams's point of view, then, Stevens is one of those who use
'complicated ritualistic forms designed to separate the work from "reality"—
such as rhyme, meter as meter and not as the essential of the work, one of its
words'. Another way of putting this is to say that Stevens's banality of form is an
abstraction from reality, a further expression of the fact that, as far as this poet is
concerned, we are always in some degree abstracted from reality. Our 'mere
being', as Stevens calls it, is—or is partly—abstract. Poetry has no special claim
on the use-values of things.

The larger claim being made here then is, as I say, that Stevens's handling of
form illustrates the conception worked out by Marx and subsequently developed
by Adorno of the shifting bias from qualitative use-values to purely
quantitative exchange-values under the kind of capitalist conditions Stevens
championed. The use-value of a commodity, writes Marx, 'being limited by the
physical properties of the commodity . . . has no existence apart from that com-
modity' (Marx, 421): i.e. use-value has a necessary relation to the thing itself. 'But
the exchange of commodities is evidently an act characterized by a total abstrac-
tion from use-value. Then one use-value is just as good as another, provided only
it be present in sufficient quantity' (422). Exchange-value has no necessary
relation to use-value—the crucial thing about it is exchangeability itself.

Likewise Stevens's verse is never dependent on the use-value of any one
specific thing (a guitar, for instance, or a pair of shears), but on the general
amenability of whatever finds its way into the poem. The one indispensable
requirement is the observation of the meter—which, as Williams complains,
is inessential, an abstract quantitative principle: i.e. 'one use-value is just as

good as another, provided only it be present in sufficient quantity'. Which is to say, near=clear=dear; or since the abstraction transcends individual poems, she=sea=C=c...

4.7.2

So far the analysis of the formal differences between Williams and Stevens in terms of the relationship between use-values and exchange-values seems to suggest that it is Stevens rather than Williams who is the dupe of a reified world. So I had better make it clear that I would *also* like to argue the reverse: namely, that the conservatism of Stevens's formal means is also a critique of innovative form and its pretension to break free of reification—what Stevens calls 'the accepted sense of things'. Stevens thinks there is an unthinking re-activism about Williams's formal prejudice in favour of things. He is trying to give too much back to them—more than they are capable of taking. It is an attempt to do away with representation—to unburden the mind of the mind. Stevens attacks the unconditioned multiplicity of points of view he finds in Williams, and the brevity of each point of view.

What Williams calls 'that peculiarity which gives a thing a character by itself' is consistent with what Madison criticized as the atomizing spirit of locality. Nothing sticks around long enough—images, things, points of view, whatever you prefer to call them, come thick and fast. They have a 'casual' variety that borders on 'miscellany'.[81] Stevens doesn't care for miscellany, what he wants to see is a settled and enduring point of view ('a single manner or mood thoroughly matured and exploited'), an anchor for the flux which is, he thinks, a part of anything. Faced with this flux we require a certain ballast from our imaginations: call it a concentration. Writing to Williams after the publication of *Al Que Quiere!* (1917), Stevens argued: 'Given a fixed point of view, realistic, imagistic or what you will, everything adjusts itself to that point of view; and the process of adjustment is a world in flux, as it should be for a poet. But to fidget with points of view leads always to new beginnings and incessant new beginnings lead to sterility' (*Imaginations*, 15). Note Stevens's distaste for 'new beginnings and incessant new beginnings'—for the revolution of use-values per se.

If Stevens is to be aligned with romanticism, which is the alignment he frequently invites, then as he saw it, it should be as a critic of romanticism. In fact it was Williams whom he saw as the romantic poet, as he wrote in 1934:

The man has spent his life in rejecting the accepted sense of things. In that, most of all, his romantic temperament appears...

---

[81] Williams, *Imaginations*, 15.

In order to understand Williams at all, it is necessary to say at once that he has a sentimental side . . . What Williams gives, on the whole, is not sentiment but the reaction from sentiment, or rather, a little sentiment, very little, together with acute reaction . . .

To a man with a sentimental side the anti-poetic is that truth, that reality to which all of us are forever fleeing. (*Opus Posthumous*, 213)

Fourteen years later, in the essay 'Imagination as Value', the terms and thinking are much the same, but the judgement (though 'abstract') is still clearer:

We must somehow cleanse the imagination of the romantic . . . The imagination is one of the great human powers. The romantic belittles it. The imagination is the liberty of the mind. The romantic is a failure to make use of that liberty. It is to the imagination what sentimentality is to feeling. It is a failure of the imagination precisely as sentimentality is a failure of feeling. The imagination is the only genius. It is intrepid and eager and the extreme of its achievement lies in abstraction. The achievement of the romantic, on the contrary, lies in minor wish-fulfillments and it is incapable of abstraction.[82]

We cannot miss here the reference to the Objectivist precepts of Pound and Williams, to be inherited, within a decade or two, by Charles Olson: *go in fear of abstractions; no ideas but in things*. Williams's romanticism is a romanticism of things, a failure to confront the reality of abstraction to which all things, as representations, tend. It is the romanticism of the concrete, the frontier, the margin, the romanticism of locality, of new beginnings and incessant new beginnings. Above all it is the romanticism of a particularity which wants to be represented and is represented at its peril. The gist of my argument is, as I've said, that what Stevens perceives in Williams's experimental verse form is use-values without exchange or property relations. We might as well say that he discovers them there, intuits them. What he apprehends in effect is their social meaning. Thus it is Stevens who discovers the truth of Williams's form, as, I am claiming, it is Williams who implicitly discovers it of Stevens.

This all brings to mind that there is something of Edmund Burke about Stevens's banality of form—the Burke who writes that 'A spirit of innovation is generally the result of a selfish temper and confined views', who finds in the continuity of artifice something like the sanction of nature: 'in what we improve we are never wholly new; in what we retain we are never wholly obsolete'.[83] In fact nothing demonstrates this more forcefully than Stevens's own particular brand of sweeping repetitiveness—than which nothing could be more natural or more abstract.

[82] Wallace Stevens, *The Necessary Angel: Essays on Reality and the Imagination* (1960; London: Faber and Faber, 1984), 138–9.
[83] Edmund Burke, *Reflections on the Revolution in France*, ed. Conor Cruise O'Brien (1790; Harmondsworth: Penguin, 1986), 119, 120.

4.8 'LIFE IS NOT DIALECTICS'

Stevens's critics have put together a detailed picture of a poet who in his politics as in his life generally attempted to stay in the democratic middle ground. He begins as a populist and ends as a typically acquiescent Cold War quietist. By the 1930s, that yardstick of a decade, he had more or less provided against his own personal economic insecurities, and had the presence of mind to steer between the rocks of left- and right-wing dogmatism without at the same time failing to apply himself to the stark political questions of the day. One limitation of these historio-biographical studies is that they depend on the author's filling in— almost as one might fill in the clues of a crossword puzzle—the poems' references to the larger world we live in, the public and political lifeworld, with the aim of demonstrating how what can sometimes seem to be Stevens's astonishingly gaudy and irreverent palette is, on the contrary, a fundamental part of the colour of reality as people at that time knew it and lived it.[84] So they end up by demonstrating the truth of Marjorie Perloff's point, made several years before the studies by Alan Filreis and James Longenbach were published, that admirers of Stevens tend to address themselves to the content, the subject matter, of the poems, and largely ignore the question of form.[85] Despite my appreciation, for instance, of Longenbach's very careful argument, I think that this failure to consider Stevens's form in proper detail, to address himself more deliberately to the nature of the verse and the character of the language, results in what is effectively an under-valuation of the poetry—of what it is and what it is capable of, politically as well as poetically.

   This of course returns us to a claim which is implicit in every part of this chapter: which is that we read Stevens differently when we read him through, or by way of, what we have learned about reading from our attention to formal innovators like Williams and Pound. To learn to read the words as Stevens weighs them, or more accurately, as his poems weigh them, is to read the poetry as it is composed, and to read it as it is composed is to attend to that part of it in which composition, the language as it acts together, thinks.

   Roughly speaking then, Longenbach attempts to recover the middle ground from Stevens's content: I am interested in whether there is a middle ground of form, extending and extended by this content. For form is also a disposition of the mind as it is engaged in a world, and there are circumstances in which the deeper or more telling thought is perhaps just this formal, this compositional

---

[84] Frank Lentricchia's approach is different again and depends more on selective narrative than on the dense accumulation of circumstantial detail. The model here might well have been the kind of dark critical storytelling practised by Stephen Greenblatt in his hugely influential *Renaissance Self-Fashioning* (1980).
[85] Marjorie Perloff, 'Pound/Stevens: Whose Era?', *The Dance of the Intellect: Studies in the Poetry of the Pound Tradition* (1985; Evanston, Ill.: Northwestern University Press, 1996), 1–32.

thought. The enigma of form in Stevens needs to be understood not in isolation but in relation to what it defined itself against: the conception of form represented by Williams. Like the creation of the American Republic, this relationship is a *dialogue*—a dialogue that is still taking place. What makes Stevens's form enigmatic rather than straightforwardly conservative or just plain dull is that its properties are a reflection on the primacy of form in Williams—his form is a reflection on what he sees as the romanticism of Williams's form. Stevens's form is not just any old form. It is a form of negation. Stevens abjures innovative form —but in his abjuring of it *thinks about it*. Moreover, his abjuring of such form extends our understanding of what form is—what the form of abjuration is, of silence, of negation. Thus there is a more powerful form in Stevens, like an aura around the apparent form: the enigma of form. Form, Stevens is saying, is not so simple as form. This may actually be a more complicated proposition than the well-known Olson–Creeley precept, namely that 'form is never more than an extension of content'.[86] Content—namely, thought—changes not just the particular form, but what form in general means. Content changes what form is.

Stevens's suspiciousness of so-called innovative form is not just a literary but also a *social criticism*. In her essay, 'Pound/Stevens: Whose Era?' Marjorie Perloff quotes the following passage from Stevens's essay 'The Relations between Poetry and Painting' (1951): 'Let me divide modern poetry into two classes, one that is modern in respect to what it says, the other that is modern in respect to form. The first kind is not interested primarily in form. The second is. The first kind is interested in form but accepts a banality of form as incidental to its language'; it is primarily interested in 'what is expressed'.[87] Perloff rightly cites this as evidence of Stevens's attitude to poetry but she passes over the larger provocation. Here is most of the passage, taking it from the beginning and up to the sentence immediately preceding the passage just quoted:

One of the characteristics of modern art is that it is uncompromising. In this it resembles modern politics, and perhaps it would appear on study, including a study of the rights of man and of women's hats and dresses, that everything modern, or possibly merely new, is, in the nature of things, uncompromising . . . Another characteristic of modern art is that it is plausible. It has a reason for everything. Even the lack of a reason becomes a reason. Picasso expresses surprise that people should ask what a picture means and says that pictures are not intended to have meanings. This explains everything. Still another characteristic of modern art is that it is bigoted. Every painter who can be defined as a modern painter becomes, by virtue of that definition, a freeman of the world of art and hence the equal of any other modern painter . . . not to be judged except by other modern painters.

We have this inability (not mere unwillingness) to compromise, this same plausibility and bigotry in modern poetry. (*Necessary Angel*, 166–7)

[86] Olson, *Collected Prose*, 240.
[87] Perloff, *Dance of the Intellect*, 8; Stevens, *Necessary Angel*, 167–8.

Stevens draws a clear if quiet parallel between uncompromising poetry and uncompromising politics—and for all the light-heartedness of the references, note the 'modern politics' he seems to be referring to: the revolutionary egalitarian politics of the eighteenth century ('rights of man', 'freeman', 'equality'). He goes on to say, after his fashion, that his characterization of both classes of modern poetry is inadequate, remarks the degree of artifice in formal banality, and ponders the intransigence of factions (169). Meanwhile the passage finds words for my contention that Stevens's compromise with form—his acceptance of banality, as elsewhere of the gaudy—is a political compromise.

This seriously playful politics of compromise finds further expression in another late article on the relations between the specialized arts and society, 'The Whole Man: Perspectives, Horizons' (1954), which also contains, as it happens, one of Stevens's only explicit references to the 'sturdy fathers' of the early Republic: 'Franklin, Washington, Jefferson, Madison' (*Opus Posthumous*, 287). (With his habitual fondness for repetition, he repeats the four names in the same order.) It is not surprising that of all the Federalists it is Madison whom Stevens names. In fact it is entirely consonant with Michael Kammen's description of the Federalists' changing reputation during the twentieth century. The 1920s and 1930s had been characterized by the 'debunking' of their motives, aims, and achievements, but after the Second World War there was a reappraisal. Reputations soared, Madison's most of all:

Finally, it is more than fortuitous that a founder hitherto neglected gained recognition in these years as an intellectual giant. James Madison emerged after World War II as the most carefully studied of American political theorists. A kind of cult figure on many campuses, he came to be regarded as the most profound, original, and far-seeing among all his peers. *Federalist* Number 10, I am sure, was more closely scrutinized in the 1950s and 1960s than either the Declaration of Independence or the Bill of Rights. Madison's apparent sophistication with interest group analysis, his realism about the nature of man as a political animal, and his profound understanding of the role of public opinion—all received lavish praise. Madison the modern pluralist, the student of governmental mechanisms, and the nationalist, had important messages for the American scene during the decades following 1945. (Kammen, 72)

The shift in focus from a revolution undone to a constitution achieved mirrored the swelling of support for, and eventual disillusionment with, radical leftist politics among American and indeed Western intellectuals during this same period.[88]

---

[88] Although Longenbach seems right to point out 'the vintage cold war rhetoric' in Stevens's later prose (*Plain Sense of Things*, 285), or else to remark his retreat into political quietism, there is a case for saying that the poet's studied moderation was always apt to take its complexion from the times; that it was bound to look more colourful against the volatile ideological backdrop of the 1930s, when, to adapt the title of Richard Pells's excellent study of the period, radical visions were still unsettling American dreams, than under the steady Western skies of anti-communist hegemony (Richard H. Pells, *Radical Visions and American Dreams* [1973]). With a nod to Daniel Bell's *The*

These allusions apart, 'The Whole Man' might just be a rather dull schematic essay, if it were not for Stevens's Socratic circuitousness, which doesn't seem to be driving at anything at all until it suddenly arrives:

What really exists is the difference between the theorist and the technician, the difference between Hamlet and Horatio, the difference between the man who can talk about pictures and the man who can afford to buy them. None of these differences involve direct and total opposites. The best technician, the purest mechanic, is necessarily something of a theorist. Hamlet was far more pushing than Horatio ever thought of being, when it came to the point. More often than the satirists admit, the man who can afford to buy pictures is entirely competent to take their measure and at the same time to take the measure both of the artist and of the dealer. (*Opus Posthumous*, 285–6)

What really exists is difference not opposition: 'Could Franklin, Washington, Jefferson, Madison have lived different lives?' Stevens asks (287). The modern artist is identified with the *specialist* and the *technician*: his opposite (the word is at best a convenience), is the *theorist*, who is not strictly identified with (there is a nice elision here), but comes within linguistic orbit of, the 'whole' or 'all-round man'—a circular Emersonian man, radiating from his own centre. 'The world is the world through its theorists' (286). To them falls the task of thinking of the whole.

Note the scenario here: the exchange-relation itself, and, in the middle of it, Stevens's phlegmatic (and Emersonian) repudiation of too much dialectical consistency or rigour. 'Life', as Emerson said, 'is not dialectics.'[89] Note also the sphinx-like deployment of that favourite technical term of Williams's, 'measure'. For Stevens, the modernist artist is in fact as mad as a scientist: his mistake is that he thinks to solve the world, the problem of the whole, through technique. But the whole can only be lived, not solved. The modern artist has got in the habit of addressing himself to other artists, the habit, as Stevens says, of bigotry (*Necessary Angel*, 167): but someone from another walk of life may see the thing better, at any rate more wholly, *because he is not an artist*: at just that point he ventures upon wholeness, or at least, since there is no *whole whole*, out of specialism. As Stevens blandly suggests, this is another way of thinking about experimental form.

End of Ideology (1960), Filreis also emphasizes the significance of 'the emerging postwar moment', when 'American intellectuals, emerging from a period of partisanship, were presented with the apparently liberating idea that ideologies had exhausted themselves and that political writing was to be outmoded' (Filreis, *Wallace Stevens and the Actual World*, 155).

[89] Emerson, 'Experience', *Essays and Lectures*, 478. Emerson expands on this, or seems to, at the beginning of the final paragraph: 'I know that the world I converse with in the city and in the farms, is not the world I *think*' (491). Observe how he unsettles things with the dazzling ghost of contradiction: 'I know that the world ... is not the world, I think.' The point is that for Emerson this is a hard-won thought, as that feinted contradiction demonstrates, and it comes at the end of one of his greatest essays, whereas for the modernists, so Stevens implies, it is rather an easy one.

The idea that in certain instances the wealthy collector, the man who can afford to buy a painting, the man who is master of exchange-relations, might fully appreciate what he has bought, or as Stevens provokingly says, might best take the measure of it—and take the measure too of the artist and the dealer—so that exchange-value and use-value and even the value of labour itself seem to float harmoniously together, was a hard one for the twentieth century to swallow. Stevens's collector here, in this mischievous cameo of exchange-relations, recalls the vastly rich and supremely enigmatic American Adam—Adam Verver—in Henry James's *The Golden Bowl* (1904). And the measure of Stevens's mischief is amply suggested by considering the disapprobation of his immediate contemporary, the critic F. O. Matthiessen, as he tries to make sense of James's benign connoisseur:

James was always ready to confess that he did not have the shadowiest notion of business; but by picking a character like Adam Verver he obligated himself to some knowledge of the type of men who were making the great American fortunes . . . Without such knowledge [James] laid himself wide open to the most serious charge that can be levelled against a great novelist, what Yvor Winters has instanced . . . as the split between manners and morals, the lack of congruity between the environment which would have produced a character and the traits which the author has imputed to him.[90]

Matthiessen's criticism is that James's collector is not enough of a robber baron. And what Stevens argues is that this is modern bigotry. The dialectical wish (which is in part, as I've said, my own critical wish) to find congruity between manners and morals, environment and character, exchange-values and aesthetic stupidity, is a form of critical compulsion ('It has a reason for everything'), when what is really needed is a leap, a break, a truly incongruous act, of imagination. Stevens's Emersonian proposition is, on the contrary, that we shall understand things better not by dialectics but in spite of them.

---

[90] F. O. Matthiessen, *Henry James: The Major Phase* (London: Oxford University Press, 1944), 89–90.

5

Robert Creeley's Lonely Crowd

At the end of canto 81, as Pound rails against vanity, he leaves it tantalizingly unclear whether or not he is also thinking of his own vanity. At the same time he spins out some gorgeous cadences, in which he reminds us of his own willingness *to do*, which is, it is intimated, inseparable from his ability to hear, or to carve out a perfect line:

> But to have done instead of not doing
>   this is not vanity
> To have, with decency, knocked
> That a Blunt should open
>   To have gathered from the air a live tradition
> or from a fine old eye the unconquered flame
> This is not vanity.
>   Here error is all in the not done,
> all in the diffidence that faltered . . .

(The Cantos, 81/535–6)

This is very fine and it is also typical of Pound's subtle lingering critical wit. For the poet is not just saying that diffidence is all very well, but what if it falters? He does indeed wish to be 'decent', as he says, to such decencies. But the underlying point, the undertow, catching hold of us in those concluding lines, is that diffidence always falters—is faltering by nature. And what Pound sets against diffidence is his essential confidence, his perfect sureness of touch—in keeping with canto 81's singling out of the great musical tradition represented by John Dowland. Diffidence may falter, but the rhythm does not.

The way Pound seems to feign humility in order to draw us in is reminiscent of a striking passage on 'modest diffidence' in *The Autobiography of Benjamin Franklin*:

I continu'd this Method some few Years, but gradually left it, retaining only the Habit of expressing my self in Terms of modest Diffidence, never using when I advance any thing that may possibly be disputed, the Words, *Certainly, undoubtedly*, or any others that give the Air of Positiveness to an Opinion; but rather say, I conceive, or I apprehend a Thing to be so or so, It appears to me, or I should think it so or so for such and such Reasons, or I imagine it to be so, or it is so if I am not mistaken. This Habit I believe has been of great

Advantage to me, when I have had occasion to inculcate my Opinions and persuade Men into Measures that I have been from time to time engag'd in promoting.[1]

Franklin goes on to quote Alexander Pope's *Essay on Criticism*, in which it is recommended 'To speak tho' sure, with seeming Diffidence'.[2] Diffidence, for Franklin, is not about being in two minds, it is about seeming to be so, while remaining single-minded.

In this chapter I want to look at a poet in whom diffidence is not fashioned or feigned, is not a mere seeming, but rather constitutes a way of being in the world, or as he would say, of coming into the world, with the implication that being is a kind of *coming* or *be-coming*, a sort of not quite being—a poet, moreover, in whom diffidence falters, but falters this time in its characteristic rhythm, or rather falters to produce its characteristic rhythm.

The poetry of Robert Creeley is not always described in such terms. For instance:

The corollary of Creeley's sense of self is a narrow drama of self-consciousness. He vacillates between self-disgust and the freedoms of attention and pure thinking. But he cannot introduce into his reflections much sense of history or a broad enough range of concerns to keep the conjecture a complex philosophical movement . . . In his poetics of thinking Creeley becomes a victim of what had been his greatest strength: his taut, ascetic language.[3]

Charles Altieri registers here in that word 'vacillates' what I am calling Creeley's diffidence, but he does so only to articulate emphatically what has become the standard criticism of his poetry, essentially enlarging on Frank O'Hara's clever observation (made with reference also to Denise Levertov), 'that where they've pared down the diction so that the experience presumably will come through as strongly as possible, it's the experience of their paring it down that comes through . . . not the experience that is the subject'.[4] The paring down of the line, the 'taut, ascetic language', is a function of the realm of 'pure thinking' which, according to Altieri, Creeley self-consciously inhabits. Apparently consciousness is so bent on purity that it has voided the 'sense of history' that sustains 'a complex philosophical movement'. Thinking is so pure that it has become fatally enervated. In what follows I want to question the assumption that such a purity of thought, attention, or consciousness is what really occurs, and I want to address a question which I think is already there, begged but not stated, in Altieri's rather polarized terms. The question that needs to be asked is this: what 'sense of history' *could*

[1] *The Autobiography of Benjamin Franklin*, ed. Leonard W. Labaree, Ralph L. Ketcham, Helen C. Boatfield, and Helene H. Fineman (New Haven: Yale University Press, 1964), 65.

[2] Ibid. 66.

[3] Charles Altieri, *Self and Sensibility in Contemporary American Poetry* (Cambridge: Cambridge University Press, 1984), 130.

[4] Edward Lucie-Smith, 'An Interview with Frank O'Hara' (1966), in Frank O'Hara, *Standing Still and Walking in New York*, ed. Donald Allen (Bolinas, Calif.: Grey Fox Press, 1975), 23.

emerge from this 'taut, ascetic language', this 'narrow drama of self-consciousness'? Critically, or even philosophically speaking, what is the history of this voiding of history? And how do we get from the masterful diffidence of a Franklin or a Pound to that qualitatively different diffidence of Creeley—in existential terms, authentically inauthentic?

In the first section of the chapter I will try to set out the distinguishing features of Creeley's language, considering its 'taut, ascetic' quality in conjunction with what I will argue is the poet's distinctive contribution to the development of the rhythmical possibilities, or 'measure', of modern American verse. This section builds on the discussion of Williams's verse in the preceding chapter. The remainder of the chapter will then examine what the poetry makes of politics and society. This will mean relating Creeley, unlikely as it may sound, to the Arendtian conception of democratic or communicative reason.

5.1 FROM WILLIAMS TO CREELEY

5.1.1

In his 'Introduction to *The New Writing in the USA*', Creeley cites as a founding or breakthrough moment his encounter with the idea of poetic form expressed by William Carlos Williams in his introduction to *The Wedge* (1944).[5] In terms that correspond to his lifelong emphasis on thingly particularity, Williams had argued that because any given speech has its own peculiar character 'the poetry it engenders will be peculiar to that speech also in its own intrinsic form' (*WCW2*, 54). In his critical writings, Creeley tends to quote from those revelatory moments in Williams's later work where the poet returns to this basic insight—to passages from *The Desert Music* (1954) in particular, which Creeley calls 'the loveliest form he left us',[6] or else from *Journey to Love* (1955), passages in which Williams tries to answer the question: 'Why | does one want to write a poem?' This is the form the question takes in the poem 'The Desert Music', where it is an offshoot of what the poet calls, with light-hearted irony, 'brains | ... scattered | aimlessly', the spontaneous contingencies of speech and conversation.[7] The poem's answer is: 'Because it's there to be written.'[8] The insistence that the poem is 'there', is already there, is an allusion to its source in speech. Or as he put it at the beginning of the poem, 'How shall we get said what must be said?' (*WCW2*, 274). But Williams never lays it on. And the poem moves easily

[5] Robert Creeley, 'Introduction to *The New Writing in the USA*', *The Collected Essays of Robert Creeley* (Berkeley and Los Angeles: University of California Press, 1989), 89–96. Subsequently cited as *Essays*.
[6] Creeley, 'I'm given to write poems', *Essays*, 500.
[7] *WCW2*, 273–84 (282).
[8] Ibid.

or 'aimlessly', unencumbered by any heavy symbolism, from the 'obscene fingers' of the begging children the poet meets in the desert, from whose crude speech he initially recoils ('Give me penny please, mister'); to their 'insistent fingers', which are associated in the end with the fingers of the poet and with the fingers of the cellist Pablo Casals, until they all form part of an 'insistent music'—there to be written.

Creeley addresses some of these concerns as well as some of Williams's vocabulary in the poem 'For W. C. W.':

> The rhyme is after
> all the repeated
> insistence.
>
> There, you say, and
> there, and there,
> and *and* becomes
>
> just so. And
> what one wants is
> what one wants,
>
> yet complexly
> as you
> say.
>
> Let's
> let it go.
> I want—
>
> Then there is—
> and,
> I want.[9]

The emphasis on 'insistence', on what is 'there', on what 'one wants', seems to recall 'The Desert Music', just quoted ('Why | does one want to write a poem?'), whereas 'complexly' and 'say' might recall, among other things, Williams's introduction to *The Wedge*: 'The arts have a *complex* relation to society' ('complexities' also occurs on the first page of *Paterson*, and the frequency of the word or its variants suggests that it was one of Williams's favourite terms, one which he instinctively reached for when he wanted to move beyond the particular without getting stuck in an idea); 'It isn't what he *says* that counts as a work of art ... What does it matter what the line "says"?'[10] There are some words here that for readers of modern American poetry have become inescapably associated with Williams,

---

    [9] Robert Creeley, *The Collected Poems of Robert Creeley: 1945–1975* (Berkeley and Los Angeles: University of California Press, 1982), 273. Hereafter cited as *Poems*.
    [10] *WCW2*, 53–4.

such as 'just' ('This Is Just to Say'), and the ubiquitous 'so' ('so much depends', 'so cold', 'so be it', etc.). Perhaps this is incidental. But it could equally be argued that none of this is merely incidental, since in the poetics of both Williams and Creeley the incidental itself is never just incidental: all contingencies have their necessity, a necessity which is found out by the poetry. On the other hand, what I take to be the primary level of coincidence is indicative of Creeley's indebtedness to certain key moments in Williams's work, the care with which he listens to the speech the other uses. What I want to look at now is how Creeley turns this experience of listening to Williams into a new and equally 'peculiar... speech', with 'its own intrinsic form'.[11]

To begin with, the definition of rhyme as 'repeated insistence', as insistent repetition, is a precise way of evoking one of the formal principles in Williams's work which serves for him, as it obviously does in 'The Desert Music', if not instead of rhyme, then in a way that broadens our conception of what a rhyme is, what a rhyme does: rhyme as the parameter of the 'field'. To take a couple of obvious examples from the beginning of Williams's poem, the repetition of such phrases as 'not to copy nature' and 'only the poem', their repetition with constant minute variation, the variation occurring not only in the combination of words ('only the poem' becoming, for instance, 'Only the counted poem', 'only the made poem'),[12] but in their position on the verse line, is the most readily apparent means by which Williams, as he puts it, 'takes words as he finds them interrelated about him and composes them' (*WCW2*, 54). Williams himself doesn't use the term repetition to describe this aspect of his art, and given that the line is so flexible and the word order so changeable, it would hardly do justice by itself to its peculiarly fluid dynamic. We might better say, in almost Heraclitean fashion, no repetition without variation, no variation without repetition. Particular combinations of acoustic and visual material are more or less repeated, with the degree of more or less determining the dynamic.

Creeley's poem, then, is a study of Williams's prosody, which subjects itself to what it studies. It is a participant study, of marvellous economy. But its use of the word 'insistence' is more than simply a rhyme with Williams's 'insistent', more than just formal repetition with formal variation, since it also alludes to the speech element in Williams's poetics as outlined in *The Wedge*: 'insistence', that is, registers the speech that the poet heard or found 'about him'.[13] This is speech in its particularity, particularity as what was spoken. Insistence therefore recalls the original spoken moment, the original pressure, as it insists upon itself, or in Charles Olson's apt words, 'which wants us to know more about it'.[14] Again, in

---

[11] Ibid.

[12] 'The Desert Music', *WCW2*, 274.

[13] See the Introduction to *The Wedge*, *WCW2*, 54: a poem's 'movement is distinguished in each case by the character of the speech from which it arises.'

[14] Olson, *Collected Prose*, 158.

the essay 'I'm given to write poems', Creeley mentions 'Williams' painfully marked insistence just before the close of "The Desert Music"' (*Essays*, 501).

What Creeley now does is to observe what happens when one such spoken or insistent moment, namely the word 'there' (as in 'because it's there') is varied and repeated: 'There, you say, and I there, and there'. The question Creeley puts here is which *there* is which (or rather, *is there*)? What has become of that original spoken pressure? And he puts it in a way that can make Jacques Derrida's contemporaneous dilations on the relationship of speech to writing—on which has precedence, or takes it—seem prolix. Moreover, out of that questioning another felt pressure emerges: 'and *and* becomes I just so'. Creeley captures here the irony of the fact that we use italics, which are in the end just a different degree of writing, to signify speech, that is, to emphasize what we mean, as for example when Williams writes: 'The arts have a *complex* relation to society... *That* might be a note on current affairs' (*WCW2*, 53). Does the repetition (with marked variation) of that repeated word 'and' constitute a moment of speech within the poem or a moment of what Williams calls 'music', 'dance'? Can Williams have it both ways? Can Creeley? For Creeley's interrogation of Williams's poetics would seem to be, up to a point, a vivid illustration of them. There are other relevant examples within this remarkably dense, yet weightless and translucent poem, such as the relationship of 'one wants' (with its implication of impersonal universality, as in Williams's timeless question 'Why I does one want to write a poem?') to 'I want' (line 15), and of 'I want' to 'and, I I want' (lines 17–18). The poem tracks another more personal level of insistence, which wants to be heard alongside, maybe even over and above, the music that indifferently, formally repeats it (the poem as a 'machine made of words'):[15] the sheer pressure of communication from Creeley to Williams; or as one might say, the want of speech.

5.1.2

I have brought Williams and Creeley together in order to establish again the actual, substantial nature of the relationship between them, the relationship there in the writing. Having done that I now want to distinguish between them, but the difference is not only a matter of the different kinds of particulars the two writers choose to work with, or of the expansiveness of one (Williams) versus the intensiveness of the other (Creeley). The difference obtains first and foremost in Creeley's use of the verse line. It is here first of all that Creeley's departure from Williams is felt, in the use of the line ending, and it represents a whole new stage in the metric of what I am referring to as the American experimental tradition. It is a stage which is as distinct and seems as wholly achieved as, in another tradition, the transition from Joyce to Beckett.

---

[15] *WCW2*, 54.

Some of the most important characteristics of the relationship between ending and meaning in Williams's line are accurately described by the English critic Donald Davie. And I find it useful to cite Davie here precisely because his terse scepticism as regards the so-called measure of American free verse purges his descriptions of any obscure indulgence. Davie is clinical and direct, which makes it easier to see what his account misses out. Speaking of the Pound–Williams tradition as a whole, he acknowledges that the first and most obvious characteristic of their work, since it is 'so much further from counting off syllables to the verse line', consists in its use of 'line endings, as apparent on the printed page and to the listening ear, to compel meaningful inflections'.[16] We can illustrate what this means by looking at a poem like 'The Sparrow', where the rhythm corresponds to the reception, in sequence, of additional items or 'inflections' of meaning (contributions to the overall picture), in the syntax of lucid idiomatic prose. Inflection seems to be the appropriate term, because there is just enough ambiguity at times to make the reader pause and revise, to give a twist to the meaning of the previous line. For example, 'the relief he feels | makes him': Williams's sensual evocation of the ecstatic relief from itching is what *makes* us believe in 'This sparrow', it is the convincing thing about him, but the sensuality is also sexual (another sense of 'made', and another sense of 'itch'), underlining the force with which he then, in the next line, '[cries] out lustily'.[17] Each separate line brings with it a new moment of meaning, which the next line completes or departs from, turns on or from. 'The Sparrow' is a good example because in it Williams seems to be giving us a slightly self-mocking image of the movement of his own voice, 'His voice, | his movements, | his habits—', and above all his *insistence* ('the insistence | of his cheep!').

At the same time, however, it is important not to overemphasize the wit, as Davie calls it, the play of ambiguity and conceit, with which Williams invests the line. The poem is not encumbered as it journeys from line to line. Each small addition to the complex of meaning tends to bring the cadence home, shaping or fulfilling it rather than overloading it. Williams on the whole tends to travel light, and the reader often has a job to keep up. But once you have learnt to keep up, then what Williams does that possibly no other twentieth-century poet writing in English does so well is to imitate the unfolding of an uninhibited attention. And I stress the term uninhibited, because when we consider the great twentieth-century poets of attention, whether Marianne Moore or Wallace Stevens, Ezra Pound or George Oppen, then it is the persistent inhibition of attention which seems to form half their subject matter. It is not simply that for Williams alone in the twentieth century, true to Whitman, nothing is unworthy of attention; more precisely, there is nothing that is worthy of it which does not receive it. It follows

---

[16] Donald Davie, 'After Sedley, After Pound', *The Poet in the Imaginary Museum: Essays of Two Decades*, ed. Barry Alpert (Manchester: Carcanet, 1977), 137–9 (138).
[17] *WCW2*, 291–5 (291–2).

that the bare receiving of it is enough. So when we find Davie claiming that 'the poet [Williams] starts at a point very far from his subject, and talks his way nervously nearer and nearer to it', with the result that 'the poem as a whole is not direct at all, but extremely oblique and circuitous in the way it approaches the subject', it seems that his conclusion is at odds with his analysis.[18] It is the presumption of a separate subject matter, which the form of the poem takes a long time to arrive at, which keeps Davie from hearing what his reading is telling him. He reads it from what he sees as its neglected centre, whereas what it sheds is an equal light, and that surely is the significance of the 'flower' as a 'figure'.[19] Attention finds in anything it touches Williams's rightful subject matter, and simultaneously exposes what Creeley would call the voice or speech of the poet (as Davie consistently notes).

Where does this leave Williams's line ending? Williams's attention is, as I say, an equal light, and the line works democratically, in the sense that all things count or have their say (his sober 'so be it' is the best twentieth-century version of Whitman's all-inclusive 'It shall be you!'). In a corresponding way, the line ending itself is not emphatic: it is neither end-stopped nor does it bear an exceptional semantic burden. Indeed it is perhaps Williams's greatest technical feat to resist, in a great deal of his best verse, the temptation of such a burden, the line as a punchline (he can write punchline poetry too of course, but it is often for deliberately comic or sardonic effect, as in 'He's dead', from 1930).[20] It follows that the line's main rhythmical task is to get the reader to move off lightly, so as to land adroitly on the next one. The deceptively casual nature of this practical equality is caught by Williams in the funny but faintly repellent image of the dog in the Preface to *Paterson*: as repellent as democracy, but also as valid. For the dog is in earnest.

> Sniffing the trees,
> just another dog
> among a lot of dogs. What
> else is there?

> (*Paterson*, 3)

Leaving aside the pun on dog/doc (Williams's profession), the introduction of the word 'What' into the line, insisting on its place, breaking up the rhyme of 'dog' with 'dogs', carrying meaning beyond the full stop, but at the same time not carrying much (refusing the burden of solitary meaning), is equality in action. The line is as important for the unobtrusive way in which it sends the reader forward, on, as for the cadence it contributes by itself. Which is why it is

---

[18] Donald Davie, 'Two Ways out of Whitman', *The Poet in the Imaginary Museum*, 132–6 (133–4).
[19] Ibid.
[20] *WCW1*, 346–8.

nonsense in speaking of Williams to speak of enjambment—as one would speak of it in Milton or Wordsworth. The line is 'just another dog I among a lot of dogs', subordinate to measure. We move *with*, then *off*, and in moving *on* again, in moving *with*, we move with the poem as a whole, as a complex. Complex is a better word than whole, for it suggests a relational activity rather than a static totality. Measure consists not in the poem as a whole ('Waken from a dream, this dream of I the whole poem'),[21] but in the relation of the lines as, at best, a *holistic activity*. In this respect the question of how we get from the word 'What' to the word 'else' is both unexceptional and exemplary.

Now it is this egalitarian poise of Williams's line that Creeley disturbs, and what happens is all the more disturbing because at first it looks as though Creeley may be doing the same sort of thing. At the beginning of an essay in which he claims that Creeley's is 'the one genuinely original verbal music in the English language in the second half of the twentieth century', Robert Hass considers the possibility that Creeley's music has its origins in a mistaken end-stopped reading of Williams.[22] In Williams's poetry the break could be 'so unnatural that it hurried you from one line to the next and, in doing so, imitated the swiftness of perception' (Hass, 391–2). The trick, as we have seen, is not to pause. However, 'whether by cunning or mistake', Creeley read Williams with 'a full pause', and in so doing discovered his own voice (ibid.). As Hass says, it's a good story. But it does not fully explain what Creeley seems to be doing if we look again at the line breaks in 'For W. C. W.':

> There, you say, and
> there, and there,   [line 5]
> and *and* becomes
>
> just so. And
> what one wants is
> what one wants,

The word with which the fourth line of the poems ends ('and'), is repeated twice at the beginning of the sixth line. But it isn't just that the word has been repeated: the repetition raises the possibility that the line ending itself has been *moved* or *transposed* (an effect which is exaggerated by the use of italics). The same thing happens with the word 'there', which marks both the beginning and the ending of the fifth line, but might also be a transposition of the beginning of the fourth line, a transposition which has cost it an upper case *t*. 'And' is transposed again, not for the last time, to line 7. Whereupon 'what' plays against 'wants' to such an extent, imitating the acoustic image and aggravating its meaning, that there is now the possibility of a further transposition (which it might be argued has

[21] *Paterson*, 199.
[22] Robert Hass, 'Creeley: His Metric', in John Wilson (ed.), *Robert Creeley's Life and Work: A Sense of Increment* (Ann Arbor: University of Michigan Press, 1987), 391–2.

already happened, to the tune in fact of three letters). The further play on 'one' and 'wants' (the incomplete pun lingering until it evokes a more general incompleteness, the sense of something *wanting* in *oneself*, which is then mirrored by the paradoxical doubling up of 'one'), intensifies the general sense of positional insecurity, of meaning shifting and regressing.

What I am arguing here is that in Creeley questions of semantic insecurity are inseparable from questions about what one might call the positive identity, the position and disposition, of his terms. You have to look to Gertrude Stein or to late Henry James to find words like these, some of the slightest monosyllables in the language, working under this sort of syntactical pressure. But Stein and James worked primarily with the prose sentence not with the verse line. Creeley builds up pressure within the verse line—to the point where it upsets our sense of what a line is and where it might end. And by attacking the beginning and the ending of the line, he can also attack the middle (the word 'and', for example, is in the middle of line 5, but is it also in the middle of line 6? and if so, is it there in the same way? Is it in the middle of the middle? Or is it simply a stammering repetition of the beginning?). In describing this effect, it hardly seems enough to assert that Creeley pursues the logic of the free verse poem to the point where he is actually interrogating it from within. The notion of his being somewhere *within* already offers the reader too much of a foothold. What happens is more extreme than that—it is more like watching a man who shifts the ground from underneath his feet while he walks upon it. The poem no sooner starts than it stops, no sooner stops than it starts (starting again where it had stopped). Moreover, in keeping with the untethering of the line ending, the automatic assumption that the poem itself will end, which is one of the basic expectations that we bring to the reading of it, begins to feel unfounded. And this is achieved in a poetry whose very smallness seemed to make finishing it a certainty. After all, here we have the shortest poems in the Pound-Williams tradition, the tradition that brought us *The Cantos*, 'A', *Paterson*, and *Maximus*, and yet there is a fundamental sense in which these little works of Robert Creeley's are perhaps the most unfinishable of the lot. Their epic interior stands out all the more ironically because of their sheer diminutiveness on the page, reminding us of Edmund Burke's observation that there is something in smallness that like its opposite massiveness partakes of the infinite and sublime.

Many of Creeley's poems involve practical reflections on their own technique, which then extend their technical preoccupations into metaphysical metaphors. 'The Rhythm' is an obvious example. But more interesting perhaps is 'The Turn', which in its mock-jauntiness, its self-lacerating and disrupted voyeurism, its refusal to let the spectator forget the camera angle, might be the poetic equivalent of a Jean-Luc Godard film—and in its characteristic brevity it would bear out Godard's claim that 'one could make a good film in twenty seconds'.[23] The technique of 'The Turn' might be compared to what has been described as one of Godard's most radical techniques: 'the jump cut, in which a section of a single continuous shot is eliminated and then what remains is spliced together, creating a completely non-naturalistic ellipsis'.[24] One is not speaking here of montage, of rapid cutting *between* scenes, but rather of the elimination of transitional moments within the *same* scene:

> Each way the turn
> twists, to be apprehended:
> now she is
> there, now she
>
> is not, goes, but   [line 5]
> did she, having gone,
> went before
> the eye saw
>
> nothing. The tree
> cannot walk, all its
> going must
> be violence.

(*Poems*, 272)

The 'turn' in this poem is the turning away of the woman, turning the corner, the turn of time ('now'), of opportunity (whose turn is it?) and the turn or crisis in the verse line, which 'twists' into the next one, or is 'apprehended' (stopped?). The poem not only betrays perception here to a cinematic ellipsis (we don't actually see the point at which she 'goes', the narrative 'twist'), it then reviews, so to speak, the perception of the ellipsis. The stop-start nature of the poem's visual drama is also played out in the relationship between line break and punctuation—between what *turns*, that is, and what *stops*. The line both turns and stops: it twists. But given that it turns, and given that the turn is always moving, one line always turning into the next, at what point does it really end, really stop? This has important implications for the rhythm of the poem. For instance, how does the stress we put on the word 'nothing' affect the stress we put or don't put on the word 'tree' (line 9)? Which end is more emphatic (line or sentence)? And what is the relation between end and emphasis?

Creeley's older contemporary George Oppen, working from within the same American free verse tradition, but using the line ending in a markedly different way, makes an interesting criticism of Creeley's verse line:

---

[23] See David A. Cook, *A History of Narrative Film* (1981; New York: W. W. Norton & Company, 1996), 546.

[24] Ibid. 534.

I think that probably a lot of the worst of modern poetry, and it would be true of some quite good poetry, such as Creeley's, uses the line-ending simply as the ending of a line, a kind of syncopation or punctuation. It's a kind of formlessness that lacks any sense of line measure.[25]

Coming from a not unsympathetic fellow poet, this is illuminating because it exemplifies what happens if the reader assumes that the line ending stops, rather than twists and turns—if one assumes that the ending merely punctuates or syncopates rather than generates a tension between the different kinds of ending (grammatical, semantic, metrical, perceptual, mortal); between where it stops and where it might have stopped (where something else stopped). It is not that Creeley doesn't use or mean the line ending as such, it's simply that having used it he automatically relates the use he makes of it to other terminal moments, moments of breaking and starting, within the same poem. The question of the relationship between the stress on 'nothing' and the stress on 'tree' is not superficial, ornamental or immaterial: it is a resonant part of the poem's concern with the relationship between 'going' and 'gone', departure and 'violence'.

> But what we want
> is not what we get.
> What we saw, we think
> we will see again?
>
> We will not. Moving,
> we will
> move, and then
> stop.

By the time we get to the end of this short poem, we have been trained, I think, to see the unsettled and ambiguous nature of that final 'stop'. Not only is the reader thrown or projected forward from it by the sheer habit of momentum, but the word 'stop' itself is echoed in the full stop, with the result that the whole thing fails, minutely, to stop where it says. This is the whole point. As Creeley puts it in the Preface to *The Gold Diggers*: 'The old assumptions of beginning and end—those very neat assertions—have fallen way completely in a place where the only actuality is life, the only end (never realised) death.'[26]

It is well known that Creeley observed the line breaks in his poems when reading them aloud, producing an end-stopped, syncopated effect. His readings were notoriously hazardous affairs, in which the pauses between lines could communicate a rare sense of hesitancy and acute vulnerability. On the other

[25] George Oppen, interview with L. S. Dembo (1968), in L. S. Dembo and Cyrena Pondrom (eds.), *The Contemporary Writer: Interviews with Sixteen Novelists and Poets* (Madison: University of Wisconsin Press 1972), 172–90 (180).

[26] Robert Creeley, *The Gold Diggers* (1954), rpt. in *The Collected Prose of Robert Creeley* (Berkeley and Los Angeles: University of California Press, 1988), 11.

hand, where critics complained that the readings did not work it was because the line breaks seemed to be too pronounced and the syncopation seemed mechanical and exaggerated. Creeley, like Frank O'Hara, tends (in O'Hara's words) to go on his nerve[27]—it is as if for this generation what one might call the sequence of the nerve had replaced the 'musical phrase' with which Pound and the Imagists had, earlier on, replaced the 'sequence of a metronome'.[28] To put the matter more bluntly, it is as if the exposed line ending becomes a metaphor or analogue for the raw nerve—which is why a bad reading of a Creeley poem can seem to harden and to cauterize the most original aspect of his written voice, the mobile impression of exposed affect: the lively trepidation of the form as it penetrates the syllable. Even in the seemingly immediate event of reading, it is writing that peers out, like something glimpsed through flesh. For in the 1960s it was also part of Creeley's virtue to have reversed the traditional priority of speech over writing, and to have done it, not in the name of writing, as in Derrida, but, more paradoxically, in the name of speech. Creeley reverses St Paul's dictum, that 'the letter killeth, but the spirit giveth life': in Creeley it is the letter which preserves both life and spirit, against the presumption of the spirit to speak through the voice.[29]

In 'A Sense of Measure' Creeley contended that 'There can no longer be a significant discussion of the metre of a poem in relation to iambs and like terms because linguistics has offered a much more detailed and sensitive register of this part of a poem's activity' (*Essays*, 487–8). His poetry, he says, seems to him to 'obtain to an unequivocal order', but he resists 'any assumption that that order can be either acknowledged or gained by intellectual assertion, or will, or some like intention to shape language to a purpose which the literal act of writing does not itself discover' (486). There are no grounds for supposing therefore that Creeley prioritized the act of reading aloud over the act of writing, that he would use the reading 'to shape language to a purpose' over and above the one which writing had already revealed. While it would be frivolous to doubt that Creeley was an honest reader, it would be equally naive to see those readings as final infallible renditions of his poems. There is sufficient reason to argue that they should be seen instead as confessed approximations, invocations, whose deliberate regularity can give the audience an insight into that deeper irregularity which is the real heartbeat of his line. 'Such senses of pattern as I would admit are those having to do with a preparatory ritual, and however vague it may sound, I mean simply that character of invocation common to both prayer and children's games' (486). It is difficult to believe that a writer who makes poetry from his distrust of patterns, or as Richard Howard puts it, from his distrust of repetition,

---

[27] O'Hara, 'Personism: A Manifesto', *Collected Poems of Frank O'Hara*, 498–9 (498).

[28] Pound, *Literary Essays*, 3.

[29] Compare Cavell's discussion of the relationship between speech and writing at the end of ch. 1 of *Senses of Walden* (29–35).

would then impose a ritual reading upon it, if that reading were not itself intercessional and preparatory, having the intention to invoke something more, 'some deeper complex of activity' (486).[30]

But we don't need to involve ourselves with Creeley's intentions as a reader of his poems in order to see that it is consistent with his more theoretical statements about poetry that what Hass would call the unnatural syncopation of his readings, which many critics note, accentuates the gap between the voice on the page and the voice, let's say, in the air. Still, it is surprising that a critic such as Altieri, who sees Creeley as a kind of Cartesian dualist, fails to see the tension between reading and measure as a further manifestation of that same purported dualism—the dualism of the poem as spoken and the poem as written, the voice of the one haunting the inevitable rituals of the other. This is one of the things at issue in one of Creeley's best known poems, 'I Keep to Myself Such Measures . . . ', which takes up the theme of childlike or prayer-like invocation: 'to I hopefully come back to II where it cannot' (*Poems*, 297). The words on the page are compared to 'rocks', stone 'markers', that 'daily . . . I accumulate position' (ibid.). But they are also like the breadcrumbs left behind by Hansel and Gretel. The poem seems to invite comparison with the hermetic Symbolist tradition explicitly inaugurated by Mallarmé, whose rhymes were also invocatory, the voice consciously abstracting itself from the song, by way of the song.[31]

One final point, however, which bears on what follows. Creeley brings to the now familiar Symbolist trope a concern with self which isn't Symbolist at all. As Marcel Raymond writes of Symbolism, and of Mallarmé in particular: 'The poet must avoid imposing a single, indisputably certain meaning at the outset; he needs "elbow room" in his expression, a "blank space" around his words, which will enable them to radiate fully; it is when their meaning is at first uncertain that they assume that strange, unfamiliar and miraculous quality.'[32] Whereas Symbolism aspires to the incantation (as Raymond puts it) of absolute meaning, Creeley tries to invoke the comparatively slight fact of his own conditional and fluctuating *presence*. He doesn't want to describe or dramatize himself ('I am not at all interested in describing anything'), to adopt a visceral confessional presence.[33] 'I keep to myself', he writes, averting the confessional. Yet there is something tantalizingly suppliant about the poem, about its whole posture, in which secrecy and exposure are functions of each other. In other words, if the Symbolists played hide-and-seek with meaning, Creeley plays it with his own existence. Both versions of this magical game require, like a child that learns to

---

[30] Richard Howard, 'Robert Creeley: "I Begin Where I Can and End When I See the Whole Thing Returning"', in Wilson (ed.), *Creeley's Life and Work*, 187–98. In 'The Writer's Situation' (1969), Creeley referred to Howard as 'perhaps the best' of modern poetry critics (*Essays*, 522).

[31] Compare the earlier poem, 'After Mallarmé', where the 'mind' has 'stones', if not rocks (*Poems*, 250).

[32] Marcel Raymond, *From Baudelaire to Surrealism* (1933; London: Peter Owen, 1957), 27.

[33] *Essays*, 488.

play under its parents' watchful eye, an imaginary audience, the presumed indulgence of a possibly invisible reader (listener or onlooker). Which implies that Creeley depends on other people out there, not readers as such (he has been careful to deny that),[34] but the active recollection of the intimate situation itself, to tolerate and bear witness to his reserved insistence—his comings and goings. 'I want to give witness not to the thought of myself—that specious concept of identity—but, rather, to what I am as simple agency, a thing evidently alive by virtue of such activity. I want, as Charles Olson says, to come into the world. Measure, then, is my testament' (*Essays*, 488). It is remarkable just how many times Creeley comes and goes in the course of these three sentences.

5.2 THE NEW AMERICAN NERVOUSNESS: RIESMAN AND HEIDEGGER

In the second section of this chapter I want to change direction, with the aim now of recovering the latent social and political intelligence that is at work in this seemingly most apolitical of modern poets. As I will try to show, contrary to appearances, the poetry is in fact inflected (literally *in-formed*—formed from within) by this intelligence. It might even be said to meet this intelligence with a secret political vision. In order to establish this I shall first expand the terms of what has so far been a mainly literary account of how Creeley's poetry works. I shall begin by summarizing the argument of one of the most persuasive accounts we have of twentieth-century American middle-class anxiety: David Riesman's *The Lonely Crowd*.[35] *The Lonely Crowd* is apposite here for several reasons: it offers us, first, a theory of anxiety within the context of modern political malaise; secondly, there are important links, as we shall see, between Riesman and Arendt, not least their Tocquevillean theoretical orientation; finally, Riesman was Creeley's immediate contemporary as a writer, and in most respects was writing about Creeley's time and place: educated white 'post-political' America. In order to clarify further what is so peculiarly American about Riesman's conception of anxiety, I shall compare it with Martin Heidegger's in some ways antithetical conception—thereby consolidating the connection with Arendt. I shall then look at one of Creeley's strongest early poems in the light of Riesman and Heidegger, and consider in what ways the questions it raises are prototypical. Before concluding I shall say something about Creeley's own more explicit, and for the most part unremarkable, comments on politics, before I try, finally, to describe once again what I see as the rather more pointed social

---

[34] See the interview 'The Art of Poetry' (1968), rpt. in *A Sense of Measure* (London: Calder and Boyars, 1972), 89.

[35] David Riesman, with Nathan Glazer and Reuel Denney, *The Lonely Crowd: A Study of the Changing American Character*, abridged edn. (1950; New Haven: Yale University Press, 1961).

and political awareness worked out in the poetry itself. To begin with, however, I must give space to Riesman and Heidegger.

5.2.1

Riesman's reputation has waned considerably since the early 1950s when he published *The Lonely Crowd*:[36] this was, first, because of his notorious contention that America at mid-century was 'near Condorcet's dream of the conquest of poverty';[37] secondly, because of his preoccupation with the middle classes; thirdly, because of his dogged liberalism; and fourthly because of his theory of individual autonomy. To take this last point first: the problem with the notion of autonomy, which Riesman adopted from the work of Erich Fromm, was that it was essentially a notion of psychological autonomy. Riesman had little constructive to say about the material conditions of autonomy, about hard politics and hard economics, and this tended to throw his assumptions about the 'conquest of poverty' and his liberal acceptance of middle-class ascendancy into ugly relief. Nevertheless, there is a darker and less disabused side to Riesman's work. Lacking the *ressentiment* of the reluctant bourgeois intellectual, he was an outstanding critical analyst of the American middle-class, and he had a rare theoretical acumen. Riesman introduced the notion of autonomy to try and solve his brilliant account of middle-class anxiety—but it is the question of anxiety which will concern us here.

In *The Lonely Crowd: A Study of the Changing American Character*, Riesman argues that there have been three broad stages in the history of American social character. The first stage was the period of what he calls 'tradition-direction'. The tradition-directed character scarcely thought of himself as an individual at all. Instead of singling him out, his personality was at best an index of his identity with, and place within, the tribal or feudal group. Within such a monolithic orthodox society, ritual and religion helped to supply people's deeper emotional and imaginative needs while they got on with the day-to-day business of living. Society was organized with centrifugal force, pulling and integrating from a hierarchical core. Eccentrics would be integrated as shamans or magicians, but for most ordinary people fear of public shame would guarantee conformity. A person who was made to feel shamed rationalized his transgression from the point of view of the group: there was no separate or heterodox space in which he could have learned to formulate his own point of view.

[36] *The Lonely Crowd* had an impact in the 1950s beyond the social sciences. Creeley himself harked back to it as recently as 1991, in the lecture 'Some Senses of the Commonplace', but in a way that suggests ruminations on the title rather than a reading of the book—always the snag of a catchy title! It also turns up in Frank O'Hara's poem 'John Button Birthday'.

[37] David Riesman, 'The Saving Remnant: An Examination of Character Structure' (1949), *Individualism Reconsidered* (New York: The Free Press, 1954), 99–120 (99).

The next stage in Riesman's history of social character is one in which tradition-direction gives way to inner-direction. As Riesman sees it, the inner-directed social character dates from around the Renaissance and Reformation and has, as we might expect, a great deal in common with the Protestant ethical type described by Max Weber. Inner-directed society is 'characterized by increased personal mobility, by a rapid accumulation of capital (teamed with devastating technological shifts), and by an almost constant *expansion*: intensive expansion in the production of goods and people, and extensive expansion in exploration, colonization, and imperialism' (*Lonely Crowd*, 14). The inner-directed character thrives on the capitalist-imperialist dynamic of society to such a degree that individual enterprise emerges as the heroic paradigm of social conformity. Competition is literally the rule. The most successful people are those 'who can manage to live socially without strict and self-evident tradition-direction' (ibid.). In Riesman's most compelling images of the inner-directed character, he sees him as being guided by a 'psychological gyroscope', or by a 'pilot [which] is not quite automatic' (16). He is 'on course', so to speak, with no clear destination. Teleology is replaced by 'experiments in self-mastery' (42).

It would be easy to object to the simplifications involved in Riesman's character types, but that would be to mistake them for the analysis which they are intended to facilitate: like Max Weber's 'ideal types', they are 'constructions necessary for analytical work' (243). With this qualification in mind they can be brought to bear on literature as well as sociology. To take a particularly obvious example, the nineteenth-century American Adam was haunted by his dramatic emergence from the tradition-directed world. The canonical works of the nineteenth-century American literature syllabus provide excellent evidence of this: one need only think of the struggle for autonomy in Frederick Douglass or Huck Finn, or most powerfully of all, perhaps, in Nathaniel Hawthorne's *The Scarlet Letter*, where the inner-directed author confronts imaginatively, through an essentially inner-directed heroine—a nineteenth-century woman having to make her way in a seventeenth-century world—the strengths and limitations of tradition-direction: the austerely integral community and its forbidding boundaries of 'shame'.

But it is the third and most ambiguous stage in Riesman's examination of social character which has the greatest bearing on my argument. This is the stage of other-direction, in which the need for self-mastery that was typical of the inner-directed has given way to an overwhelming need for approval from others. '*What is common to all the other-directed people is that their contemporaries are the source of direction for the individual—either those known to him or those with whom he is indirectly acquainted, through friends and through the mass media*' (21; emphasis in the original). The other-directed person is determined through and through by an 'exceptional sensitivity to the actions and wishes of others' (22). In other words, if the inner-directed person is guided or steadied by the gyroscope that keeps him upright, the other-directed person is guided by radar

(25). As with tradition-direction and inner-direction, the social mindset of other-direction is handed down from parent to child. The emotional key to it is anxiety: 'what the other-directed child does "learn" from his parents is anxiety—the emotional tuning appropriate to his other-directed adjustment' (51).[38]

Riesman is endlessly ambivalent about other-direction. The problem with it is that it has by definition no self-reliant moral core: you live in a state of constant anxiety, driven hither and thither by a craven desire for approval. As a result the public world of the other-directed is the advertising world, the PR world, where success depends on how you package and present yourself. But even here the wish to stand out as such is 'muted' by the pressures of peer-group opinion (118). And since human aggression and competitiveness cannot be phased out, we get the scorpion-like circuit of what Riesman calls 'antagonistic cooperation'; 'marginal differentiation' in the theatre of consumption. A world of false modesties. The gist of Riesman's analysis is contained in the Sartre-like claim that 'The problem for people in America today is other people' (p. xxi). But the problem could also be seen as a challenge. When the second edition of *The Lonely Crowd* was published Riesman observed that he had not taken the trouble to spell out what seems genuinely valuable about other-direction: its openness, mobility and willingness to change, its social sensitivity and tolerance, its symbiotic mutuality. The difficulty here is that what makes the other-directed person valuable is, from a different angle, the same thing that makes him problematic: 'The other-directed person wants to be loved rather than esteemed; he wants not

---

[38] One clue to the ongoing value of Riesman's conception of other-direction was the success of Christopher Lasch's *The Culture of Narcissism*, which despite Lasch's brief acknowledgement of it seemed to be essentially a polemical update of Riesman's critique. 'The new narcissist is haunted not by guilt but by anxiety', wrote Lasch, *The Culture of Narcissism: American Life in An Age of Diminishing Expectations* (1979; New York: W. W. Norton, 1991), p. xvi. 'Narcissism', he explained, 'represents the psychological dimension of...dependence. Notwithstanding his occasional illusions of omnipotence the narcissist depends on others to validate his self-esteem. He cannot live without an admiring audience...For the narcissist, the world is a mirror, whereas the rugged individualist saw it as an empty wilderness to be shaped to his own design' (10). Elsewhere Lasch suggests that Riesman *mistook* what the latter called 'the bland surface of American sociability' (along with other critics of the forties and fifties, such as Margaret Mead and Erich Fromm), for the *deeper reality* (64). This is not a very generous or imaginative reading. What Riesman struggles with in what is much the best part of *The Lonely Crowd*, the first two-thirds of it, is the way in which surface and depth interpenetrate and simulate each other: so that it becomes very difficult to retain an authentic critical hold on depth; to know what depth is when you've got it or are in it. The generally acknowledged inadequacy of Riesman's notion of 'autonomy' only points up the lasting excellence of what precedes it. While Riesman clearly began his analysis of other-direction on a hostile critical footing (the structure of the book alone makes that clear), in the actual process of writing he was unable to evaluate it conclusively or to surmount it. It is this ambivalence which conveys the sense of the writer locked into his historical moment; a thoughtful man trying to get a grip. For a more rounded and disinterested assessment of Riesman, see Richard H. Pells, *The Liberal Mind in a Conservative Age: American Intellectuals in the 1940s and 1950s* (New York: Harper & Row, 1985). Pells puts Riesman's thought in the context of the work of his contemporaries, the likes of William Whyte, Richard Hofstadter, Dwight Macdonald, and Daniel Bell, but he has a keen eye too for what singles it out.

to gull or impress, let alone oppress, others but, in the current phrase, to relate to them; he seeks less a snobbish status in the eyes of others than assurance of being emotionally in tune with them. He lives in a glass house, not behind lace or velvet curtains' (p. xx). Riesman gives guarded expression here to the utopian potential in the democratic psyche of other-direction. No one uses anybody else: everyone loves and relates: together we abjure the instrumental aspect of human relationships. But the image is loaded with irony. For the admirable qualities here—love, relationship, being emotionally in tune—are, first of all, qualities we associate with the intimate sphere rather than with the thorny question of power in a democracy; while, to compound the irony, such a one-sided image of intimate relations discreetly ignores the more instrumental (power-ridden) side of sexual love. It is at this point that Riesman's analysis comes into its own. For it is precisely the continuance of this increasingly bourgeois assumption—the assumption of a working boundary between public and private life—that enables him to make one of his most searching criticisms. What happens, Riesman asks, when the public world begins to conduct itself like an extension of the intimate one? What happens then to public affairs? For Riesman the moment is fraught with deception. Power, in all its decisiveness, ceases to face up to itself in just those areas—business, politics—where in reality it will not go away, where one way or another the decision gets made. (Of course something similar happens in the intimate sphere; but the ramifications are supposedly more contained—more *intimate...*)

Given the inescapability of this question of power it was perhaps inevitable that the bulk of Riesman's critical analysis dwelt on the larger social world of other-directed America: on its educational, political, and economic life, rather than its intimate private life. But Riesman is not only concerned with the wider social and political world. He is equally anxious about the fate of his once private world, and he is deeply pessimistic about what becomes of the authentic experience of intimacy, given that it is the prototype of that 'superficial intimacy' which he now finds characteristic of society at large. In other words, if we can be superficially intimate with people we do not know, how shall we keep this new guise of intimacy from affecting our relationships with people we supposedly do? 'While the game of post office is old, the breakdown of privacy for reasonably serious love-making is new... Whereas etiquette built barriers between people, socialized exchange of consumer taste requires that privacy either be given up, or be kept, like a liberal theologian's God, in some interstices of one's nature' (76). Unlike Hannah Arendt at the end of the decade, Riesman is not concerned to give a historical explanation for the erosion of the distinction between the public and the private, or for its replacement by the more obscure distinction between the intimate and the social. Lacking Arendt's philosophical and historical sweep, Riesman is more interested in characterizing the situation than accounting for it. What particularly interests him, and what his analysis of other-direction is all about, is the emergence of a mutant form of intimacy, 'exceptional sensitivity', within society at large. This is not intimacy proper, but looks like it, and must, given time, change its very nature. At the same time, it is true to say that there is in Riesman, as there is in Arendt, the classical belief (which both writers share with Tocqueville) that an almost Manichaean public-private distinction could be essential to the viable working of democracy. From this point of view the anxiety which Riesman sees as the characteristic emotional climate of modern America is the anxiety of a people which has come adrift of its agonistic democratic moorings and which, without first knowing itself, gets more like itself every day.

It is into this context that I would like to insert the work of Robert Creeley, which I see as being an attempt to reconstitute the intimate or private world; an attempt to recover something of its utopian potential. The problem for Creeley, however, an aspect of the problem confronted by Riesman, is that privacy cannot simply exist by itself, independently of the public or larger social world: rather, it exists in relation, or in contradistinction, to the world it is defined, or defines itself, against. My argument is, consequently—and the consequence is paradox-ical—that Creeley tends to project a utopian polity onto an exclusive and antis-ocial intimacy, while at the same time the anxiety that is characteristic of society at large, the society Creeley thinks to exclude, seeps back into his poetry, where it then provides the key to its distinctive form. In other words, the shape and measure of Creeley's poetry, the hallmark of a writer who is frequently dismissed as whimsical or ethereal, and who is even seen by his admirers as politically indifferent, is, I am arguing, profoundly and problematically social.

5.2.2

Now before I turn back to Creeley, I would like to clarify what is so historically significant, and in the first instance so American, about the anxiety with which Riesman is concerned. To do this I want to compare Riesman's discussion of anxiety with Martin Heidegger's classic discussion of it in *Being and Time*, from 1927. This is probably the most influential philosophical explanation of the origin and significance of anxiety in its twentieth-century European cast. But a comparison of the two works shows the extent to which Riesman's discussion, unlike Heidegger's, takes for granted an imperilled democratic context. Democ-racy is its given, its shaky ground. At the same time, there is something in Heidegger's severe attempt to purge privacy of all corrupting influence that will help us to measure the authentic private tendency in Creeley.

Like Riesman, Heidegger is very much concerned with people as a problem. For both, 'the world is always the one that I share with Others': 'By "Others" we do not mean everyone else but me—those over against whom the "I" stands out. They are rather those from whom, for the most part, one does *not* distinguish oneself—those among whom one is too' (*Being and Time*, 154–5). For Heideg-ger, our everyday way of going about our business in the world includes within it, as a kind of unconscious foreknowledge, a working apprehension of what Arendt will call the 'web of human relationships'. All our activities touch other people's lives: but that hardly says enough, because, in fact, the nature of the contact helps to shape the activity. At some point, however, active *relationship-to* tends to sink into passive *identification-with*. Thus for Heidegger the most problematical others in our lives are not the people we define ourselves against, but the ones we unconsciously identify with—those from whom we fail to mark ourselves off. The world is a *with-world* (*Mitwelt*), and within this with-world, Heidegger sets out to distinguish what he calls the *authentic* (*eigentlich*) way of being there with Others from the inauthentic. For Heidegger the inauthentic is the insidious realm in which one fails to move beyond this too given fact of the Other (for it cannot be disputed that *'they are there too, and there with it'*),[39] to an encounter with oneself—*an encounter which can only be had by oneself.*

One of the key terms, and at any rate the determinant emotion, in Heidegger's solution to the burden of the Other is his conception of anxiety. And this is where the comparison with Riesman is most revealing. For Riesman, anxiety is occasioned, first and foremost, by a lack of self-mastery in our relationship to others. Anxiety occurs because of others, but it is not anxiety about others (how are they doing?), but about ourselves as we need to be seen by others (how do they think we are doing?). The anxious radar of other-direction is concerned with how we are received, with whether we are on the same wavelength. Hence its endlessly sensitive obsession with signs, indications that we seem to be loved. The sense of authenticity is out of our hands. For Heidegger, on the other hand, far from being 'a societal emotion, the product of an overly sensitized relationship to others, '"real" anxiety is rare' and one of the things that can still distinguish us from Others (*Being and Time*, 234). It is an alternative to that 'concernful solicitude' for the Other which Heidegger sees as luring one away from the real problem of being here oneself: 'the kind of knowing-oneself which is essential and closest, demands that one become acquainted with oneself' (161). Anxiety occurs only where we have started on such an acquaintance. As Heidegger puts it, 'anxiety individualizes' (235).[40] So, whereas Riesman sees anxiety as a problem, the soft underbelly of an emasculated democracy, Heidegger, on the contrary, vindicates it: *anxiety is an authentic alternative to democracy.*

It is something broadly akin to what Riesman calls other-direction which structures what Heidegger sees as our inauthentic way of Being-in-the-world. In our ordinary, everyday absorption in the world, in our self-forgetful concern with it, we are already absorbed in Being-with-one-another, and in this 'everyday Being-with-one-another' we stand, without realizing it, 'in *subjection* [*Botmässig-keit*] to Others' (*Being and Time*, 164). The telltale form of this subjection is what Heidegger calls *das Man*, one, the 'they', the insidious 'dictatorship' of the impersonal average (*der Durchschnitt*), whose conduits are public space and

[39] *Being and Time*, 154.
[40] *'Angst . . . vereinzelt'* (*Sein und Zeit*, 190–1).

public opinion (ibid.). We get an interesting example of what Heidegger means by this when he makes an oblique attack on the institutionalized concern of the then nascent welfare state: i.e. on solicitude for the Other (*Fürsorge*) as a 'factical social arrangement' (157–8). Predictably, Heidegger's attack on the public sphere (*die Öffentlichkeit*) is less ambivalent than Riesman's, precisely because for Riesman the existence of an alternative to public life, authentic privacy, is also questionable: the contamination of one has led, democratically one might say, to the contamination of the other. Heidegger, however, steps right out of the fallen public world into his very own kind of intimacy: in anxiety, he writes, 'Dasein finds itself *face to face* with the "nothing" of the possible impossibility of its existence', with the 'constant *threat* arising' out of the 'indefinite certainty of death' (310). Thus for Heidegger the anxiety which is really anxiety-unto-death is the means of sanctioning individual verity. It has nothing to do with society. For Riesman, on the contrary, anxiety is social, a *democratic anxiety*, in a society from which the stronger sense of self, still apparent in Heidegger's notion of authentic *Dasein*, disappears.

Given the scarcity of concrete social reference in *Being and Time* it comes as a shock to realize that Heidegger actually sees the inauthentic public realm as broadly identifiable with the emergent welfare state. In Germany, leftist social theorists like Habermas, trying to lift the Heideggerian cloud after the Second World War, will more or less begin by analysing the terms of this equation.[41] On the American side, where radical political thinking was in the process of recoiling from Stalin rather than from Hitler, and so from the Popular Front line of the 1930s, Riesman's substitution of his three character types for 'the conventional Marxist categories of feudalism, industrial capitalism, and socialism', enabled him, as Richard Pells argues, to address the psychological make-up of what America had got *instead* of socialism: the mindset, or psyche, of an intangible equality, which blandly existed *inside* consumer capitalism.[42] 'Thus Riesman was almost alone among post-war intellectuals in translating the doctrine of pluralism—the alleged source of America's democratic ideals and pragmatic temperament—into an explanation of modern political passivity' (Pells, 244). Within twelve years of its publication both Habermas and Arendt were quoting Riesman in their classic studies of the public sphere. Whatever their differences,

[41] See esp. Jürgen Habermas, *The Structural Transformation of the Public Sphere* (1962). Habermas does not mention Heidegger at all in this book, but given the historical circumstances, and the legacy of Heidegger's relationship with National Socialism, which, under Hitler and Goebbels, gutted what was left of the democratic public sphere, reverting instead to a dismal version of what Habermas calls 'representative publicness'—the projection of power on the obliging crowd—it is a pregnant silence. In his later work, Habermas's contempt is explicit: 'Heidegger's critical judgements on "*das Man*," on the dictatorship of the public realm and the impotence of the private sphere, on technocracy and mass civilization, are without any originality whatsoever, because they belong to a repertoire of opinions typical of a certain generation of German mandarins' (*Philosophical Discourse of Modernity*, 140).

[42] Pells, *The Liberal Mind in a Conservative Age*, 240.

all three writers took the untidy circumstances of an unfulfilled or self-contradictory democracy, a democracy that in Adorno's terms was not identical with its concept, as *their* circumstances.[43]

5.3 'POEM FOR D. H. LAWRENCE'

Let me try to summarize the significance of the foregoing discussion. One way of understanding Robert Creeley's writing is to see it as an attempt to get back to a state of substantial intimacy: *to return*—'to "return" not to oneself as some egocentric centre, but to experience oneself as *in* the world, thus, through this agency or fact we call, variously, "poetry"' (*Essays*, 498). Sharing the reservations of both Riesman and Heidegger about the modern public world, Creeley is looking for a less lonely and forbidding version of Heideggerian privacy, less anxious perhaps, and more expressly dialogical; in a word more intimate. For Creeley the authentic human realm is the intimate one. Nevertheless, the historical situation he is stuck with is the one described by Riesman. As Riesman sees it, contemporary intimacy knows no bounds: with its values transplanted into the larger public world intimacy is always potentially hollow at the core. So, given that Creeley's language and subject matter are so insistently intimate, how does the problem of other-direction manifest itself in his poetry? Where is Creeley's society, and what form does it take?

To begin with, it will help to look at Creeley at what seems to be his most explicitly Heideggerian.

Heidegger writes in *Being and Time* that, '"The Others" whom one thus designates [as Others] in order to cover up the fact of one's belonging to them essentially oneself, are those who proximally and for the most part *"are there"* in everyday Being-with-one-another' (164). Heidegger calls this problem of deceptive existential space *Abständigkeit* (translated into ugly English as 'distantiality'—whereas in the German the sense of standing off or aloof is much starker, and sounds less technical), and it is fundamental to his whole conception of it that he could also conceive of a lived alternative, a realm of authentic selfhood.

The earliest poem in which Creeley explicitly confronts the question of the Other is 'Poem for D. H. Lawrence', from 1948 (*Poems*, 7–8). The confrontation here is markedly abstract, its style closer perhaps to Wallace Stevens

---

[43] After Arendt moved to the United States, she and Riesman were inevitably drawn together as politically engaged Jewish intellectuals, and in 1948 collaborated on a proposal to be submitted to the United Nations on Palestine. Riesman also commented in detail on a draft manuscript of part of *The Origins of Totalitarianism*, and he wanted Arendt to write a chapter of what would become *The Lonely Crowd*. There were differences, of course, quite apart from the obvious one that Arendt's overall achievement is immeasurably greater. For one thing, Arendt made it clear to Riesman that she saw herself as a radical, not as a liberal. See Young-Bruehl, *Hannah Arendt: For Love of the World*, 230, 251–2, 255–6.

than to Williams.[44] There are two key features to my discussion of it, which can be classified first of all as matters of form and content, and this form/content division corresponds, I think, to a technical problem within the poem itself, which Creeley only resolved later on. 'Poem for D. H. Lawrence' begins with three lines in italics, poised quite deliberately between epigraph and beginning:

> *I would begin by explaining*
> *that by reason of being*
> *I am and no other.*

We might begin here by observing that 'being' is an anagram of 'begin', a pun which Heidegger himself might have appreciated.[45] In Creeley's poem, however, the Heideggerian realm of authentic selfhood, where the self communes with being from the beginning, and not with *das Man* (the Others, the 'they'), is illusory, and its illusory nature is already ironized by the wish to explain—for to whom does one explain but to others?

As the poem proceeds, the problems of authenticity and *Abständigkeit* prove real enough to Creeley, but the issue of authenticity turns instead, in accordance with the ascendancy of other-direction, on the question of authentic relationship. Creeley explores a central aspect of this question of relationship, focusing on the way in which any distance that one puts between self and others is undone by one's self-othering, so to speak, in self-consciousness. Which is to say that within the everyday environment of being-with-one-another, the self's attempt to keep its distance is undone by the relational nature of self-consciousness. And it is undone not just because I compulsively relate the distance I've achieved back to my point of departure in being-with-one-another, but more importantly, because in the divisive inner space of self-consciousness, I feel that I am both myself—I—and *another*. I am, to put it crudely, both the self that is conscious (the self as consciousness) and the self of which I am conscious. In other words, in becoming conscious of myself, and in thus relating to myself, I introduce an element of the other into what strives to be a single-minded non-relational 'I'.[46] Creeley captures this problem of the other in the image of 'the figure drawn by the window':

---

[44] Perhaps the poem it most obviously recalls, in the way it recapitulates and varies, composes and discomposes, a limited number of elements, for example the state of the light, the time of day, movement and stillness, picturing as it were an 'indecipherable cause' (Creeley's 'not to know how they came there'), with the items harmonized stanza by stanza, is Stevens's 'Thirteen Ways of Looking at a Blackbird' (*Collected Poems*, 92–5).

[45] The pun doesn't work in German, unfortunately, though Heidegger is already playing, from the outset, with the proximity of *Sinn* (meaning) and *Sein* (being).

[46] The now classic formulation of this idea is of course to be found in Jacques Lacan's paper, 'The mirror stage as formative of the function of the I' (1949), *Écrits*, trans. Alan Sheridan (New York: Norton, 1977), 1–7.

Always the self returns to
self-consciousness, seeing
the figure drawn by the window
by its own hand, standing
alone and unwanted by others.

Creeley presents the reader with an image of self-consciousness which, *purely in that it is self-conscious*, seems to come apart in the mind. From the moment it is self-conscious, the self is not one integral self, but (leaving aside the question of whether it ever was), an onion-like layering of half-transparent selves, a Russian doll made up of insidious reflections, each one problematizing the almost-identical claims of the other. '[S]tanding I alone' suggests *not wanting others*, what Riesman calls inner-direction, but 'unwanted by others' suggests something else: other-direction-despite-itself, the masquerade of what Heidegger calls standing off or aloof (*Abständigkeit*), posing, however, as Heideggerian man. We seem to have an image of embattled self-reliance. A more appropriate way of describing the effect, however, given the language in which the poem is couched, is to say that it actually unpicks the pretensions of self-reliance from inside what has always been its greatest sanctuary: philosophical abstraction. It is here perhaps above all that the poem invites comparison with the grand parodic manner of Wallace Stevens.

I would argue that when Creeley refers to self-consciousness he refers to something more diffuse than post-Cartesian philosophical self-consciousness. The larger contextual referent is society, not philosophy. In Descartes, self-consciousness is a sign that the mind is on the right track: it denotes the successful turning inward of reflecting consciousness. As Charles Taylor puts it: 'what I now meet is myself: I achieve a clarity and fulness of self-presence that was lacking before.'[47] We might say that in Descartes self-consciousness is inner-directed: it is the gyroscope steadily lighting on itself. But Creeley's self-consciousness is radically different, and emerges in the interstices between 'I', let us say, and 'myself'; interstices to which Descartes, as Nietzsche observed, was epistemologically oblivious. In Creeley, that is, the idea of what Taylor calls a self that is fully present to itself already posits a space *within the self* where, as I have argued, the problematics of other-direction can take hold. In the twentieth century the self that is fully present to itself is not just itself: it cannot take itself for granted in that way, and indeed its being present to itself renders it, in our modern other-directed world, present to itself as an other. From Descartes until at least the end of the nineteenth century self-consciousness is a corollary of philosophical certainty. But for Creeley self-consciousness is, on the contrary, a source of anxiety, and this makes Creeley typical of what has happened to the world inside our heads by the middle of the twentieth century: every recess of it has been

[47] Taylor, *Sources of the Self*, 157.

invaded. The 'problem of other people' has been internalized and the line which divides internal from external has become almost impossible to call.

The question of authenticity, for Creeley, as I've said, is no longer a question of how to be authentically on one's own, as it is in Heidegger: the question is rather one of an authentic relationship to others, authentic other-direction so to speak. 'I am given as a man to work with what is most intimate to me—these senses of relationship among people. I think, for myself at least, the world is most evident and most intense in these relationships.'[48] This gives an interesting twist to the status of self-consciousness. Given the ubiquitousness in Creeley's writing of the relationship to others—'these senses of relationship among people'—*self-consciousness emerges as the archetypal form of inauthentic relationship*: a 'specious concept of identity', which conceals from itself its divided and relational nature. Self-presence comes between me and the world. It is a form of obstructive self-othering, which must be warded off like a ghost. 'I want to give witness not to the thought of myself—that specious concept of identity—but, rather, to what I am as simple agency, a thing evidently alive by virtue of such activity. I want, as Charles Olson says, to come into the world.' The reference to Olson is instructive. Indeed, for Olson also, self-consciousness, giving witness to the thought of oneself, is the hubris of Western man. The antidote is to renew one's relationship to the working world of objects in all their particularity. By reactivating particularity in its particularity, self-consciousness is humbled out of sight. If we can usefully speak of Olson as other-directed, extrovert even, we must say that his principal others are things—and even Olson's people, in their role as others, come principally under the sign of things: people are objects, in the best sense of the word.[49]

For Creeley, on the other hand, the others by and to whom he is directed, are always people, first and foremost. And this accounts for one of the most striking differences between the two men's work, which is that in spite of the luminous tendency out and away from the self that we register in Olson's writing, the ego remains, scraped clean of its self-absorption, more or less intact. The gyroscope, as it were, is still spinning and standing. Even at his most troubled and moving, as in the magnificent 'Maximus, to himself', there is still something confidently inner-directed about the first person from which Olson means to venture out: it is 'I' with which he starts; 'I' who 'was slow'; I who 'stood estranged'; 'I' who 'note[s] in others'; 'I' who 'look[s] out' and 'know[s] the quarters I of the weather'; and 'I' who finally 'speak[s]' of 'undone business'.[50] It brings to mind Leland's (Joseph Cotton's) comment to the young Charles Foster Kane (Orson Welles):

[48] Creeley, *A Sense of Measure*, 100.
[49] See Olson, 'Projective Verse': 'For a man is himself an object, whatever he may take to be his advantages' (*Collected Prose*, 247).
[50] Charles Olson, *The Maximus Poems*, ed. George F. Butterick (Berkeley and Los Angeles: University of California Press, 1983), 56–7.

'that's the second sentence you've started with "I" ...'. Despite the fact that 'the single | is not easily | known', the trouble, the uneasiness, has not got inside, so as to disturb the very bearings of the verse form itself (*Maximus Poems*, 56–7). In Creeley's most typical poetry, on the contrary, the problem of the other reaches all the way back inside, and gives it its distinctive hesitant voice.

And yet one of the most striking things about 'Poem for D. H. Lawrence', as compared to Creeley's later work, is that it is so *formally untypical*: it is as formally untypical as its subject matter is untypically explicit. This is certainly inseparable from the fact that it first appeared in 1948, very early on in the Creeley oeuvre. However, before I spell out what is meant here by formally untypical, we should observe its truly typical features. And what is typical above all is the use of repetition with constant minute variation:

> In the beginning was this self,
> perhaps, without the figure,
> without the consciousness of self
> or figure or evening. In the
> beginning was this self only,
> alone and unwanted by others.
>
> In the beginning was that and this
> is different, is changed and how
> it is changed is not known but felt.
> It is felt by the self and the self
> is feeling, is changed by feeling,
> but not known, is changed, is felt.

The idea of an original point in time, a 'beginning', where the self flourished feelingly and unself-consciously, without worrying about or being worried by others, and without worrying about itself (i.e. without seeing itself as a 'figure'), is rendered more and more elusive by the repetition of the word 'beginning'. On the one hand the poem seems to be saying, in true Emersonian fashion, that if there ever was such a moment of primary, unknown—i.e. unself-conscious— feeling, then we can only have access to it in so far as it occurs again, i.e. whenever we feel something new ('changed', 'different'). On the other hand, is it possible to feel anything at all anymore without the intrusion of socially induced self-conscious expectations about what we are supposed to feel—about what that feeling should be like: will it feel primary and unself-conscious? will it feel 'different'? The contradiction here is that the whole idea of difference would seem to imply a degree of rather self-conscious knowing, as against unself-conscious feeling. 'Felt' is a sort of pun on 'self', on that Lawrentian ethos of the self which identifies it with its most unself-conscious feeling ('felt by the self and the self | is feeling'): but this pun, if we can call it that, is also deeply sceptical. The very conflation of the words as signifiers emphasizes the artificiality of fusing their far from identical concepts. Likewise the repetition of the phrase 'in the beginning', like the repetition of 'remembering' in stanza 5, and the host of repetitions throughout the poem, always varying what they repeat (or what they remember), makes the positive identification of a primordial moment—the last occasion at which one was not self-conscious—all the more unlikely.

In this respect then the formal properties of the poem are typical of the mature Creeley we had been looking at earlier and comparing with Williams. That is: *particular combinations of acoustic and visual material are more or less repeated, with the degree of more or less determining the dynamic.* The conspicuous difference, however, is that in 'Poem for D. H. Lawrence' the fundamental compositional unit is the stanza rather than the line. Although Creeley does play with some of the line endings ('and how' is a nice example), there is a marked pause at the end of each stanza, a period actually, of a different weight and duration altogether from the pause at the end of the line, and each time this happens the turbulence engendered by the dense play of repetition and variation is temporarily resolved. The net effect of this is to give the poem a formal stability, of stanzas beginning and ending, which is largely irrelevant to, and therefore overrides, what we can begin to speak of separately as the poem's subject matter. It follows that this part of the poem's form, the relationship between the rhythm, the stanza and the line, is neither an expression nor an extension of the self-consciousness the poem is effectively 'about'. Form and content have split.

In Creeley's finest poetry the form of the poem is always answerable to the content, and it has no answer, so to speak, that is independent of the content. What this means is that if the subject matter of the poem is the relationship between self and others, or the relationship, more accurately, between a self-consciously self-othering self and others, then the very form of the poem will be an expression, line by line, of the selfsame relationship. And the key to this is in the fully realized diffidence of the Creeley line ending, where whatever is disappointed by it (the Creeley line too, like Joyce's pier, is a disappointed bridge), or elicited by it, or set into motion by it, even if it's nothing at all, is not rounded off or contained by the integral harmonies of the adjacent line or surrounding stanza. The Creeley line has no confidence in itself—it badly wants to be liked, to make sense. It wants the person to whom it is addressed to understand why it hesitates and stops when it does—or why it *seems* to hesitate and stop when it doesn't. But what I have called the person to whom it is addressed cannot simply be referred to as the reader. Creeley himself has said: 'I don't think that "possible readers" are really the context in which poetry is written.'[51] But having said that, he went on to say, in the same interview, that his sense, or *intimation*, of relationship to others *is* the material, nevertheless, of which his poetry is made (*Sense of Measure*, 100). So it seems as though we are

---

[51] *Sense of Measure*, 89.

speaking of an addressee with whom the poetry is always already intimate from the moment of its articulation: that is, the poetry is not conceived from some solitary vantage point and then addressed to the intimate sphere; it is written in and out of intimacy and in each of its hesitations testifies to it. Other-direction is internal to its form.

Part of what I am arguing then is that Creeley's poetry from the 1950s onwards was immersed in a quest to find a form more adequate to its thematic preoccupations: once this form was achieved, its subject matter became less separable and distinct. And although Creeley was, as 'Lawrence' indicates, just as equipped to be a philosophical poet as Stevens, his thinking was increasingly disciplined by the specific moment of the poem, and had to be thought with the vocabulary at hand—in other words with *any* vocabulary; whereas Stevens's thinking, even at its most anarchic, depends (as Creeley's 'Lawrence' also does) upon the privileged vocabulary of the philosophers—the traditional, recogniz-able terms. Furthermore, the difference between the two poets in this respect corresponds directly to the significance of speech in Creeley's work: the fluid movement in and out of spoken idiom, the sense of poems occurring alongside or incorporating dialogue, just as film unfolds, visually, alongside dialogue. And now we can see that there is something different even about the materials from which 'Lawrence' is made, quite apart from the formal fact of how it uses line and stanza: I refer to the pointed absence of registered speech or spoken register (which renders ironical that initial vow to explain). The subsequent access of speech in Creeley's work, and the simultaneous resistance to privileged philo-sophical idiom, correspond to a further consolidation of the shift I mentioned earlier—away from the narrow philosophical referent toward the broader social referent.

5.4 LANGUAGE, POLITICS, COMMONPLACES

It is interesting to note Creeley's use of the word 'world'.[52] It enables him to imply a much larger world than any his poetry will ever deal with directly. Poetry experiences the intimate world, and it experiences the larger world only by way of the intimate one. Before I make a final attempt to describe this experience, I want to pause over some of Creeley's more explicit comments about politics, poetry, and language generally.

Creeley's general attitude to public life did not change fundamentally over the years. In 1969, with the election of Richard Nixon marking the end of that hopeful fickle half-progressive, spectacularly violent decade, the poet had this to say about the writer's situation—and it's worth quoting him at length:

[52] See 'The World', *Poems*, 328–9.

Possibly political agency is regaining an active contest. But really the advanced younger people of this moment are, if anything, *post*-political, just that the available political agencies seem to them so bankrupt. The militant part of the black community might be the one active revolutionary group still intent on political possibilities. I know that many of the young showed an active commitment to Eugene McCarthy's leadership in the circumstances of the 1968 election, but I question, even with reluctance, that that had initially to do with political occasion or possibility. More, I think, they wanted renewal of a kind of *presence*, in public life, possessed of a demonstrable integrity, even one apart from the usual conditions of political activity. They wanted someone to be literally there—and this was, curiously, not the case either with Kennedy or Nixon. Both were finally part of a system the young have every reason to distrust, as, God knows, the elders might equally.

Obviously the disaster of the national commitment to the war in Vietnam is the largest 'political' counter of the past few years, and it served to energize political agencies in every sense. But again, I'm very intrigued by the hippie culture, so to speak, and its decisively apolitical character. It's as though a very deep shift in the conception of human relations and use of the environment were taking place—and indeed I believe very much that it is. We've come to that time when, as Williams said, we must either change our 'wishes' or perish. I don't feel that present insistence on ecological problems is simply a new game. We have literally to change our minds. In this respect, drugs in the culture have really two, among other, clear possibilities: (1) either to reveal a oneness in all manifestations of life-form of whatever order and thus change the mind by that revelation (certainly the most useful information to be gained from taking LSD); or (2) to kill anxiety, to lull intuitive perception of inherent peril, to simply get out of the 'world' one is actually in—and in this respect the elders are as committed to this use of chemical agency as any of the young.

In any case, I don't see that art and politics, or that order of present experience involved with the post-political, should all be kept separate. I don't see how they can be. One can't, perhaps, entirely respect an art committed to propagandizing or to a use of life not clearly initiated in its own activity. But when men and women are outraged by political malfeasance, it's hardly likely that their art will not make that quite clear.

As far as my own art is concerned—I've not been able to write directly to a purpose of political involvement. It's not given me in my own nature to be able to do so, but I hope I've made clear where I stood nonetheless.[53]

Much of the terminology and most of the emphasis are typical of Creeley: the key words such as 'activity', 'agency', 'possibility', 'occasion', 'presence', 'human relations', 'insistence', 'involvement', 'nature' as it is 'given'. Most typically of all, no one word is permitted to nominate or signify the immediate experiential complex: it's as if the substantial experience of life is always moving between words, the immediate is always in the process of mutating. The opening is a good example: 'Possibly political agency is regaining an active contest.' Conditions and nuances ripple through the sentence. Creeley not only refuses to say that politics, as agency, is an activity, as he understands the term, he refuses to confine the meaning of activity to one term (the adjective 'active')—the burden is projected

---

[53] 'The Writer's Situation', *Essays*, 517–18.

forward onto 'contest', in such a way, however, that the noun is not so much enabled to mean as *activated, complicated*—i.e. brought into complex relationship. The language is mimetic, and intimates what it means not through its separate words but through their combined activity. The same thing happens further on, when Creeley refers to an art committed 'to a use of life not clearly initiated in its own activity': the precise meaning of this takes some pinning down. Of course we may attempt to paraphrase, along the lines perhaps of: an art which is not actively at one with life itself—but this would still leave the central concept, activity, unsolved. The qualifications that Creeley somehow injects into the definitive moment take too consistent a form to be dismissed as mere casual vagueness. Their imprecision seems meditated, practised, and deliberate. The reader can see Creeley as coy, or can see him as practising, as I have said, such a refinement of the scope of speech and consciousness that he becomes, at his best, the minimalistic heir of Henry James and Gertrude Stein.

There are other things worth pointing out in the passage: first, the almost Arendtian conception of the public sphere as, ideally, the realm of appearances, *presences* ('they wanted renewal of a kind of *presence*, in public life'), as distinct from the futile realm of presidential power-politics (Kennedy and Nixon were 'curiously' not 'there'); secondly, the conviction as to the existence of an intelligent post-political consensus, and thirdly, the parallel awareness of the delusory potential of the counter-culture: 'to kill anxiety ... to simply get out of the "world" one is actually in'.[54] The reference to anxiety needs, I hope, little further comment.

Allowing for a gap of twenty years, and yet at the same time bearing in mind that Creeley came of age politically just before *The Lonely Crowd* appeared, the poet's conception of a post-political counter-culture might be related, with some qualifications, to Riesman's description of other-directed political 'indifferents'; educated, middle-class, and at once 'cynical' and 'tolerant'. According to Riesman,

This apathy cuts two ways. It tends to deprive them of the capacity for enthusiasm and for genuine political involvement, but it also helps protect them from many of the fairy tales about politics that have mobilized people in the past for political adventures. And while the tradition-directed person can sometimes be roused, in his inexperience, into indignation, and is even sometimes hungry for political indoctrination ... the modern indifferent has built up a fairly high and often fairly useful immunity to politics—though not to cynical attacks on 'politics.' (*Lonely Crowd*, 171)

What Riesman could not have foreseen was that during the 1960s cynicism would be mitigated by a new communitarianism and a revived ontology of nature, the metaphysical ecology of the 'hippie-culture', which harked back to Emerson and Thoreau, and was also in tune with the later Heidegger. Was this

---

[54] Compare Lasch on how, during the 1960s, 'radical politics filled empty lives, provided a sense of meaning and purpose' (*Culture of Narcissism*, 7).

something altogether new and distinct—or had cynicism reached a new pitch of tolerance in which the feeling of impotence had taken root and blossomed? As regards the political process, Riesman's contention that the circles of withdrawal are self-confirming seems valid: 'It is not only that he withdraws emotional allegiance from a political scene that strikes him as too complex and too unmanageable—it strikes him so in part precisely because he has withdrawn' (*Lonely Crowd*, 183).[55]

Nevertheless, Creeley's position—positioning might in fact be a better word—in this 1969 interview is more interestingly stated, more involved and involving, than a much later but otherwise comparable statement that he made in 1991, when he was reflecting on the first Gulf War. In the transcription of this lecture, entitled 'Some Senses of the Commonplace', it is the punning use of commonplace which is used, as world was used earlier, to mediate the vexed relationship between public and private, social and intimate. Thus: 'Commonplaces are truly—I mean, we're *in* a common place. It's unimaginable that humans shouldn't insistently be in common places ... Because there's almost no variation of significant kind in the way that people do seem to need people.'[56] The commonplace is the *Mitwelt* of Heideggerian phenomenology, that unmappable habitation of half-forgotten half-determinate interrelationship: a togetherness that conditions us even when we are spatially apart. 'The relationships in fact are as dense as they could be ... Everything's related' ('Commonplace', 89). But clearly the commonplace is also the commonplace of banality—a media-saturated global village in which everything can be communicated except lived experience:

There's then the question of whether we have our President in common at such juncture. Well, it isn't that he is *not* in common, so to speak; but he is not evident in either the information or the experience that seems to be the case. And if he *is* evident, he is not evident the way that we—speaking again for myself—can find a common place with. It isn't that I can't be in the same room with him, but I can't find a place to be the way that he presumes the world to be, or thinks of the world as a place to act. I don't have questions at all, necessarily, about his sincerity, his commitment, even his intelligence. But I have absolute *confusion* in reaction to the presumption of the world he feels is the necessary case. (90)

---

[55] Compare Thomas Pynchon, *The Crying of Lot 49* (1967; London: Picador, 1979), 86: 'For here were God knew how many citizens, deliberately choosing not to communicate by US Mail. It was not an act of treason, nor possibly even of defiance. But it was a calculated withdrawal, from the life of the Republic, from its machinery. Whatever else was being denied them out of hate, indifference to the power of their vote, loopholes, simple ignorance, this withdrawal was their own, unpublicized, private.' Perhaps nobody expressed this attitude of 'withdrawal' more powerfully in the 1960s than Pynchon, in whom the anarchism and disillusionment of Thoreau on the one hand, and the Beats on the other, is somehow combined with the puerile comedy of a Robert Crumb cartoon and a Heideggerian feeling for human authenticity as a lonely being-toward-death.

[56] Robert Creeley, 'Some Senses of the Commonplace', in Tom Clark, *Robert Creeley and the Genius of the American Common Place: Together With the Poet's Own 'Autobiography'* (New York: New Directions, 1993), 83–116 (89).

Creeley's method here is of course ironical, stretching the common to include what is uncommon: the mind of the President, the (first) Gulf War, and so on. But there are problems too with these sorts of language games. For a start there is the hunch that for a poet like Creeley the game is too easy; the suspicion that by now the irony is so introverted and genteel it amounts to what Benjamin calls 'indolence of the heart'.

In addition there is a failure to trouble the dominant terms by bringing in conspicuous and intractable detail: as for instance in 'Poem for D. H. Lawrence' where to remember the figure by the window is, quite suddenly, 'to see the thing like money' (line 27). Or we might contrast an appropriate moment from George Oppen's 'Of Being Numerous', where a US helicopter in Vietnam signifies:

> An event as ordinary
> As a President.
>
> A plume of smoke, visible at a distance
> In which people burn.

> (*NCP*, 173)

Oppen incorporates just enough detail into the lines, and just enough imagination, to put an irresolvable critical pressure on words like 'event' (is a President an event in the way that a bomb is?), 'ordinary' (which then activates the pun: what exactly is an ordinary *precedent*?), 'plume' (wings of fire?), 'people', and, above all, perhaps, on the phrase 'visible at a distance', in which there is equal scope for aesthetics ('Objectivist'), binoculars (military), television, and total detachment.

Creeley ends the lecture with some warily accommodating remarks about language:

What's interesting in our rhetorical habits—I mean, listen to the President of the United States or anyone else—is that the language is intensely common ... It endlessly comes back to clichés, to idioms, to banality, triteness, triviality, and hackneyed phrasing; because, frankly, that is the most valuable conduit for information that we possess ... [T]he nouns need a grounding element. And they are taken basically from commonly experienced idioms that are the most commonplace of the language situation. And then you wrench and break the syntax, e.g. in primarily the verb structure; or you keep the ground localized in the idiom, you keep that the commonplace, and you wrench the syntax to keep the bonding apparent, to keep the thing moving. ('Commonplace', 115–16)

This invocation of a common American language, which recalls Whitman's great Preface to *Leaves of Grass*, where poets, presidents, 'or anyone else' could meet, equally, as Whitman would say, does seem to describe some of the characteristics of the public language of the then President, George Bush (Senior). Certainly in the following quotation, where the President is responding to a question on education, he patently grounds himself in a thicket of hackneyed phrases, and yet brings a startling life to them by, as Creeley says, wrenching the syntax and keeping the thing moving:

Well, I'm going to kick that one right into the end zone of the Secretary of Education. But, yes, we have all—he travels a great deal, goes abroad. We have a lot of people in the department that does that. We're having an international—this is not as much education as dealing with the environment—a big international conference coming up. And we get it all the time—exchanges of ideas. But I think we've got—we set out there—and I want to give credit to your Governor McWherter and to your former Governor Lamar Alexander—we've gotten great ideas for a national goals program from—in this country—from the governors who were responding to, maybe, the principal of your high school for heaven's sake.[57]

Thus isolated there is a peculiar poetry in a speech like this, with its stark jerks and incomplete figures, and the remarkable way it interrupts itself without ever once establishing a line. It shatters what Pound called the fortress of syntax, but it does not reduce it to rubble: there is a communicative thrust there, a push, in Olson's words, that wants to mobilize the fragments; and, in so far as it wants to, does—even if it isn't clear where they arrive. The President communicates the desire to communicate, as well as an appealing recognition of the fact that messages don't always get through. This is most apparent in the final sentence; in the swing from the humble qualifier, 'maybe', to the thumping invocation of the heavens. One has the sense that Bush Senior, inarticulate as he was, had some intimation of what it was like for the person trying to understand him. There is some baffled empathy there.[58]

By contrast, from a rhetorical point of view, Creeley himself, in his lecture on the commonplace, says nothing as complicated as the passage just quoted. Where Bush disperses meaning, and resists the nominal, Creeley does exactly the opposite: he gathers meaning into the nominal ('the commonplace') and depends on irony to offset stasis. Significantly, this is also the opposite of his style in the 1960s interview, where he himself was much too wary, too doubtful, to allow any one word, least of all a noun, to take on the burden of nominating either the political context itself or the range of possible political activities. Creeley's allusion to Bush's rhetoric is deliberately kind (a Whitman-like extension of the common touch), but perhaps a little too kind. In the passage just quoted not only does the President seem to be more alive to the inadequacy of the

---

[57] Maureen Dowd, 'The Language Thing', *New York Times Magazine*, 29 July 1990, 32; qtd. in David Merwin, *The President of the United States* (Hemel Hempstead: Harvester, 1993), 234.

[58] See Richard Rose, *The Postmodern President: George Bush Meets the World*, 2nd edn. (Chatham, NJ: Chatham House Publishers, Inc., 1991), 309–10: Rose wrote that Bush Senior's 'fractured half sentences and opaque metaphors leave unclear what his own views are'. Without discounting the tactical value of obfuscation, he interpreted this as largely indicative of the President's uncertainty. Noting that his language had been interpreted as 'reflecting an underlying psychological need for approval and a deep aversion to political controversy', Rose claimed that 'the President places himself above politics, which is about advancing controversial values'. In short, the man Rose called the 'postmodern President' was exactly what Riesman would have called an other-directed President.

communicative commonplace, he becomes by virtue of that—at least for a fleeting moment—the more interesting poet.

5.5 DIFFIDENCE

In the concluding pages of this chapter I want to go back to the poetry and to bring into focus the main point I made earlier, namely that Creeley tends to project a utopian polity onto an antisocial intimacy, but that this ideal is contradicted by the actual form of the poetry, which bears witness to an anxiety that is unthinkable *without* society; an anxiety which is social (or societal) at heart. I can best demonstrate what I mean by this by taking one of Creeley's most typical poems of the 1960s, 'To Bobbie':

> What can occur
> invests the weather, also,
> but the trees, again,
> are in bloom.
>
> The day will not
> be less than that. I
> am writing to you,
> wishing to be rid of
>
> these confusions. You
> have so largely
> let me continue, not
> as indulgence but
>
> then to say I
> have said, and will,
> anything is so
> hard, at this moment.
>
> In my mind, as
> ever, you occur. Your
> face is such
> delight, I can
>
> see the lines there
> as the finest
> mark of ourselves.
> Your skin at moments
>
> is translucent. I
> want to make love
> to you, now. The world
> is the trees, you,

> I cannot change it,
> the weather
> occurs, the mind
> is not its only witness.
>
> (*Poems*, 337)

Some broad remarks to begin with. The poem is an attempt to re-establish relationship, to create a secure emotional environment, to bring desire into the fold, to recall a satisfying intimacy. It wants to open the 'world' up by shrinking it down. The poet tells himself that the woman is as natural as the weather—like it she 'occurs' and recurs. As in all love poetry, time and desire play together, with language mimicking each treacherous 'moment'. Thus: 'I I want to make love I to you, now': the poem uses a comma, which may or may not be casual, inadvertent (what would inadvertent mean here? As if desire were deliberate . . .), to dramatize what seems like the gap ('these confusions') between the wish to make love and the 'now' of its consummation. 'How soon is now?' as the song puts it. There is a cumulative rapport between 'I' and 'you' or 'your', words which alternately punctuate the poem and carry as much rhythmic weight as the line endings with which they sometimes coincide. And this rapport echoes the joke about doubling in the poem's title (Bobbie being not only the name of Creeley's wife but another version of his own name). There are some superb figurative moments, of the kind that language seems to achieve all the more effectively when it appears to eschew figures altogether. For example:

> Your
> face is such
> delight, I can
>
> see the lines there

The poem is now written in the 'fine' wrinkles on the woman's brow: a nice conceit on what Sir Philip Sidney calls the Aristotelian 'fore-conceit'. Sweetest of all, however, is the ending of the poem, where the art consists in the unobtrusive transition from one obvious referent for 'its', the 'weather', to another, less obvious, the 'mind'. Creeley manages to say in seven gnomic words what Merleau-Ponty spent a lifetime saying: 'the mind I is not its only witness'.

In sum, then, the poem exhibits extraordinary craft and control. It is concerned with the dialectic of absence and presence that is part of a loving relationship. The poem doesn't hesitate to refer its own need for reassurance to a childlike dependence on a 'largely' mothering figure ('You I have so largely I let me continue')—whose bountiful presence is large enough (has largesse enough) to free the poet from the mental trap of solipsism.

The release from solipsism into intimacy is the closest thing we shall find in Creeley to a political ideal: he would like to base his politics on intimacy. But on an intimacy which has been purged of everything Heidegger would have laid at the door of *das Man*: i.e. its market-driven, televised, banalized public image. But purged also of what Heidegger did not grasp: the endless inhibitions of a spineless tortuous self-consciousness. This is something Riesman implicitly apprehends in the structure of other-direction, but he does not fully explicate it. Creeley, however, is one of its minute witnesses. And to undo self-consciousness by way of itself seems to be the prevailing effort of his poems, to get back once again to an uninhibited intimacy. But while intimacy remains the nearest thing we have to a political ideal in Creeley, he refuses to claim a politics for it. Intimacy goes hand in hand with political apostasy. But political apostasy is, as we have seen, double-edged. The evocation and interrogation of intimacy, which provides, as I say, the occasion of each poem, gradually betrays the fact that intimacy embeds itself in a society whose relationship to it is both inimical and parasitical. Intimacy—which had been by definition a refuge from society—is now the very manner of society, which both copies and confuses it.

So it is that Creeley's quest for intimacy is pursued at every turn by the dark side of political apostasy, by society in the coldest broadest sense, which tracks the poet's pursuit of intimacy in the least articulate, and ironically the most original feature of his poems: their line endings. To see this we have to consider what Creeley's line endings are doing within the almost Winnicottian loving-and-holding environment of poems like 'To Bobbie', with their delicate recollection of not fully replenished emotional security. The reassurance for which insecurity searches in the intimate realm bears witness line by line to another more comprehensive insecurity. The insecurity of the lover and the insecurity of society coincide. One can be temporarily abated, the other cannot: one is specific but the other is systemic. Insecurity not only affects the poet's breathing, it is what he breathes and how he breathes it: it is that voice of his which he recognizes when he enters the field of composition. For it is invariably at the diffident moment, when there is no exceptional reason for it, that Creeley hears the line end. In 'To Bobbie' the rhythmic tension accrues word by word rather than line by line: but it accrues word by word *because* of the line ending: it is the line ending which both establishes and epitomizes the fate of every word. And while this rhythmic tension is carefully adapted to the subject matter of the poem, and thoroughly integral to it, it also audibly, visibly exceeds it. There is a temptation to say that this excessive diffidence is what the poetry is really about—but *about* was never the right word. It is, so to speak, the thing one is left with, and it bears witness to something besides the more or less modernist art forms to which the commentators usually refer (jazz syncopation, montage, abstract painting, etc.).

Creeley takes with him into the intimate sphere the memory of a society that has been infantilized by a half-hearted promise of equality: a promise whose only fruit, as Riesman argues, has been psychological rather than material (a socialism of the mind—a socialism of manners). His line endings invite the reading voice (including his own) to coincide with the page, in the knowledge that there is nothing necessary about the coincidence—to the point in fact where the poem actually forms its rhythm out of trepidation. To put it more starkly: the line has, in Riesman's terms, no strong sense of inner-direction; it *looks* inner-directed, but its whole orientation is towards an other—an other it may never reach. Because it can never be sure of the other, it has to gamble on communication and assent. Hence the diffidence. And it is in the line ending that this diffidence is most keenly felt. For even diffidence develops a rhythm.

6

'Ferocious Mumbling in Public':
George Oppen

In the first chapter of this book I looked at how the nature of seeing, in Tocqueville, expresses the Frenchman's own alienation from the democratic conditions he meant to understand. I then examined how the visual faculty in Whitman, which otherwise threatens to be no less dominant, and might have turned out to be no less problematic, is complicated by posture and embodiment. I then argued that this complexity embodies or expresses a democratic disposition or relation. In this final chapter I look at George Oppen, for whom seeing figures almost as prominently as it does in Whitman, only to show that in this case too vision is complicated by something else, something more. The claim is that in Oppen's poetry too in the end the democratic situation is shared rather than merely contemplated—which is to say shared rather than alienated. In the concluding section I consider Oppen in the light of two of his most remarkable contemporaries, a novelist and a poet—Richard Wright and Muriel Rukeyser.

6.1 ANOTHER LOOK AT OPPEN AND HEIDEGGER

> If I were to describe reality as I found it, I would have to include my arm.
> Bertrand Russell[1]

For all its brevity, the opening poem of George Oppen's prismatic first collection, *Discrete Series* (1934), is exquisitely modulated: one seemingly digressive sentence in which by the final line everything—literally—has come into focus. Although it was written when he was only 21 years old, it is witness to a contradiction that would remain central to his poetry for the duration of his remarkable career:

> The knowledge not of sorrow, you were
>   saying, but of boredom,
> Is—aside from reading speaking
>   smoking—

---

[1] Qtd. in George Oppen, 'The Mind's Own Place' (1963), rpt. in *Selected Prose, Daybooks, and Papers*, ed. Stephen Cope (Berkeley and Los Angeles: University of California Press, 2007), 30–1.

> Of what, Maude Blessingbourne it was,
>   wished to know when, having risen,
> 'approached the window as if to see
>   what really was going on';
> And saw rain falling, in the distance
>   more slowly;
> The road clear from her past the window-
>   glass—
> Of the world, weather-swept, with which
>   one shares the century.

> (*NCP*, 5)

Readers familiar with the range of Oppen's poetry cannot fail to recognize here a number of talismanic words and themes: 'knowledge'; the deftly isolated 'Is'; 'really'; 'distance'; 'clear'; 'window'; 'world'; 'swept'; 'one shares'. The poem presents a snapshot of bourgeois curiosity, as instanced by Henry James's character Maude Blessingbourne, impelled across the sitting room by her Socratic 'wish to know': we would like 'to see what really [is] going on'—even if our surroundings are not altogether conducive, are apt to hide more than they reveal. The emphasis on *seeing* seems tentative at first (the slight pause at 'see', where the line breaks or bends), but is then reinforced by the peculiar emphasis on 'really' (this last being the pause of the master, Henry James, which for aficionados may seem to vibrate a little more because Oppen has minutely altered, as if in the style of James himself, James's syntax).[2] The importance of seeing is underlined further by the fact that Maude 'saw rain falling' and by the two references to 'window'. The mediation of the window-glass between self and world, subject and object, or in Emersonian terms, me and not-me, makes, as James also made, a point which is more readily associated with Georg Lukács's Marxist interpretation of Kantian thought. In Kant, as we saw in Chapter 4, the breach between subject and object is both symbolized and yet reassuringly contained by the purer inaccessibility of the thing-in-itself. Lukács contends that this Kantian settlement is a supreme example of the bourgeois reification and mystification of knowledge.[3] The window seems transparent and yet it is a screen. Maude's

---

[2] See Henry James, 'The Story in It', *Daisy Miller, Pandora, The Patagonia and Other Tales* (New York: Charles Scribner's Sons, 1909), 409–35 (410): 'She . . . approached the window as if to see what was really going on.'

[3] Lukács's celebrated analysis of Kantian epistemology is to be found in the essay 'Reification and the Consciousness of the Proletariat', particularly the middle section, 'The Antinomies of Bourgeois Thought', in *History and Class Consciousness: Studies in Marxist Dialectics*, trans. Rodney Livingstone (1968; London: Merlin Press, 1974), 110–49. Fredric Jameson summarizes it very well: 'For Lukács, however, this dilemma of classical philosophy, to which Kant's system is a monument, derives from an even more fundamental, prephilosophical attitude toward the world which is ultimately socio-economic in character: namely, from the tendency of the middle classes to understand our relationship to external objects (and consequently our *knowledge* of those objects) in static and contemplative fashion. It is as though our primary relationship to the things of the

alienation from the world she 'wished to know' is emphasized by the ambiguous relationship between the natural world—Emerson's nature—as represented by 'rain falling'; and the man-made world hinted at by 'road' and 'swept'. For the sake of the leisured bourgeois's aesthetic pleasure and innocence, labour is reassuringly hidden from its work: there is not a person in sight.

In contradistinction to this intense concentration on seeing, which dominates the poem, there is, just briefly, right at the start, an invocation of speech: 'you were saying'; followed by a passing reference to 'speaking'; followed finally by the quotation marks around the quotation from James, which could just make it seem, for a moment, in this drawing-room context, as though the quoted words might be part of what 'you were saying'. Although this is significant, as we shall see, and might seem to support Michael Davidson's claim, in the Introduction to his handsome edition of the poems, that Oppen 'places his faith in parts of speech and speech acts' (p. xxxii), the pre-eminence of seeing in the poem remains, I think, indisputable. Nor can it be said to be untypical. So that the other half of Davidson's argument, that 'Oppen's aesthetics is decidedly nonvisual', is harder to accept (ibid.). On the contrary, that aesthetic experience expresses itself visually is a touchstone of his poetry from beginning to end. In fact it may be doubted whether any twentieth-century English-language poet has more vigorously or eloquently espoused the importance of looking and seeing. The superb 'Guest Room', from *This in Which* (1965), is a good example: 'The virtue of the mind ‖ Is that emotion ‖ Which causes I To see' (*NCP*, 107),[4] Oppen writes, before presenting us with an instance of exactly what he means by that:

> Of the dawn
> Over Frisco
> Lighting the large hills
> And the very small coves
> At their feet, and we

outside world were not one of making or use, but rather that of a motionless gaze, in a moment of time suspended, across a gap which it subsequently becomes impossible for thought to bridge. The dilemma of the thing-in-itself becomes, then, a kind of optical illusion or false problem, a kind of distorted reflection of this initially immobile situation which is the privileged moment of middle-class knowledge' (*Marxism and Form*, 185). Where this chapter departs from Lukács and Jameson, as will become more obvious as it unfolds, is in respect of their restrictedly Marxist conception of what constitutes societal *motion*, a *mobile situation*, knowing as a shared human process or action.

[4] Oppen echoes these lines and spells out their meaning in his interview with L. S. Dembo: 'The mind is capable not only of thinking but has an emotional root that forces it to look, to think, to see. The most tremendous and compelling emotion we possess is the one that forces us to look, to know, if we can, to see. The difference between just the neuro-sensitivity of the eye and the act of seeing is one over which we have no control. It is a tremendous emotional response, which fills us with the experience we describe as seeing, not with the experience of some twitching nerves in the eyeball. It can only be interpreted emotionally, and those who lack it I despair of' (Interview with Dembo, *Contemporary Writer*, 186). Dembo would later describe Oppen as 'a poet who is committed to his eyes'. L. S. Dembo, 'The Existential World of George Oppen', *Iowa Review*, 3/1 (1972), 64–91 (69).

Perched in the dawn wind
Of that coast like leaves
Of the most recent weed—And yet the things

That happen! Signs,
Promises—we took it
As sign, as promise

Still for nothing wavered,
Nothing begged or was unreal, the thing
Happening, filling our eyesight
Out to the horizon—I remember the sky
And the moving sea.

(109–10)

A word, first of all, about the form, for a passage like this also illustrates what Oppen understands by 'the objectification of the poem, the making an object of the poem'.[5] It is poetry composed of repeated sounds, of the small subtle echoes which paper it together. To take just the first verse paragraph: there is 'of' and 'over'; 'Frisco' and 'coves'; 'dawn' and 'wind'; 'feet' and 'we'; 'coast' and 'most'; 'coves', 'leaves', and 'recent weed'. The phrasing is simple, but it is also adhesive and synthetic. Its simplicities are refined and matched beyond the broad range of banality; their music is careful and confined. Nor should we make the mistake of supposing that the poetry eschews all play, for it balances wittily 'large' and 'small', 'feet' and 'perched', 'leaves' and 'weed'. After this literary intricacy, there is something Wordsworthian about the exclamatory ordinariness of, 'And yet the things || That happen!' And certainly it would be true to say that Oppen is no less an ordinary language philosopher than the great English Romantic poet. But nor is he any less a visual poet either—and like Wordsworth he often invokes the power of the eye by revolving negatively around it:

Tho the world
Is the obvious, the seen
And unforeseeable,
That which one cannot
Not see

Which the first eyes
Saw—

('Of Being Numerous',
NCP, 185)

As 'Guest Room' reaches its climax, the 'thing' that 'happen[s]', as Oppen puts it, fills the eyesight, right out to the Emersonian horizon, remaining as a memory of sky and 'moving sea'. Its fullness (as in Wordsworth again) is also a kind of blankness—vision at the very limit.

---

[5] Interview with Dembo, 173.

The Wordsworthian image of the promontory, of seeing as a promontory, occurs again, differently, in 'World, World—':

> Failure, worse failure, nothing seen
> From prominence,
> Too much seen in the ditch.
>
> Those who will not look
> Tho they feel on their skins
> Are not pierced;
>
> One cannot count them
> Tho they are present.

(NCP, 159)

Just as in 'Guest Room', Oppen again takes seeing as the proof of deeper feeling. Those who are 'not pierced', who do not look, will themselves *not pierce*, will themselves *not be seen*: they will be merely 'present'.

The image of seeing in the ditch recurs in the later sequence 'Route':

> Cars on the highway filled with speech,
> People talk, they talk to each other;
>
> Imagine a man in the ditch,
> The wheels of the overturned wreck
> Still spinning—
>
> I don't mean he despairs, I mean if he does not
> He sees in the manner of poetry

(NCP, 198)

Which in turn echoes 'Of Being Numerous':

> One must not come to feel that he has a thousand threads
>   in his hands,
> He must somehow see the one thing;
> This is the level of art

(NCP, 180)

Nevertheless, the passage from 'Route' does also set the faculty of speech alongside this vision of authentic or responsive seeing: 'Cars on the highway filled with speech | People talk, they talk to each other'. We are back at that dramatic juxtaposition, which is such a striking feature of the first poem of *Discrete Series*: speech and seeing in apparent opposition, as the supposed clarities of seeing come up against the opacities of language. 'Words cannot be wholly transparent. And that is the "heartlessness" of words.'[6] Indeed, the passage I've just quoted

---

[6] 'Route', *NCP*, 194.

from 'Of Being Numerous', with its vindication of focused seeing, begins with the magnificent understatement: 'It is difficult now to speak of poetry' (*NCP*, 180). This conflict—for the poetry expresses it as a conflict, as for instance in the line, 'I *speak* of tourists. But what we *see* is there'[7]—is responsible for the uniquely discursive, ruminative, sometimes downright argumentative tone of Oppen's work after the twenty-five-year interruption of his poetic career that was to follow the publication of *Discrete Series*. The conflict is in the lack of synchrony between two ways of knowing or relating to the world—which as it were butt up against each other. If his were simply a visual aesthetic or a dialogical aesthetic, or just graduated from one to the other, the poetry would not have that grave but almost quizzical sense of someone trying to communicate against the odds which makes it sound, as Pound had said, like nobody else (*NCP*, 4). In the mature poetry, the two aesthetic impulses exist side-by-side, baffling and provoking each other, vexing, as Wordsworth says, their own creation.

I want now to go back to *Discrete Series* and that opening poem. For in the light of what has just been said, it is a remarkable feature of the book that after those first direct references to familiar speech in the book's opening lines, 'you were saying' and 'aside from . . . speaking', the words *speak, speech, say, talk, tell,* and their variants, which more or less establish the tone of Oppen's greatest poetry, from the 1960s on, have no part in it. (Such terms are something quite different from the poet's use of direct quotation, of which there are several more instances in *Discrete Series*. I am referring to the way in which the poetry draws attention not only to what is said but also to the act of speaking.) In fact, in spite of the ironic picture of Maude Blessingbourne going to the window, it is the visual attitude that dominates the book, albeit in a richly complicated sense. To clarify what I mean by this and spell out its larger significance I want to turn to the philosopher with whose work Oppen has to some extent come to be associated, Martin Heidegger. My purpose here is not to read Oppen's first book in the light of his own later reading of Heidegger, as if that were all Heidegger had to say to the poetry, but to show how the latter's thinking can illuminate it in any case.[8] At the same time we get to see the rather magnificent way in which Oppen's poetry can illuminate Heidegger. A consideration of how these two writers converge will also shed light on Oppen's early Marxist orientation while simultaneously bringing the limits of that into view.

Critical commentary on Oppen and Heidegger tends to begin understandably with 'The knowledge not of sorrow, you were | saying, but of boredom'. As Davidson writes: 'Although it is unlikely that he could have known it when he

---

[7] 'Historic Pun', *NCP*, 189 (my emphasis).
[8] For the history of Oppen's knowledge of Heidegger, see 'Appendix A: Oppen's Reading of Heidegger', in Peter Nicholls, *George Oppen and the Fate of Modernism* (Oxford: Oxford University Press, 2007), 194–6.

wrote this poem in the late 1920s, Oppen's concept of boredom anticipates Heidegger's idea as stated in his acceptance speech for the chair of philosophy at Freiburg in 1929' (*NCP*, 359). In this chapter I want to look at another Heideggerian category or concept through which we can usefully read the poem, the notion of the 'worldhood of the world' (*die Weltlichkeit der Welt*). The poem ends with reference to a world that is somehow *shared* ('the world, weather-swept, with which I one shares the century')—and in the later poems already quoted above it will be apparent that some idea or image of the world also figures strongly. *World* is one of those words that seem to exert a kind of gravitational pull on Oppen. He is drawn to it repeatedly, repetitively.

Heidegger's discussion of the worldhood of the world turns on the distinction between what he calls readiness-to-hand (*Zuhandenheit*) and presence-at-hand (*Vorhandenheit*). Though they are often intertwined, these essentially constitute two different ways of experiencing the world. A human being will typically alternate between the two experiences, finding himself in the one as much as in the other. It is important to bear in mind that for Heidegger, as for Arendt, the world is in the main a world of things. It is the world we make and have made. But it is also a world in which we are always already concerned. As Heidegger expresses it, we are always alongside the world, even when it strikes us as being *just there* in a way that might leave us feeling quite remote from it, quite detached. And this is what seems to have occurred to Maude Blessingbourne. As if we felt we should have to cross the drawing room and get to the window— or even, God forbid, go outside—just to re-establish our connections with it. At such moments, precisely those moments in which we wish most to know it, and feel most detached, the world is present-at-hand:

We must keep in mind that knowing is grounded beforehand in a Being-already-alongside-the-world, which is essentially constitutive for Dasein's Being . . . This Being-already-alongside is not just a fixed staring at something that is purely present-at-hand. Being-in-the-world, as concern, is *fascinated by* the world with which it is concerned. If knowing is to be possible as a way of determining the nature of the present-at-hand by observing it, then there must first be a *deficiency* in our having-to-do with the world concernfully. When concern holds back [Sichenthalten] from any kind of producing, manipulating, and the like, it puts itself into what is now the sole remaining mode of Being-in, the mode of just tarrying alongside. . . . [das Nur-noch-weilen bei . . .] This kind of Being towards the world is one which lets us encounter entities within-the-world purely in the *way they look* (εἶδος), just that; *on the basis* of this kind of Being, and *as* a mode of it, looking explicitly at what we encounter is possible. Looking *at* something in this way is sometimes a definite way of taking up a direction towards something— of setting our sights towards what is present-at-hand. It takes over a 'view-point' in advance from the entity which it encounters. Such looking-at enters the mode of dwelling autonomously alongside entities within-the-world. In this kind of '*dwelling*' as a holding-oneself-back from any manipulation or utilization, the *perception* of the present-at-hand is consummated. (*Being and Time*, 88–9)

In passages such as this Heidegger seems quite close, as Oppen does, to Lukács's critique of the whole philosophical or epistemological project of *knowing the world* by standing back and thinking about it as a bourgeois daydream. Similarly, despite his failure to address directly the extent to which labour is divided from itself and alienated from its product, Heidegger's account of the ready-to-hand seems also broadly compatible, up to a point, with the supreme place Marxian thinking accords to work as the authentic measure of the world. Of course, as *Being and Time* proceeds, so Heidegger will be at pains to show us how authentic *Dasein* raises itself above this absorbedly concerned Being-in-the-world. But that is as yet some way off, and in the meantime the centrality of work to the first half of *Being and Time* needs to be noted, for the Oppen of *Discrete Series* also shares, or wants to share, the Marxian valuation of work.

Here is Heidegger, then, on the ready-to-hand:

> In dealings such as this, where something is put to use, our concern subordinates itself to the "in-order-to" which is constitutive for the equipment we are employing at the time; the less we just stare at the hammer-Thing, and the more we seize hold of it and use it, the more primordial does our relationship to it become, and the more unveiledly is it encountered as that which it is—as equipment. The hammering itself uncovers the specific 'manipulability' ["Handlichkeit"] of the hammer. The kind of Being which equipment possesses—in which it manifests itself in its own right—we call "*readiness-to-hand*" [*Zuhandenheit*]. Only because equipment has *this* 'Being-in-itself' and does not merely occur, is it manipulable in the broadest sense and at our disposal. No matter how sharply we just *look* [Nur-noch-*hinsehen*] at the 'outward appearance' ["Aussehen"] of Things in whatever form this takes, we cannot discover anything ready-to-hand. If we look at Things just 'theoretically', we can get along without understanding readiness-to-hand. But when we deal with them by using them and manipulating them, this activity is not a blind one; it has its own kind of sight, by which our manipulation is guided and from which it acquires its specific Thingly character. (*Being and Time*, 98)

In other words, we get to know the world through our dealings with it. A thing only reveals what sort of thing it is when we use it for that purpose in respect of which we took hold of it in the first place: when we manipulate it as an instrument or tool. To know a thing is to know what it is for. And this is a kind of knowledge that is prior to any kind of theoretical knowledge, in which we stand back from the thing and think about it. When we deal with things in such a way as to reveal what Heidegger would call their very being as things, we may not even look at them at all—we may not be conscious *of being conscious* of them. But it is precisely then that we are closest to them and, even though we haven't looked at them, see them most clearly. It is in the nature of the thing as thing to be unobtrusive and inconspicuous. And this happens the more easily because a thing never stands alone: it belongs to a context of things (the totality of equipment, Heidegger calls it) brought together by that set of purposes with which we are concerned.

By contrast, when things occur within our field of vision as it were, but outside what Heidegger characterizes as our concernful dealings with the world, they again take on the character of being not ready-to-hand but just present-at-hand. We do not know how to take hold of them or to what purpose. The English translation of Heidegger's *Vorhandenheit* has at least the virtue of suggesting, no less than the German (wherein the prefix *vor* draws attention to one's being *before* a thing, spatially and temporally), the ineptitude of hands that are as it were blind to their task: as if a hand should look rather than lay hold. For Heidegger, as we have implied, the history of Western philosophy since Plato is founded on just such a misunderstanding of the nature of being and of the being of things. It is a misunderstanding epitomized, within the pages of *Being and Time*, by the philosophy of Descartes. In effect, philosophy has expected its eyes to grasp and its hands to see.[9]

Presence-at-hand refers not to a property of things but to the way in which the world we are concerned with is revealed to us. Something that is ready-to-hand can suddenly take on the character of being disconcertingly present-at-hand. Where this happens, the unexpectedly present-at-hand character of what was ordinarily ready-to-hand manifests itself in one of three ways: as *conspicuousness*, *obtrusiveness*, or *obstinacy*. Here is Heidegger again:

> When its unusability is thus discovered, equipment becomes conspicuous. This *conspicuousness* presents the ready-to-hand equipment as in a certain un-readiness-to-hand. But this implies that what cannot be used just lies there; it shows itself as an equipmental Thing which looks so and so, and which, in its readiness-to-hand as looking that way, has constantly been present-at-hand too. Pure presence-at-hand announces itself in such equipment, but only to withdraw to the readiness-to-hand of something with which one concerns oneself—that is to say, of the sort of thing we find when we put it back into repair . . .
>
> We not only come up against unusable things *within* what is ready-to-hand already: we also find things which are missing—which not only are not 'handy' ["handlich"] but are not 'to hand' ["zur Hand"] at all. Again, to miss something in this way amounts to coming across something un-ready-to-hand. When we notice what is un-ready-to-hand, that which is ready-to-hand enters the mode of *obtrusiveness* . . .
>
> The un-ready-to-hand can [also] be encountered . . . as something un-ready-to-hand which is *not* missing at all and *not* unusable, but which 'stands in the way' of our concern. That to which our concern refuses to turn, that for which it has 'no time', is something *un*-ready-to-hand in the manner of what does not belong here, of what has not as yet been attended to. Anything which is un-ready-to-hand in this way is disturbing to us, and enables us to see the *obstinacy* of that with which we must concern ourselves in the first instance before we do anything else. (*Being and Time*, 102–3)

When the world of our concern becomes un-ready-to-hand, it comes across as being, as Heidegger's translators admirably put, just-present-at-hand-and-no-more.

---

[9] See esp. the passage on 'seeing' in *Being and Time*, pt. 1, ch. 5, sect. 36, under the subheading 'Curiosity' (*die Neugier*), pp. 214–17.

I want to propose that in *Discrete Series* Oppen was already embarked upon an investigation of what Heidegger understood as the relationship between *Vorhandenheit* and *Zuhandenheit*, as the intensity of his phenomenological prowess carried him beyond the usual Marxist categories. The poetry presents us with an instrumental world at the moment it falls into desuetude—an instrumental world as it becomes, as Heidegger says, conspicuous, obstinate, and obtrusive. Take for example the second poem in the book:

> White. From the
> Under arm of T
>
> The red globe.
>
> Up
> Down. Round
> Shiny fixed
> Alternatives
>
> From the quiet
>
> Stone floor . . .
>
> (*NCP*, 6)

In a letter to the English poet Charles Tomlinson, Oppen explained that the poem refers to a 'contrivance' that would be commonly found over the door of an elevator in 1930s New York.[10] It presents us with a device that has reverted from its use-value in the interdependent context of elevator, office, building, and so on, what Heidegger calls the world as equipment, and stands before us now in its puzzling presence—prior to any use. Its shininess draws attention to this superficial visual character of its being—its conspicuousness; it stands in our way, obstinately 'fixed'; something 'with which we must concern ourselves in the first instance before we do anything else' (i.e. enter the lift, pass to the office, get on with the day). Oppen accentuates the paradox of its being there like that, unready-to-hand, by tacitly adducing and yet overtly ignoring the fact that one operates the lift not by looking at it but by touching it. There is no mention of hands or fingers: it is as if the 'alternatives' are merely alternatives for the eyes, which in their turn reflect the 'Round | Shiny' nature of the mechanical lights. The effect of the omission of hands and fingers is aggravated by the reference to the 'under arm' of the device (there is even an obscure sensuality about it—the 'under arm' perhaps suggesting for a moment the 'white' of flesh). But in truth it has no limbs at all—which mirrors the fact that whoever stands before it may be supposed, for the duration of the poem, to stand there helplessly, unable to lift a finger, as if having temporarily forgotten what to do. The poem deliberately

---

[10] *The Selected Letters of George Oppen*, ed. Rachel Blau DuPlessis (Durham, NC: Duke University Press, 1990), 90.

suggests that in this abstracted state one stares at the device as one might stare at a difficult poem—the eye going blindly 'Up | Down'. Meanwhile, just as the reference to 'globe' recalls again Oppen's preoccupation with the worldhood of the world, the closing image of the 'quiet | Stone floor' suggests an underlying silent reality: the quietness of Being, of meaning that goes unheard.

The poem reads as if it could be an extreme revision of William Carlos Williams's most famous poem, 'The Red Wheelbarrow' (1923). Oppen has, for a start, drawn on the same colour-scheme, white and red. But he takes his equipment from an urban environment, not a potentially nostalgic rural one.[11] Williams's poem beautifully captures the *interdependence* of tool and context—the phenomenological impossibility so to speak of minutely itemizing the complex ways in which a livelihood, not just a farm, but a whole chain of being, depends on one of its parts: the humble wheelbarrow. Here is the worldhood of the world, then, in its readiness to hand. However, the further wonder of the phrase 'so much' is that Williams also invites us to consider that the poem too may depend on our ability to recall this complex interdependence, even if it seems to depend purely on its formal appearance on the page. The word 'depends' hangs exquisitely, and the poem hangs (depends) from it.

Williams's poem recalls us, then, to the inconspicuousness of the ready-to-hand, the eminently forgettable nature of the working world. Williams is no fool. He knows that he runs the risk of betraying that world by thus posing it aesthetically. But he solves this problem by presenting the poem as *his work*. So the chain of being is secured. Oppen's poem by contrast shows us what happens when the chain is broken—in that abstract or distracted moment when the working world doesn't work, when the tool merely shines. Whereupon we recall that in the decade that had passed since the publication of Williams's poem the working world had changed catastrophically. By 1933 a third of the American labour force was unemployed. The Great Depression had set in—work had come to a standstill. So much of what had once been ready-to-hand was now, in the words of Heidegger's translators, just-present-at-hand-and-no-more.

It is remarkable just how often images of arms, hands, and fingers occur in *Discrete Series*. Even in the third poem of the book, where they are not directly mentioned, they are an inescapable or hidden part of the poet's satirical reflections on the relationship between masturbation and big business. And in the fourth poem, a glance inside an automobile continues the satire of consumerist machismo, with the driver's 'hand on the sword-hilt' (*NCP*, 8). In the fifth, a woman brushes her hair (*NCP*, 9). In 'Who comes is occupied', the poet observes the middle-aged driver of a 'steam-shovel cab': 'his arms fingers continually— | Turned with the cab' (*NCP*, 14). In the next poem, 'Party on Shipboard', an arm is waved (*NCP*, 15). In the poem beginning, 'Semaphoring chorus' a man and

[11] Oppen cites 'The Red Wheelbarrow' in the interview with Dembo when reflecting on what he sees as his differences from Williams (180), as well as in his only published essay, from 1963, 'The Mind's Own Place' (32).

woman remove their gloves (*NCP*, 17). In 'She lies, hip high', there are 'arms hands fingers'—seeming to float in the air (*NCP*, 20). Another poem bears witness to 'your elbow on a car-edge' (*NCP*, 28). And in 'Drawing', not only the title, but also the reference to 'paper, turned', invoke dexterity, manual action (*NCP*, 33). And yet there is a sense in which the action of all these hands is abortive or truncated, cut off from the world as a whole; that is to say, not really related to an interrelated world ('incapable of contact | Save in incidents', in the words of 'Party on Shipboard'). Thus the hands and arms occur like amputations, or what the final poem calls 'Successive | Happenings' (*NCP*, 35). The book ends appropriately with two bracketed words: '(the telephone)'—which is, in the first place, an image of the perilousness of speech (is communication by telephone speech? is speech by telephone communication?), but is also, in the second place, an image of the strange part played by hands in the general disconnect. Oppen would be cautious of Heidegger's nostalgia for the golden age of manual workmanship—he is too rooted now in this abortive modern world. But what *Discrete Series* captures perfectly is the present-at-hand character of this world. For in this book even hands are not ready-to-hand. They are more seen than used—or seen at the very moment when their use becomes questionable. (It is interesting to compare this separation of hands and eyes with their coordination in Whitman as described in Chapter 1.)

This detached or amputated character of Oppen's hands and limbs is matched by the intense but fragmentary nature of the poet's gaze; by the sense of bodies, especially women's bodies, coming apart ('Your face unaccented, your mouth a mouth?'); bodies atomized, itemized ('Your hips a possession | ... | Your breasts | Pertain to lingerie').[12] Eyes themselves float free of all surrounding flesh. Here are three examples, taken from separate poems:

> From a crowd a white powdered face,
> Eyes and mouth making three—
> Awaited—locally—a date.
>
> (*NCP*, 25)

> Near your eyes—
> Love at the pelvis
> Reaches the generic, gratuitous
>   (Your eyes like snail-tracks)
>
> (*NCP*, 26)

> In this place, two geraniums
> In your window-box
> Are his life's eyes.
>
> (*NCP*, 34)

---

[12] *NCP*, 28–9.

These disembodied eyes (or eyes becoming disembodied), reflect the apparently disembodied observations of the poet—or to put it more strongly they reflect the visual apparatus of the poet at the moment he finds himself alongside a world turned present-at-hand. Even love-making seems a mode of separation rather than togetherness: hands-free, as it were: 'We slide in separate hard grooves' (*NCP*, 26).

It is the car, however, which emerges as the most powerful source of the recurrent images of the world as equipment. The car as an epistemological site (that is to say, a paradigm of our knowledge of the world, the place from which we view it and which informs that view), is the successor to the drawing room where we encountered Maude Blessingbourne:

> Closed car—closed in glass—
> At the curb,
> Unapplied and empty:
> A thing among others
>
> (*NCP*, 13)

This seems like textbook Heidegger, pared down in Oppen's distinctive style. But of course the poet was not reading *Sein und Zeit* when he wrote this—it would not be translated for another thirty years. He is just bringing his existential metaphysical proclivity to bear on something like Marx's notion of use-value. But the effect is the same. The car is 'empty' (of passengers first of all but also of meaning) because it is 'unapplied', because it is not in use. And its not being in use spreads like a contagion to the other things around it: its relation of not being in relation, of not being active or applied. Drive it, however, and it is transformed: 'Moving in traffic | This thing is less strange—' (ibid.). As Heidegger puts it, speaking of the difference between finding something unusable and putting it back into repair: 'When its unusability is thus discovered, equipment becomes conspicuous ... Pure presence-at-hand announces itself in such equipment, but only to withdraw to the readiness-to-hand of something with which one concerns oneself—that is to say, of the sort of thing we find when we put it back into repair ... '

What is also wonderful is that Oppen does not say the car is *not strange* but that it is 'less strange'. The strangeness does not go away entirely. It can resurface at any moment, like 'the face, still within it, | Between glasses' (*NCP*, 13). 'Between glasses' is succinctness itself: the face between spectacles, and between windscreen and windows. Here is another remarkable image of a car:

> Nothing can equal in polish and obscured
>   origin that dark instrument
> A car
>   (Which.
> Ease; the hand on the sword-hilt
>
> (*NCP*, 8)

Again Oppen captures beautifully the way in which the thing ('instrument') unapplied gleams before the eye, stands out against the background of its obscured origin, in the high polish of its conspicuousness. 'The hand on the sword-hilt' is poised ambiguously between application and inertia: between readiness-to-hand and presence-at-hand; between inconspicuousness and pompous visualization. Oppen catches himself not just using the gear-stick but also looking at it, fascinated, mystified.

6.2 'POETRY DEFINED AS A JOB, A PIECE OF WORK'

We're committed, Mary and I, as artists, and therefore very seriously, to the common, the un-doped, the un-staged, the plain and ordinary daylight . . .
    I believe we can't be astonished by any hallucination whatever. Whereas we are totally astonished by daylight, by any brick in a brick wall we focus on . . .
    And astonishment—which is a form of stubbornness—is the core of our lives.

Oppen, *Selected Letters*, 105

6.2.1

'The shock is metaphysical', Oppen wrote, when he returned to writing a quarter of a century after publishing *Discrete Series*.[13] Which is to say, shock is metaphysical.[14] That said, Oppen does not try to shock the reader but to pinpoint as nearly as possible the 'circumstances' that seemed to obtain when he himself was shocked. If the reader is astonished, it must be because the poet was astonished, and not because the latter set out to astonish him. As he would express it in the later sequence, 'Route' (another sequence in which cars figure prominently),

A picture seen from within. The picture is unstable, a
moving picture, unlimited drift. Still the picture
exists.

The circumstances:

(*NCP*, 197)

Another deceptively straightforward remark from the same poem sums up the distinctive inward bent of Oppen's aesthetics of shock, in other words its

---

[13] 'Return', *NCP*, 47.
[14] Oppen explained what he meant by metaphysics in a long letter to Julian Zimet, in 1959: 'I cannot really think twenty minutes about anything without coming to a metaphysical agony in the back of my mind . . . I do not see how it is possible to pretend to be "Beyond metaphysics" What's your love for anyone, or mine? . . . What are any of us worked up about — — — if not metaphysics!' (*Selected Letters*, 29, 33).

taciturnity: 'Well', he writes, 'hardly an epiphany, but there the thing is all the same' (199). The reader may well feel that the focal point of a given poem, the thing looked at or referred to ('the word it, never more powerful than in this moment', as Oppen says, saying it flatly and without power), is 'hardly an epiphany': the epiphany, if there is one, will consist in the apprehension of what Oppen apprehends and cannot say: 'but there the thing is all the same'. There is a capitulation here, i.e. a giving up on saying more and an obstinate pointing.[15] We may not apprehend the thing as such ('it'): but we are more likely to apprehend it when we imagine another mind in the process of apprehending it, or in the process of remembering that it apprehended it before. It is after this fashion that Oppen speaks; communicates or fails to communicate an epiphany. The main difference between the early and the later poetry consists in his much greater willingness to digress before the reader on the problems of communication and the limits (the comparative smallness, the modesty) of what he has to communicate.[16]

[15] This is confirmed by Peter Nicholls, who quotes a late interview with Oppen, from 1978: 'what I'm doing is making that Heideggerian gesture of "pointing"': this could be 'an allusion', Nicholls notes, 'to the account of "saying" given in [Heidegger's] *On the Way to Language*: "we understand saying in terms of showing, pointing out, signalling"' (*George Oppen and the Fate of Modernism*, 74). Nicholls comments aptly: 'This "pointing" is not even primarily to objects designated by words but to the event of language itself . . . Oppen's "pointing", his way of shifting emphasis from the content of his words to the pure fact of their utterance, implies a poetics of being that does not now require the impacted syntax of *Discrete Series* and can thus produce more fluent and expanded structures' (74).

[16] Here I seem to be at variance with Nicholls, who, as he reflects on Oppen's return to poetry following his exile in Mexico, in *George Oppen and the Fate of Modernism*, quotes revealingly from the poet's unpublished notes: 'I have resigned myself to coming on stage, to *talking* for silence is impossible', writes Oppen (57). Nicholls adds: 'The distinction here is clarified by another unpublished note, where [Oppen] observes: " 'Discrete': I had tried NOT to speak not to talk" ' (57). However, Nicholls argues that 'it is the distant, partly forgotten *Discrete Series*, with its *refusal* of "talking" and "coming on stage" that seems intermittently to present itself to him as a more effective and fuller realization of . . . [those] ideas . . . which would direct much of the work to come' (57). In so far as I find that the quotations are very much in keeping with the spirit of the work to come, I have to disagree. While Nicholls's study is invaluable for its wealth of useful quotation, and I have learned a great deal from his precise historical commentary, when it comes to reading the poems the author seems much too ready to defer to Oppen's unpublished papers. Again and again, the task of interpretation, of thinking poetically—with the poem as it exists—seems to be displaced onto this or that quotation from the archive, somewhat against the grain of Nicholls's own lucid outline of Heideggerian poetical thinking (72). Yet nowhere in the book is there any consideration of what the significance of this method of interpretation might be—philosophically, critically, historically. Michael Davidson, by contrast, puts just this issue at the very centre of his thoughtful discussion of Oppen in *Ghostlier Demarcations: Modern Poetry and the Material Word* (Berkeley and Los Angeles: University of California Press, 1997), which Nicholls doesn't cite. It's worth quoting Davidson at length: 'As one-time curator of the Archive for New Poetry, I had a unique chance to view Oppen's papers in their pristine state, before they were divided up into separate categories according to genre (manuscripts, notes, correspondence, daybooks, etc). When I first opened the boxes in which the papers were sent, I was not prepared for the chaos that appeared . . . Prose and poetry were interspersed with grocery lists, phone numbers, quotations from philosophers, observations on films, tables of contents from books (his own and others). Every conceivable type of paper had been used . . .' (76). As Davidson suggests: 'Once we have seen the poem in this

Discrete Series is the least expansive of books, in contrast for example to *Spring and All*, which latter gains immeasurably, as a whole, from the improvised prose reflections—those expansions—between poems, where the irrepressible Williams seems to enter into dialogue with the problems the reader is going to have when reading him, giving word to one's exasperations and excitements. But then the focus of Williams's book is the dynamics of interrelation, the condition that 'so much depends'. This is the revelation that the prose contagiously enacts. Whereas the focus of Oppen's book is how, given the complexity of our world, and the adhesive complexity of our relations to it, the glue can suddenly come away, leaving the world merely *present. The presence of the world*, the poems seem to say, *is no explanation of the world*. As we began by remarking, it is only in the very first poem of the book that there is an approximation to something like the expansive tone—and even then it is partly an illusion, a sleight of hand, fostered by the half-expansive, half-knowing reference, to the minutely expansive figure of Henry James.

There is by now a shelf or two of commentary on the so-called Objectivist poets which points up the historical inaccuracy involved in trying to think of Objectivism as a shared aesthetic programme.[17] Nevertheless, there is little doubt that Oppen was influenced by Louis Zukofsky during the 1930s and in agreement with him, as he repeatedly acknowledged, about the basic principles of what both men were willing to call, if not Objectivism, then 'objectification'.[18] For Zukofsky this meant, 'the arrangement, into one apprehended unit, of minor units of sincerity—in other words, the resolving of words and their ideation into structure'.[19] Oppen recalls this language of form in the opening lines of the final poem of *Discrete Series*: 'Written structure, | Shape of art' (*NCP*, 35).[20] Likewise sincerity was what the poet started from: 'beginning from imagism as a position

context, it becomes very difficult to isolate it from its written environment. Indeed, can we speak of "poetry" at all when so much of it is embedded in other quotations, prose remarks, and observations? Does Oppen's oeuvre end in the work we know as *The Collected Poems*, or does it end on the page where it began?' (66–7). There may not be one answer to these questions, but if the poet's archive is to be made the fulcrum of critical interpretation then it seems essential to ask them.

[17] The obvious starting point for any enquiring reader would be the *Man and Poet* volumes published since 1979 by the National Poetry Foundation of the University of Maine at Orono.

[18] '"He taught me everything," said George', recalled his wife Mary in her memoir, writing about the breakdown of Oppen's friendship with Zukofsky in the 1960s. Mary Oppen, *Meaning a Life: An Autobiography* (Santa Rosa, Calif.: Black Sparrow Press, 1978), 208. Charles Tomlinson has written sympathetically about their relationship in 'Objectivists: Zukofsky and Oppen', in *Some Americans: A Personal Record* (Berkeley and Los Angeles: University of California Press, 1981), 45–73.

[19] Zukofsky, *Prepositions+*, 194.

[20] The lines read like a distillation of part of Zukofsky's not quite definitive essay of 1931, 'Sincerity and Objectification': 'In sincerity shapes appear concomitants of word combinations, precursors of . . . completed sound or structure, melody or form. Writing occurs which is the detail, not mirage, of seeing, of thinking with the things as they exist, and of directing them along a line of melody. Shapes suggest themselves, and the mind senses and receives awareness' (*Prepositions+*, 194).

of honesty. The first question at the time in poetry was simply the question of honesty, of sincerity', Oppen recalled; it was what one had to work with or, as Zukofsky says, resolve. In the interview with Dembo, Oppen was eloquent and forthright: 'That's what "objectivist" really means. There's been tremendous misunderstanding about that. People assume it means the psychologically objective in attitude. It actually means the objectification of the poem, the making an object of the poem' (173). This *making an object* was also what the most celebrated of the Objectivists, Williams, was talking about in his revelatory discussion of Poe in *In the American Grain*: 'He sought by stress upon construction to hold the loose-strung mass off even at the cost of an icy coldness of appearance; it was the first need of his time, an escape from the formless mass he hated . . . to get from sentiment to form' (221).

Objectification, then, seems to be a very good instance of what Marjorie Perloff sees as the constructionist tendency within high modernism.[21] Scholars and critics concur that, whatever else it was, constructionism, making an object, arranging a structure, was modernism's response to the vagaries of romantic subjectivity. From the constructionist point of view, the legacy of romanticism looked like glorified self-expression, too absorbed by its transcendental navel to attend to the renovation of its concrete objects and forms. In *The Theory of the Novel* Lukács argued that the true medium of transcendence (the ordinary transcendence of 'an ordinary human being in the midst of ordinary life') was, on the contrary, these concrete objects and forms. It was precisely by attending to them, and not by chasing the tail of its subjectivity, that humanity would best express and transcend itself, recover its spirit or grace. In his account of what he calls the 'minor epic' Lukács describes 'the subject's form-giving, structuring, de-limiting act' whose 'lyricism is still pure selection', and where, as the work proceeds, 'the utter arbitrariness of chance' is 'balanced by clear, uncommented, purely objective depiction': 'Such lyricism is here the last epic unity; it is not the swallowing of a solitary "I" in the object-free contemplation of its own self, nor is it the dissolving of the object into sensations and moods; it is born out of form, it creates form, and it sustains everything that has been given form in such a work.'[22] Although Lukács writes here about the short story he could just as easily be speaking of the objectification of 'minor units of sincerity' in a poem, as Oppen and Zukofsky understood it.[23] For what Lukács has mainly taken from Hegel, Oppen and Zukofsky have taken from Marx—but not just from Marx: they have drawn more generally on a particular model of human action, one which has exerted an extraordinary influence on humanity's historical

---

[21] Perloff, *The Dance of the Intellect*, 23.

[22] Lukács, *Theory of the Novel*, 51.

[23] Oppen recalled in a letter that 'Zukofsky wrote . . . of "sincerity" as the "epic quality"' (*Selected Letters*, 82). My Lukácsian reading of Objectivism, which harks back to my discussion of Pound in Ch. 2 above, is anticipated by Zukofsky in his brilliant essay of 1929, 'Ezra Pound' (*Prepositions+*, 67–83; esp. 76–7).

understanding of how it works and creates.[24] In what follows I will refer to this as
the work paradigm, or the 'intentional-teleological model of action': what Zu-
kofsky calls 'poetry defined as a job, a piece of work'.[25] The larger argument I wish
to make is that what Oppen comes to see, shortly after he publishes *Discrete Series*,
as the inadequacy of poetry as a type of action, has to do with the inadequacy of
the work or intentional-teleological paradigm, the paradigm on which Objectivist
poetics quite demonstrably draws: in other words, it has to do with a recognition
of the limitations of conceiving of poetry as a kind of making or work.

6.2.2

In *Critique, Norm, and Utopia: A Study of the Foundations of Critical Theory*, the
philosopher Seyla Benhabib describes the failures and inadequacies of the 'inten-
tional-teleological model of action' in the thought of Hegel, Marx, and their
followers. In the case of Hegel action takes the form of externalization, to which
there are essentially three stages: (1) the stage of impure 'inwardness', of inward-
ness tending outwards, where there is as yet only obscure purpose or intention;
(2) the expression or externalization of that inwardness; (3) the movement or
process that realizes the unity of (1) and (2).[26] This may seem a little too concise,
but looking back at Lukács we can see the stages unfolding: first there is the
moment of 'pure selection', before the intentions, purposes, contents of con-
sciousness, have been given form: the artist has simply chanced on something, as
it might seem arbitrarily, without yet realizing what he has done—for what he
has done will only become apparent in time, through his work; next there is the
process, choice of means, by which 'the subject' gives the material form, his
'form-giving, structuring, delimiting act'; finally, there is the finished work itself,

---

[24] Oppen wrote to John Crawford that 'The "Marxism" of Discrete Series is, was felt as, the
struggle against the loss of the commonplace' (*Selected Letters*, 254). As Mary Oppen explained,
'Both of us refer to Marx as something basic from which to proceed.' Burton Hatlen and Tom
Mandel, 'Poetry and Politics: A Conversation with George and Mary Oppen', in Burton Hatlen
(ed.), *George Oppen: Man and Poet* (Orono, Me.: National Poetry Foundation, 1981), 28. For
Zukofsky's reading of Marx, see Louis Zukofsky, *'A'* (Berkeley and Los Angeles: University of
California Press, 1978), most explicitly sect. 8, beginning 'And of labour' (p. 43).
[25] Zukofsky, '"Recencies" in Poetry' (1932), in *Prepositions+*, 203–15 (207). The essay as
reprinted ends: 'The good poems of today are—*as jobs*—not far from the good poems of
yesterday' (215, my emphasis).
[26] See G. W. F. Hegel, *Phenomenology of Spirit*, trans. A. V. Miller, with analysis of the text and
foreword by J. N. Findlay (Oxford: Oxford University Press, 1977), 490: 'Spirit, however, has
shown itself to us to be neither merely the withdrawal of self-consciousness into its pure inwardness,
nor the mere submergence of self-consciousness into substance, and the non-being of its [moment
of] difference; but Spirit is *this movement* of the Self which empties itself of itself and sinks itself into
its substance, and also, as Subject, has gone out of that substance into itself, making the substance
into an object and a content at the same time as it cancels this difference between objectivity and
content . . . The "I" has neither to cling to itself in the *form* of *self-consciousness* as against the form of
substantiality and objectivity, as if it were afraid of the externalization of itself: the power of Spirit
lies rather in remaining the selfsame Spirit in its externalization.'

wherein individual action and the activity of Spirit coincide. (As Hegel writes: the 'I' must not 'cling to itself in the *form* of *self-consciousness* as against the form of substantiality and objectivity, as if it were afraid of the externalization of itself').[27] In sum the artist extends himself, transcends himself, and returns to himself, in this the externalized object of his art.[28]

That at least is the theory. But there is something unsatisfactory about it, as the Hegelian dialectic proceeds to show. After all, what guarantee is there that the work of art as it is realized will correspond to my intentions; that the exteriority will express my interiority, and that Spirit will so to speak be externalized through me—just as I am through my art? Benhabib writes:

This manifestation of oneself to others entails their comprehending my intentions and motives correctly in a process of mutual understanding and interpretation. And it is precisely this *interpretive* aspect of expressive action that leads Hegel to see it as an ontologically inadequate form.

For Hegel, the dialectic, even the fate, of acting and doing consists in that, in this movement from interior to exterior, from purpose to its realization, the self can fail to express itself. The realization may fail to correspond to the intention; the purpose may be frustrated by reality.[29]

Hegel's solution to this problem, as Benhabib argues, is ultimately to refer all action back to Spirit, which is to say, to the intentional *telos* itself. 'The action of Spirit is to be its own "work"; . . . reality must be appropriated in such a way that the dialectic of action, the incongruence between deed and intention, is eliminated' (87). Only in the action of Spirit are intention and realization one and the same; and only if they are the same can Spirit be said to act. So the only real work is Spirit's work, or to express it in a way that will take on more significance shortly, the only real *action* is *work*.

Benhabib sums up as follows what she sees as the blinkeredness inherent in Hegel's account of the inadequacy of action:

To be an acting agent is to live in this interpreted world where one's own understanding of one's deeds is but one point of view, one interpretive framework, among others. In this sense, it is even misleading to speak of 'misinterpretation', as if the standpoint of the agent, her or his interpretation of what she or he was doing, was the only relevant one. Very often, we come to learn *what* we have done through others' understanding and interpretation of, and reaction to, our actions. Human actions, unlike objects and things,

---

[27] See n. 26 above.

[28] The coincidence of work, self, and Spirit is at best temporary; it can only be understood as process, as movement. Lukács tries to express this paradox as follows: 'The concept of totality for the epic is not a transcendental one . . . it is not born out of the form itself, but is empirical and metaphysical, combining transcendence and immanence inseparably within itself' (*Theory of the Novel*, 49). The empiricism of epic art commits it to the fragmentary and incomplete, and there, and only there, is its totality. The dialectic resumes. The epic is as incomplete as history itself.

[29] Seyla Benhabib, *Critique, Norm, and Utopia: A Study of the Foundations of Critical Theory* (New York: Columbia University Press, 1986), 86.

are not the property of their agents, or their 'work.' They do not embody or express a univocal meaning or purpose. Such a meaning or purpose can only be determined interpretively; in this sense, human action is fundamentally indeterminate. Hegel criticizes this indeterminacy of action in order to show the antinomies of moral consciousness. But what he reveals thereby is his profound ontological rejection of lived intersubjectivity in the name of an objectifying philosophical discourse.[30]

Hegel has no time for what Benhabib calls 'lived intersubjectivity', which he can only see as an inadequate, unsatisfactory realm, where the great cycle of externalization is stopped short, stranded. Action is undone by the *interpretation of action*, that is by the inevitable impertinence of other subjects, other selves, who fail to recognize the expressive self's true *telos* and intention; who fail to see the subject in the object. But what makes Hegel think that the interpretative act of others is not one of the rightful ends of action, a valid form of understanding and responding to it? From this rejected perspective, what you and I make of an action is a critical and constitutive part of it. The realm of lived intersubjectivity is indeed, as Hegel thinks, the realm of action. But instead of seeing this as marking the failure of action, we might ask instead why it is that Hegel thinks there is a realm (call it the realm of Spirit, truth, or reciprocal recognition) above and beyond the intersubjective realm. Why does he privilege the singular subject over subjects plural? Why does the celebrated notion of reciprocal recognition not allow for some mis-recognition? Happening simultaneously and more or less alongside it? Some reciprocity agreeably lost? A little bit of discord to liven up the accord? As I noted in Chapter 1, something similar happens in Tocqueville's critique of democracy, where from the outset democracy is understood and variously figured not as lived intersubjectivity but as a homogeneous collective singular subject. Tocqueville improperly infers subjective identity—democracy reproducing itself in its own image—from political equality. This enables him to argue that democracy is something quite different from freedom, for freedom as he understands it depends on the give and take of difference—in other words on *lived intersubjectivity*. But the supposition that democracy was not also a form of lived intersubjectivity (not less so, at any rate, than any other form of society) was always premature.

Like Hegel's dialectic of externalization, Marx's theory of objectification also presupposes a singular, homogeneous subject, now the collective subject of the human species itself. For Marx, 'Objectification is the externalization of the essential powers of the individual' (*Critique, Norm, and Utopia*, 56). The question is: is individual activity a process of 'self-confirmation or self-denial?' (ibid.) As Benhabib says, 'Marx names objectifying activity that denies and stultifies the powers and capacities of the self "alienated" activity' (ibid.). So the next question is, how does the individual reappropriate his alienated activity? Well, he can only reappropriate it by way of the collective subject of history:

---

[30] Benhabib, *Critique, Norm, and Utopia*, 87–8.

Marx remains loyal to Hegel's philosophy of the subject: not only is objectification understood as self-expression through externalization, but the subject of this activity is said to be a collective singular, the species itself. Indeed, the statement objectification is self-expression presupposes this collective singular subject, because for concrete individuals objectification and labour can be forms of self-realization, if at all, only when in their empirical life conditions they approximate the universal attributes characterizing species essence . . .

On the one hand, history is the becoming and self-production of 'man', of the collective singular subject, and on the other hand, empirical history is the alienation of concrete individuals from their essential species attributes. When viewed from the standpoint of the collective singular, history is objectification and self-expression; when viewed from the standpoint of the individual, it is self-negation and alienated objectification . . . The point is that history can appear as such, both as the becoming of a goal and in need of attaining this goal, when its *unity* is attributed to the presence of a *collective singular* subject and its *diversity* to the life conditions of empirical individuals. This collective singular is both substance and subject: history is the process through which it becomes, its capacities unfold, and it is also what humans ought to be in the future. Empirical individuals can become the subject of the historical process only if, in their collective life conditions, they reappropriate the idealized properties of species being. (56–7)

In Oppen's *Discrete Series* history as 'self-negation and alienated objectification' is revealed through the presence-at-hand of the world, the truncation of the latter's readiness-to-hand. The poems are exemplary instances of this kind of objectification. At the same time, the poetry gestures beyond the individual to the species, what Oppen will come to call 'of being numerous' (there is a premonition of this phrase in 'Party on Shipboard').[31] What enables it to do this is of course the *fragmentary* form itself: for the fragment represents both the breaking down of the individual (of Maude Blessingbourne, for example) and the breaking in of numerousness. The more one is aware of this numerousness, the peopled world—that 'with which one shares'—the more one is reconfigured by it. The perspective of Maude Blessingbourne gives way to that of the poet: or rather gives way to that of the poems.

Nevertheless, in his exploration of the vicissitudes of the categories of readiness-to-hand and presence-at-hand, of the world as it oscillates between them, Oppen the Objectivist is still tied, like Heidegger himself, to the intentional-teleological model of action, the paradigm of work. It is no surprise then that Benhabib's most trenchant and far-reaching criticism of that paradigm might be usefully applied to *Discrete Series*, as it might also be applied, with important qualifications, to *Being and Time*:

Yet this model of action is a monological one. It privileges the subject–object relation and abstracts from the dimension of subject–subject relations and from the social context of action. In the first place: purposeful or intentional activity is described with the help of

[31] *NCP*, 15.

a *prelinguistic* model. One proceeds from a reflecting consciousness formulating its intentions and goals. While Hegel describes this activity of reflection as 'the repositing of contents of consciousness', Marx resorts to the metaphor of 'the image which the architect has before the eyes of his mind'. Goals, intentions, and purposes are described in mentalistic language as 'contents' of consciousness, as 'images', as what is 'before the eyes of the mind'. One abstracts from the linguistic mediation of these goals, purposes, and intentions through a propositional form. But the answer to the question 'What do you intend, wish, want to do?' is not 'I want to bring about a content of my consciousness called X or an image Y', but a reply of the sort 'I intend to get an education', 'I wish to help her', 'I want to build a bridge or a private home in the Bauhaus style', etc. The contents or images of consciousness are linguistically mediated propositional expressions ... The [work] model privileges the subject–object relation and abstracts from the shared, social world in which humans attain their identity as persons through linguistically mediated socialization. (135–6)

It is precisely Benhabib's Arendtian sense of a 'shared, social world in which humans attain their identity as persons through linguistically mediated socialization' which is left out of *Discrete Series* and in fact underlines that book's dazzlingly alienated objectifications.[32] Likewise it is worth noting that in *Being and Time* Heidegger gives only the most damningly limited account of the linguistically mediated socialization that belongs in any full account of Being-in-the-world as Being-with-others. This is despite the fact that he too was trying to get away from the 'subject–object relation' as philosophy traditionally conceived it and the domination of 'reflecting consciousness'. But Heidegger's solution took the form of Being, not the form of 'subject–subject relations and ... the social context of action'. It is as if speech were merely 'gossip' or 'idle talk'—and as if gossip or idle talk were merely just that (*Being and Time*, 211–14).[33] Meanwhile the few fragments of speech that Oppen records ('"My hair, scalp—"'; '"O—" ‖ "Tomorrow?"—'), hang uselessly in the air, as disconnected from the world as the mouthpiece of the 'telephone' (which, as I noted above, is the book's final word).

When Oppen finally starts to write poetry again, after the twenty-five-year break which follows *Discrete Series*, and comes to reflect, in these new poems, on

---

[32] The distinction Benhabib makes between teleological work and the indeterminacy of action is fundamentally Arendtian, and lies at the very heart of *The Human Condition*, though it should be said that within the pages of *Critique, Norm, and Utopia*, it is only in a footnote, really, that Benhabib makes that clear (367 n. 23).

[33] Habermas puts it very well: 'At the centre of the first section of *Being and Time* stands the analysis of the concept of the world', which Heidegger explicates 'as a network of concepts reminiscent of Pragmatism' (*Philosophical Discourse of Modernity*, 148). Heidegger's originality, Habermas contends, consists in the use he 'makes of this concept of world for a critique of the philosophy of consciousness' (ibid.). But this originality is in turn undermined 'because from the start he degrades the background structures of the lifeworld', which Habermas argues are 'structures of linguistic intersubjectivity ... in which subjects capable of speech and action come to a mutual understanding about something in the world' (149). For Heidegger, however, these are mere 'structures of average everyday existence ... inauthentic Dasein' (ibid.).

what the Objectivists were about, it is the world of 'linguistically mediated socialization', that he now invokes and sets alongside—I might almost say *against*, so great is the difference it makes—the original Objectivist emphases on sincerity and objectification, honesty and making. The change of tack is announced in 'Leviathan'—like an amendment to the poet's constitution:

> Truth also is the pursuit of it:
> Like happiness, and it will not stand.
>
> Even the verse begins to eat away
> In the acid. Pursuit, pursuit;
>
> A wind moves a little,
> Moving in a circle, very cold.
>
> How shall we say?
> In ordinary discourse—
>
> We must talk now. I am no longer sure of the words,
> The clockwork of the world. What is inexplicable
>
> Is the 'preponderance of objects'. The sky lights
> Daily with that predominance
>
> And we have become the present.
>
> We must talk now. Fear
> Is fear. But we abandon one another.

(NCP, 89)

To begin with, the phrase in quotation marks, 'the "preponderance of objects"', is surely a felicitous misremembering of a passage from Zukofsky's essay 'Sincerity and Objectification': 'the facts carried by one word are, in view of the *preponderance of facts* carried by combinations of words, not sufficiently explicit to warrant a realization of rested totality such as might be designated an art form'.[34] That the poet should substitute *objects* for *facts* is entirely fitting, as the poem telescopes Zukofsky's argument and refers us back explicitly to the terms 'objectification' and 'Objectivist' and their part in Oppen's history. There may be other references here too to the Objectivist ethos. As against the Objectivist insistence on the poem's 'solidity', its 'rested totality', there is a menacing awareness of process and decay: 'it will not stand'; it 'eat[s] away | In the acid'. The reference to the 'clockwork of the world' recalls another of Zukofsky's essays, 'A Statement for Poetry', from 1950, as well as two other well-known

---

[34] *Prepositions+*, 194–5 (my emphasis). Nicholls suggests that the phrase may recall a passage from Heidegger's *Introduction to Metaphysics*, which Oppen had marked, where Heidegger speaks of 'the preponderant power of being [which] bursts in its appearing' (*George Oppen and the Fate of Modernism*, 71).

formulations, both of which are cited in that later essay. Zukofsky quotes the first, from Williams, directly: 'A contemporary American poet says: "A poem is a small (or large) machine made of words."'[35] The second is Pound's famous advice for Imagists: 'To compose in the sequence of the musical phrase, not in sequence of a metronome' (*Literary Essays*, 3). Zukofsky echoes or reiterates this, when he writes that the poet 'does not measure with handbook, and is not a pendulum' (*Prepositions+*, 23).

The evocation in 'Leviathan' of *becoming the present* may recall another striking passage from 'Sincerity and Objectification': 'Writing occurs which is the detail, not mirage, of seeing, of thinking with the things as they exist . . . Shapes suggest themselves, and the mind senses and receives awareness' (194). To become the present is, then, to think with the things as they exist: 'keeping time with existence' (20); to sense and receive awareness. (The concluding passages of 'Guest Room', quoted earlier, and of 'A Narrative', both of them written within a few years of 'Leviathan', represent more detailed amplifications of this idea—and in both of them of course 'the detail, not mirage, of seeing' is indicative of the receptive mind.)

However, the real power of 'Leviathan' comes not from its recall of Objectivist aesthetics, but from its references to speech and the need for speech: 'How shall we say? | In ordinary discourse', and the repeated 'We must talk now'—which could mean several things: we didn't talk *before*; we haven't talked *yet*; it's what we say *now* that matters; and something is *still* preventing us from speaking. Similarly, 'I am no longer sure of the words' can mean: I am not sure what to say; I am not sure how to say it; and also, since the phrase 'no longer' introduces an element of retrospection: I am *no longer* as sure in my choice of words as I used to be, as I was for example when I was an Objectivist—i.e. they *no longer* convince me of their rested totality. It is with *The Materials*, then, his second book (1962), in which 'Leviathan' is the final poem, that Oppen begins to move beyond the work model of action, the subject–object relation; and to let in or explore that very different, more uncertain kind of action that is speech—i.e. the subject–subject relation and its linguistic mediations. We cannot know if he intended to juxtapose the two: the action of work and the action of speech. But in its concern for speech the book raises the question: what does speech tell us about our relation to the world that for instance work, or Objectivism, did not tell us?

That the poet had more than an inkling that he was heading this way is suggested by his own comments on 'Leviathan' in a letter to his half-sister, June Oppen Degnan:

Tho I've said that Leviathan is my defense not of the work, but of my role, still it is obvious that the poems arise from my own need to write them. I do not know that they are of *use*. It is possible that they contribute only to the process which is stripping people of their defenses. I don't know and I don't know of any way in which it might be possible to get beyond what is said in them. And yet it is clear that the poems are not written in total isolation, and could not be. (*Selected Letters,* 98–9)

Here is another richly moving instance of Oppen's confrontation with both the necessity and the limitations of his will as an artist; he cannot make the work *work,* he cannot realize or guarantee its 'use'. And yet instead of seeing what Benhabib calls 'the incongruence between deed and intention' as marking the failure of the poems, he recognizes that what it really does is to mark the limits of his role in relation to them: 'I don't know', he concedes, how he could have said more. Of course he does not. In the solitude of his work the poet is tempted by solipsism, self-sufficiency. But he finds a way to see beyond it: 'it is clear that the poems are not written in total isolation and could not be.' At this point in the letter he turns away from the intentional-teleological model to recognize the intersubjective, interpretative context: 'If a writer manages to write, he does have some belief, some hope, in a way of life which he is creating or helping to create. There is no serious writer who is not concerned that there should be at least some editors and publishers who have broken altogether with the conception of literature as part of the entertainment industry, and are able to regard literature as a process of thought' (99).

The very first poem of *The Materials* evokes the confrontation between intention and interpretation. The book begins with an image of men: an image not of men working but of them *talking,* which is all the more powerful for its recognition of the way that talk ranges beyond what any speaker *intends*:

> The men talking
> Near the room's center. They have said
> More than they had intended.
>
> ('Eclogue', *NCP*, 39)

The next poem, 'Image of the Engine', returns us to the world of work, and to the breakdown or failure of work, which was discussed earlier in relation to Heidegger:

> Likely as not a ruined head gasket
> Spitting at every power stroke, if not a crank shaft
> Bearing knocking at the roots of the thing like a pile-driver:
> A machine involved with itself, a concentrated
> Hot lump of a machine
> Geared in the loose mechanics of the world with the valves
>   jumping
> And the heavy frenzy of the pistons. When the thing stops,
> Is stopped, with the last slow cough
> In the manifold, the flywheel blundering
> Against compression, stopping, finally
> Stopped...
>
> (*NCP*, 40)

The poem is not one of Oppen's best by any means, but like many lesser poems it is useful for the light it can shed on better ones. The second section considers the image of engine failure as a familiar metaphor for mortality:

> Endlessly, endlessly,
> The definition of mortality
>
> The image of the engine
>
> That stops.
> We cannot live on that.
> I know that no one would live out
> Thirty years, fifty years if the world were ending
> With his life.
> The machine stares out,
> Stares out
> With all its eyes
>
> (40–1)

As Oppen says, 'We cannot live on that'—which I take it means we cannot live on that image, that metaphor. The 'engine' (Williams's machine made of words again) does justice neither to mortality nor to the life that shapes and is shaped by it. The somewhat strained image of the mortal machine staring out (anticipating the much sharper image of the wild deer in 'Psalm'), is interesting, however, because of the connection it makes between the failure of man's instruments (including, one might say, this particular metaphor) and the sudden and conspicuous presence-at-hand of the world. A world that is not in repair, as Heidegger argues, is a world that one stares at.

6.3 'MORE THAN POLITICS REALLY'

In 1934 Oppen made the decision to stop writing poetry and in 1935 he and Mary joined the Communist Party as committed activists. They would remain card-carrying members right through the McCarthy era, although 'in [their] heads', as Mary wrote to Rachel Blau Duplessis, they had left the Party by 1946.[36] As DuPlessis relates, the FBI began watching the Oppens in 1941—and kept an eye on them for the next twenty-five years (p. xv). The passage of the Smith Act in 1940 had made it possible to indict Communist leaders for conspiracy to overthrow the government and in 1949 the FBI began to harass the Oppens in their home. 'Visits from a neat, unobtrusive car with two gray flannel-suited young men with F.B.I. credentials and notebooks became routine'

---

[36] DuPlessis, Introduction, *Selected Letters of George Oppen*, p. vii–xx (xv).

(*Meaning a Life*, 193). In 1950, 'fearing further and increasing levels of harass-ment', the couple 'went into political exile in Mexico' (DuPlessis, p. xvi). They remained there for most of the following decade. It was not until 1958 that Oppen 'bought a pad of paper and some pencils and started to write *The Materials*' (*Meaning a Life*, 202). I have no new information to add to the existing accounts of what Oppen calls 'the life of [those] times' (*NCP*, 140).[37] My purpose is instead to show how these two opposing paradigms of action, the work paradigm, and the intersubjective paradigm, both make their presence felt in Oppen's attempts to explain his actions. They produce as it were conflicting registers, conflicting ways of seeing. Consider the interview with Dembo:

I think it was fifteen million families that were faced with the threat of immediate starvation. It wasn't a business that one simply read about in the newspaper. You stepped out your door and found men who had nothing to eat. I'm not moralizing now—and I've been through this before—but for some people it was simply impossible not to do something. I've written an essay that appeared in *Kulchur* 10 ['The Mind's Own Place'] in which I explained that I didn't believe in political poetry or poetry as being politically efficacious. I don't even believe in the honesty of a man saying, 'Well, I'm a poet and I will make my contribution to the cause by writing poems about it.' I don't believe that's any more honest than to make wooden nutmegs because you happen to be a woodworker. If you decide to do something politically, you do something that has political efficacy. And if you decide to write poetry, then you write poetry, not something that you hope, or deceive yourself into believing, can save people who are suffering. That was the dilemma of the thirties. In a way I gave up poetry because of the pressures of what for the moment I'll call conscience. But there were some things I had to live through, some things I had to think my way through, some things I had to try out—and it was more than politics, really; it was the whole experience of working in factories, of having a child, and so on. Absurd to ask myself whether what I undertook was right or wrong or right for the artist and the rest of that. Hugh Kenner interrupted my explanation to him of these years by saying, 'In brief, it took twenty-five years to write the next poem.' Which is the way to say it. (187)

In the first place Oppen wants to think in clear-cut categorical terms. There is poetry on the one hand, and politics on the other, and each is characterized by a particular kind of *work*—that is to say, by the manipulation of certain means to certain ends. Politics means doing 'something politically efficacious', in the same way that writing poetry means writing poetry and being a woodworker means making wooden nutmegs. The complicated motivations behind twenty-five years of not writing poetry get to be defined according to Objectivist criteria: '"In brief,

---

[37] Nicholls has been responsible for the most thorough 'attempt to bring together what little information we have about the period of exile' and to flesh out the Oppens' own 'rather reticent and colourless accounts of their time', originally in the essay 'George Oppen in Exile: Mexico and Maritain', *Journal of American Studies*, 39/1 (2005), 1–18 (2, 7), the substance of which is incorporated into *George Oppen and the Fate of Modernism*, along with his other published essays on the poet.

it took twenty-five years to write the next poem." Which is the way to say it.' Oppen's interlocutor provides him with a way of formally resolving, of objectifying, the sincerities of a lifetime: '*the way* to say it'. What won't go into words gets cut out. This desire to simplify, to clarify ('I have not and never did have any motive of poetry I But to achieve clarity'),[38] is part of the overwhelming motivation of Oppen's major poetry: 'One must not come to feel that he has a thousand threads in his hands, I He must somehow see the one thing'.[39] And these ideas of clarity, of seeing the one thing, and by extension of *one way to say it*, reflect not only a visual aesthetic but also a visually oriented epistemology.

Yet, there is also, throughout the passage, striking evidence that Oppen realizes that nothing is as clear-cut as the distinctions he would like to make. The explanation constantly undercuts or qualifies itself: 'in a way I gave up writing poetry because of'; 'what for the moment I'll call'; 'it was more than politics, really; it was the whole experience . . . and so on'. All these discursive gestures, like the repetition of the phrase 'some things', deliberately gesturing beyond any specific thing that the speaker says, actively draw upon the listener's willingness to enter, experientially and emotionally, into that indefiniteness, that vagueness, which is of course the vagueness of a life ('a thousand threads'). From the point of view of this intersubjective or discursive paradigm, what Kenner finally says is less significant than the fact that he interrupts.

The paradox we confront is that two very different notions of politics seem here to exist side-by-side. There is politics as a particular kind of work, a particular kind of externalization. And there is that altogether more indefinite realm of politics, which will not admit of closure, and where the course of any action can be changed or extended by how it is interpreted by others. (As Benahbib puts it: 'Very often, we come to learn *what* we have done through others' understanding and interpretation of, and reaction to, our actions.') From this point of view, the statement 'It was more than politics, really' expresses the paradoxical truth of action as such. Politics is always *more than politics*—for who can say where it ends; who can have the last word on anything he or she has done? The life of politics will not be delineated totally or perfectly; it will not, in Objectivist terms, be laid to rest.[40]

We have to keep in mind that Oppen is looking back many years later on his association with Communism and some thirty years after the period of his overt political activism. At the same time, this in itself might be said to illustrate the whole point about action and interpretation. *Discrete Series* is not a work of

---

[38] *NCP*, 193.

[39] *NCP*, 180.

[40] Davidson puts it very well, reflecting on 'that trinity of concerns that informs Oppen's entire life: politics, epistemology, and poetics . . . As he meditated on the contradictions in American politics, so he drafted poems; as he drafted poems, so he thought about the relationship of old age to love' (*Ghostlier Demarcations*, 78).

explicit political commitment, but the way in which it makes sense of experience is, as we have seen, consistent with the instrumentalist Marxist world-view that seems to have contributed to Oppen's decision to stop writing poetry.[41] For Oppen, poetry and political commitment are very different things. Nevertheless, what they do have in common is that they are both forms of work, having definite ends; i.e. they are both forms, in Benhabib's terms, of intentional-teleological externalization. Yet this is a position that the poetry itself, after 1958, increasingly complicates and contradicts.

However, as Marjorie Perloff sceptically remarks, 'It has been argued, most notably by Burton Hatlen, that Oppen's poetic stance is specifically Marxist.'[42] And Perloff quotes from Hatlen as he sets out his case for what he sees as Oppen's essentially consistent Marxism:

Oppen's is a 'materialist' poetry in its rigorous refusal to surrender to what I would call the 'transcendental temptation'. The very title of *The Materials* testifies to Oppen's commitment to the physical world. But for Oppen as for Marx the physical world is not simply a given. Rather it is 'in process', as human labour reshapes the raw materials of nature. The *people* exerting their *labour* upon the *material* world—out of this matrix, Marx and Oppen agree, emerges the human life-world . . . 'Truth' for [Oppen] exists, if it exists at all, neither in 'nature' nor in the splendid solitude of the reflective mind, but only in the collective, ongoing life of the people '*en masse*' (as Whitman liked to say), as they collectively make through their labour the only world we can know . . . In this affirmation Oppen's poetry, even long after he and Mary left the Communist Party, represents, not a repudiation of or an alternative to the political commitments of Oppen's middle years, but rather an extension of these commitments back into poetry.[43]

I agree with Perloff that such an interpretation seems to be 'wishful thinking' ('Shipwreck', 195), but it is also in my view a categorical straitjacket, bringing with it a kind of blindness or deafness. For note also how Hatlen's emphasis prioritizes the work paradigm described by Benhabib—the intentional-teleological model of action—and passes over, doesn't cite, takes for granted, the spoken or linguistic nature of our lived intersubjectivity. Yet it is precisely to this realm, the realm of lived intersubjectivity, that Oppen's complicatedly confused and contradictory statements about what he was doing when he gave up writing direct us (something that comes across in Perloff's own discussion).[44] And they

---

[41] My conclusion here chimes with that of Nicholls, who writes: 'Motivated as it was by the exigencies of the time, Oppen's decision to abandon poetry for politics was also, we might infer, bound up with a set of assumptions about poetic *form*.' Peter Nicholls, 'George Oppen and "that primitive, Hegel"', *Paideuma*, 32 (2003), 351–75 (352).

[42] Marjorie Perloff, 'The Shipwreck of the Singular: George Oppen's "Of Being Numerous"', *Ironwood*, 13/2 (Fall 1985), 193–204 (194).

[43] Burton Hatlen, 'Not Altogether Lone in a Lone Universe: George Oppen's *The Materials*', *George Oppen: Man and Poet*, 325–57 (331–2).

[44] I should make it clear, however, that I disagree almost as strongly with Perloff's interpretation of Oppen's major work: 'A good deal has been written about Oppen's relationship to the masses,

direct us there not because there is some underlying truth beyond the contradictions but because history, like politics, is like that.

6.4 'OF BEING NUMEROUS'

> Like Zukofsky, he saw the humorous side of things, but he listened more.
> His speech was less fluent, more meditative; it was exact with a pondered
> exactness like his poetry.
>
> Tomlinson, *Some Americans*, 62

> What have we argued about? what have we done?
> 'Of Being Numerous'

It is a remarkable thing that Oppen's artistic silence, while not in itself art, has only seemed to underline the silence of art in the face of politics—so that the silences in the poems and the long silence of the artist have appeared, in some enigmatical way, to be in communion with one another. From an Arendtian point of view, however, this sense of enfolding silences is an illusion, which may be more usefully considered by way of the notion that action, political action, is essentially ephemeral. It exists in the moment of its recognition, above all in the transience of speech, then it disappears: whereas art aspires to the permanency of things, the durability of objects.

Neither of these interpretations, however, seems to account by itself for the complicated, contradictory, yet somehow inextricable relation between speech and objectification, between action and work, between communication and things, at the heart of Oppen's masterpiece 'Of Being Numerous', published ten years after he resumed writing. *Discrete Series* drew attention to the presence-at-hand of things in a working world that doesn't work, a world in which speech barely seems to exist. It pictures a world of alienated use-values, a world which is seen and not heard. People don't talk, they just wave. On the very rare occasions where speech is invoked, it is virtually reified—it is just another strange thing ('My hair, scalp—'). 'Of Being Numerous' reveals a different world. Here the 'existence of things' is not just a function of the mind's eye, or an extension of their use-values: here the reality of things is also an effect of speech. We know that the world is there not only because we see it, or because we use it, but also because we talk about it—and this is the case even if what we talk about is, to some extent, the seeing and the using of it. The opening sections of 'Of Being Numerous' illustrate the point:

but, at least in "Of Being Numerous", the point is that that there is no relationship' ('Shipwreck', 197). This is much too simple, and much too easy to assert.

1

There are things
We live among 'and to see them
Is to know ourselves'.

Occurrence, a part
Of an infinite series,

The sad marvels;

Of this was told
A tale of our wickedness.
It is not our wickedness.

'You remember that old town we went to, and we sat in the
ruined window, and we tried to imagine that we belonged to
those times—It is dead and it is not dead, and you cannot
imagine either its life or its death; the earth speaks and the
salamander speaks, the Spring comes and only obscures it—'

2

So spoke of the existence of things,
An unmanageable pantheon

Absolute, but they say
Arid.

(*NCP*, 163)

The poem begins, then, with some seemingly rather terse statements about our knowledge of the world, and with some allusions, apparently, to *Discrete Series*, including the punning 'Occurrence, a part'—we live among things that are *apart*, but which are nevertheless *parts*—an 'infinite *series*'. (This may recall Oppen's explanation to Dembo: 'A discrete series is a series of terms each of which is empirically derived, each one of which is empirically true.')[45] The lines command attention because of that Wittgenstein-like combination of terseness, audacity, and intensity with which Oppen confronts the world. Even so, what enlivens the plainness of the opening proposition is not the second proposition, which is yet another expression of the sovereignty of visual metaphors in the domain of metaphysics and epistemology, but the fact that the second proposition is in speech marks—which brings to the lines the drama of discursive juxtaposition, an intimation of speech. Where we might have had the solipsistic mood of Wittgenstein's *Tractatus*, we have instead, in contradistinction, an evocation of other persons. That word 'we' suddenly feels like 'we'. There are things we live among, and voices we live among. The question is: what is the relationship between these voices and these things?

[45] Interview with Dembo, 174.

This concern with the underlying significance of speech is amplified in lines 7 and 8 with the allusions to storytelling. It also seems that the peripheral evocation of speech lends a different force to the contradictory, 'It is not our wickedness'. We then move into a longer quotation, of magnificently mysterious prose. According to Davidson, this is Mary Oppen talking about the French poet Yves Bonnefoy (*NCP*, 380)—but of course we don't need to know that for its significance to register. The passage cements the communicative plural subject at the core of the poem ('we' now falls inside the quotation marks, is as it were embraced by them), it exemplifies the force of narrative alluded to in lines 7 and 8, and it introduces the verb *speak*—which supported by the verbs *say, talk, tell,* and *listen* will provide the poem with its most poignant motif and the nearest thing it will offer by way of an answer to the problem of human numerousness.

When the second section of the poem begins, speech is now explicitly to the fore: 'So *spoke* of the existence of things' (my emphasis). In a sense it reruns the beginning of the poem, but from the point of view of speech. In other words, there are things we live among, and there is the speech we conduct about the things we live among. The things we say or 'they say' (line 17). What we tend to forget—and what the poem may be said to have forgotten as it started and rediscovered as it went on—is that the things we live among are unimaginable without that speech.

And just as speech is a means of apprehending the multiplicity of things ('An unmanageable pantheon'), in their multiplicity, so it is a means of getting a handle on the multiplicity of persons—that is to say, a means of turning the raw stuff of multiplicity into recognizable (or significant, or communicative) plurality:

> But I will listen to a man, I will listen to a man, and when I
> speak I will speak, tho he will fail and I will fail. But I will
> listen to him speak. The shuffling of a crowd is nothing—
> well, nothing but the many that we are, but nothing.
>
> (167–8)

Thus section 10 picks up the prose rhythms of section 1, in the repetition of 'speak' ('the earth speaks and the salamander speaks'). Speaking and listening, albeit with the attendant risk of failing, offers an alternative to the 'shuffling', the meaningless numbers, of the crowd. It is a middle way, between 'many' (punning both on *man* and *men*) and 'nothing'.

The next section (11) enlarges on this central image of communicative action. The poem does not deny the importance of vision and the visual representation of knowledge, it just complicates it. The section begins with images of light and seeing: 'You could look from any window' (168). The image of the Empire State Building appears to recall the waving arm of 'Party on Shipboard'. Then, suddenly, among the hollow and immobile buildings, the poem calls for speech: 'Speak || If you can || Speak' (168). This is the third section of the poem so far in which the present tense of 'speak' has appeared, and as in the previous instances it is immediately repeated. Here the repetition, besides picking up those earlier repetitions, gives ballast to the one-word line and sustains the poem's musical form—the revelation of the poem as object.

It continues:

> Phyllis—not neo-classic,
> The girl's name is Phyllis—
>
> Coming home from her first job
> On the bus in the bare civic interior
> Among those people, the small doors
> Opening on the night at the curb
> Her heart, she told me, suddenly tight with happiness—
>
> (169)

The name Phyllis appears to allude to Book Four of Williams's *Paterson* (the 'Idyl' of Corydon and Phyllis); the bus recalls the beginning of Book Three. The English poet Charles Tomlinson has read the section as 'a direct challenge' to *The Waste Land's* depiction of 'squalid sexual encounter'—a reading which is not incompatible with the allusion to Williams.[46] But the critical thing about the encounter with Phyllis is the role of speech: 'Her heart, she told me, suddenly tight with happiness—'. (This passage is variously recalled in section 29: 'We say happiness, happiness and are not | Satisfied'; 'I can tell myself, and I tell myself', with its remarkable echo of Whitman.) Was that then the speech for which the poem called? That the 'girl's name is Phyllis' already draws our attention to the intimacy of the spoken word, the spoken name, while Oppen's 'not neo-classic' is typical of the way he uses contradiction to evoke the contrariness, impatience, difference, the sometimes passionate irascibility, of someone speaking.

The section concludes with another, larger evocation of the spoken word—that is to say, the spoken world: 'To talk of the house and the neighborhood and the docks | | And it is not "art"'. There is a certain imprecision here, which is too easily overlooked and yet it is very much a part of Oppen's characteristic style. Does he mean that 'talk' is not 'art'? Or that this talk that is the poem is not art? Or that the 'house and the neighborhood and the docks' are not art? Or is he talking about that kind of talk in which an artist or poet says that such-and-such a thing is not art? Thus once again the poet implicates himself, in his impassioned vagueness and contradictoriness.

It is hardly necessary to go through every section of the poem in which speech figures, even if there were space. However, it is worth noting that in the next section (12), where Oppen presents us with anthropological images of a primitive people—

> They made small objects
> Of wood and the bones of fish
> And of stone.
>
> (*NCP*, 169)

---

[46] Charles Tomlinson, Introduction, *Poems of George Oppen (1908–1984)* (Newcastle upon Tyne: Cloudforms, 1990), 8–13 (11).

he doesn't just describe a world of objects and tools, but also a world that is animated by talk:

> They talked,
> Families talked.
> They gathered in council
> And spoke, carrying objects.
> They were credulous,
> Their things shone in the forest.
>
> (170)

It is easy to see here a memento of those original primitive Objectivist poets, Oppen's friends, who also 'made small objects', but where before Oppen seemed to think that he could make the things of the world shine without recourse to speech, he now seems to be saying that speaking and shining go together.

As often as not it is the difficulty of speaking that Oppen invokes. 'How talk | Distantly of "The People"', he asks: 'Cars | | Echo like history | Down walled avenues | In which one cannot speak' (171). Sometimes the problem is too many people talking at once, or talking to themselves, the problem of talk about talk: '— and the mad, too, speak only of conspiracy | and people talking—' (186). But it isn't only the words 'speak' and 'talk' that are under pressure. Watch what happens in section 17 to the word 'say':

> The roots of words
> Dim in the subways
>
> There is madness in the number
> Of the living
> 'A state of matter'
>
> There is nobody here but us chickens
>
> Anti-ontology—
>
> He wants to say
> His life is real,
> No one can say why
>
> It is not easy to speak
>
> A ferocious mumbling, in public
> Of rootless speech
>
> (172–3)

Because of the Spartan character of the writing, the tendency of Oppen's meanings to range, to open up, also reacts back upon the words, producing simultaneously an intensification. They have as it were an expansive concentration. 'No one can say why' the man's 'life is real'; but also, 'No one can say why' *he wants to say it*. What do we mean by real? What makes us want to speak of it? What is there to say? 'It is not easy to speak' recalls us to 'Speak ‖ If you can ‖ Speak' and anticipates 'It is difficult now to speak of poetry'—the extraordinary opening line of what is perhaps the most telling part of the entire poem, section 27.

Oppen puts more pressure on the word 'say' in the section immediately before this last, another critical passage and the longest part of the poem. There the poet addresses himself explicitly to the question of the relation between poet and society:

> They carry nativeness
> To a conclusion
> In suicide.
>
> We want to defend
> Limitation
> And do not know how.
>
> Stupid to say merely
> That poets should not lead their lives
> Among poets,
>
> They have lost the metaphysical sense
> Of the future, they feel themselves
> The end of a chain
>
> Of lives, singles lives
> And we know that lives
> Are single
>
> And cannot defend
> The metaphysic
> On which rest
>
> The boundaries
> Of our distances.
> We want to say
>
> 'Common sense'
> And cannot.

(177–8)

The idea of limitation refers to legal and existential limits, social and geographical frontiers, and the ethics and aesthetics of discretion. Limitation informs the empirical derivations of *Discrete Series*, underlies Oppen's concept of objectification (what he refers to, in 'Route', as 'A limited, limiting clarity': i.e. clarity given definition), and enables us to make a distinction between different kinds of life and praxis—between being a poet, for example, and 'doing something politically'. The trouble is that metaphysically at least, these limitations seem to have become indefensible (as we saw for example when we looked at

Benhabib's critique of Arendt in Chapter 3): but we feel, at the level of common sense, that there are distinctions to be made. The poetry is animated by this sense of lived contradiction: 'Stupid to say merely | That poets should not lead their lives | Among poets'. It is not primarily as poets *but as people* that poets—such as Oppen—live among other people. They are poets in their capacity as poets—but before they are poets, they are of course people. And people are always living among people. A poem is, as language, a product of people who are poets and people who are not, and people, so to speak, who are both. It would be 'stupid' even to appear to suggest that it might be otherwise—that poets could somehow lead their lives exclusively among other poets; or that poets might be poets *all their lives*. It is all very well to say 'we know that lives | are single': but the trouble is that we no longer know what 'single' means. We 'cannot defend | ... | The boundaries | Of our distances'—Oppen's use of the inclusive plural pronoun being a case in point.

Yet, Oppen risks the stupidity of merely saying. In other words he risks the stupidity of poetry, sets it against the intelligence of metaphysics. His defiant stupidity corresponds to Wallace Stevens's contestation that poetry is an unofficial view of being—one that has more to say to common sense than to philosophy; one that talks to philosophy by way of common sense. Not for the first time in Oppen's mature work we may perhaps be reminded of Wordsworth's famous definition of a poet as a man speaking to men. Though there is an altogether more acute sense now that such speech is in jeopardy. The passage declines to let the matter rest, to come to a standstill. Words and doubts tumble on, and once again the pressure falls on the word 'say':

> We want to say
>
> 'Common sense'
> And cannot. We stand on
>
> That denial

'We want to say' takes us back immediately of course to the man in section 17 who 'wants to say | His life is real'; just as the word 'cannot' recalls us, for instance, to 'Speak || If you can || Speak' (section 11); to 'one cannot speak' (section 14); and to 'one may honorably keep | His distance | If he can' (section 13). But the crucial point surely is that Oppen *says* 'Common sense'—in common-sense fashion as it were—and, as the lineation emphasizes, even *before* he says that we 'cannot' say it. He does indeed 'stand on' (the vowel sounds picking up and elongating the vowel sounds of 'cannot'), 'That denial'—in all its contradictory senses.

As was argued earlier then, Oppen is in dialogue throughout *Of Being Numerous* with his youthful Objectivist aesthetics and his earlier political and ethical distinctions. He doesn't repudiate them or wholly contradict them—there is no absolute self-conscious philosophical position: he argues with them and is in conversation with them. It is this primacy of dialogue that really matters, that gives the book its character and gives to Oppen's own voice its surprising modulations and its most dramatic and compelling resonance. In the great section 27 Oppen again takes up this question of choices and distinctions, what he calls here 'different order[s] of experience'—and once again he attempts to set art apart:

It is difficult now to speak of poetry—

about those who have recognized the range of choice or those who have lived within the life they were born to—. It is not precisely a question of profundity but a different order of experience. One would have to tell what happens in a life, what choices present themselves, what the world is for us, what happens in time, what thought is in the course of a life and therefore what art is, and the isolation of the actual. (*NCP*, 180)

As the section continues these different orders of experience seem to be figured as the rooms in a building ('I would want to talk of rooms and of what they look out on'), then as floors or levels ('This is the level of art | There are other levels').[47] But what is wonderful about the passage just quoted is how the halting syntax fails to separate out what it claims must be separated, and so complicates or undermines its own existential didacticism. In the attempt 'to speak of poetry' we talk about 'life', and in the attempt 'to tell what happens in a life' we end up talking about 'what art is'. The different orders of experience merge, events overlap, one thing blends into another, which begs the whole question of 'the isolation of the actual', 'the level of art'.

The opening line is, by the way, perhaps the greatest understatement in a body of work that is crafted out of understatements. It is worth thinking about the number of things the line is saying. 'It is difficult now to speak of poetry—': as if it were more difficult 'now', in 1968, than in 1934, when Oppen gave up writing! It could also mean that it is difficult to speak of poetry without speaking of everything else—as the same passage goes on to demonstrate. Or it could mean that it is difficult because, as the poem has been telling us all along, it is difficult anyway to speak of *anything* (compare 'Route': 'One man could not understand me because I was saying simple things').[48] It could also mean that it is difficult because poetry's relationship to speech is difficult. Or it could mean, for a Jewish writer like Oppen, and a veteran of the Second World War, what Adorno meant when he said that 'to write poetry after Auschwitz is barbaric'.[49] Or it could mean what Muriel Rukeyser meant when she said that there was a widespread cultural fear of poetry—an embarrassment, a resistance.

---

[47] *NCP*, 180.
[48] *NCP*, 197.
[49] Theodor W. Adorno, 'Cultural Criticism and Society' (1951), *Prisms*, 19–34 (34). A decade later Adorno refused to 'soften' his words: Theodor W. Adorno, 'Commitment', *Notes to Literature*, vol. 2, ed. Rolf Tiedemann, trans. Shierry Weber Nicholsen (New York: Columbia University Press, 1992), 76–94 (87).

Yet poetry is not speech, much as it might long to speak or seem to enter into dialogue with speech. The emphasis on difficulty throughout of 'Of Being Numerous', the reiteration of the terms 'can' and 'cannot', is a way of saying that poetry speaks and fails to speak—as if this acknowledgement of poetry's difficulty vis-à-vis speech might bring it closer, despite itself, to the state of speech as such.

6.5 FELLOW TRAVELLERS: RICHARD WRIGHT AND MURIEL RUKEYSER

6.5.1

The literary historian Alan Wald has observed:

The Communist movement, which had fewer than 20,000 members in the early Depression years, managed to telescope, crystallize, and articulate concerns felt by a far greater number of individuals, becoming for many an institutionalised conscience. The process, of course, was variegated, because Communist ideology and activism struck a chord among writers with diverse literary sensibilities who were at disparate stages in their careers... Poets felt obliged to make contributions through their writing, by collaborating on cultural projects, or, in a few instances, by abandoning poetry for full-time Party activities, as was the case for many years with Walter Lowenfels, George Oppen... and A. B. Magil.[50]

As we have seen, Marxism informs the terms in which Oppen first sought to understand his decision to stop writing poetry. But there were other ways in which that decision might be understood, as he increasingly conceded—the 'thousand threads' (echoing Hamlet's 'thousand natural shocks'), which complicate, as always, the clear-cut either/or, the 'to be or not to be'. So it is not surprising that Oppen begins to distance himself from Marxism, or begins to find some distance opening up between himself and Marxism—begins to expand upon it and to digress within it—in the years before he moves away from, expands upon, digresses from, Objectivism. There is not a clean break with Objectivism, any more than there is a clean break with Marxism, for the idea of a clean break is itself an Objectivist concept: instead there is a continuing dialogue with both. But the dialogue is exactly what makes all the difference. When Oppen cites that very first poem of *Discrete Series* in 'Of Being Numerous', quoting not any line but the one about *seeing* ('approached the window as if to see'), and adds, 'I should have written, not the rain | Of a nineteenth century day, but the motes | In the air, the dust', he risks unmaking the thing he had made (*NCP*, 186). Its 'rested totality' (Zukofsky) is rendered unfinished, restless. The

[50] Alan M. Wald, *Exiles from a Future Time: The Forging of the Mid-Twentieth-Century Literary Left* (Chapel Hill: University of North Carolina Press, 2002), 17.

poem seems to hesitate, its outline doubles. The poet enters into dialogue with his earlier work and switches the emphasis away from the object in isolation to the dialogue about objects and between them. 'What have we argued about?' he writes, further down the page; 'what have we done?' It is for *argument* to decide what has been *done*.

Oppen's drift beyond Marxism can be measured by the way his poetry embraces, accommodates and seizes dramatically on speech—what Benhabib calls the realm of 'lived intersubjectivity', what Arendt calls the domain of speech and action. Indeed, it is no exaggeration to say that to come across *Of Being Numerous* after *Discrete Series* is, leaving aside for a moment the intervening volumes *The Materials* and *This in Which*, a bit like traversing the interval between silent cinema and the Golden Age of Hollywood 'Talkies'. The parallel is not arbitrary—for in cinema also of course an almost wholly visual apprehension of the world was animated dramatically by the intervention of speech.[51]

However, I want to press home this argument about Marxist objectification on the one hand, and speech and action on the other, by looking, briefly and finally, at two American writers who were contemporary with Oppen and whose experiences of the relationship between art and politics provide some valuable points of comparison.

6.5.2

The novelist Richard Wright was born in the same year as Oppen and also joined the Communist Party in the 1930s, just a couple of years before the Oppens. His social background was very different. He was an African American, and his family, which was originally from the South, was poor. There is no evidence, to my knowledge, that the two men ever met. But given Wright's colour and celebrity, and Oppen's relative obscurity and abrupt silence, that is hardly surprising. Like Oppen, Wright was also drawn to existentialist thought: indirectly at first, through Dostoevsky, but eventually he read Albert Camus and Jean-Paul Sartre and according to Michel Fabre he even discussed Heidegger with Hannah Arendt.[52] Because of the success that he enjoyed as a writer, particularly an African American writer, especially after the publication of *Native Son* in 1940, his identification with the Communist Party and his subsequent rejection of it were public matters in a way that Oppen's allegiances were not. Disillusioned, during the war, with the Party's softening attitude on civil rights

---

[51] In his thinking about art Zukofsky was much more responsive to the cinema than Oppen, and wrote perceptively about it—but interestingly it was the silent cinema, the cinema of Chaplin above all, that he loved. See his essay '*Modern Times*'—the title of a movie in which Charlie sings but doesn't talk (*Prepositions+*, 57–64).

[52] Michel Fabre, *The Unfinished Quest of Richard Wright*, trans. Isabel Barzun (1973; Urbana: University of Illinois Press, 1993), 299.

issues, particularly its willingness to tolerate segregation in the army, Wright broke with the Communists in the early 1940s.

Plainly influenced by Theodore Dreiser's *An American Tragedy* (1925) and by Dostoevsky's *Crime and Punishment* (1866), Wright's most important novel, *Native Son*, tells the story of a poor uneducated black youth, Bigger Thomas, who, in a fit of panic, kills the daughter of a liberal-minded white property millionaire a matter of hours after getting a job as the family chauffeur. Since he instantly foresees what he will be accused of, he tries to destroy the evidence. Gradually he identifies with his crime, seeing it almost as a liberation. He embraces the 'Fate', as Wright puts it, of killer and fugitive. Until he is caught and tried, the action is related principally from Bigger's violent, frequently inarticulate point of view. At his trial, however, Bigger is defended by an eloquent left-wing Jewish lawyer, Boris Max, whose lengthy social analysis abruptly displaces Bigger's perspective. While no one seriously doubts that Max's speech expresses a broadly Marxist ideological standpoint, what his intervention means within the dramatic context of the novel is open to debate. One school of thought, almost certainly influenced by Ralph Ellison's somewhat later satire of the Communist 'Brotherhood' in *Invisible Man* (1952), sees it as deliberately ironic: a satire of dogmatic ideology, that treats Bigger as a social object rather than recognizing him as a unique individual with a distinctive human experience.

At the other extreme, critics as respected as Fabre, Wright's biographer, have assumed that Max is meant to articulate the novelist's hard-line Marxist critique of American race relations: 'Wright does use Max as the spokesman for his Marxist analysis of the social situation in the United States, and he is inclined to equate racial and social prejudice as both being fostered by economic exploitation.'[53] Of course, what Fabre calls Wright's 'Marxist analysis' is not necessarily the dramatic analysis worked out in the novel as a whole. We don't have to see Max as a cold-blooded precursor of Ellison's totalitarian puppets to understand that the drama at the close of the novel turns on the dialogical distance between what Max says in the courtroom and what Bigger tries to say to him immediately afterwards.

At the close of Max's long speech, we are told categorically that Bigger 'had not understood the speech': 'Bigger was not at that moment really bothered about whether Max's speech had saved his life or not. He was hugging the proud thought that Max had made the speech all for him, to save his life. It was not the meaning of the speech that gave him pride, but the mere act of it.'[54] What moves

---

[53] Fabre, *Unfinished Quest of Richard Wright*, 184. As he notes, 'Wright's liberal admirers have tended to minimize the extent and sincerity of his commitment to the Party, while many Communists reproached him for not adopting a true Communist perspective because he did not portray the masses as revolutionary' (ibid.).
[54] Richard Wright, *Native Son* (1940; New York: HarperPerennial, 1993), 473.

Bigger about the speech is not its content but its utterance: not what it says, but that it was said at all. But that isn't of course why Max has spoken.

Nevertheless, it gives a clue to what follows, when Bigger tries to speak to the spent and withdrawn lawyer in the silence of his death cell:

Silently, Bigger shook hands with him. Max was before him, quiet, white, solid, real . . .

There was silence . . . Well, why didn't he [Bigger] speak now? . . . He stopped trying, and in the very moment he stopped, he heard himself talking with tight throat, in tense, involuntary whispers; he was trusting the sound of his voice rather than the sense of his words to carry his meaning . . .

Under the pressure of a feeling of futility, his voice trailed off . . . His lips moved, but no words came. . . .

'I'm glad I got to know you before I go!' he said with almost a shout; then was silent, for that was not what he had wanted to say. (Wright, 491–2, 494)

In the course of the intermittent silence and despair, Max himself also speaks, or as Wright says, mumbles: 'But Bigger had not heard him. In him again, imperiously, was the desire to talk, to tell; his hands were lifted in mid-air and when he spoke he tried to charge into the tone of his words what he *himself* wanted to hear, what *he* needed' (496). The old Marxist is uneasy before the young man's need for some sort of last-minute, eschatological reckoning: 'Bigger knew that Max would rather not have him talk like this; but he could not help it. He had to die and he had to talk' (496). Bigger succeeds neither in saying what he wants to say, nor in hearing what he wants to hear. Furthermore, Wright makes it clear that both men are in their different ways acutely conscious of their existential solitude. Bigger wants to hear himself speak, and 'what he wanted to say was stronger in him when he was alone' (492); while Max tries to quiet him with the slightly self-pitying truism that 'men die alone' (496).

However, Wright's great achievement here consists in the writing's revelation of a communicative imperative that exists quite apart from the consolations of existential isolation. Max's speech doesn't get through to Bigger, but the fact that *he speaks* gets through ('the mere act of it'). Similarly, Bigger cannot say to Max what he wants to say to him when he is alone, but that is not more significant than the fact that Max's presence still draws Bigger into speaking—spontaneously and *involuntarily*, as Wright points out. And even if what Bigger wants to say is also something he himself primarily wants to hear, the fact remains that the other man's presence is somehow crucial to this process. He wants to hear himself speak in the presence of another—which is to say, that he *can* only speak in the presence of another; and this presence of the other is more important finally than whether or not he or she understands what is said. Wright demonstrates that Oppen's 'I will listen to a man, I will listen to a man, and when I speak I will speak, tho he will fail and I will fail', is not only, as it half purports to be, a statement of the futility of the communicative situation: it is also, as the poem increasingly realizes, a description of the communicative situation as such, in which there is commonly a measure of failure, or at the very least of the *feeling* of failure. Emphatic as it is, Oppen's 'tho' by no means negates the force of 'speak' and 'listen'. On the contrary, these words carry more force because the word 'fail' is so emphatic: we fail and fail again, but still we speak, still we listen. To fail is not to fail outright. To feel that one did not say what one wanted to say is no proof that one said nothing. Wright's magnificently concise declaration, 'He had to die and he had to talk', probably gains some of its power from its unconscious substitution of *talk* for *live* (as who should say, he had to live and he had to die), and its rich intuitive identification of life and talk. (Compare Wright's existential Cartesian punning, 'For real, I am',[55] with Oppen's 'He wants to say | His life is real, | No one can say why'.)

That speech enacts more than it means is a critical point for Arendt. The conviction that 'these two human capacities', action and speech, she writes, 'belonged together and are the highest of all seems to have preceded the *polis* and was already present in pre-Socratic thought... Speech and action were considered to be coeval and coequal, of the same rank and the same kind... [F]inding the right words at the right moment, quite apart from the information or communication they may convey, is action' (*HC*, 25–6).

So what is it that speech is doing in Bigger's particular situation, given that it demonstrably fails, in Arendt's words, to convey information or communication? The answer is that its action is to reveal the other person's presence: it reveals him, simply, as someone who is *there*—who wants to say his life is real, though no one can say why—and he (that is Bigger), can only express this reality, can only *say it*, in so far as there is someone else *there* too. The whole conclusion of the novel is about this disclosure of Bigger, as an 'acting and speaking agent' (Arendt), to Max—who, as fifty years of commentary has pointed out, has somehow missed it. This revelation is not to be confused with presuming to understand him ('he will fail and I will fail'), it is simply about bearing witness to him: the acknowledgement of the other person's existence rather than the comprehension of it. As Arendt writes:

This revelatory quality of speech and action comes to the fore where people are *with* others and neither for nor against them—that is, in sheer human togetherness. Although nobody knows whom he reveals when he discloses himself in deed or word, he must be willing to risk the disclosure...

The basic error of all materialism in politics... is to overlook the inevitability with which men disclose themselves as subjects, as distinct and unique persons, even when they wholly concentrate upon reaching an altogether worldly, material object. (*HC*, 180, 183)

<hr />

[55] Wright, *Native Son*, 502.

What Wright and Oppen have in common, then, is the realization that the alternative to Marxism is the space of speech and action; or to put it another way, and going back to Bigger's cell, the alternative to Marxism is talk—or rather life. Like Oppen, Wright doesn't abandon Marxism: he enters into dialogue with it. Or rather, he enters into dialogue. For this is not a dialogue about Marxism (no one pretends that Max and Bigger are arguing about Marx). It is a dialogue that takes place alongside Marxism and does things Marxism cannot do. For it is more concerned with the revelation of the acting and speaking agent (Bigger, say, or Phyllis) than with raising the proletariat to historical self-consciousness. Wright of course enters into dialogue as early as 1940—while he is still a committed member of the Communist Party. Oppen enters into dialogue in 1958. Wright enters into dialogue and in a sense it saves his writing. Oppen enters into dialogue and begins to write again.

6.5.3

Though he has almost nothing to say about Oppen in his study of the 'mid-twentieth-century literary left', *Exiles from a Future Time*, Alan Wald writes enthusiastically of Muriel Rukeyser, a poet with whom Oppen would seem at first to have much in common. Just five years younger, Rukeyser came, like him, from a solidly middle-class East Coast Jewish family: like him she enjoyed the relative luxury of a college education which she left prematurely, without graduating; and like him she was drawn to left-wing radicalism and experimental modernist poetry. Her first book, *Theory of Flight* (1935) came out just a year after his. Oppen appears to have owned two volumes of Rukeyser's poetry, but I'm not aware that they knew each other personally.[56] Their respective critics and admirers have not sought to compare them.[57] And it's easy to see why. Rukeyser was no Objectivist, and she published her first poems in *New Masses*, the sort of ideological organ that the Oppens distrusted.[58]

There were other significant differences. In spite of Rukeyser's having been, as Wald puts it, 'pro-Communist for nearly two decades' (300), she never joined the Party:

Most likely she was a member of the Young Communist League in the early 1930s, but after 1940 she became increasingly independent...

In the political biography she later imparted to her son, she said that she had come close to joining in the mid-1930s—to the point of taking out an application—but had

---

[56] 'George Oppen's Library: A Bibliography', George Oppen Papers, the Mandeville Special Collections, University of California at San Diego.

[57] Davidson discusses both poets in *Ghostlier Demarcations*, but does not compare them.

[58] 'We stayed carefully away from people who wrote for *New Masses*', Oppen recalled. 'A Conversation with George Oppen', with Charles Amirkhanian and David Gitin, *Ironwood*, 5 (1975), 23.

pulled back at the last minute from a desire to protect her creative autonomy. By 1940, however, she was adamant about her independence from the Communist Party in her correspondence, although there is no public record of her dissociating herself from the Party's slavish pro-Soviet policies during the next decade. (Wald, 302)

Wald discusses the conflict between Rukeyser's determinedly innovative poetic practice, which he agrees 'might convincingly be dubbed "modernist"', and the outright aversion to modernism 'within the Communist cultural leadership' (309). He cites an important contemporary essay by John Malcolm Brinnin, 'The Social Poet and the Problem of Communication' (1943),[59] in which the critic examines the three volumes of poetry Rukeyser published in the 1930s and traces her 'move from an emphasis on straightforward declarations, often in urban speech, toward the increasing use of images of psychological and surrealist character, as well as a change in the use of symbols from those that were public and universal to those more "privately conceived and privately endowed"' (Wald, 308). Sixty years apart, Wald and Brinnin concur that Rukeyser succeeds in avoiding the kind of poetry that is effectively little more than 'radical journalism' in verse, 'a kind of poetic commentary' on 'the Party line', without retreating completely into formal opacity and hermetic subjectivity (ibid.).

Another way of putting this is to say that for Rukeyser the history of subjectivity, the foregrounding of the self in its discursive depth, becomes part of the living history the poet confronts. It's not a way of avoiding history, politics, society, but another means of addressing them; it is a way of acknowledging her subjective immersion in them. Still, it is easy to see what Brinnin was getting at when he talked about the straightforwardness of Rukeyser's more public verse. It leaps out at us in the unabashed ideological crudity of such poems from that first book as 'Thousands of Days', 'Metaphor to Action', and 'Cats and a Cock'.[60] This last poem, for instance, is certainly very remote from Oppen's understanding, during the 1930s, of the categorical gulf between poetry and politics:

> there is a labor
> before reunion.
> Poets, pickets,
> prepare for dawn![61]

There is no marked difference here, for Rukeyser, between the labour of poets and pickets; their trades union will be a 'reunion'. This kind of punning, by means

---

[59] John Malcolm Brinnin, 'Muriel Rukeyser: The Social Poet and the Problem of Communication', *Poetry: A Magazine of Verse*, 56/4 (1943), 554–75.

[60] For an account of how 'reviewers were divided over the "proletarianism" of *Theory of Flight*', see Louise Kertesz, *The Poetic Vision of Muriel Rukeyser* (Baton Rouge: Louisiana State University Press, 1980), 96–7.

[61] *The Collected Poems of Muriel Rukeyser*, ed. Janet E. Kaufman and Anna F. Herzog, with Jan Heller Levi (Pittsburgh: University of Pittsburgh Press, 2005), 64.

of which the two types of labour are united, recurs further on: 'poetry, picket-line', she writes, as if committed poets pen *picket-lines* (*Collected Poems*, 65). As the poem rises to a crescendo, 'masses recognize masses' and 'mouth sets on mouth' (68). Here the problem of numerousness is no problem at all:

> Tomorrow's Mayday.—How many are we?
>   We'll be everyone.
>
> .   .   .   .
>
> poets and pickets contriving a valid country,
> :   Mayday moment, forever provoking new
>   belief and blooming.
>
>   (68)

Nevertheless, such strident gaucherie cannot stand for the book as a whole, and it needs to be seen in the context of certain characteristic continuities—above all Rukeyser's lifelong concern with speech and voice, which runs through her work like a signature. Indeed it is because of Rukeyser's dedication to something like the bravery and vulnerability of the voice that from to time she is apt to make excessively 'straightforward declarations'—especially of an ideological kind. It is all part of a fearless and most un-snobbish insistence on human solidarity ('We'll be everyone'). But if the heady straightforwardness of 'Cats and a Cock' is illustrative of the pitfalls of openness, of Rukeyser's passionately candid disposition, then a remarkable early poem such as 'Effort at Speech between Two People' exemplifies its special strength. Here in fact the greater the candidness, the greater the nuance, as the poem casts a spell of unforced and intimate obscurity. Rukeyser, it turns out, has a voice like no other:

> :   Speak to me.   Take my hand.   What are you now?
>   I will tell you all.   I will conceal nothing.
>   When I was three, a little child read a story about a rabbit
>   who died, in the story, and I crawled under a chair   :
>   a pink rabbit   :   it was my birthday, and a candle
>   burnt a sore spot on my finger, and I was told to be happy.
>
> :   Oh, grow to know me.   I am not happy.   I will be open:
>   Now I am thinking of white sails against a sky like music,
>   like glad horns blowing, and birds tilting, and an arm about me.
>   There was one I loved, who wanted to live, sailing.
>
> :   Speak to me.   Take my hand.   What are you now?
>   When I was nine, I was fruitily sentimental,
>   fluid   :   and my widowed aunt played Chopin,
>   and I bent my head on the painted woodwork, and wept.
>   I want now to be close to you.   I would
>   link the minutes of my days close, somehow, to your days.

:   I am not happy.   I will be open.
    I have liked lamps in evening corners, and quiet poems.
    There has been fear in my life.   Sometimes I speculate
    On what a tragedy his life was, really.

:   Take my hand.   Fist my mind in your hand.   What are you now?
    When I was fourteen, I had dreams of suicide,
    and I stood at a steep window, at sunset, hoping toward death :
    if the light had not melted clouds and plains to beauty,
    if light had not transformed that day, I would have leapt.
    I am unhappy.   I am lonely.   Speak to me.

:   I will be open.   I think he never loved me:
    he loved the bright beaches, the little lips of foam
    that ride small waves, he loved the veer of gulls:
    he said with a gay mouth: I love you.   Grow to know me.

:   What are you now?   If we could touch one another,
    if these our separate entities could come to grips,
    clenched like a Chinese puzzle . . . yesterday
    I stood in a crowded street that was live with people,
    and no one spoke a word, and the morning shone.
    Everyone silent, moving. . . . Take my hand.   Speak to me.

(*Collected Poems*, 9–10)

It's not clear whether there are one or two voices here. There's a sense of subtle contradiction. Thematic continuities, the repetition of certain phrases, seem to suggest one voice. But visually, typographically, at least, the poem suggests two voices alternating—the first speaking in groups of six lines, the second in groups of four. However, it might be just one person talking to herself, with ceremonious pauses, trying to imagine the presence of another—or trying to draw another (silent) person out: perhaps by means of intimate confession (talking for instance about someone else). The ironic burden of the speech is 'Speak to me'. But if the speaker means, as she says, to be open, it doesn't follow that she is really open to the person she is with. The colons suggest openness—but they are also an ironic image: two separate points in space.

Because of these uncertainties the title of the poem is important: what it presents is not necessarily speech but an 'effort at speech'; this effort takes place in some sense 'between two people', which suggests that it depends on both of them. And this is the case even if one person is just talking to herself, in the process of attempting to speak with another: for what ensues goes on *between* them. 'People' is interesting too: people who are in a sense learning to speak. Are we people if we cannot yet speak? Or are we still children (as some of the childlike imagery and feelings may suggest)? And are children people?

Perhaps the poem is also an allegory of reading—or of what someone might like to get from a poem. The reader wants the poem to speak to her, the poem claims it 'will be open'. It is the poem's suggestiveness and ambiguity on all these matters that make it eloquent and affecting, and allow it at the same time to keep a certain distance, to leave, as it says, a space between. The poem's formal power comes from its alternating repetition of certain commonplace phrases, which, thus stylized, seem to shed their banality—an effect which casts a spell in turn over the commonplace intimacies that the people seek (and perhaps fail) to exchange.

Language and rhythm clearly recall a passage from T. S. Eliot's *The Waste Land*, the deadly exchange between the lovers in 'A Game of Chess': 'Stay with me. I Speak to me. Why do you never speak? Speak'.[62] We may also feel that this is a passage that haunts the encounter with Phyllis in 'Of Being Numerous' ('Speak || If you can || Speak').[63] If Oppen recalls Eliot, it is not to suggest that communication is easier than Eliot's poem implies. But the 'effort at speech' is more important to him than some ironical judgement on the interlocutors. Rukeyser's response is different again. She is fascinated first of all by the drama of the situation. But where Eliot sees his twosome as broken isolates, who express the half-heartedness of a dying culture, Rukeyser, under the influence of Marx and psychoanalysis, sees them as repressed. Fear is the keynote: 'There has been fear in my life', the poem says. The whole book cries out not just for a revolution of the proletariat but also for a revolution of the unconscious—to cast off this fear.[64] Seen in this context the 'effort at speech' is, though the people concerned may not realize it, just 'this latest effort to revolution'.[65]

The casting of the unconscious as a kind of proletariat figures strongly in 'The Gyroscope': 'Air mocks, and desire whirls outward in strict frenzy' (*Collected Poems*, 25); 'The dynamics of desire are explained I in terms of action outward and reaction to a core' (ibid.). Or, as the first poem in *Theory of Flight* puts it, with another of those characteristic heavy-handed puns, this time explicitly linking the sexual and the political: 'Not Sappho, Sacco. I Rebellion pioneered among our lives'.[66] When desire finds the courage to speak ('dynamiting the structure of our loves'), it *flies*. This is Rukeyser's 'Theory of Flight':

---

[62] T. S. Eliot, *Collected Poems 1909–1962* (1963; London: Faber and Faber, 1974), p. 67, lines 111–12.

[63] Perhaps Oppen was also thinking of the encounter with the Hyacinth girl: 'I could not I Speak . . . Looking into the heart of light, the silence' (Eliot, p. 64, lines 38–41). There are echoes of Eliot throughout early Rukeyser, notably for instance in 'First Elegy. Rotten Lake', discussed later in the present chapter.

[64] It will remain a constant theme of her work. See e.g. the 'Third Elegy. The Fear of Form' (*Collected Poems*, 304–7), or 'Moment of Proof', which begins: 'The fear of poetry is the I fear' (ibid. 155). 'The Fear of Poetry' is also the title of the first subsection of Part One of Rukeyser's book *The Life of Poetry*. 'Fear-led and led again to fear', she writes in her apologia, 'The Motive of All of It' (1948), which ends by invoking 'Lenin with his cry of Dare We Win' (*Collected Poems*, 260). The word also occurs of course in one of the best-known lines of Eliot's *Waste Land*: 'I will show you fear in a handful of dust' (Eliot, line 30).

[65] 'The Lynchings of Jesus', *Collected Poems*, 25.

[66] 'Poem Out of Childhood', *Collected Poems*, 3.

Master in the plane shouts 'Contact'   :
master on the ground   :   'Contact!'
          he looks up   :   'Now?' whispering   :   'Now'.
          'Yes', she says.   'Do'.
          Say yes, people.
          Say yes.
          YES.

(*Collected Poems*, 48)

Clumsy as this flying-machine imagery is, and unsuccessful as I think the
poem is, it is interesting for its gendering of the historical dialectic; for its attempt
to establish 'contact' *between two people*; for its use of direct speech; and for its
running together of the mass social and the individually sexual—as the voice
which encourages the people seems to speak with the voice of Molly Bloom.[67]

One cannot see Rukeyser plain, I think, without addressing her prolixity. It is
as much a feature of her work as brevity is a feature of Oppen's or Creeley's. The
poems, the longer ones in particular, have a way of pouring forth. 'Our days pour
down. | I am pouring my poems', she wrote late in her life (*Collected Poems*, 482).
Her poetry floods the page and seems capable of taking up anything in its path.
From one angle it seems to roar forward; from another to meander copiously. Yet
in the middle of this prolixity the poet finds her voice, and couldn't find it, one
feels, without first indulging that prolixity.

At various points in her writing Rukeyser recalls her visit to Spain in the
summer of 1936 to report on the Anti-Fascist Olympic Games. The Spanish
Civil War broke out days before she arrived, and her recollections cluster around
her eventual evacuation from the country and the question, as it was then raised
for her, of poetry's place in what she would come to call 'the first century of
world wars' (*Collected Poems*, 430): the question, which was also Oppen's
question, of the relation of poetry to politics, to ideology in action. Here are
two slightly different accounts she gives of an incident during the evacuation
when that question seemed as it were to form on the night air. The first comes
from the introduction to *The Life of Poetry* (1949):

We were on a small ship, five times past our capacity in refugees, sailing for the first port
at peace. On the deck that night, people talked quietly about what they had just seen and
what it might mean to the world . . . There were long pauses between those broken images
of life, spoken in language after language.

Suddenly, throwing his question into talk not at all leading up to it—not seeming to—
a man—a printer, several times a refugee—asked, 'And poetry—among all this—where is
there a place for poetry?'

Then I began to say what I believe. (2–3)

---

[67] See Joyce, *Ulysses*. Oppen also, as it happens, wittily invoked Molly's final words when asked
by the poet Sharon Olds about his Jewishness (*Selected Letters*, 323).

The introduction ends right there. So all we get is Rukeyser's announcement that *she began to speak*. On the one hand, it is of course a way of suggesting that the book, *The Life of Poetry*, contains all she said or had meant to say that night. On the other hand, the fact that she doesn't tell us what she said, that she leaves everything to the imagination, puts the emphasis on the act of speaking rather than on what was said: the act of speaking before others, speech as a form of action and disclosure, through which one appears dramatically before the world, in the Arendtian sense.

In a poem called 'Mediterranean', published just over a decade earlier in *U.S. 1* (1938), Rukeyser had already recalled in detail the night of the evacuation and, in the darkness, the printer's sudden question:

> Escape, dark on the water, an overloaded ship.
> Crowded the deck. Spoke little. Down to dinner.
> Quiet on the sea: no guns.
> The printer said, In Paris there is time,
> but where's its place now; where is poetry?
>
>> This is the sea of war; the first frontier
>> blank on the maps, blank sea; Minoan boats
>> maybe achieved this shore;
>> mountains whose slope divides
>> one race, old insurrections, Narbo, now
>> moves at the coloured beach
>> destroyer wardog. 'Do not burn the church,
>> compañeros, it is beautiful. Besides,
>> it brings tourists.' They smashed only the image
>> madness and persecution.
>> Exterminating wish; they forced the door,
>> lifted the rifle, broke the garden window,
>> removed only the drawings: cross and wrath.
>> Whenever we think of these, the poem is,
>> that week, the beginning, exile
>> remembered in continual poetry.
>
> Voyage and exile, a midnight cold return,
> dark to our left mountains begin the sky.
>
> .   .   .   .
>
> The poem is the fact, memory fails
> under and seething lifts and will not pass.

(*Collected Poems*, 146–7)

It is difficult not to quote at length the passage following the question, which may also give a hint as to what I called Rukeyser's prolixity—difficult not because of the detail, which is concrete enough, but because of the abstractions about poetry that frame it. The story is told here with markedly different emphases: the question about poetry's place is obscured initially by uncertainty about the referent of 'its' (one could be forgiven for taking this to mean: where's time's place? or even where, now, is Paris's place?), and by the semicolon. In *The Life of Poetry* by contrast there is no ambiguity about the referent—as the noun both opens and closes the question, giving it some of the terse force of Hölderlin's question, *'wozu Dichter...?'*

Following the description of the voyage, which in keeping with the question plays on the page-like blankness of maps and sea, there appear to be two attempts to give an answer. The first begins, 'Whenever we think of these, the poem is'—i.e. whenever we think of these details the poem takes place. But such force as this has is blunted again by the failure to make the point crisply, the idea instead is dragged out repetitively: 'remembered in continual poetry'. Here it's not clear whether she means that the memory of the events creates poetry continually (in which case, how seriously can we take the word 'continual'?), or that poetry continues, and continues to remember. I call this prolix because the poem doesn't seem to be interested in developing the nuances, the differences, or sustaining the tension between them. It seems content to be dimly aware of them. For after another verse paragraph the poem generalizes again: 'the poem is the fact', etc. In two lines we get a whole string, or rather several strings, of verbs: *being, failing under, seething, lifting* (or *seething while lifting*), *willing,* and *not passing,* whose relationship to one another is vague and produces no particular image. At the same time, interestingly, Rukeyser makes no mention of engaging with the printer or his question directly, right there and then. There is no 'Then I began to say' ... The poet didn't find her voice, or doesn't relate if she found it, and her retrospective attempts to answer the question lack precision and conviction—or express conviction without precision, which is just as bad. (What Yeats said about people is just as true sometimes of poems: 'The worst are full of passionate intensity.')

A year later, in another striking, if characteristically uneven poem, 'First Elegy. Rotten Lake', originally from her third book, *A Turning Wind* (1939), Rukeyser recalled again, more briefly this time, her visit to Spain.[68] Essentially a testament to the writer's 'unfinished spirit', the 'amazing desire I that keeps [her] alive', the poem is an affirmation of action, of the will to survive, and a repudiation of the world of Eliot's 'Gerontion' and *The Waste Land,* whose voices and imagery haunt it. Now one of the things that is remarkable about this poem and enables it to work is, once again, the role of speaking and saying: for example, the poet's private cautioning: '(don't say it!)'; 'the poet I and his wife, those who say Survive'; the description of those who 'lose their hands and voices, never I get used to the world':

> Walking at night, they are asked Are you your best friend's
> best friend? and must say No, not yet, they are
> love's vulnerable, and they go down to Rotten Lake
> hoping for wonders.

[68] *Collected Poems,* 299–301.

At last, in the poem's final stanzas the poet writes: 'I say in my own voice. These prophecies I may all come true':

> [I] cry I want!   I want!   rising among the world
> to gain my converted wish, the amazing desire
> that keeps me alive, though the face be still, be still,
> the slow dilated heart know nothing but lack,
> now I begin again the private rising,
> the ride to survival of that consuming bird
> beating, up from dead lakes, ascents of fire.

Here again we have the familiar imagery of desire and flight, not an aeroplane this time but the mythical phoenix that rises from death; that rises from 'lack' (punning on the 'rotten lake' of the title). The word 'rising' is repeated, for it refers both to the rising of the bird and the rising of the poet's voice, her 'private rising', crying 'I want! I want!' We note also the reference to 'beating'—the beating of wings, of the heart, and of the poem finding its rhythm.

The importance to Rukeyser of *saying in her own voice* is given forthright expression in 'Suicide Blues', from her fourth book, *Beast in View* (1944):

> I want to speak in my voice!
> I want to speak in my real voice!
>
> This street leads into the white wind
> I am not yet ready to go there.
> Not in my real voice.
>
> The river.   Do you know where the river springs?
> The river issues from a tall man,
> From his real voice.
>
> Do you know where the river is flowing?
> The river flows into a singing woman,
> In her real voice.
>
> Are you able to imagine truth?
> Evil has conspired a world of death,
> An unreal voice.
>
> The death-world killed me when the flowers shine,
> In spring, in front of the little children,
> It threw me burning out of the window
> And all my enemies phoned my friends,
> But my legs went running around that building
> Dancing to the suicide blues.
>
> They flung me into the sea
>
> The sunlight ran all over my face,
> The water was blue the water was dark brown

And my severed head swam around that ship
Three times around and it wouldn't go down.

Too much life, my darling, embraces and strong veins,
Every sense speaking in my real voice,
Too many flowers, a too-knowing sun,
Too much life to kill.

                                    (*Collected Poems*, 216–17)

The poem pursues the same themes as 'Rotten Lake': desire, survival, rebirth, life as process, journeying, the pettiness of other people that tries to undermine us, and above all of course the significance of speaking in your real voice—of not tuning in to death's 'unreal voice'. As with the earlier poem, Rukeyser's extremely confident use of the first-person pronoun is very much part of that 'real voice'. She hears herself speak.

We know that the voices in Rukeyser's poetry aren't always hers. As she writes in 'Correspondences' (*A Turning Wind*): 'a lyric poet has his voices, audible | as separate lives' (*Collected Poems*, 167). We can't possibly do justice to all of them. This is certainly not the place, for instance, to survey the voices included in the documentary sequence *The Book of the Dead* (1938). Instead I will just give a few more striking instances, beginning with that third book, *A Turning Wind*. The 'Fourth Elegy. The Refugees' specifically relates the question of voice to the dilemma of the melting pot: 'I want to write for my race.   But what race will you speak, | being American?' (*Collected Poems*, 307). Note how the verb *to write* is automatically converted into the verb *to speak*. The brilliant and vivid 'Nuns in the Wind' begins:

As I came out of the New York Public Library
you said your influence on my style would be noticed
and from now on there would be happy poems.

                                    (*Collected Poems*, 161)

The speaker says other things, before the poet says, in her *real voice*: 'Well, I said suddenly in the tall and abstract room, | time to wake up' (162). In 'The Victims, a Play for the Home', Rukeyser again uses the voice to confront questions of authenticity and inauthenticity: 'if anything is said, it is what others said', she writes: 'The player thinks: Who speaks for me?' (ibid. 176). In 'Judith', there is 'a dark woman at a telephone | thinking ... | ... saying to her friend' (ibid. 179). And in the sequence of 'Lives' that concludes the book, Rukeyser imagines the voices of, among others: J. Willard Gibbs ('said, "Mathematics *is* a language"');[69] Whitman ('Whitman forever saying, "Identify"');[70] the soul ('The soul says to the self: I will withdraw');[71] John Jay Chapman ('His soul rises screaming in the shape

---

[69] *Collected Poems*, 182.
[70] Ibid. 183.   [71] Ibid. 185.

of an eagle. I He says, quietly and exactly, "This will never do"');[72] Chapman speaking of Whitman ('He speaks of Whitman as tramp');[73] Ann Burlak ('Let her be seen, a voice on a platform, heard I as a city is heard);[74] 'She speaks to the ten greatest American women');[75] and finally Charles Ives ('Knowing the voices of the country', and sounding for a moment not a little like George Oppen: 'To whom do I speak today?').[76]

This presence of the voice in Rukeyser, the invocation of speech, was to the very last a prominent feature of her work. *Waterlily Fire* (1962) begins with a poem called 'The Speaking Tree' and ends with the words 'I speak to you You speak to me' (*Collected Poems*, 410). The volume *Speed of Darkness* (1968) ends with the words:

> Who will speak these days,
> if not I,
> if not you?
>
> (*Collected Poems*, 468)

It is impossible to cite as many instances as one would like to, to enumerate so many voices. 'Martin Luther King, Malcolm X' contains the arresting image, 'he is shot through the voice', and ends by invoking 'my black voice bleeding' (ibid. 494). A poem called 'The Outer Banks' speaks of 'all my voices' (ibid. 450). Another poem called, simply, 'Voices' begins with the words 'Voices of all our voices' (ibid. 475). Throughout these poems the poet Rukeyser recalls is not Eliot of course but Whitman, the writer she celebrates as 'the poet of possibility', the poet of democratic hope (*Life of Poetry*, 61, 83):

> Through me many long dumb voices,
> Voices of the interminable generations of prisoners and slaves,
> Voices of the diseas'd and despairing and of thieves and dwarfs,
> Voices of cycles of preparation and accretion . . .
>
> .   .   .   .
>
> Through me forbidden voices,
> Voices of sexes and lusts, voices veil'd and I remove the veil,
> Voices indecent by me clarified and transfigur'd
>
> ('Song of Myself', lines 508–18)

It is fair to assume that the example of Whitman is also behind such stark lines as 'Never to despise I the clitoris in her least speech'.[77]

---

[72] Ibid. 188.   [73] Ibid. 189.
[74] Ibid. 191.   [75] Ibid. 193.
[76] Ibid. 195–6. Cf. Oppen, 'Route': 'Whom shall I speak to' (*NCP*, 200).
[77] 'Despisals', *Collected Poems*, 472. See Whitman's open letter to Emerson of 1856, *Leaves of Grass*, 739: 'Infidelism usurps most with fœtid polite face: among the rest infidelism about sex . . . I say that the body of a man or woman, the main matter, is so far quite unexpressed in poems; but that the body is to be expressed, and sex is.'

I conclude this discussion of Rukeyser by quoting another late poem which returns us explicitly to these questions of the relationship between poetry and politics and the role of speech. It is called 'The Artist as Social Critic' and comes from the sequence 'Searching/Not Searching' (1973):

> They have asked me to speak in public
> and set me a subject.
>
> I hate anything that begins   :   the artist as . . .
> and as for 'social critic'
> at the last quarter of the twentieth century
> I know what that is:
>
> late at night, among radio music
> the voice of my son speaking half-world away
> coming clear on the radio into my room
> out of blazing Belfast.
>
> Long enough for me to walk around
> in that strong voice.
>
> (*Collected Poems*, 484)

It seems fair to imagine that a poem as Spartan as this would have found favour even with Oppen. And it reflects on problems he recognized and addressed: the problem of speaking in public; the problem of distance; what it means to speak as an artist (we may recall such lines of Oppen's as 'And it is not "art"', or 'It is difficult now to speak of poetry'); more profoundly, what it is in one that does speak; and the way love (her son) and hate ('I hate anything that') bear down on that; and what any of this has to do with war ('blazing Belfast': think of Oppen's great lines, 'There is a simple ego in a lyric, | A strange one in war').[78] There is an ironic drama to the poem's displacements and parallels. The woman who is to speak is spoken to: the speaker becomes the audience, listening to a radio 'half-world away'.

It may be felt that Rukeyser portrays in a more vivid, more concretely personal way what it feels like to be moved by the speaking of another voice (and she is quite literally moved: she *walks around*). But the central point is that for both poets it is finally speech which communes or mediates between persons and worlds, or which if it doesn't exactly make a world, makes sense of our place within it ('my room', 'blazing Belfast'). There is no guarantee that a given speech will get through or 'come clear', or that it will be clear for 'long enough' ('he will fail and I will fail'). That is the risk one takes. Still, this indefinite realm of speech, this 'effort at speech', is where, in Rukeyser's words, we best 'tend toward democracy'. As she wrote, thinking of Whitman, 'we are a people tending toward democracy at the level of hope' (*Life of Poetry*, 61)—a statement that captures

[78] *NCP*, 53.

perfectly the idea that democracy, like intersubjectivity, is not a fixed state but a tendency, an action, a process.

For Rukeyser then, speech was always a much more significant measure of reality than political ideology. It is the touchstone of her place in the world, both of her part in it and of her receptivity to it. Unlike Oppen and Wright, and indeed unlike many others, she did not join the Communist Party—remaining instead a true radical, as I've said, in the Arendtian sense.[79] Unlike Oppen also she never abandoned writing. More importantly she never felt, as Oppen did, that poetry and politics were absolutely distinct—for both of them were pervaded by and answered to the middle ground of speech. Speech had played an almost insignificant part in Oppen's first book. But it was his admission of that middle ground, and readmittance to it, that produced some of the most moving American poetry of the 1960s, and perhaps in 'Of Being Numerous'—his song of our selves—the greatest *short* long poem in the language since *The Waste Land.*

[79] See Young-Bruehl, 256.

Conclusion
'Your Marvellous Appearances': Frank O'Hara

Public silence indeed is nothing

So we confront the fact with stage craft
And the available poses

Of greatness

> Oppen, 'Monument', *NCP*, 145

Near the beginning of her last major work, *The Life of the Mind*, Hannah Arendt makes the following simple but startling claim: 'It is indeed as though everything that is alive—in addition to the fact that its surface is made for appearance, fit to be seen and meant to appear to others—has an *urge to appear*' (1. 29). She argues that things do not appear because they exist, as we have been led to suppose—as if appearance were a mere attribute of Being—rather they exist because they appear: or rather, *they exist in order to appear.* 'Could it not be that appearances are not there for the sake of the life process but, on the contrary, that the life process is there for the sake of appearances? Since we live in an *appearing* world, is it not much more plausible that the relevant and the meaningful in this world of ours should be located precisely on the surface?' (1.27)—that is to say, in what she had called in *The Human Condition*, the 'space of appearance'.

Within the space of appearance everything that appears must appear to someone. 'Nothing and nobody exists in this world', she claims, 'whose very being does not presuppose a *spectator*' (1.19). Viewed in this way, our inner life matters so much less than our apparent, manifest, public life—our life out there in the world. As George Oppen put it, in the aptly entitled 'World, World—': 'The self is no mystery, the mystery is | That there is something for us to stand on' (*NCP*, 159). Indeed, even our inner life is shot through with an urge to appear; it gathers itself up, concentrates itself, in order to reveal itself—which is so manifestly true even of writers as inward as Emily Dickinson or Lorine Niedecker that one somehow neglects to consider the significance of the fact: even the most inward life is impelled urgently outward. 'To be alive means to be possessed by an urge toward self-display which answers the fact of one's own appearingness' (*Life of the Mind*, 1.21). In this world of appearances, the fact that we appear to

one another from as many different angles as there are persons to perceive us—
that we are open to interpretation, that we *open up* to interpretation—is measure
of our freedom and corresponds to our plurality: 'Seeming corresponds', Arendt
writes, 'to the fact that every appearance, its identity notwithstanding, is per-
ceived by a plurality of persons' (1.21). Thus the 'primacy of appearances'
underwrites our pluralism. 'Nothing perhaps is more surprising in this world
of ours than the almost infinite diversity of its appearances' (1.20). In sharp
contrast, our 'inside organs', if we could see them, would 'all look alike' (1.29).

The political arrangement that most nearly corresponds to this pluralism, this
diversity, is democracy: 'nothing that is', Arendt writes, 'insofar as it appears, exists
in the singular ... Not man but men inhabit this planet' (1.19). In the opening
chapter of this book I argued that Tocqueville's epistemological apparatus caused
him to underestimate the capacity of democratic society to create, sustain, and
recognize human diversity. Ironically, although he was one of the first great political
thinkers to address himself to what he believed was going to be an unstoppable
democratic revolution, he feared that democracy would result in the annihilation
somehow of what for Arendt is one of the inescapable givens of the human
condition—its multifarious plurality. Equality, Tocqueville thought, would mark
the end of all distinction, whereas for Arendt distinction or distinctions, since they
have their basis in the fundamental human condition of plurality, are the very stuff
of life, the one thing we can depend on—*with or without democracy*. Democracy just
means that more people are free to enjoy their diversity or to express it publicly. The
public domain itself exists in the plural: there are untold publics within the so-called
public; the space of appearance is effectively many spaces.

In the long introductory essay for their controversial translation of *Democracy
in America*, Mansfield and Winthrop write that Tocqueville 'seems to have
understood the desire to distinguish oneself as essentially political' (p. xxi).
'Political freedom in republics', Tocqueville felt, 'clears the way for those few
who desire to distinguish themselves and sharpens their hunger for greatness'
(p. xxii). Tocqueville knew himself to be one of 'those few'. As the democratic
revolution rolled on, however, he faced a dilemma: for the 'greatness of that
democratic revolution' had 'inspired the passion for equality and produced the
growing equality of conditions that are hardly welcoming, even profoundly
hostile, to human greatness' (p. xxiv).

I want to propose that greatness in the monumental aristocratic sense in which
Tocqueville understood it is essentially distinction, or distinctiveness, writ large
—the variety and difference of the many, something which we generally experi-
ence at close quarters, idealized, gigantized, and fetishized in the few. Another
way of putting this would be to say that the so-called many only ever appear a few
at a time, i.e. gather and create a space of appearance. Tocqueville mistakes *a few*
for *the few*. Captive to a monumental picture of the past, in which the world is all
one stage, he could not begin to entertain the possibility that there might be fews,
spaces, incommensurable stages. He could see the revolution thundering towards

him, but only from the perspective of what T. S. Eliot called 'an ideal order'. For the desire to distinguish oneself, the desire to be considered great, is indeed political, as Tocqueville thought, but that is because it is also, after all, merely an exaggerated development, of the original, primary urge to appear, as described by Arendt—out of which the political emerges. We might say that the attribution of greatness to others is an immature or inflated form of the more fundamental human aptitude to recognize others. It's as if recognition is always great, in and of itself, but where there is no recognition, greatness is, accordingly, apt to be exaggerated, as Oppen's poem 'Monument' eloquently states: 'Public silence indeed is nothing || So we confront the fact with stagecraft', i.e. with 'poses || Of greatness'. We want to appear, as Arendt says, and to recognize what appears—in demotic terms, to see and be seen.

I would like to illustrate this argument by looking briefly and finally at a poet who, whatever politics he practised in his life, would not ordinarily be thought of as a political poet at all: Frank O'Hara.[1] There are other reasons why O'Hara provides a fitting place to end. He inherits Whitman's sensitive flamboyance and queered manliness, just as he inherits his Manhattan, which turns out to be a strikingly different place from the New York of Oppen's 'Of Being Numerous', with which it is almost contemporaneous. But like Oppen he also offers a refreshingly different way of conceiving of the space of appearance while still hanging on to some features, fully democratized now, of the Poundian universe.

One needn't spend very long in the company of O'Hara's vast *Collected Poems* to see that he is vividly concerned with the nature and fate of human greatness and the ubiquitousness and variety of our appearances—in short the heroism of modern life. A good place to start is with the poem 'On Seeing Larry Rivers' *Washington Crossing the Delaware* at the Museum of Modern Art'.[2] The poem begins by taking up a stock image of greatness, that of the revolutionary hero George Washington: 'Now that our hero has come back to us'. It was Washington who, in his apparent greatness personified the greatness of the American cause: he is the 'Dear father of our country'. As is well known, the poem conjures an image at several removes from 'the physical event' of the crossing of the Delaware: it is O'Hara's ebullient response to Larry Rivers's playfully sceptical response to Emanuel Leutze's grandiose connivance in legendary history.[3]

---

[1] See Brad Gooch, *City Poet: The Life and Times of Frank O'Hara* (New York: Alfred A. Knopf, 1993), 425–6: in his life, O'Hara 'was more naturally and temperamentally engaged than most of the other New York School poets', Gooch writes, citing Amiri Baraka ('Frank at least had a political sense'), Bill Berkson ('I said, "You're just being a sentimental Communist"'), and Kenneth Koch ('Frank is a revolutionary poet without a revolution'), all to that effect.

[2] O'Hara, *Collected Poems*, 233–4.

[3] 'If there was anyone who could be relied on to produce a large, efficient, patriotic machine whose meaning would be over no one's head, that person was Leutze', Robert Hughes writes, in respect of the German-born nineteenth-century painter: *American Visions: The Epic History of Art in America* (London: Harvill Press, 1999), 192. According to O'Hara's biographer, Rivers described undertaking his painting as 'like getting into the ring with Tolstoy' (Gooch, 238). Marjorie Perloff

But this ultimately matters less, I think, than the way the poem still poses the question of what kind of figure individual greatness cuts, which is to say what kind of recognition might be possible now, in this 'nation of persons' (*persons*, note, not citizens) where freedom is 'secular and intimate', and less portentously visible than a romantic history painting or, as O'Hara puts it, the 'sighting [of] a redcoat': since we can no longer turn to paintings of the Founding Fathers for an image of our liberty, it has become harder to 'See how free we are!'

We can observe similar concerns at work in one of O'Hara's most ambitious poems, 'In Memory of My Feelings', where once again, against a pop-art historical backcloth, the question of what greatness means is posed. In this world there are still heroes, but 'The hero, trying to unhitch his parachute, | stumbles over me'; and there are still statues: but only 'the cancerous | statue which my body could no longer contain' (*Collected Poems*, 256–7). The monument is diseased, rather than the body. Yet the question of greatness persists, mainly, it seems, thanks to art: the poem makes reference, for instance, to 'a great Courbet', an artist famously, if ambiguously, associated with what T. J. Clark has called 'the image of the people',[4] and the French Revolution of 1848 (whose socialist threat so exercised Tocqueville).[5] This question of greatness persists alongside (is to be found in the same passage as) the question of what O'Hara calls, with offhand vagueness, 'our democracy' (*Collected Poems*, 256). We note that whereas a painting is identified with Courbet, a public statue is identified with no one at all. There's no indication in the poem that O'Hara cares whether Courbet was a socialist, but clearly the painter is appropriate to the poem's general democratic ambience.[6] And given the centrality of the theme of plurality, it's clear that 'our democracy' has something to do with 'what is always and everywhere | present, the scene of my selves, the occasion of these ruses' (257): i.e. democracy is, or is partly, the occasion of our multiplicity and variety, it is the indefinable, insubstantial, all-pervasive monument ('in memory of') to our innumerable 'feelings' and our several 'lives':

> Grace
> to be born and live as variously as possible. The conception
> of the masque barely suggests the sordid identifications.
> I am a Hittite in love with a horse. I don't know what blood's

---

comments: 'Although O'Hara's poem is especially witty if read in conjunction with Rivers's painting, it can be read quite independently as a pastiche on a Major Event in American History'. Marjorie Perloff, *Frank O'Hara, Poet Among Painters* (1977; Chicago: University of Chicago Press, 1998), 85.

[4] See T. J. Clark, *Image of the People: Gustave Courbet and the 1848 Revolution* (London: Thames and Hudson, 1973).

[5] See Alexis de Tocqueville, *Recollections*, trans. George Lawrence, ed. J. P. Mayer and A. P. Kerr (New York: Anchor Books, 1971).

[6] See, however, 'After Courbet', which makes what is for O'Hara a rare, if surreal, reference to social class ('the gentle sentiment of a class') and, as always, to the appearance of 'great forms' (O'Hara, *Collected Poems*, 287, 289).

in me I feel like an African prince I am a girl walking downstairs
in a red pleated dress with heels I am a champion taking a fall
I am a jockey with a sprained ass-hole I am the light mist
                              in which a face appears
and it is another face of blonde I am a baboon eating a banana
I am a dictator looking at his wife I am a doctor eating a child
and the child's mother smiling I am a Chinaman climbing a mountain
I am a child smelling his father's underwear I am an Indian
sleeping on a scalp
                    and my pony is stamping in the birches,
and I've just caught sight of the *Niña*, the *Pinta* and the *Santa Maria*.
              What land is this, so free?

                                                              (256)

The enigmatic notion of grace, where this passage begins, was also a great favourite of another highly sensitive genius of America's secular post-war intimacy, Robert Creeley. Historical pastiche is undoubtedly operative here, but not just pastiche—freedom is also operative ('What land is this, so free?'), the freedom for example of pastiche itself, of short-lived identifications, whimsical or heartfelt or both. 'Grace to be born and live as variously as possible': in Arendt's terms, grace to be born and *appear* as variously as possible; in psychoanalytic terms, grace to identify as variously as possible (the poem strikingly recalls Whitman's 'There Was a Child Went Forth'); in secular political terms, grace to enjoy the varieties of this democratic experience. As O'Hara says, the 'conception | of the masque barely suggests the sordid identifications': in other words, this is not pantomime, this is *variety* . . . the acting out of our plurality, as we encounter it abroad and in ourselves. Before O'Hara no one in American letters had expressed this idea more succinctly than Wallace Stevens:

> And out of what one sees and hears and out
> Of what one feels, who could have thought to make
> So many selves, so many sensuous worlds,
> As if the air, the mid-day air, was swarming
> With the metaphysical changes that occur,
> Merely in living as and where we live.[7]

Stevens's irony is beautifully present in that 'who could have thought to make', a question the spirit of which is best glossed perhaps by quoting Arendt: 'Nobody so far has succeeded in *living* in a world that does not manifest itself of its own accord' (*Life of the Mind*, 1.26). Appearances are their own gift to the world. They surprise us out of ourselves, into new selves.

O'Hara's catalogue of his manifestations is reminiscent of the empathetic disposition of Whitman ('that object I became'), whom he calls, pointedly, 'my great predecessor'. It may be helpful, I think, to consider an analogous movement from another of O'Hara's poems, 'To the Film Industry in Crisis',

---

[7] Wallace Stevens, 'Esthétique du Mal', *Collected Poems* 326.

where the poet evokes a galaxy of Hollywood stars, cascading as he does so down the page in a waterfall of wit—limpid, luminous, and loving:

> Ginger Rogers with her pageboy bob like a sausage
> on her shuffling shoulders, peach-melba-voiced Fred Astaire of the feet,
> Erich von Stroheim, the seducer of mountain-climbers' gasping spouses,
> the Tarzans, each and every one of you (I cannot bring myself to prefer
> Johnny Weissmuller to Lex Barker, I cannot!), Mae West in a furry sled,
> her bordello radiance and bland remarks, Rudolph Valentino of the moon,
> its crushing passions, and moonlike, too, the gentle Norma Shearer,
>
>   .   .   .   .
>
> Joseph Cotton puzzling and Orson Welles puzzled and Dolores del Rio
> eating orchids for lunch and breaking mirrors, Gloria Swanson reclining,
> and Jean Harlow reclining and wiggling, and Alice Faye reclining
> and wiggling and singing
>
>   (*Collected Poems*, 232)

What O'Hara does here, as with the list of his identifications earlier, is to conjure or project these stars in their phenomenal *appearances* ('so many selves, so many sensuous worlds')—and notice how once again he comes back to the question of greatness: 'and to all you others, the great, the near-great, the featured, the extras | . . . | Long may you illumine space with your marvellous appearances' (ibid.). This is cinema as space of appearance and as proto-democratic space: for the poet tells us that he loves them all *equally* ('I cannot bring myself to prefer | Johnny Weissmuller to Lex Barker, I cannot!'), just as he loves, and loves to celebrate, their differences—if only by the difference of a word here or there (as 'reclining and wiggling' is different from 'reclining and wiggling and singing', as 'puzzled' is different from 'puzzling'). To take a line from the poem that celebrates 'Whitman my great predecessor': 'if there is fortuity it's in the love we bear each other's differences'.[8]

'To the Film Industry in Crisis' also illustrates another way, fundamental to O'Hara, whereby appearances appear: by way of names, the resonance of proper nouns. O'Hara's poetry is littered with names, from famous names to the names of friends, friends who were famous and friends who were not so: 'the great, the near-great' and 'the extras'. Sometimes we are given the whole name ('John Button Birthday', 'Poem Read at Joan Mitchell's'), sometimes just a part, a familiar first name ('For Grace, After a Party'), or, as in the case of John Ashbery, a nickname ('Ashes on Saturday Afternoon'). Easily the most important names are those of persons, but the names of buildings, places, books, paintings also figure strongly. Altogether they lend the poetry that opaque glittering quality, as of something half transparent, half impenetrable, which in accordance with what Merleau-Ponty calls the 'paradox of immanence and transcendence', whereby the

---

[8] 'Ode: Salute to the French Negro Poets', *Collected Poems*, 305.

wholeness of things appears to us only in parts that simultaneously and paradox-
ically promise us the whole, smacks of the texture of reality.[9] The profusion of
names in his work is, then, part of the poetry's way of being in the world, or
going about the world, or going about New York—its richly efflorescent surface.
It is what Allen Ginsberg was getting at when he described O'Hara's poetry as
'deep gossip',[10] and it is not entirely dissimilar to the way names eventually
function in Pound's *Cantos*, as they drift from the didactic level to the level of
everyday life. O'Hara, incidentally, has a feeling like Pound's for the elegiac
resonance of names, as in 'A Step Away from Them':

> First
> Bunny died, then John Latouche,
> then Jackson Pollock. But is the
> earth as full as life was full, of them?
>
> (*Collected Poems*, 258)

Compare this to the moment in *The Cantos*, where Pound, names, via 'The
Seafarer', those 'Lordly men' who 'are to earth o'ergiven' (74/446). There's an
interesting complication of tone there, as Pound names the first of these men,
'Fordie' (Ford Madox Ford), and so combines the solemnity of his Old English
original with those altogether more familiar manners that declare him to be the
countryman of Whitman.

'The poet names the thing because he sees it, or comes one step nearer to it
than any other', Emerson wrote: 'By virtue of this science the poet is the Namer,
or Language-maker, naming things sometimes after their appearance, sometimes
after their essence, and giving to everyone its own name and not another's.'[11]
O'Hara is just such a poet as Emerson describes, the poet as Namer, with the
qualification that in his world, as in Arendt's, *essence* also *appears*, whether of
someone or something. Names are perhaps the single most characteristic way
whereby O'Hara registers and celebrates the world's appearingness—we might
even say that it is because he names them that he is, in a famous phrase, 'needed
by things'.[12] It seems at least arguable that this freedom to name names is one of
the evidences of what Tocqueville envisaged as democratic people getting excited
about themselves. 'To be alive means to be possessed by an urge toward self-
display which answers the fact of one's own appearingness': naming is, in a
complementary way, a species of recognition. And we might recall that for

---

[9] Merleau-Ponty, *Primacy of Perception*, 16.
[10] *Homage to Frank O'Hara*, ed. Bill Berkson and Joe LeSueur (1978; Bolinas, Calif.: Big Sky,
1988), 63, 149.
[11] Emerson, 'The Poet', *Essays and Lectures*, 456–7. For a different take on O'Hara's use of
names, see Lytle Shaw, *Frank O'Hara: The Poetics of Coterie* (Iowa City: University of Iowa Press,
2006).
[12] 'Meditations in an Emergency', 197.

Whitman to be able to name himself ('Walt Whitman, a kosmos, of Manhattan the son') was to 'give the sign of democracy'.[13]

O'Hara has great fun with names: in 'A Step Away from Them' he gives his heart a name ('it is Poems by Pierre Reverdy'); 'Why I Am Not a Painter' highlights less the apparent arbitrariness of names (a poem called 'Oranges', a painting called 'Sardines'),[14] than the luckiness of them—the freedom, as in a poem, to find the word that fits—the separation of signifier and signified dissolved in a democratic gesture; in 'A True Account of Talking to the Sun at Fire Island', the Sun wakes the poet up, addresses him as Frank, and even manages a corny pun on his name:

> 'Frankly I wanted to tell you
> I like your poetry. I see a lot
> on my rounds and you're okay. You may
> not be the greatest thing on earth, but
> you're different.'

> (*Collected Poems*, 306)

Once again the abiding themes of greatness and difference bubble to the surface—but here, as in 'To the Film Industry in Crisis' there is an underlying sense that difference will do, that greatness is just difference writ large. The poem plays out, in comic cathartic fashion, O'Hara's desire for recognition, his 'urge to appear' (Arendt), to step out into the light. He understands Tocqueville's fear that equality of conditions might be the death of us: 'To be equal? It's the worst! | Are we just muddy instants?'[15]—to which it may be rejoined that he knows unlike Tocqueville that it is just a fear.

Recognitions and appearances acquire additional significance in a poem like 'At the Old Place', where one of the things that is being recognized is one's own or a friend's or 'Someone' else's sexuality:

> Joe is restless, and so am I, so restless.
> Button's buddy lips frame 'L G T TH O P?'
> across the bar. 'Yes!' I cry, for dancing's
> my soul delight. (Feet! feet!) 'Come on!'
>
> Through the streets we skip like swallows.
> Howard malingers. (Come on, Howard.) Ashes
> malingers. (Come on, J.A.) Dick malingers.
> (Come on, Dick.) Alvin darts ahead. (Wait up,
> Alvin.) Jack, Earl and Someone don't come.

---

[13] 'Song of Myself', lines 497 and 506.
[14] *Collected Poems*, 261–2.
[15] 'Ode', *Collected Poems*, 196.

Down the dark stairs drifts the steaming cha-
cha-cha. Through the urine and smoke we charge
to the floor. Wrapped in Ashes' arms I glide.
(It's heaven!) Button lindys with me. (It's
heaven!) Joe's two-steps, too, are incredible,
and then a fast rhumba with Alvin, like skipping
on toothpicks. And the interminable intermissions,

we have them. Jack, Earl and Someone drift
guiltily in. 'I knew they were gay
the minute I laid eyes on them!' screams John.
How ashamed they are of us! we hope.

(*Collected Poems*, 223–4)

This 'wonderful poem', as Stuart Byron described it, underscores once again the prominence of names in O'Hara's armoury.[16] It's as if he is trying to find out just how far he can get in a poem—how far he can run a poem—on little more than names. And in this case he is using names that are not—that certainly were not—household names, public names. What Arendt's friend W. H. Auden said of private faces in public places is now made to apply to names, as we feel O'Hara's intimacy with these persons yet have no choice but to respect their privacy (we are told precious little in fact besides their names). The poem illustrates perfectly the way he likes to dance with names (one of the dances cited in the poem even has a name that sounds like the name of a person, a woman or perhaps an effeminate man: to 'lindy'), and to engage them in the irregular play of repetition that he, like Creeley, has learned from Williams, and then developed in his singular and spectacular way.

Within this playful context the poem touches lightly but distinctly on the question of sexual identification and appearance, the question of coming out, or not—which invokes another space of appearance, or in this case a conjunction of overlapping spaces: the openly gay (relatively openly, since this poem dates back some thirteen years before Stonewall) and the apparently gay. As I argued in Chapter 1, the willingness to accommodate or encourage sexual difference can be, under certain circumstances, the difference which underwrites democracy— the difference at the heart of difference. As O'Hara writes in 'Meditations in an Emergency': 'Heterosexuality! you are inexorably approaching. (How discourage her?)': O'Hara's fear here, like Tocqueville's, is that we could all end up the same (unlike Tocqueville he meets it with a joke).

For O'Hara, ultimately, however, sexuality is just one context, as art is another, in which the more fundamental matters of appearing different and

---

[16] As Byron noted, the poem was omitted from *The Selected Poems of Frank O'Hara*, ed. Donald Allen (New York: Vintage Books, 1974). Stuart Byron, 'Frank O'Hara: Poetic "Queertalk"', in Jim Elledge (ed.), *Frank O'Hara: To Be True to a City* (Ann Arbor: University of Michigan Press, 1993), 68.

recognizing difference can arise. Coming out is only a special aspect of a wider concern with stepping out into the light or waking up to it ('each day's light has more significance these days', he writes, sounding like a twentieth-century Keats).[17] The atmosphere of morning or lunchtime light that shines through so many of O'Hara's poems represents a more workaday version of Pound's 'all things that are are lights' (*Cantos*, 74/443). The poems are lit up by the radiance of appearances, as if illumined from within by a demotic but revitalized public domain. O'Hara's masterpiece in this vein is 'A Step Away from Them', where the lightness, charm, and fragility of life on earth ('Neon in daylight is a | great pleasure... | ...as are light bulbs in daylight') is contrasted with the under-world which is just 'a step away'. But a more raggedy and rather less well-known poem such as his 'Ode to Willem de Kooning' enlarges on this theme of living-as-appearing, picking up its Homeric as well as its democratic resonances. The poem begins, 'Beyond the sunrise | where the black begins', where 'an enormous city | is sending up its shutters' and the poet tries, yet again, 'to seize upon greatness' (*Collected Poems*, 283–4):

> A bus crashes into a milk truck
>   and the girl goes skating up the avenue
> with streaming hair
>   roaring through fluttering newspapers
> and their Athenian contradictions
>   for democracy is joined
> with stunning collapsible savages, all natural and relaxed and free
>
> as the day zooms into space and only darkness lights our lives,
> with few flags flaming, imperishable courage and the gentle will
> which is the individual dawn of genius rising from its bed
>
>   (285)

What O'Hara understands by democracy ('all natural and relaxed and free') is vague, but it has something to do with our bearing witness to one another, and with the feeling that 'life's marvellous', just as it appears, to the extent that it appears, and in so far as one wakes up in time to see it. Democracy is unimagin-able without its seat in consciousness—in what he calls in 'In Favour of One's Time', 'the mirrored room of this consciousness': i.e. they extend one another.[18] We wake up, as Thoreau would say, when we see a bus collide with a milk truck, watch a girl tearing down the avenue on skates, or look at a canvas by an artist like de Kooning. As he writes of our time—our time here on earth—in that same poem ('In Favour of One's Time'): 'it's practically a blaze of pure sensi-bility'. The pun here is critical: life, democracy, this age or time, is practically, *pragmatically*, a mode of consciousness.

---

[17] 'Getting Up Ahead of Someone (Sun)', *Collected Poems*, 341.
[18] *Collected Poems*, 341–2.

List of Works Cited

Adams, Henry, *The Education of Henry Adams* (1918; Boston: Houghton Mifflin Company, 1973).

Adorno, Theodor W., *The Culture Industry: Selected Essays on Mass Culture*, ed. J. M. Bernstein (London: Routledge, 1991).

——*Minima Moralia: Reflections from Damaged Life*, trans. E. F. N. Jephcott (London: Verso, 1978).

——*Minima Moralia: Reflexionen aus dem beschädigten Leben* (1951; Frankfurt am Main: Suhrkamp Verlag, 1997).

——*Notes to Literature*, vol. 2, ed. Rolf Tiedemann, trans. Shierry Weber Nicholsen (New York: Columbia University Press, 1992).

——*Prisms*, trans. Samuel and Shierry Weber (Cambridge, Mass.: MIT Press, 1994).

Alldritt, Keith, *The Poet as Spy: The Life and Wild Times of Basil Bunting* (London: Aurum Press, 1998).

Altieri, Charles, *Self and Sensibility in Contemporary American Poetry* (Cambridge: Cambridge University Press, 1984).

Arendt, Hannah, *The Human Condition* (Chicago: University of Chicago Press, 1958).

——*The Life of the Mind*, 1. *Thinking*; 2. *Willing*, 1-vol. edn., ed. Mary McCarthy (San Diego, Calif.: Harcourt Brace & Company, 1978).

——*Men in Dark Times* (San Diego, Calif.: Harcourt Brace & Company, 1983).

——*On Revolution* (1963; Harmondsworth: Penguin, 1973).

——*The Origins of Totalitarianism* (1951; San Diego, Calif.: Harcourt Brace & Company, 1975).

Aristotle, *The Politics*, trans. T. A. Sinclair, rev. Trevor J. Saunders (Harmondsworth: Penguin, 1992).

Bachelard, Gaston, *The Poetics of Space*, trans. Maria Jolas (1964; Boston: Beacon Press, 1994).

Bailyn, Bernard, *The Ideological Origins of the American Revolution*, enlarged edn. (Cambridge, Mass.: The Belknap Press of the University of Harvard Press, 1992).

——Dallek, Robert, Davis, David Brion, Donald, David Herbert, Thomas, John L., and Wood, Gordon S., *The Great Republic: A History of the American People*, vol. 1 (1977; Lexington, Ky.: D. C. Heath, 1992).

Bell, Vereen, and Lerner, Laurence (eds.), *On Modern Poetry: Essays Presented to Donald Davie* (Nashville: Vanderbilt University Press, 1988).

Benhabib, Seyla, *Critique, Norm, and Utopia: A Study of the Foundations of Critical Theory* (New York: Columbia University Press, 1986).

——*The Reluctant Modernism of Hannah Arendt* (Thousand Oaks, Calif.: Sage, 1996).

Benjamin, Walter, *One Way Street and Other Writings*, trans. Edmund Jephcott and Kingsley Shorter (London: Verso, 1985).

Bercovitch, Sacvan, *The American Jeremiad* (Madison: University of Wisconsin Press, 1978).

——*The Rites of Assent: Transformations in the Symbolic Construction of America* (New York: Routledge, 1993).

Berkson, Bill, and LeSueur, Joe (eds.), *Homage to Frank O'Hara* (1978; Bolinas, Calif.: Big Sky, 1988).

Bernstein, Michael, *The Tale of the Tribe: Ezra Pound and the Modern Verse Epic* (Princeton: Princeton University Press, 1980).

Bishop, Elizabeth, *Complete Poems 1927–1979* (New York: Farrer, Straus and Giroux, 1983).

Blake, William, *The Complete Poetry and Prose*, ed. David Erdman (Berkeley and Los Angeles: University of California Press, 1982).

Bloom, Harold, *Wallace Stevens: The Poems of Our Climate* (Ithaca, NY: Cornell University Press, 1977).

Bowles, Paul, *Let It Come Down* (1952; Santa Rosa, Calif.: Black Sparrow Press, 1990).

Brinnin, John Malcolm, 'Muriel Rukeyser: The Social Poet and the Problem of Communication', *Poetry: A Magazine of Verse*, 56/4 (1943), 554–75.

Burke, Carolyn, *Becoming Modern: The Life of Mina Loy* (New York: Farrar, Straus and Giroux, 1996).

Burke, Edmund, *Reflections on the Revolution in France*, ed. Conor Cruise O'Brien (1790; Harmondsworth: Penguin, 1986).

Bush, Clive, *Halfway to Revolution: Investigation and Crisis in the Work of Henry Adams, William James and Gertrude Stein* (New Haven: Yale University Press, 1991).

Canovan, Margaret, *Hannah Arendt: A Reinterpretation of Her Political Thought* (Cambridge: Cambridge University Press, 1992).

Capps, Jack L., *Emily Dickinson's Reading: 1836–1886* (Cambridge, Mass.: Harvard University Press, 1966).

Casey, Edward S., *The Fate of Place: A Philosophical History* (Berkeley and Los Angeles: University of California Press, 1997).

Cavell, Stanley, *Pursuits of Happiness: The Hollywood Comedy of Remarriage* (Cambridge, Mass.: Harvard University Press, 1981).

—— *The Senses of Walden* (1972; Chicago: University of Chicago Press, 1992).

Chauncey, Jr., George, 'From Sexual Inversion to Homosexuality: Medicine and the Changing Conceptualization of Female Deviance', *Salmagundi*, 58–9 (Fall 1982-Winter 1983).

Clark, T. J., *Image of the People: Gustave Courbet and the 1848 Revolution* (London: Thames and Hudson, 1973).

Clark, Tom, *Robert Creeley and the Genius of the American Common Place: Together with the Poet's Own 'Autobiography'* (New York: New Directions, 1993).

Conrad, Bryce, *Refiguring America: A Study of William Carlos Williams'* In the American Grain (Urbana: University of Illinois Press, 1990).

Cook, David A., *A History of Narrative Film* (1981; New York: W. W. Norton & Company, 1996).

Cornell, Julian, *The Trial of Ezra Pound: A Documented Account of the Treason Case by the Defendant's Lawyer* (London: Faber and Faber, 1967).

Countryman, Edward, *The American Revolution* (London: I. B. Tauris & Co. Ltd, 1986).

Cox, Kenneth, *Collected Studies in the Use of English* (London: Agenda Editions, 2001).

Creeley, Robert, *The Collected Essays of Robert Creeley* (Berkeley and Los Angeles: University of California Press, 1989).

—— *The Collected Poems of Robert Creeley: 1945–1975* (Berkeley and Los Angeles: University of California Press, 1982).

—— *The Collected Prose of Robert Creeley* (Berkeley and Los Angeles: University of California Press, 1988).

—— *A Sense of Measure* (London: Calder and Boyars, 1972).

Davidson, Michael, *Ghostlier Demarcations: Modern Poetry and the Material Word* (Berkeley and Los Angeles: University of California Press, 1997).

—— *Guys Like Us: Citing Masculinity in Cold War Poetics* (Chicago: University of Chicago Press, 2004).

Davie, Donald, *Poet as Sculptor* (London: Routledge & Kegan Paul, 1965).

—— *The Poet in the Imaginary Museum: Essays of Two Decades*, ed. Barry Alpert (Manchester: Carcanet, 1977).

Dembo, L. S., 'The Existential World of George Oppen', *Iowa Review*, 3/1 (1972), 64–91.

—— and Pondrom, Cyrena (eds.), *The Contemporary Writer: Interviews with Sixteen Novelists and Poets* (Madison: University of Wisconsin Press, 1972).

Dickinson, Emily, *The Complete Poems of Emily Dickinson*, ed. Thomas H. Johnson (London: Faber and Faber, 1970).

—— *The Letters of Emily Dickinson*, ed. Thomas H. Johnson, associate ed. Theodora Ward (1957; Cambridge, Mass.: The Belknap Press of the University of Harvard Press, 1986).

Dijkstra, Bram, *Cubism, Stieglitz and the Early Poetry of William Carlos Williams* (Princeton: Princeton University Press, 1969).

Duffey, Bernard, *A Poetry of Presence: The Writing of William Carlos Williams* (Madison: University of Wisconsin Press, 1986).

DuPlessis, Rachel Blau, and Quatermain, Peter (eds.), *The Objectivist Nexus: Essays in Cultural Poetics* (Tuscaloo: University of Alabama Press, 1999).

Eisenstadt, Abraham S. (ed.), *Reconsidering Tocqueville's Democracy in America* (New Brunswick, NJ: Rutgers University Press, 1988).

Eliot, T. S., *Collected Poems 1909–1962* (1963; London: Faber and Faber, 1974).

Elledge, Jim (ed.), *Frank O'Hara: To Be True to a City* (Ann Arbor: University of Michigan Press, 1993).

Else, Gerald F., *Aristotle's Poetics: The Argument* (Cambridge, Mass.: Harvard University Press, 1967).

Emerson, Ralph Waldo, *Essays and Lectures*, ed. Joel Porte (New York: Library of America, 1983).

Erkkila, Betsy, *Whitman: The Political Poet* (New York: Oxford University Press, 1989).

—— and Grossman, Jay (eds.), *Breaking Bounds: Whitman and American Cultural Studies* (New York: Oxford University Press, 1996).

Fabre, Michel, *The Unfinished Quest of Richard Wright*, trans. Isabel Barzun (1973; Urbana: University of Illinois Press, 1993).

Farr, Judith, *The Passion of Emily Dickinson* (Cambridge, Mass.: Harvard University Press, 1992).

Filreis, Alan, *Modernism from Right to Left: Wallace Stevens, the Thirties, and Literary Radicalism* (Cambridge: Cambridge University Press, 1994).

—— *Wallace Stevens and the Actual World* (Princeton: Princeton University Press, 1991).

Fitzgerald, F. Scott, *The Great Gatsby* (1926; Harmondsworth: Penguin, 1990).

Flory, Wendy Stallard, *The American Ezra Pound* (New Haven: Yale University Press, 1988).

Franklin, Benjamin, *The Autobiography of Benjamin Franklin*, ed. Leonard W. Labaree, Ralph L. Ketcham, Helen C. Boatfield, and Helene H. Fineman (New Haven: Yale University Press, 1964).

Fredman, Stephen, *The Grounding of American Poetry: Charles Olson and the Emersonian Tradition* (Cambridge: Cambridge University Press, 1993).

Freud, Sigmund, *The Pelican Freud Library*, 7. *On Sexuality*, ed. Angela Richards (Harmondsworth: Penguin, 1977).

—— *The Penguin Freud Library*, 11. *On Metapsychology*, ed. Angela Richards (1984; Harmondsworth: Penguin, 1991).

—— *The Penguin Freud Library*, 12. *Civilization, Society and Religion*, ed. Albert Dickson (1985; Harmondsworth: Penguin, 1991).

—— *The Penguin Freud Library*, 14. *Art and Literature*, ed. Albert Dickson (1985; Harmondsworth: Penguin, 1990).

Fried, Michael, *Courbet's Realism* (Chicago: University of Chicago Press, 1992).

Gilman, Charlotte Perkins, *Women and Economics: A Study of the Economic Relation Between Men and Women as a Factor in Social Evolution* (1898; Berkeley and Los Angeles: University of California Press, 1998).

Gilmore, Michael T., *American Romanticism and the Marketplace* (Chicago: University of Chicago Press, 1985).

Goldhammer, Arthur, 'Remarks on the Mansfield-Winthrop Translation', <http://www. people.fas.harvard.edu/~agoldham/articles/Mansfield.htm> last accessed 2 December 2008.

Gooch, Brad, *City Poet: The Life and Times of Frank O'Hara* (New York: Alfred A. Knopf, 1993).

Greene, Theodore Meyer (ed.), *Kant: Selections* (London: Charles Scribner's Sons, 1929).

Greenspan, Ezra (ed.), *The Cambridge Companion to Walt Whitman* (Cambridge: Cambridge University Press, 1995).

Habermas, Jürgen, *The Philosophical Discourse of Modernity*, trans. Frederick Lawrence (Cambridge: Polity Press, 1987).

—— *The Structural Transformation of the Public Sphere: An Inquiry into a Category of Bourgeois Society*, trans. Thomas Burger with the assistance of Frederick Lawrence (1962; Cambridge: Polity Press, 1992).

—— *The Theory of Communicative Action*, 1. *Reason and the Rationalization of Society*, trans. Thomas McCarthy (London: Heinemann, 1984).

Harrington, Joseph, *Poetry and the Public: The Social Form of U.S. Poetics* (Middletown, Conn.: Wesleyan University Press, 2002).

Hartz, Louis, *The Liberal Tradition in America* (New York: Harcourt, Brace & Company, 1953).

Hatlen, Burton (ed.), *George Oppen: Man and Poet* (Orono, Me.: National Poetry Foundation, 1981).

Hawthorne, Nathaniel, *The Scarlet Letter*, ed. Seymour Gross, Sculley Bradley, Richmond Croom Beatty, and E. Hudson Long (1850; New York: W. W. Norton & Company, 1988).

Hegel, G. W. F., *Phenomenology of Spirit*, trans. A. V. Miller, with analysis of the text and foreword by J. N. Findlay (Oxford: Oxford University Press, 1977).

Heidegger, Martin, *Being and Time*, trans. John Macquarrie and Edward Robinson (Oxford: Basil Blackwell, 1962).

——— *Poetry, Language, Thought*, trans. Alfred Hofstadter (New York: Harper & Row, 1975).

——— *Sein und Zeit* (1927; Tübingen: Max Niemeyer Verlag, 1993).

Hofstadter, Richard, *The American Political Tradition* (1948; New York: Vintage Books, 1989).

Hughes, Robert, *American Visions: The Epic History of Art in America* (London: Harvill Press, 1999).

Hyde, Lewis, *The Gift: Imagination and the Erotic Life of Property* (New York: Vintage Books, 1983).

James, Henry, *The Bostonians*, ed. Charles R. Anderson (1886; Harmondsworth: Penguin, 1984).

——— *Daisy Miller, Pandora, The Patagonia and Other Tales* (New York: Charles Scribner's Sons, 1909).

Jameson, Fredric, *Marxism and Form: Twentieth-Century Dialectical Theories of Literature* (Princeton: Princeton University Press, 1974).

——— *The Political Unconscious: Narrative as a Socially Symbolic Act* (1981; London: Routledge, 1989).

Joyce, James, *Ulysses* (1922; Harmondsworth: Penguin, 1986).

Kammen, Michael, *A Season of Youth: The American Revolution and the Historical Imagination* (1978; Ithaca, NY: Cornell University Press, 1988).

Kant, Immanuel, *Critique of Pure Reason*, trans. and ed. Paul Guyer and Allen W. Wood (1781; 1787; Cambridge: Cambridge University Press, 1999).

Kearns, George, *Guide to Ezra Pound's Selected Cantos* (Folkestone: Dawson, 1980).

Kertesz, Louise, *The Poetic Vision of Muriel Rukeyser* (Baton Rouge: Louisiana State University Press, 1980).

Kinnahan, Linda A., *Poetics of the Feminine: Authority and Literary Tradition in William Carlos Williams, Mina Loy, Denise Levertov, and Kathleen Fraser* (Cambridge: Cambridge University Press, 1994).

King, Richard H., *Race, Culture, and the Intellectuals, 1940–1970* (Washington: Woodrow Wilson Center Press; Baltimore: Johns Hopkins University Press, 2004).

Kouidis, Virginia, *Mina Loy: American Modernist Poet* (Baton Rouge: Louisiana State University Press, 1980).

Kristeva, Julia, *Hannah Arendt*, trans. Ross Guberman (New York: Columbia University Press, 2001).

——— *Melanie Klein*, trans. Ross Guberman (New York: Columbia University Press, 2001).

Lacan, Jacques, *Écrits*, trans. Alan Sheridan (New York: Norton, 1977).

Laplanche, Jean, and Pontalis, Jean-Bertrand, *The Language of Psychoanalysis*, trans. Donald Nicholson-Smith (1973; London: Karnac Books, 1988).

Lasch, Christopher, *The Culture of Narcissism: American Life in An Age of Diminishing Expectations* (1979; New York: Norton, 1991).

Lawrence, D. H., *Studies in Classic American Literature* (1923; Harmondsworth: Penguin, 1971).

Lentricchia, Frank, *Modernist Quartet* (Cambridge: Cambridge University Press, 1994).

Longenbach, James, *Modernist Poetics of History: Pound, Eliot, and the Sense of the Past* (Princeton: Princeton University Press, 1987).

Longenbach, James, *Wallace Stevens: The Plain Sense of Things* (New York: Oxford University Press, 1991).

Loy, Mina, *The Last Lunar Baedeker*, ed. Roger L. Conover (Manchester: Carcanet, 1985).

—— *The Lost Lunar Baedeker*, ed. Roger L. Conover (New York: Noonday Press, 1997).

Lukács, Georg, *History and Class Consciousness: Studies in Marxist Dialectics*, trans. Rodney Livingstone (1968; London: Merlin Press, 1974).

—— *The Theory of the Novel*, trans. Anna Bostock (London: Merlin, 1971).

MacIntyre, Alasdair, *After Virtue: A Study in Moral Theory* (1981; London: Duckworth, 1985).

—— *A Short History of Ethics* (London: Routledge & Kegan Paul, 1967).

Madison, James, Hamilton, Alexander, and Jay, John, *The Federalist Papers*, ed. Isaac Kramnick (1788; Harmondsworth: Penguin, 1987).

Mariani, Paul, *William Carlos Williams: A New World Naked* (New York: McGraw-Hill Book Company, 1981).

Martin, Robert K., *The Homosexual Tradition in American Poetry* (Austin: University of Texas Press, 1979).

Marx, Karl, *Selected Writings*, ed. David McLellan (Oxford: Oxford University Press, 1977).

Matthiessen, F. O., *The American Renaissance: Art and Expression in the Age of Emerson and Whitman* (London: Oxford University Press, 1941).

—— *Henry James: The Major Phase* (London: Oxford University Press, 1944).

Mehta, J. L., *The Philosophy of Martin Heidegger* (New York: Harper & Row, 1971).

Melville, Herman, *Moby Dick; Or, the Whale*, ed. Harold Beaver (1851; Harmondsworth: Penguin, 1972).

Merleau-Ponty, Maurice, *The Primacy of Perception* (Evanston, Ill.: Northwestern University Press, 1964).

Merwin, David, *The President of the United States* (Hemel Hempstead: Harvester, 1993).

Michaels, Walter Benn, and Pease, Donald E. (eds.), *The American Renaissance Reconsidered* (Baltimore: Johns Hopkins University Press, 1985).

Moon, Michael, *Disseminating Whitman: Revision and Corporeality in Leaves of Grass* (Cambridge, Mass.: Harvard University Press, 1991).

Moore, Marianne, *Complete Poems* (New York: Macmillan Company; Viking Press, 1967).

Mudge, Jean McClure, *Emily Dickinson and the Image of Home* (Amherst: University of Massachusetts Press, 1975).

Mulhall, Stephen, *Stanley Cavell: Philosophy's Recounting of the Ordinary* (Oxford, Clarendon: 1994).

New, Elisa, *The Line's Eye: Poetic Experience, American Sight* (Cambridge, Mass.: Harvard University Press, 1998).

Nicholls, Peter, 'George Oppen and "that primitive, Hegel"', *Paideuma*, 32 (2003), 351–75.

—— *George Oppen and the Fate of Modernism* (Oxford: Oxford University Press, 2007).

—— 'George Oppen in Exile: Mexico and Maritain', *Journal of American Studies*, 39/1 (2005), 1–18.

Niedecker, Lorine, *Collected Works*, ed. Jenny Penberthy (Berkeley and Los Angeles: University of California Press, 2002).

O'Hara, Frank, *Collected Poems of Frank O'Hara*, ed. Donald Allen (New York: Alfred A. Knopf, 1971).

—— *The Selected Poems of Frank O'Hara*, ed. Donald Allen (New York: Vintage Books, 1974).

—— *Standing Still and Walking in New York*, ed. Donald Allen (Bolinas, Calif.: Grey Fox Press, 1975).

Olson, Charles, *Collected Prose*, ed. Donald Allen and Benjamin Friedlander (Berkeley and Los Angeles: University of California Press, 1997).

—— *The Maximus Poems*, ed. George F. Butterick (Berkeley and Los Angeles: University of California Press, 1983).

Oppen, George, *New Collected Poems*, ed. Michael Davidson (New York: New Directions, 2002).

—— *Poems of George Oppen (1908–1984)*, ed. Charles Tomlinson (Newcastle upon Tyne: Cloudforms, 1990).

—— *The Selected Letters of George Oppen*, ed. Rachel Blau DuPlessis (Durham, NC: Duke University Press, 1990).

—— *Selected Prose, Daybooks, and Papers*, ed. Stephen Cope (Berkeley and Los Angeles: University of California Press, 2007).

'George Oppen's Library: A Bibliography', George Oppen Papers, the Mandeville Special Collections, University of California at San Diego.

'A Conversation with George Oppen', with Charles Amirkhanian and David Gitin, *Ironwood*, 5 (1975), 21–4.

Oppen, Mary, *Meaning a Life: An Autobiography* (Santa Rosa, Calif.: Black Sparrow Press, 1978).

Ott, Hugo, *Martin Heidegger: A Political Life*, trans. Allan Blunden (London: HarperCollins Publishers, 1993).

Pells, Richard H., *Radical Visions and American Dreams: Culture and Social Thought in the Depression Years* (New York: Harper & Row, 1973).

—— *The Liberal Mind in a Conservative Age: American Intellectuals in the 1940s and 1950s* (New York: Harper & Row, 1985).

Perloff, Marjorie, *The Dance of the Intellect: Studies in the Poetry of the Pound Tradition* (1985; Evanston, Ill.: Northwestern University Press, 1996).

—— *Frank O'Hara, Poet Among Painters* (1977; Chicago: University of Chicago Press, 1998).

—— *Poetry On and Off the Page: Essays for Emergent Occasions* (Evanston, Ill.: Northwestern University Press, 1998).

—— 'The Shipwreck of the Singular: George Oppen's "Of Being Numerous" ', *Ironwood*, 13/2 (Fall 1985), 193–204.

Phillips, Adam, *Winnicott* (London: Fontana, 1988).

Plato, *The Republic*, trans. F. M. Cornford (Oxford: Clarendon Press, 1941).

Porter, Carolyn, *Seeing and Being: The Plight of the Participant Observer in Emerson, James, Adams, and Faulkner* (Middletown, Conn.: Wesleyan University Press, 1981).

Potter, Rachel, *Modernism and Democracy: Literary Culture 1900–1930* (Oxford: Oxford University Press, 2006).

Pound, Ezra, *The Cantos* (1954; London: Faber and Faber, 1987).

—— *Collected Shorter Poems* (London: Faber and Faber, 1968).

Pound, Ezra, *Gaudier-Brzeska: A Memoir* (1916; New York: New Directions, 1970).
—— *Guide to Kulchur* (1938; London: Peter Owen, 1978).
—— *Jefferson and/or Mussolini* (1935; New York: Liveright, 1970).
—— *The Literary Essays of Ezra Pound*, ed. T. S. Eliot (London: Faber and Faber, 1954).
—— *Selected Prose 1909–1965*, ed. William Cookson (London: Faber, 1973).
Pynchon, Thomas, *The Crying of Lot 49* (1967; London: Picador, 1979).
Raymond, Marcel, *From Baudelaire to Surrealism* (1933; London: Peter Owen, 1957).
Redman, Tim, *Ezra Pound and Italian Fascism* (Cambridge: Cambridge University Press, 1991).
Reiss, Hans (ed.), *Kant's Political Writings*, trans. H. B. Nisbet (Cambridge: Cambridge University Press, 1970).
Richardson, Joan, *Wallace Stevens: The Later Years, 1923–1955* (New York: William Morrow, 1986).
Ricoeur, Paul, *Freud and Philosophy: An Essay on Interpretation*, trans. Denis Savage (New Haven: Yale University Press, 1970).
Riddel, Joseph, *The Clairvoyant Eye: The Poetry and Poetics of Wallace Stevens* (Baton Rouge: Louisiana State University Press, 1965).
Rieff, Philip, *Freud: The Mind of the Moralist* (London: Victor Gollanz Ltd, 1959).
Riesman, David, *Individualism Reconsidered* (New York: The Free Press, 1954).
—— with Nathan Glazer and Reuel Denney, *The Lonely Crowd: A Study of the Changing American Character*, abridged edn. (1950; New Haven: Yale University Press, 1961).
Roll, Eric, *A History of Economic Thought* (1938; London: Faber and Faber, 1992).
Rorty, Richard, *Philosophy and the Mirror of Nature* (Oxford: Basil Blackwell, 1980).
Rose, Gillian, *The Melancholy Science: An Introduction to the Thought of Theodor W. Adorno* (London: Macmillan, 1978).
Rose, Richard, *The Postmodern President: George Bush Meets the World*, 2nd edn. (Chatham, NJ: Chatham House Publishers, Inc., 1991).
Rukeyser, Muriel, *The Collected Poems of Muriel Rukeyser*, ed. Janet E. Kaufman and Anna F. Herzog, with Jan Heller Levi (Pittsburgh: University of Pittsburgh Press, 2005).
—— *The Life of Poetry* (1949; Ashfield, Mass.: Paris Press, 1996).
Ruthven, K. K., *A Guide to Ezra Pound's* Personae *(1926)* (Berkeley and Los Angeles: University of California Press, 1969).
Schleifer, James T., *The Making of Tocqueville's* Democracy in America (Chapel Hill: University of North Carolina Press, 1980).
Sedgwick, Eve Kosofsky, *Epistemology of the Closet* (Berkeley and Los Angeles: University of California Press, 1990).
Shaw, Lytle, *Frank O'Hara: The Poetics of Coterie* (Iowa City: University of Iowa Press, 2006).
Stevens, Wallace, *Collected Poems* (1954; London: Faber and Faber, 1984).
—— *Collected Poetry and Prose*, ed. Frank Kermode and Joan Richardson (New York: Library of America, 1997).
—— *The Necessary Angel: Essays on Reality and the Imagination* (1960; London: Faber and Faber, 1984), 138–9.
—— *Opus Posthumous*, revised, enlarged and corrected edn., ed. Milton J. Bates (1957; New York: Alfred A. Knopf, 1989).

Strauss, Leo, *What Is Political Philosophy? and Other Studies* (1959; Chicago: University of Chicago Press, 1988).

Szalay, Michael, *New Deal Modernism: American Literature and the Invention of the Welfare State* (Durham, NC: Duke University Press, 2000).

Taylor, Charles, *Sources of the Self: The Making of the Modern Identity* (Cambridge: Cambridge University Press, 1992).

Terrell, Carroll F., *A Companion to* The Cantos *of Ezra Pound* (Berkeley and Los Angeles: University of California Press, 1993).

Thoreau, Henry David, *Walden and Civil Disobedience*, ed. Owen Thomas (1854; New York: W. W. Norton & Company, 1966).

Tocqueville, Alexis de, *Democracy in America*, trans. George Lawrence, ed. J. P. Mayer (1966; London: Fontana, 1994).

——*Democracy in America*, trans. and ed. Harvey C. Mansfield and Delba Winthrop (Chicago: University of Chicago Press, 2000).

——*Œuvres complètes*, 1. *De la Démocratie en Amérique*, ed. J. P. Mayer, 2 vols. (Paris: Gallimard, 1961).

——*Recollections*, trans. George Lawrence, ed. J. P. Mayer and A. P. Kerr (New York: Anchor Books, 1971).

Tomlinson, Charles, *Some Americans: A Personal Record* (Berkeley and Los Angeles: University of California Press, 1981).

Traubel, Horace, *With Walt Whitman in Camden*, vol. 2 (New York: D. Appleton and Company, 1908).

Tsvetaeva, Marina, *Selected Poems*, trans. Elaine Feinstein (Oxford: Oxford University Press, 1993).

Vidal, Gore, *Burr: A Novel* (New York: Random House, 1973).

Wald, Alan M., *Exiles from a Future Time: The Forging of the Mid-Twentieth-Century Literary Left* (Chapel Hill: University of North Carolina Press, 2002).

Watson, Steven, *Strange Bedfellows: The First American Avant-Garde* (New York: Abbeville Press Publishers, 1991).

Weber, Max, *The Protestant Ethic and the Spirit of Capitalism*, trans. Talcott Parsons (1930; London: Routledge, 1992).

Whitman, Walt, *Leaves of Grass*, ed. Sculley Bradley and Harold W. Blodgett (New York: W. W. Norton and Company 1973).

——*Poetry and Prose*, ed. Justin Kaplan (New York: Library of America, 1982).

Wiggershaus, Rolf, *The Frankfurt School: Its History, Theories and Political Significance*, trans. Michael Robertson (Cambridge: Polity Press, 1994).

Williams, William Carlos, *The Collected Poems*, 1. *1909–1939*, ed. A. Walton Litz and Christopher MacGowan (Manchester: Carcanet, 1987).

——*The Collected Poems*, 2. *1939–1962*, ed. Christopher MacGowan (Manchester: Carcanet, 1988).

——*The Embodiment of Knowledge*, ed. Ron Loewinsohn (New York: New Directions, 1974).

——*Imaginations*, ed. Webster Schott (New York: New Directions, 1971).

——*In the American Grain* (1925; New York: New Directions, 1956).

——*Paterson*, ed. Christopher MacGowan (1992; New York: New Directions, 1995).

——*Selected Essays* (1954; New York: New Directions, 1969).

Wilson, John (ed.), *Robert Creeley's Life and Work: A Sense of Increment* (Ann Arbor: University of Michigan Press, 1987).

Winnicott, D. W., *The Family and Individual Development* (1965; London: Brunner-Routledge, 2001).

—— *The Maturational Processes and the Facilitating Environment: Studies in the Theory of Emotional Development* (1965; London: Karnac Books, 1990).

—— *Through Paediatrics to Psychoanalysis: Collected Papers* (1975; London: Karnac Books, 1992).

Wood, Gordon S., *The Creation of the American Republic 1776–1787* (1969; Chapel Hill: University of North Carolina Press, 1998).

Woolf, Virginia, *A Room of One's Own* (1929; London: Grafton, 1977).

Wright, Richard, *Native Son* (1940; New York: HarperPerennial, 1993).

Young-Bruehl, Elisabeth, *Hannah Arendt: For Love of the World* (New Haven: Yale University Press, 1982).

Zukofsky, Louis, *'A'* (Berkeley and Los Angeles: University of California Press, 1978).

—— *Prepositions+: The Collected Critical Essays*, additional prose, ed. Mark Scroggins (Hanover, NH: Wesleyan University Press, 2000).

Index